Date Due

BRODART, INC.   Cat. No. 23 233   Printed in U.S.A.

D1400711

OPTIONS FOR THE FUTURE

OPTIONS FOR THE FUTURE

A Comparative
Analysis of
Policy-Oriented
Forecasts

Thomas E. Jones

Foreword by
Anthony J. Wiener

PRAEGER

PRAEGER SPECIAL STUDIES • PRAEGER SCIENTIFIC

Library of Congress Cataloging in Publication Data

Jones, Thomas E.   1937–
    Options for the future.

    Bibliography: p.
    Includes index.
    1. Forecasting.   I. Title.
H61.4.J66   003   80–11615

ISBN 0-03-053846-7
ISBN 0-03-053841-6 (pbk.)

Published in 1980 by Praeger Publishers
CBS Educational and Professional Publishing
A Division of CBS, Inc.
521 Fifth Avenue, New York, New York 10017 U.S.A.

0123456789   145   987654321

Printed in the United States of America

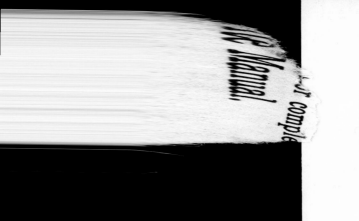
To the analysts whose policy-oriented forecasts I examine in this study. They have undertaken a crucial and extremely difficult task, the steady improvement of which depends on the most vigorous criticism. If their accomplishments seem uneven, it is not for lack of talent or effort. A new, comprehensive discipline should not be expected to grow from a seedling to maturity within a single decade.

FOREWORD
Anthony J. Wiener

Primitive man was also concerned and confused about the future. Certain phenomena, like the rising and setting of the sun, the movements of the moon, the stars, and even the planets, the changes in climate from season to season, the general lifecycle of people, animals, and plants (patterns of birth, growth, maturity, decline, and death) were, within broad limits, predictable. But there were many puzzles. For example, the planets looked like the stars, but did not remain in constellations; the moon changed shape and could not be seen at all on some nights; some winters were colder than others, some summers hotter; some plants, animals, and people lived longer than others. It was hard to know when it would rain or snow; when accidents or illnesses would disable or kill; when babies would be born or when any particular individual would die; when enemies or predators would attack; when there would be forest fires or floods or droughts; when "luck" or "fate" or "the gods" would be good or bad.

Hardest of all, then as now, was to know the difference between what could be predicted and what could not. Primitives searched everywhere for signs and portents that would help them cope with the unknown dangers and opportunities that the future would bring. They also searched for and found explanations—differently in each culture, and fanciful and far-fetched by modern scientific standards, though still believed today by perhaps a majority of the world's people. Their explanations for mysteries were generally found in supernatural forces, in the wishes and conflicts of anthropomorphic gods and demons, and in myths to answer the hardest questions: What was the Beginning? What determines "fate"? Where does the sun go when it disappears on one side of the sky, only to reappear from almost the opposite direction? Where do the spirits of people go after their bodies die? How will people ultimately be rewarded for virtue and punished for wrong-doing in the "next world," if not in this? Are there ways to approach supernatural forces properly to gain their intervention? And how will everything finally end?

As societies confronted these cosmic uncertainties, witch doctors, oracles, soothsayers, priests, astrologers, astronomers and other scientists, fortune-tellers, and councils of wise elders flourished. But oracles spoke in riddles, and tea-leaves, goat's entrails, palm wrinkles, the Zodiac, and the judgments of the wise men were often wrong. Sometimes efforts to predict were severely punished, either for being fraudulent and misleading, or, more often, for being subversive of established authority. Galileo was forced to recant. The 17th century Massachusetts law under which the witches of Salem were burned at the stake or crushed under rocks prescribed cruel and unusual forms of capital punishment for many kinds of witchcraft. Any extraordinary knowledge of the future was prima facie evidence of communication with the Devil.

In 1980, our situation is not different enough. After hundreds of thousands of years of deep ambivalence about the capacity to foresee, it would be surprising indeed for social attitudes to change radically. Nothing important enough has happened yet. Only a small minority of the world's population, in the almost infinitesimal fraction of human history comprised of the last few centuries, has participated in the Scientific Revolution. That is not enough to bring about a triumph of rationality, even among the few hundred people who know most about the subject.

Ambivalence persists. On the one hand, we would like to know so many things. How will the Arms Race finally end? Can the world survive indefinitely while weapons grow increasingly destructive, sophisticated, and widespread and, at the same time, competing nationalisms and ethnic hostilities persist? What about the population? The carrying capacity of the global environment? The energy crisis? The future of world food supply? Mythology will not answer such questions. Yet we need answers, not only in order to frame current policies, but also to satisfy our ancient and continuing concern about eschatology, the Final Days, individual death, judgment, heaven or hell, and the ultimate end of man as a species.

We also need to make decisions: global, national, corporate, and personal. These decisions can have extremely long-term consequences. Jerusalem and Damascus (and perhaps many other cities) were first setted more than five thousand years ago. The Appian Way remains a highway after two thousand years. The U.S. Constitution is nearly two centuries old and might govern our national politics and personal liberties for many more centuries. As individuals, we enter marriage contracts, beget children, buy houses, borrow 20- or 30-year mortgages, decide on a career for a lifetime, buy life insurance, pay into Social Security and other pension plans, and make many other decisions which will have consequences in decades far ahead, about which we have great uncertainty.

It would be *so* helpful if we really knew what to expect. People are eager for predictions about the weather, the stock market, the inflation rate, the energy supply, the best jobs for the 1990s, the probability of nuclear war, and so on. In our decisions, we make implicit assumptions about the long-term future. When we don't know what to assume we tend to assume continuity.

Everyone who purports to have answers to such questions gets a hearing— especially scientists who have earned good reputations in technical fields and who now wish to participate in more troubling subjects.

The ambivalence toward such forecasts persists. On the one hand, we want and desperately need good predictions; on the other hand, we distrust (for good reasons) those who attempt to supply them. While erroneous speculations about the future are no longer capital offenses, they continue to bring ridicule and scorn, whether in scholarly journals or in the humorous excerpts from old predictions of the present which *The New Yorker* now and then prints at the bottom of its pages under the heading, "The Clouded Crystal Ball." People want to know what the "experts" anticipate, but at the same time they are relieved when "even the experts are wrong." If the experts can be debunked, then perhaps it is less painful to be almost completely at a loss as to what the future may hold.

The future does not yet exist; it presents us with no data; we cannot study it by means of the "scientific method" in the usual sense. The yearning for "data" is understandable, but it leads to an over-emphasis of what can be quantified (such as the current expectations of a group) and, therefore, to distorted judgments. How can we improve our judgments about the future? Only by making them on the basis of the best possible information and analysis of everything that is likely to make an important difference to the alternative outcomes of options among which we (as individuals, corporations, governments, etc.) must decide. And only by recognizing that at best we can never do better than improve our judgments; about most important things, we can never be certain.

All this has been pointed out by most of the writers whose works are examined by Thomas E. Jones in this book. For example, in *The Year 2000: A Framework for Speculation* (1967) Herman Kahn and I devoted a substantial portion of an unusually long book to discussion of methodology, emphasizing uncertainty alternative futures, potential disasters, and above all explicating the difference between trying to improve long-term policy planning, which was our purpose, and making either optimistic or pessimistic predictions about the future, which was not.

Moreover, we tried to make it clear that extrapolation of past trends was only a methodological device for establishing a scenario that would be extremely surprising if it did occur but that is useful as a starting point from which to consider major branch-points, or discontinuities, and the alternative situations which would result. Daniel Bell, in his introduction to our book and again in his own book, *The Coming of Post-Industrial Society: A Venture into Social Forecasting* (1973) also emphasized these points, stressing the impossibility and uselessness of specific, isolated "predictions", the irrelevance of attempting to characterize the future either "optimistically" or "pessimistically", and the need instead for a coherent, integrated understanding of the entire system the future of which is being "forecasted."

In *Options for the Future*, Dr. Jones makes a major contribution to the improvement of long-term policy decisions. He moves quickly past the obvious differences of opinion among the authors and attempts something much more important: a systematic comparison of the implicit assumptions underlying each forecast. Merely noting disagreements would provide only a survey of the field—a useful work but not one which would improve the quality of future work in social forecasting. Analyzing the underlying chains of reasoning, even when they have not been made explicit, that lead to the disagreements, shifts the debate from conclusions, which invite mere repetition, to assumptions, which invite further analysis and clarification.

The measure of the importance of anyone's work in any field of knowledge is the extent to which later writers in that field are influenced by it and must take it into consideration. I believe this book is extremely important, by that standard, to everyone concerned with social forecasting, long-range planning, or simply speculating, as an intelligent person must, about his own future, his children's future, and the future of his society. Dr. Jones has dug carefully beneath the surface of what has been written. Although I would disagree with him at many points, I feel he has to an impressive degree uncovered not merely the obvious differences, but also the differences in unstated methodological and substantive assumptions and in implicit social values that lead to divergent conclusions.

After the publication of this book, no serious writer on long-range planning or social forecasting will want, or be allowed by serious critics, to shirk his responsibility to undertake an analysis of his own work. While it would be foolish to think that some journalists and many idealogues (including some academics, of course) will (or even should) henceforth refrain from producing sensationalist, one-idea books intended to frighten a mass audience about the future, or some potential future, I believe it is realistic to judge that in this book, as far as serious work is concerned, Dr. Jones has changed the field. He has made unmistakeable the need to shift emphasis away from arguments for predictive conclusions towards analysis of the whole set of judgments from which such conclusions must emerge.

PREFACE

While studying for a doctorate at the New School for Social Research in New York City, I became aware of a significant gap in the rapidly expanding literature on policy-oriented forecasting and planning. Nowhere could I find a thorough comparative analysis of conflicting forecasts in terms of their incompatible assumptions. I undertook such an analysis in my dissertation, which served as a springboard for this book.

In view of the increasing importance of forecasting for shaping the future, political and business leaders, educated professionals, students, and others cannot afford to ignore the debate about which forecasts are more suitable for policy formulation. Hence, I have sought to make this book accessible to the widest possible audience without compromising the rigor needed to establish plausible conclusions. By evaluating the relative usefulness of representative types of forecasts, I derive a number of conclusions about crucial issues in the much-publicized, ongoing controversy concerning the likely consequences of the continued global growth of population and industrialization. Still, my aim is not just to assess today's most important forecasts and issues but to help a broad spectrum of readers develop the capacity to assess tomorrow's.

To tailor this study to the interests of university students and readers generally, I have extensively revised the original dissertation. I have added new material and have deleted much of the background information concerning the current methods of forecasting and the origin and development of the renewed interest in the future. I have also omitted most of my evaluation of the potential for improving forecasting. Any reader who is interested in these topics or in detailed documentation of them may wish to consult my dissertation, "Forecasts by Representative Futurists: A Sociological Analysis" (New School for Social Research, New York City, January 1975; available from University Microfilms, Ann Arbor, Michigan.)

A complete list of people who have offered perceptive advice or provided other forms of assistance during my preparation of the manuscript would cover several pages. Therefore, I can only express my gratitude to them collectively and single out a few who made especially valuable contributions.

The future-oriented approach of Benjamin Nelson, the recently deceased historical sociologist who directed my dissertation research, exerted a strong influence on my evaluation of forecasts. At the dissertation stage David Muchnick raised constructive criticisms that led me to improve my analysis. I also appreciate the Dissertation Fellowship awarded by the National Science Foundation (NSF), as well as the assistance furnished by Robert Lamson and Joseph Coates, who worked for NSF at that time.

Among the many analysts whose comments enabled me to enhance the quality of the manuscript are Bernard Cazas, Draper Kauffman, Andrew Lipinski,

John McHale, Edward Cornish, James Bright, Robert Ayres, Alexander King, Clark Souers, Theodore Gordon, Willis Harman, Robert Burton, Anthony Fedanzo, Carl Madden, Charles Wolf, David Miller, Jib Fowles, and Joëlle Brink. Olaf Helmer, Zbigniew Brzezinski, Anthony Wiener, Daniel Bell, and Willis Harman and O. W. Markley submitted useful reviews of the chapters that analyze their respective forecasts. My evaluation of ecological problems and prospects depends in part on observations made by Glenn Seaborg, Hans Bethe, Thomas Wilson, Gerald Feinberg, Margaret Mead, John Dooher, Burns Weston, Ervin Laszlo, and others who reviewed essays that I wrote for the Club of Rome's Goals for Global Society project while working as a Research Fellow at the United Nations Institute for Training and Research (UNITAR). I am grateful for the comments of Anthony Wiener, O. W. Markley, and Robert Prehoda on the final draft of this book. Richard Lamb, Dennis Pirages, Richard Coe, Wesley Thomas, Robert Bland, and Robert Burton offered useful editorial assistance.

I especially appreciate the high quality of the work performed by the following personnel at Praeger in preparing the book for publication: Lynda Sharp and Mary Curtis, for editorial guidance; Ann Dichter, for advice concerning the market; Susan Badger, for her excellent copyediting of the final manuscript; and Benedette Knopik, for efficiently coordinating the project.

I am particularly indebted to John Pessolano, whose percpetive editing of the entire manuscript significantly improved both its literary quality and its line of argumentation.

John Pessolano, Wesley Thomas, and Roy Mason helped in the selection of the graphics; Barbara Lea and Robert Burton, in the preparation of the index. Virginia Ritchie typed the final draft; Eva Thomas, an earlier draft; and Janis Wolf, the dissertation. My parents, Ernest E. Jones and Martha Hiemke Jones, and many other friends provided the understanding and encouragement that helped to bring this analysis of forecasts to fruition.

CONTENTS

LIST OF TABLES

LIST OF FIGURES

LIST OF ACRONYMS

ABM	antiballistic missile
DDT	dichloro-diphenyl-trichloro-ethane
EPA	Environmental Protection Agency
EPRC	Educational Policy Research Center
FAO	Food and Agriculture Organization
FAR	Field Anomaly Relaxation Method
GNP	gross national product
GWP	gross world product
IFF	Institute for the Future
MIT	Massachusetts Institute of Technology
MOIRA	Model of International Relations in Agriculture
NASA	National Aeronautics and Space Administration
NPG	negative population growth
NSF	National Science Foundation
OPEC	Organization of Petroleum Exporting Countries
PCB	polychlorobiphenyls
R&D	research and development
SALT	Strategic Arms Limitation Treaty
SDS	Students for a Democratic Society
SRI	Stanford Research Institute
SST	supersonic transport
UNITAR	United Nations Institute for Training and Research
WOMP	World Order Models Project

OPTIONS
FOR THE
FUTURE

1

INTRODUCTION: OVERVIEW OF CONTEMPORARY FORECASTING

We are all poised in the transition from the old world to the new—literally on the hinge of the greatest evolutionary transformation in the human condition.

John McHale

Since World War II, the pace, constancy, and geographical extent of change have increased enormously. Most contemporary change is either deliberate or a consequence of deliberate change. "What is distinctive about the middle of the twentieth century," Daniel Bell (1967a) states, "is the deliberate intervention of human instruments, principally government, to control change for specified ends" (p. xxvi). Regardless of whether such ends are achieved, pursuit of them begets side effects. Many of the far-reaching consequences of intentional change have been unintended, unanticipated, and undesirable. In short, controlled change has spawned unsettling types and amounts of uncontrolled change.

The present decade has brought more than its quota of unexpected occurrences, including the 1973/74 energy crisis and the vexing problems that it left in its wake, the persistent union of supposedly incompatible inflation and recession, and the Watergate burglary cover-up. Prominent among surprises precipitated by rapid, uncoordinated change are those that stem from the implementation of new technologies. Who in Henry Ford's day suspected that the automobile would not only generate high levels of smog and exacerbate urban congestion but also revolutionize sexual mores by functioning as a "bedroom on wheels"? Today, energy experts argue vehemently about the future impact of much more potent technologies, such as nuclear power installations (see Figure 1.1).

The undesirable consequences of runaway change dramatize the need to use forecasting and planning to control change wisely. This, however, is by no means an easy undertaking. Cautious analysts who seek to peer into the future

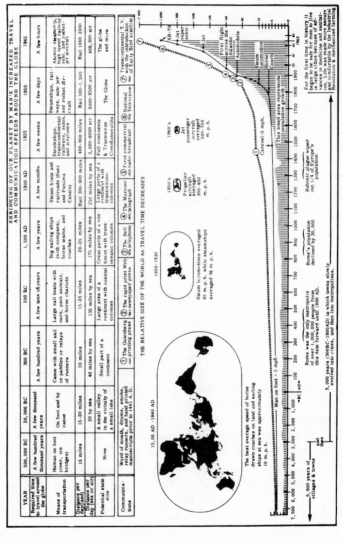

Figure 1.1. John McHale graphically depicts rapid innovations in transportation and communication technology and the consequent progressive "shrinkage" of the experienced world (McHale 1972b, p. 3). (Reprinted from WORLD FACTS AND TRENDS, Second Edition, by John McHale, courtesy of Macmillan Publishing Co., Inc. Copyright © 1971, 1972 by John McHale. Data are from THE ECOLOGICAL CONTEXT [1970] by John McHale, courtesy of George Braziller, Inc.)

2

are understandably tempted to abandon the enterprise because of the obstacles obscuring clear vision. To put it facetiously, only people who fear that success would spoil them might be strongly motivated to become forecasters. Yet, instead of permitting obstacles to intimidate them, growing numbers of forecasters have risen to meet the challenge. Sociologist John McHale (1969) observes that "the new prophets of our future are no small band of messianic oracles adrift in the wilderness, but represent rather a wide cross section of our liveliest contemporary minds." (p. 297).

What kinds of sweeping changes do these forecasters envision? How adequate are their policy-oriented forecasts? To what extent can conflicts between incompatible forecasts be resolved by assessing the divergent assumptions on which these forecasts are based? How, if at all, can forecasts be improved? Such difficult but important questions give rise to my comparative evaluation of important, representative forecasts. This analysis of different ways of envisaging the future seeks to illuminate the puzzling question of what the future can, should, and probably will be like.

TODAY'S STUDY OF THE FUTURE

Though there has always been some interest in the future, the intensity and distinguishing features of this interest have fluctuated. The ancients employed predictive devices that ranged from crystal balls to astrological charts—and even to the entrails of animals. Kings sought advice from oracles before battles. Prophecy was typically geared to discovering one's fate rather than to "inventing" the future by choosing between various possible futures. An inquirer consulted a revered oracle without carefully examining the methodology by which this expert formulated forecasts. Indeed, this methodology was usually shrouded in mystery and mysticism. All too often, people committed to living by the crystal ball were forced to survive on a diet of shattered glass.

Policy-oriented forecasting of a purportedly scientific genre emerged shortly after the French Revolution. The aspirations, but not the methods, of Saint-Simon, Comte, and Condorcet foreshadowed those of many current forecasters. Pessimistic forecasts resembling those of the English clergyman Thomas Malthus have been resuscitated recently by analysts who fear that we will soon encounter limits to population and industrial growth on this finite planet. Other contributors to the development of forecasting include science fiction writers, utopians, and political satirists, such as Jonathan Swift, Jules Verne, Edward Bellamy, H. G. Wells, George Orwell, and Aldous Huxley. Recurrently, social scientists—especially Max Weber, Alexis de Tocqueville, William Ogburn, and Harold Lasswell—have achieved varying degrees of success in establishing their forecasts on a thorough understanding of societal development.

Unifying Traits despite Diversity

Present-day forecasters seek insight into societal development in order to become increasingly "rational" in the forecasting-planning process. The novelty of their systematic efforts centers in their claim to improved interdisciplinary methods that facilitate the formulation of forecasts of policy-oriented possible futures.

This contemporary study of the future still lacks a generally accepted name. The most commonly used terms, at least in the United States, are *future(s) studies, futures research, futurists, futurism,* and *futurology.* Others include *futuribles, prognostics, future analysis, mellonology, futurics,* and *forecasting.* Cornish et al (1977a), who carefully analyzed competing names, concluded that *"futurism* . . . appears to be the most appropriate term for the mood or movement that focuses on the future" (p. xi). Not to be confused with the early twentieth century Italian artistic-literary movement that bore the same name, futurism emphasizes:

The time period between the immediate and the extremely distant future,
The interconnectedness of events both in space and time,
The plasticity of the future to human designs,
The efficacy of images of the future in shaping present actions and thereby the future itself, and
The importance of values and art as well as science in dealing with the future (p. 154).

From futurism emerges a set of specific activities dubbed "futures studies" (or "futuristics"): nonmystical efforts to identify, analyze, and evaluate possible future changes in human life and the world (p. 155). Practitioners of futurism are generally called "futurists."

This nomenclature is probably the best available. Yet it leaves considerable doubt as to whether the use of *futurism* or *futures studies* is more suitable in numerous instances, for both terms can be applied to many of the same activities. To avoid being distracted by such semantic issues, I employ the broader term *futurism* more frequently. Any reader who objects to the ideological overtones sounded by the "ism" in *futurism* may substitute a preferred term.

Although many futurists try to be as scientific as possible, few consider their embryonic discipline to be a bona fide science. Unlike science, futurism:

Lacks rigorous, well-established methods;
Incorporates philosophical, artistic, and socioeconomic endeavors;
Requires the creation of the primary objects that it studies and, hence, is heavily dependent on imagination to devise these "alternative futures";
Seeks to project a variety of such futures rather than to predict a single future on the basis of scientific laws; and

Is more aligned to action than to the pursuit of theoretical knowledge for its own sake (see Cornish et al. 1977a, pp. 154–56).

The desire to pinpoint such unifying threads in the fabric of futurism should not obscure its heterogeneity. The complexity of futurism is manifested by its various organizations, interests, problems and issues, areas of study, methods of forecasting, images of the future, types of forecasts, and clients. Within futurism we can contrast official with ad hoc groups, national with international groups, specialized with generalized, elite with participatory, technocratic with humanist, ideologically orthodox with antiestablishment, individualistic with collectivist groups, and so on. Among the divergent interests being subserved are governmental, technocratic, ideological, individualistic, and humanist interests. Such differences, as well as similarities, become more intelligible when perceived in the light of the origin and development of futurism.

Origin and Development

Since its sudden upshot during the early 1960s in the United States, France, and elsewhere, the study of the future has been gaining momentum. Yet it did not spring up in a vacuum, as some descriptions of its origin might incline one to believe. Rather, its seeds germinated in the fertile soil prepared by research during the middle and late 1950s.

The forecasting methodology employed by geophysicist Harrison Brown (1954) displays striking similarities to that of many ecologically oriented forecasters today. Brown, who had participated in the Manhattan Project, delineated alternative futures and proposed planned change to deal with the nuclear genie that had escaped from its bottle. Brown and some of his colleagues at the California Institute of Technology (Cal Tech) initiated an ongoing series of future-oriented conferences for major corporations.

The RAND Corporation, a pioneer think-tank founded in 1946, engaged in interdisciplinary policy research on national defense, space technology, and other issues of public concern. During the 1950s, RAND personnel such as Herman Kahn and Olaf Helmer helped to develop forecasting methodology. They also perceived that the nuclear age called for long-range, comprehensive social forecasting as well as technological, military, and political forecasting. Still, the forecasting sparked by Brown at Cal Tech was broader in regard to its ecological, global, social, and imaginative motifs.

Both at RAND and elsewhere, work on the U.S. space program required sophisticated forecasting and evoked Promethean images of the future. Successes in space suggest that the sky is now the starting point rather than the limit.

RAND served as a principal springboard for futures studies in the United States. In 1961 Kahn left RAND to found the Hudson Institute, a private think-tank patterned after RAND. He also became a particularly important member of the American Academy of Arts and Sciences' "Commission on the Year 2000." Helmer, another RAND alumnus, served as the first president of the Institute for the Future (IFF). The IFF was established in 1967 with the aid of a Ford Foundation grant. Theodore Gordon, who had worked on a RAND project, became vice-president of the IFF and in 1971 left to establish the Futures Group. Resemblances among some forecasts formulated at these institutions can be traced in part to RAND's parental influence, which is not strong enough to prevent other forecasts from differing markedly from each other.

The Stanford Research Institute (SRI) opened a Long-Range Planning Service in 1958 and the future-oriented Educational Policy Research Center (EPRC) a decade later. The EPRC, directed by Willis Harman, was in turn made part of the Center for the Study of Social Policy, which Harman also headed until recently. Forecasts formulated by Harman's group conflict with Hudson Institute forecasts in regard to the long-term continuity of recently dominant trends.

Activities at Cal Tech, RAND, and the SRI were high points in the gradual developments that made possible the takeoff point of futures studies around 1962. The influence of Bertrand de Jouvenel's International Futuribles Committee and France's experience in national short-range planning should not be discounted, nor should the lesser but significant influence of Great Britain's Arthur Clarke and Sir George Thompson. However, the United States has constituted the principal center of the futures research industry. Most large private and public organizations in this country maintain their own forecasting-planning groups or rely on the services of outside agencies.

In many socialist and market-economy countries, programs sponsored and funded by governments as well as by national academies of science manifest a growing concern to devise better theoretical frameworks for forecasting and planning. Moreover, on either side of the cold war's "iron curtain," nonestablishment futurists such as R. Buckminster Fuller and Andrei Sakharov have devised forecasts that differ from typical ones made by think-tank personnel for governments and businesses. Several international futurist organizations, including the Club of Rome, focus their attention on interrelated global problems. International conferences have been held in Oslo (1967), Kyoto (1970), and Bucharest (1972). The World Future Society, which has over 50,000 members (1977) and maintains its headquarters in Washington, D.C., continues to play a highly visible role in the internationalization of futurism as well as in its coordination and popularization.

On the basis of his extensive survey, John McHale (1972a) concludes that futurism has expanded from an enclave of professional forecasters into a burgeoning social movement that is attracting people from virtually all walks of life (pp. i-ii). Together with the ecology movement, best-sellers such as Toffler's *Future Shock* (1970) have rekindled public interest in the future. *The Limits to Growth* (1972), a readable paperback produced by a Club of Rome project at Massachusetts Institute of Technology, helped to touch off the "growth controversy." This controversy, which concerns the extent to which further industrial and population growth can be sustained on our small planet, has received broad press and magazine coverage.

Thus futurism exhibits at least some of the markings of an intellectual discipline, a beginning international concern, and a popular social movement. Yet none of these developments is as closely correlated with the others as one might suspect nor as unified conceptually and organizationally. Because of the explosive mixtures of futurists with different backgrounds, interests, and outlooks, diversity is a pervasive hallmark of futurism. Debates on critical issues trigger major schisms and countermovements.

The most vehement criticisms, however, frequently come from opponents of futurism, as suggested by the title of Robert Nisbet's (1968) article, "The Year 2000 and All That." Nisbet denounces the new forecasting methodologies as specious expertise. Typical neo-Marxist sociologists, such as Arthur Mendel (1969), regard the bulk of futures research as unjustifiable ideology used by technocratic elites to perpetuate their own interests. When polemical caricaturizations of futurism provoke emotionally charged counterattacks, futurists and their adversaries tend to exchange volleys across the gulf of misunderstandings (*Commentary* September 1968).

Futurism continues to proliferate rapidly despite internal divisions and pointed criticisms hurled by its antagonists. This leads us to inquire: Is futurism likely to develop much further, or is it just a passing fad that has no anchor to keep it from being swept away by the winds of criticism? To venture even a provisional answer to this question, we need to account for the accelerated growth of this field of activity.

Explanation of Rapid Growth

Any thorough explanation of the rapid growth of forecasting efforts since the early 1960s would take into account many interrelated forces, including several that Daniel Bell (1965) identified 15 years ago:

Increasing commitment to economic growth (to which we may add current challenges to economic growth),
Introduction of planning into nearly every aspect of government and business,
Emphasis on science and research, and
Technological innovations, particularly computers, that permit construction of improved forecasting models.

Joseph Coates (1971), now of the U.S. government's Office of Technology Assessment, argues that such trends as the following have made it virtually mandatory that society develop new early warning techniques and improved aids to planning and decision making:

Enhanced power of human beings over nature,

The larger scale of human enterprise,

The throw-away economy with its huge demands for limited raw materials and its stupendous waste disposal problem,

Growing interconnectedness of social institutions, with concomitant vulnerability of society to disruption,

A shift in the values of affluent society toward disgust with the degradation of unpolluted, beautiful surroundings by technology's less esthetic by-products, and

Increasing scientific knowledge that has improved the human ability to anticipate future consequences of actions (pp. 225-31).

Analysis of these forces and others discloses two very general ones that stand out as spurs to the development of futurism: the increasingly perceived social need to control swift, turbulent change and improvements in forecasting methodology. The first force has significantly shaped the character of futurism and its methodology.

THE NEED TO CONTROL CHANGE

Consequences of Shortsighted, Deliberate Change

Contemporary political and economic policy formation is remarkably fixated on achieving narrowly defined short-term benefits, rather akin to a compulsive gambler playing dice with the cash needed to pay a doctor to perform a vital operation. Not only are adopted policies frequently self-serving and short-sighted; many of their consequences are unintended and unanticipated. National and global problems have been aggravated by such policies as the use of food and natural resources as political and economic weapons, devotion to rapid industrial growth, and sale of nuclear technology to foreign nations. A continuation of these policies by governments and businesses could easily result in widespread famines in poor countries, severe energy shortages as well as extensive environmental deterioration from pollution, and nuclear proliferation accompanied by increased likelihood of nuclear war.

The driving force behind the policies that intensify interrelated problems in our interpenetrating world is the pursuit of short-term self-interest by autonomous governments and businesses. Decisions aimed at achieving short-term objectives beneficial to one component of a social system can easily trigger immediate or longer-term consequences that are harmful to another component or to the system as a whole. Government and business decision makers have often displayed little concern that their policies may produce widespread or long-term counterproductive consequences. Their increased attention to the results of future studies has just begun to correct this deficiency.

Even when politicians and businessmen acknowledge that they should bring broader considerations into play in making decisions, they often find this difficult to do. Preference for narrow-perspective goals is usually more conducive to political or corporate success and is sometimes required for survival. The resultant tendency to discount the wider context and the more distant future is reinforced by the lack of generally accepted criteria for balancing immediate needs with, for instance, the well-being of future generations.

Moreover, numerous secondary, tertiary, and subsequent consequences of deliberate change are difficult, and in some cases virtually impossible, to anticipate. Hence even well-intentioned policies have frequently yielded unwanted consequences (see Table 1.1).

Furthermore, the speed, complexity, and disorderly character of change constitute further impediments to wide-perspective decision making. Change is proceeding at rates that have started to induce "future shock," a term Alvin Toffler (1970) coined to describe the stress and disorientation that people experience when subjected to excessive amounts of change in too short a time (p. 2). Admittedly, Toffler's analysis fails to stress the turbulence of change and appears to shortchange the human capability to adapt to rapid change. Yet such change, which restructures the character of society and renders old behavioral patterns outmoded, has tended to outdistance efforts to cope rationally with its upsetting consequences. Paradoxically, at the very time when policy decisions have become more important, they have also become harder to make intelligently. Confused, somewhat alienated, caught between obsolete-but-sanctioned traditional values and functional-but-anxiety-producing new ones, and fearful of the future, many decision makers and other citizens are prone to shrink from the task of forecasting and planning. However, failure to perform this task amounts of passive acceptance of those crises that could otherwise be averted or managed successfully. An example of this is the insufficient, inadequite forecasting, planning, and decision making that set the stage for the national energy crisis in the United States in 1973/74.

Need to Control Science-Based Technology

Unless efforts to control today's change are founded on knowledge of its underlying dynamics, they stand little chance of success. Many forces besides narrow-perspective decision making contribute directly or indirectly to change. Among them, the accelerating revolution in science-based technology is a primary instigator. Inventors employ breakthroughs in theoretical science to devise revolutionary technologies, the implementation of which often touches off sweeping changes. Recognition of this is not equivalent to technological determinism, which is simplistic.

From the end of World War II onward, science-based technologies have exerted potent impacts on human beings and their cultures, institutions, and

TABLE 1.1

Several Sociocultural Consequences, Most of Them Unintended and Hidden, of Television

First-order consequences	People have a new source of entertainment and enlightenment in their homes.
Second-order consequences	People stay home more, rather than going out to local clubs and bars where they would meet other people in their community.
Third-order consequences	As in the case of the automobile and improved refrigeration, television tends to keep residents of a community from meeting and getting to know each other. Television also makes people less dependent on each other for entertainment.
Fourth-order consequences	Strangers to each other, community members find it difficult to unite to deal with common problems. Individuals find themselves increasingly isolated and alienated from their neighbors. Moreover, television caters to the increased desire for entertainment to fill the time made available when people do not need to shop so often.
Fifth-order consequences	Isolated from their neighbors, members of a family depend more on each other for satisfaction of most of their psychological needs.
Sixth-order consequences	When spouses are unable to meet heavy psychological demands that each makes on the other, frustration occurs. This may lead to divorce.

Source: Adapted from Cornish et al. 1977a, pp. 75–76. (Courtesy of Edward Cornish and members of the World Future Society, *An Introduction to the Study of the Future*, 1977, published by the World Future Society.)

environments. For instance, the harnessing of atomic energy for military purposes has significantly altered international relations by inducing the still-escalating nuclear weapons race and the balance of terror. The U.S. space program has not only landed astronauts on the moon but has spun off satellites that have revolutionized the global communications system. Technologies based on breakthroughs in organic chemistry have brought about serious pollution in the United States. Modern technologies, many of which were not derived from breakthroughs in theoretical science, have engendered a wide range of consequences. Most people who have experienced these consequences have regarded some as predominantly beneficial and others as harmful. Still others have been hard to evaluate because of their complexities and mixed values. We can illustrate this by a brief list of consequences:

Unprecedented industrial development accompanied by rising standards of living,
Attainment of food security in Western nations,
Depletion of nonrenewable natural resources,
Pervasive pollution of air, land, and sea, destroying or endangering myriad species of flora and fauna,
Broadening income disparities between most of the rich and poor countries,
Eradication of many formerly widespread diseases,
A sharp rise in global population, primarily occasioned by reduction of infant mortality rates and extension of life-spans unbalanced by an equivalent decrease in birthrates,
Rampaging urbanization in developing countries,
Automation-induced unemployment,
Greatly expanded opportunities for education and other forms of self-actualization, including personal selection of social roles and life-styles by citizens of Western democracies,
Breakdown of traditional cultural systems of beliefs and values that maintained social cohesion; consequences of personal frustration and depression, anomie and alienation, and antisocial violence, and
Increasing susceptibility of local markets to "outside" influences, leading to loss of the stability provided by relatively local autonomy.

Judged merely by the standard of apparent technological feasibility, prospects for the future dwarf present realities.* Various sociocultural† forces interfere with the full realization of technological potential and could foreclose options. One example of such a restrictive force is failure to provide sufficient

---

The Year 2000 lists 100 technical innovations deemed very likely in the last third of the twentieth century, 25 less likely but important possibilities, and 10 "far-out" possibilities (Kahn and Wiener 1967, pp. 51–56). Also relevant is *Profiles of the Future* (Clarke 1973).

†Though the term *sociocultural* is rather cumbersome, I use it to emphasize the intertwined social and cultural aspects of many phenomena (Nelson 1969). *Socio* refers to institutional arrangements, *cultural*, to symbolic guidance systems (for instance, directives of the nation-state system, capitalism, and Hinduism), to lifeways (largely derived from such systems) that have been learned and may be transmitted, and to various products of human creation. In many of the instances in which I write about "change," a more accurate expression would be "sociocultural processes."

funds or effective leadership for research and development of those feasible technologies that promise to be most beneficial for the human race. Another is resistance by vested interests to the rapid implementation of a superior new technology when such implementation would depreciate their present capital. Intelligent, cooperative efforts can weaken the grasp of such powerful restrictions.

Despite contrary sociocultural forces, the technological capacity to bring about alternative futures to the benefit or detriment of vast numbers of people will probably continue to increase significantly. The recent interlinking of chains of developments in computer technology and telecommunications provides the technical capability for "information societies." In principle such societies could range from participatory democracies to totalitarian regimes, depending upon who controls and uses the information. Looming on the horizon is the extensive use of single-cell protein for food, lasers for military and peaceful purposes, completely automated air-ground warfare, and widespread recycling of discarded products. Also likely are technologies for processing lower-grade rock for minerals, effective control of one's own brain states by pushing buttons on a console linked to the brain by electrodes, and the availability of household robots for performing menial tasks. Even mining the moon and human genetic engineering appear to be technologically feasible. In addition to material and biological technologies, psychological and intellectual technologies (exemplified by biofeedback training and systems analysis) promise to mold the future.

To meet projected increases in demand for energy, the Atomic Energy Commission backed by the Nixon administration opted for "fast-breeder" reactors. These nuclear reactors would not only expand the energy supply; they would produce large amounts of highly toxic plutonium, which is difficult to dispose of safely. Since fissionable plutonium could be easily diverted to the construction of nuclear weapons, wipespread implementation of breeders would promote nuclear proliferation and pose the threat of theft by terrorists. Hence, the Carter administration has sought to suspend the multibillion-dollar breeder development program.

More benign are other prospective technologies funded by the Department of Energy, including two possible sources of abundant energy: solar electric energy converters and controlled thermonuclear fusion reactors. The consequences of the economic feasibility of either would be revolutionary. Affordable, nonpolluting solar electric energy, for instance, could be used to diminish pollution while increasing energy generation and the availability of raw materials, thus making much sustainable industrial growth feasible for the world.

During the rest of this century, the impact of new technology and attendant future shock may not continue to increase at as high a rate as has been experienced during the last three and one-half decades. John Platt suggests that technological changes will have decreasing influence because:

Instantaneous telecommunication speeds cannot be exceeded.
The 10^6 increase in data processing has already altered lifeways so significantly that further speedups will not have a commensurate influence.

The 10^2 rise in the speed of air travel and energy use has helped to make people accustomed to rapid change (Shane 1973, pp. 6-8).

Alternatively, we can imagine how technological breakthroughs or disastrous consequences of technologies could stimulate swift technological change before the year 2000. Some of the technologies that may be extensively implemented during the next century could cause the rate of impact to soar. Yet even if Platt's contention proves to be correct and Toffler's rather low estimate of the human capacity to adapt to swift change is confirmed, this will not obviate the pressing need to control change by choosing wisely among technologies.

Control of Change by Forecasting and Planning

The choice of one technology rather than another may lead to a radically different set of consequences, as illustrated by typical estimates of differential impacts of the breeder reactor, solar electric energy converters, and coal-fired power generators. Employment of certain technologies has secured extensive gains but at frightful costs. For instance, the dropping of atomic bombs on Hiroshima and Nagasaki ended World War II quickly but took a tragic toll of Japanese civilians and opened a Pandora's box: the nuclear "balance of terror."

To benefit from technology's power to shape alternative futures instead of being victimized by it, human beings need to assume responsibility for using it wisely. This calls for major changes. Too often decisions oriented toward developing and using technologies to attain short-term goals of specific interest groups exacerbate problems elsewhere in the system sooner or later. Societies—indeed, all humanity—can ill afford continued indifference to such decision making. Similarly, the counterproductive consequences of shortsighted choice among nontechnological goals and strategies render it unacceptable.

Rather than engaging in such narrow-perspective decision making and responding to resulting crises only after they have arisen, polities could make concerted efforts to anticipate crises. Some threatened crises could thereby be prevented and others confined within manageable boundaries. Otherwise, a rampage of chaotic changes might overwhelm the capacity for intelligent policy formulation. Crises could become so intractable that no attempt at amelioration could yield satisfactory results.

Thus, the revolution in science-based technology makes it imperative that contemporary societies employ comprehensive, long-range planning to control change.

One way to replace constricted, myopic decision making with systematic "precrisis management" is to rely on "technology assessment." Like the Environmental Impact Statement, technology assessment seeks to minimize the risks inherent in technological innovation by preparing advance estimates of the character and probabilities of the differential consequences that could flow from implementation. These estimates facilitate not only the avoidance or reduction of crises but also the selection of desirable alternative futures from a wide range of options.

Whether planned change achieves its goals depends largely on the quality of the forecasts on which it is based. Accordingly, the primary wellspring of the resurgent concern with forecasting is the perceived need to steer our epoch's turbulent change away from disasters and toward beneficial goals. Hence, futurists' forecasts had best be scrutinized for ways of bridling runaway change. Indeed, much of the motivation powering the growth of futurism has sprung from successes of researchers in improving forecasting methodology since the mid-1950s and from the related belief that the methodological capacity for adequately forecasting and controlling change may be in the offing. Nonetheless, almost all futurists now recognize the urgent need for further improvements.

IMPROVED METHODOLOGY

A Central Goal of Futurism

Projection of Policy-Oriented Alternative Futures

Futurists' methodological advances are by no means limited to specific forecasting methods but extend to their distinctive overall approach. Hence, we begin by inquiring: Can an examination of what futurists do and the goals that they pursue disclose any central methodological goal?

Ideally, futurists analyze policy issues in terms of alternative futures, describing each future and specifying the kinds of policy decisions, decision points, and events appropriate to attaining or avoiding it. Moreover, they suggest ways of coping with undesirable futures that may prove to be unavoidable. By broadening and illuminating the range of possible choices, this procedure tends to raise the level of policy discussion. Forecasting, despite its conjectural nature, is a socially valuable activity if it furnishes enough insight into possibilities, probabilities, and preferences to produce appreciably better policy formulation. Accordingly, *a central goal* of policy-relevant futurism is to project systematically a representative range of "alternative future histories" of varying degrees of probability and desirability and to suggest events and policy decisions by which each could be achieved or avoided, thereby providing policy makers and other citizens with insights that could enhance the quality of societal policy choices.

This general characterization depicts many futurists' basic orientation, although the aspirations of others are somewhat less ambitious. Degrees of probability and desirability are not always assigned to alternative futures. Forecasts sometimes omit transitional steps linking such futures with the present. Not all forecasters project an equally wide range of futures, nor do they all manifest an attitude as tentative as the characterization suggests. Instead of sketching broad future contexts, certain forecasters sometimes estimate dates by which particular technological innovations seem likely. Yet even then, inquiry focuses on possible developments rather than on the description of a single predetermined future.

These qualifications are compatible with our characterization of a "forecast" as a projection of a possible future or of a set of such futures. A good forecast summarizes present experience, which is historically grounded and ongoing, in ways that specify choices suitable for attaining broad societal goals or specific goals of various institutions within societies.

This overall futurist approach constitutes a general improvement in forecasting methodology. Forecasting, planning, implementation, and the interfaces between them offer the opportunity for much further development. However, the methodology and its applications have by no means attained the status of a genuine science or even of a mature art that controls change wisely. Yet formidable obstacles interfere with attempts to make the complicated forecasting-planning-implementation process sufficiently effective to ameliorate threatening international and national problems.

Need for Increased Application to Policy Making

We should not suppose that most policy makers, especially those in the U.S. government, are waiting downstream for futurists' insights. The faith in the future that has always characterized U.S. citizens has not required holistic, long-range planning but seems to have gratuitously presupposed that the host of decisions made to secure individuals' short-term self-interest would somehow benefit society in the long run. In spite of many government contracts with futurist think-tanks, passage of the important National Environmental Policy Act of 1969, and significant progress made by the establishment of the Office of Technology Assessment (1972) as well as by the House "foresight" requirement for congressional committees (1974), the use of long-range forecasting for planning has hardly begun to be integrated into the U.S. political system. Either of two future-oriented bills presented to Congress, Senator Vance Hartke's National Growth Policy Planning Act of 1972 or Senator Hubert Humphrey's Balanced National Growth and Development Act of 1972 (reintroduced in 1974), would have contributed to this integration had it been passed (Hartke 1972; Humphrey 1972). The Humphrey-Javitts bill (1976) sought to institutionalize long-range forecasting and planning in the government. The Congressional Clearinghouse on the Future was formed (1976) to encourage the development of foresight and the use of the resources of the Futures Research Group of the Congressional Research Service, the Office of Technology Assessment, and the Congressional Budget Office to evaluate the expected future impacts of legislation.

Some countries have progressed more rapidly than the United States in the use of forecasting for planning. Of the market-economy countries, France is a leader in incorporating forecasting and planning into its political system. Japan's recent progress in national planning is remarkable.

Does the aim of basing societal choices and extensive planning on forecasting dovetail with the principles of U.S. democracy? The query arises whether institutions will be organized in ways that promote responsible use of technological power while preventing authoritarian controls. Futurism is sometimes depicted merely as the attempt to anticipate and shape the future. In a democracy, however, anticipating and shaping are institutionally differentiated roles. These roles overlap, in practice, for several futurists are governmental decision makers, and forecasts sometimes function as "self-fulfilling prophecies." Indeed, the ultimate goal of futurism in a democracy is to shape the future wisely. Yet shaping that pertains to distinctly societal choices should be decided upon and carried out primarily through political processes. Apart from such choices, businesses, various social organizations, and individual people may also shape the future by their decisions and actions.

Most U.S. futurists stress the need to stimulate inputs from all segments of the populace concerning the desirability of alternative futures. Some of these futurists favor extensive public participation in future-oriented decision making. Still other futurists convey the impression that they would prefer to do the primary decision making themselves rather than entrust it to politicians and businessmen.

Having the polity shape and implement policies does run the serious risk that maximization of short-term benefits will prevail over policies required to meet long-term needs. Yet centralization of these roles, though perhaps more appealing for rapid implementation, has generally proved rather inefficient and inflexible when applied in Communist countries. Even if it were to become more efficient, many citizens of Western democracies would be willing to relinquish some efficiency to keep it relatively participatory. The likelihood of securing sufficient unanimity to implement policies both effectively and voluntarily can be increased by adopting the following strategy. Forecasters and planners need to detect current forms of behavior that are oriented toward distinctly undesirable outcomes for collectivities and, then, to design constructive policy changes that promote perceived commonalities of interest.

Contrast with Traditional "Genius Forecasting"

Now that we have characterized an overall methodological goal and analyzed how its ultimate aim of enhancing the quality of societal policy choices can be implemented in harmony with democratic principles, let us look more closely at methodological innovations that distinguish futurists' projections of alternative futures from most previous forecasting. Throughout the ages, much more attention has been devoted to obtaining forecasts from experts than to investigating and carefully evaluating whatever methods they may have used. *Genius forecasting* is the catchall term for a host of intuitive methods that, instead of following explicit rules, depend on insight and luck. Although genius forecasting still plays an important role in futurism, emphasis falls upon relatively formalized forecasting methods that employ objective procedures. Such procedures can be publicly checked and then improved. Even the use of genius forecasting by futurists is usually connected with more formalized methods.

Accompanying this shift from intuitive toward formalized methods is a parallel shift from prediction to projection. Whereas many genius forecasts have attempted to predict specific events, futurists' methods reveal a propensity to project a range of policy-oriented possible lines of development leading to alternative "contexts". In other words, a futurist's forecast may sketch various ways in which changes in such general features as resources, lifeways, and institutions could produce new contexts: structural sociocultural changes that create new frameworks for human interaction. For instance, a greatly restricted supply of petroleum and other natural resources might induce an industrially advanced democracy to switch to an authoritarian regime geared to enforcing frugality domestically and using force to obtain resources from abroad.

Tentative projections of a plurality of long-range contexts are far easier to justify than predictions of many kinds of specific distant events. An example is a forecast of the range of feasible structural changes in U.S. society by the year 2000, as contrasted with a prediction of who shall be the vice-president then. Even if an analyst could narrow the field of likely contenders for the nomination to a handful, which is clearly impossible, such unforeseeable events as a bullet or a campaign faux pas could invalidate a prediction. Conversely, contextual changes represent general shifts that tend to overcome countervailing forces, usually proceed at a relatively slow pace, and hence are less difficult to forecast.

Furthermore, projection is better fitted to aiding decision makers than is prediction. Projection of different contexts can facilitate choice among alternative policies, particularly when forecasters perceptively delineate choice points leading to each of the contexts.

Typical alternative futures are, therefore, basically contexts. Nonetheless, particular events that are possible—such as a key technological breakthrough or a nuclear war—often enter into characterizations of such futures, as do policy choices. Futurists sometimes try to estimate the likelihood of such occurrences.

The newer methodology consists of many partially interrelated methods that are intended to establish forecasts on a rational foundation. Analysts have enumerated over a hundred different methods, but these methods can be assigned to a few categories on the basis of similarities. Since a given method is more appropriate for some uses than for others, an evaluation of it should take this into account.

Exploratory Forecasting

The term *exploratory forecasting* implies no future facts waiting to be discovered but refers to attempts to delineate alternative futures that may occur. Forecasters project these futures on the basis of the present situation, which they interpret as emergent from the womb of the past and pregnant with various potentialities for the future.

Typically, forecasters begin by projecting fundamental types of futures that might occur at a given time and place. For each of these alternative futures, they then devise "scenarios" or plausible developmental sequences of events and decisions showing how it might come about. The result can be visualized as a tree of alternative future histories that at various times and in different ways branch away from the trunk of currently dominant societal trends. Then forecasters may assign degrees of probability and desirability to each possible future. Finally, they may recommend which future should be sought.

To formulate such exploratory forecasts of long-range, comprehensive futures, futurists have generally employed three basic types of methods: "trend extrapolation," "modeling," and the "Delphi technique." Futurists often enhance these methods by using them in conjunction with another method, "scenario writing."

Trend Extrapolation

Trends depict persistent developmental tendencies of large-scale, aggregate processes. Like established contexts, long-range trends have regularly prevailed

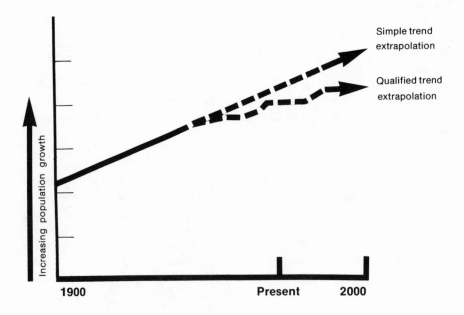

Figure 1.2. Examples of simple trend extrapolation and qualified trend extrapolation (see Chapter 3). (Constructed by the author.)

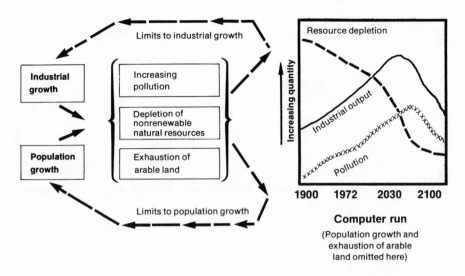

Figure 1.3. Example of modeling. Simplified version of Meadows's World3 model (see Chapter 7). (Constructed by the author.)

against obstacles that often block the continuation of sequences of specific events. Hence provisional inference from trends to alternative future contexts is far more warranted methodologically than confident prediction of distant events. A futurist may, for instance, project the rate and trajectory of the trend in electronic information technology (computers and communications media) to estimate the fundamental structural changes that this trend may bring about in U.S. society and culture by the year 2000.

"Simple trend extrapolation" assumes that the forces producing the trend will not change and that no external forces will interfere with the direction or rate of the trend (see Figure 1.2). "Qualified trend extrapolation," which tries to take into account possible changes in the basic causes of the trend, is more trustworthy. Yet a forecaster can easily ignore or misconstrue forces that could alter trends. Trend extrapolation needs to be used in conjunction with scenarios that reveal ways in which the trend may proceed.

Modeling

Futurists may map forces that might modify the rate or direction of a trend in a nonmathematical or a computer "model": a simplified analogue of the dynamic functioning of a complex system. By observing how components of the model interact, they can project ways in which the elements that comprise this system seem likely to interact in the future and how this may affect the system as a whole. Moreover, they can judge how the structure of the system influences

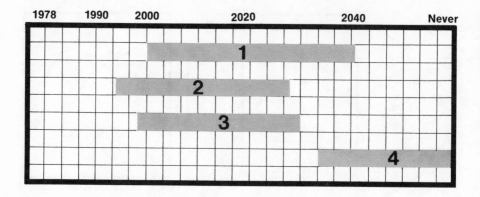

I. Chemical control of the aging process   3. Biochemicals to stimulate growth of new organs

2. Controlled thermo-nuclear power   4. Use of E.S.P. in communication

Consensus of panel on economically feasible new technologies

Figure 1.4. Example of the Delphi technique (see Chapter 2). (Constructed by the author.)

its behavior. To chart alternative futures, they can introduce into their model possible decisions, policies, or other developments that vary its causal assumptions (see Figure 1.3).

Since modeling is attuned to interacting forces in systems, it can suggest how forces might radically alter the direction of a trend. From a theoretical viewpoint, modeling is the best method by far. However, complex systems are difficult to model accurately.

The Delphi Technique

The Delphi technique is the most prominent of the so-called consensus methods for systematically soliciting and collating opinions of experts about any aspect of the future. Since anonymous respondents to questionnaires may revise their forecasts after receiving additional information concerning the forecasts of other respondents, successive rounds of a Delphi inquiry tend to generate increasing consensus among panel members. The Delphi technique is useful for systematically sampling expert opinion. Yet it ultimately depends on the intuitive genius forecasts of the experts and is more oriented toward forecasting particular items than contexts. The "cross-impact matrix" method, a form of modeling, can be employed to elicit intuitive estimates of potential causal interactions between items forecast in a Delphi inquiry, thus encouraging reappraisal of the probability of each item (see Figure 1.4).

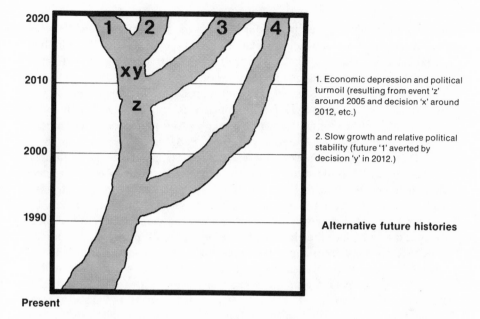

Figure 1.5. Example of scenario writing, with a "tree" of alternative future histories (see Chapter 6). (Constructed by the author.)

Scenario Writing

To make an alternative future more plausible, a forecast may invent a credible story of a potential course of developments leading to it. Of special importance in many scenarios are sequential decision points that govern policy. Whereas scenarios can be derived from such methods as computer modeling, they often result from insightful storytelling and thus embody a high degree of genius forecasting (see Figure 1.5).

Normative Forecasting

The primary aim of some forecasters is to project alternative futures of various degrees of likelihood; of others, to avoid undesirable futures and to actualize some desirable one. Appropriate to achieving the first aim is the general method of *exploratory forecasting*; to achieving the second, *normative forecasting* (also branded *normative planning*). Exploratory forecasting seeks to describe the kinds of futures that are relatively likely or unlikely to come about. Intentional, explicit evaluation enters into an exploratory forecast only as the last step, if at all. Normative forecasting *prescribes* what the future should or should not be like and then delineates paths for reaching or avoiding the selected future. Though some forecasts involve intentional mixes of exploratory and normative forecasting, the distinctions between the two processes and between the resulting forecasts are fundamental. The two types of forecast differ in their purpose and, consequently, in their design requirements, their selection of significant data, and their validation (Jones and Washburn 1978).

To decrease the danger that the beautiful maidens of normative theory will be ravished by a gang of ugly facts, normative forecasting should be founded upon, or at least be compatible with, the exploratory projection of sets of relatively likely and less likely alternative futures. Early in the forecasting process, normative forecasting focuses on the preference ordering of alternative futures. If none of the plausible futures seems sufficiently desirable, a forecaster may attempt to construct such a future. At any rate, a preferred future is posited as a goal. Next, the forecaster is obliged to make the selected future more likely by devising scenarios that specify feasible paths to it and then to select one of these paths as the best. Since the preferred future, or the "target projection," is usually quite unlikely apart from appropriate policy changes and an intelligently implemented program designed to achieve it, normative forecasting is unreliable unless it includes perspicacious planning. Even then, unanticipated events may block attainment of the goal. Yet this method provides a means of translating forecasting into planning. The implementation of such planning sometimes "creates the future" by shaping it to conform to chosen goals. An instance of normative forecasting and planning is furnished by President John F. Kennedy's decision to land astronauts on the moon and the consequent planning performed by Project Apollo.

CONFLICTS WITHIN FUTURISM

Incompatible Forecasts

The uncertainties and the realities of our technologically shaped epoch evoke both utopian hopes and depressing fears. Technological potentialities encourage images of a world in which poverty, disease, malnutrition, and war would be minimized. Dangerous by-products of technological change—pollution, natural resource depletion, food shortages, overpopulation, nuclear weapons proliferation, the widening gap between rich and poor countries, and the possibility of totalitarian surveillance—arouse anxiety that catastrophes may occur causing unprecedented suffering. Nearly all forecasts acknowledge the possibility of both promising and perilous, though not necessarily utopian or catastrophic, alternative futures.

Many, but not all, futurists agree that breakthroughs in electronic information technology (computers and telecommunications) and "intellectual technology" (the substitution of problem-solving rules for reliance on intuition in decision making) have begun to transform the United States into a postindustrial society or an "information society." As computerized automation takes over the tasks of material production, the work force shifts increasingly into the service sectors of the economy. On the basis of possibilities opened up by electronic information technology, a small elite that controls the information could govern postindustrial society; or, on the contrary, such a society could employ decentralized, participatory decision making on many important issues. Zbigniew Brzezinski (1968) contends that the movement to this new form of society will be comparable with the industrial revolution in its impact, which will drastically alter the essence of individual and social existence.

Despite their agreement that the United States is becoming a postindustrial society, postindustrial theorists disagree concerning several future characteristics of this type of society: likely diffusion and degree of development, probable duration, general desirability, best form of government, and so on. Some futurists believe that countervailing forces are likely to nip the shift to postindustrial society in the bud. Thus a societal metamorphosis appears to be unfolding, but the type of butterfly or moth our present caterpillar will become remains in doubt, as does the completion of this transformation.

Futurists' images of the most likely kind of future vary considerably. Moreover, we can distinguish forecasts from one another by so many different criteria that any typology of forecasts is bound to be somewhat simplistic. A fundamental cleavage, however, differentiates two types of images of the future: "continuous progressive evolution" and "discontinuous change." As O. W. Markley (1971) perceives, a crucial gap separates those who anticipate a continuation of present trends and those who insist that a drastic change is inevitable and possibly desirable (p. 9). Typically, but not invariably, forecasters who concentrate on *developmental futures* manifest various degrees of optimism. Conversely, forecasters of *turning-point futures* tend to display considerable pessimism about the directions of current trends. Yet they range from decidedly optimistic to moderately pessimistic concerning the capability of human beings to control dangerous trends, resolve interrelated global problems, and create desirable futures (see Figure 1.6).

Some futurists, such as Herman Kahn (1972) argue that current trends, anticipated technological breakthroughs, and an enlightened "business as usual" orientation should be relied upon to bestow increasing global affluence. Admittedly, a full-scale thermonuclear war or other cataclysm might prevent the attainment of postindustrial culture on a global scale. These futurists believe, however, that such catastrophes will probably be avoided by the rational management of change.

Opposing this image of the future as relatively continuous development from the present are futurists such as Willis Harman (1976) and Dennis Meadows (1972). They view present trends and interrelated problems as pushing toward undesirable futures and possible disasters. To achieve a desirable future, human beings must deliberately intervene to change certain values, institutions, and trends. "Technological fixes" must be supplemented by value changes that would

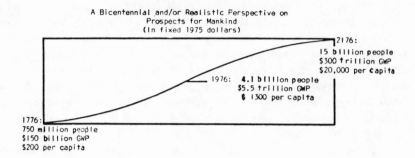

A Bicentennial and/or Realistic Perspective on
Prospects for Mankind
(In fixed 1975 dollars)

2176:
15 billion people
$300 trillion GWP
$20,000 per capita

1976: 4.1 billion people
$5.5 trillion GWP
$ 1300 per capita

1776:
750 million people
$150 billion GWP
$200 per capita

"The great transition" (Kahn, Brown, and Martel, 1976, p. 6).

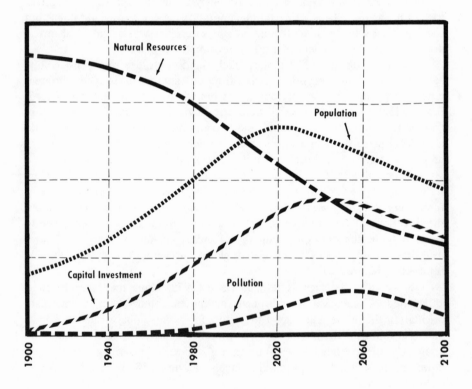

"Limits to growth" forecasts of Forrester and Meadows (*Futurist*, August 1971).

Figure 1.6. Examples of a developmental future and a turning-point future. (See Chapters 7 and 8.)

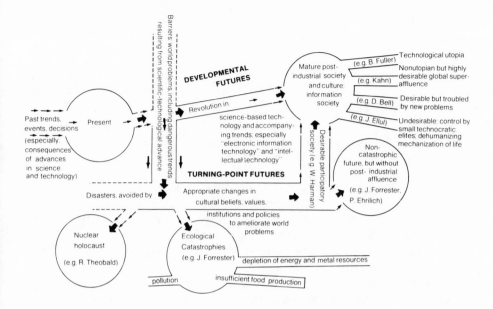

Figure 1.7. Simplified diagram of forecasts of developmental futures that involve relatively continuous evolution to one of the types of postindustrial society, as contrasted with forecasts of turning-point futures formulated by "provisional catastrophists." (Constructed by the author.)

transform present sociocultural systems. Thus, for these futurists, both desirable and undesirable futures tend to be discontinuous with, and radically different from, the present (see Figure 1.7).

This division of forecasters into two opposing camps on the basis of their images of the most likely type of future should not obscure major differences among those within each camp. Some who consider discontinuous futures to be more likely disagree markedly about those futures and about methodology. Similar disagreements set forecasters of relatively continuous futures apart from each other. Differences between members of a camp can even exceed differences that separate some of them from certain members of the other camp. For instance, Harman and Meadows appear to differ more than Harman and Anthony J. Wiener, who coauthored *The Year 2000* (1967) with Kahn. Although Wiener's forecasting centers attention on relatively continuous futures, he, unlike Kahn, does not argue that they are more likely.

Thus, complications arise because some forecasters have not committed themselves concerning the likelihood of the kind of futures they typically project. Still another problem is posed by the question: How abrupt should a change from present trends be to qualify as a discontinuity? In the absence of shared criteria, one forecaster's discontinuity may be another's continuity. Rather than undermining the primary distinction between forecasts of developmental and turning-point futures, such qualifications illustrate the need to distinguish various shades and grades of differences.

Major Controversies

The clash between proponents of forecasts of likely developmental and turning-point futures centers in disputes concerning:

Methodological assumptions that affect the type of future projected,
Influence of forecasters' implicit beliefs and values on their forecasts,
The directions in which trends are moving as well as the human ability to cope with problems and bring about fundamental planned changes,
The projected outcomes of extensive nuclear proliferation and of an increasing gap between rich and poor countries,
Consequences of continued industrial and population growth, and
The feasibility and advisability of widespread participation in decision making.

The last two disputes call for explanation at this point. The "growth controversy" has generated a countermovement within futurism as has the "participation controversy."

Of primary concern among futurists today is the growth controversy. A key issue is expressed by the question: Do such factors as the pollution absorption capacity of the global environment, the finite amount of potentially arable land, and the depletion of nonrenewable natural resources threaten to limit global industrial development and population growth drastically within the next century? Optimists such as Herman Kahn (1972) contend that technological innovations and rational policies can push back limits to growth, thus bringing huge increases in the global material standard of living. Conversely, "provisional catastrophists" such as Dennis Meadows (1972) claim that the human race may be in imminent danger of encountering limits to the exponential growth of industrialization and population. "Overshoots" of the earth's carrying capacity of industrialization and population could trigger global collapses of both. To avoid such overshoots, Meadows avers, human beings must soon stabilize both industrialization and population around the zero-growth level.

Central to the growth controversy is the question of whether enough reasonably priced energy will be generated to sustain a growing global industrial system and to supply sufficient food to an expanding population without producing excessive amounts of pollution. Hence, the energy debate has become especially prominent. Another crucial aspect of the growth controversy concerns the extent to which current limits to sustainable economic growth inhere in unnecessarily restrictive sociocultural constraints. These constraints, which result from such ecologically unsound practices as failure to recycle waste, would be loosened by appropriate changes in policies, institutions, goals, and cultural beliefs and values. Futurists argue about which changes are appropriate and about how they could be facilitated.

In the participation controversy, the most basic issue concerns the distribution of power in postindustrial society. Much debate focuses on the question: Should decision making in postindustrial society be done by relatively small groups of experts, or should electronic information technology be used to involve citizens in the decision-making process? Normative forecasts that favor the latter alternative require a more fundamental departure from current trends. Zbigniew Brzezinski (1968) is a proponent of an elitist, technocratic, "meritocratic" democracy; Robert Theobald (1976a), of a discontinuous future of participatory democracy.

As might be expected, the participation controversy is by no means limited to the primary debate about the postindustrial distribution of power but extends to all forms of decision making everywhere at all future times. In particular, it focuses on the question of who should have the decision-making power to enact policies designed to cope with global problems, such as nuclear proliferation and the ecological problems that have given rise to the growth controversy.

Strands of U.S. Futurism

Efforts to isolate strands of U.S. futurism must be viewed against the backdrop of its complex diversity. Just as members of a family differ from one another to various degrees in a number of salient respects, so futurists differ from each other. Diverse criteria for classifying futurists would yield correspondingly different strands of futurism. When the criterion is divergence of forecasts as judged primarily by conflicting positions in the growth and participation controversies, the following four strands can be roughly differentiated in terms of four divergent clusters of similar forecasts. This categorization does not profess to preclude much diversity within strands or areas in which some strands overlap others.

The *establishment strand* expects relatively continuous progress toward postindustrial society governed by a meritocratic elite. Strongly influenced by previous work at the RAND Corporation, this large establishment-oriented strand developed social forecasting but neglected ecological problems until recently. One leading institutional contributor to the development of this strand is the Hudson Institute. Another is the American Academy of Arts and Sciences' "Commission on the Year 2000," chaired by Daniel Bell.

The smaller, less-institutionalized *participatory strand* emerged during the 1960s and early 1970s as a challenge to the meritocratic elitism of forecasts by the establishment strand. Such provisional catastrophists as Robert Theobald use normative forecasting to show how elitist forms of postindustrial society might be avoided and participatory forms created.

The *ecologically optimistic strand* was fairly prominent during the 1960s and continues to be heard. Composed of diverse substrands, this basically nonestablishment strand includes those science fiction writers and "blue-sky prophets" who paint portraits of technological utopias. An important substrand propounds full-fledged technological optimism and "utopia-or-oblivion" provisional catastrophism. The centers of this substrand have been the Committee for the Future, recently dissolved, and the World Resources Inventory, launched at Southern Illinois University in 1962 by Buckminster Fuller and John McHale. The Committee for the Future significantly overlapped the participatory strand.

The fourth strand, which is pessimistic concerning the directions of current ecological trends, may be termed the *ecological provisional catastrophist strand*. Many of its forecasts issue warnings about ecological catastrophes that could be avoided or decreased in impact by fundamental cultural and institutional changes. Hence this strand, which combines social and ecological forecasting, emphasizes the likelihood of turning-point futures. It began to emerge in the late 1960s, touched off the growth controversy, and became a powerful countermovement within futurism during the early 1970s. This challenge to both the establishment and the ecologically optimistic strands opposes the so-called business as usual orientation and ardent technological optimism. Paradoxically, an important part of this attack is launched from the heart of the establishment, as exemplified by the forecast formulated by Jay Forrester in 1971 at the Massachusetts Institute of Technology.

COMPARATIVE EVALUATION OF SELECTED FORECASTS

Decision makers and other citizens are currently confronted with incompatible policy-oriented forecasts but have little rationale for deciding among them. This has produced considerable perplexity about which forecasts provide the most suitable guidelines for action. Hence, we need perceptive comparative evaluations of forecasts to help dispel such confusion. I seek to provide such an evaluation.

Criteria for Evaluating Forecasts

General Considerations

Anyone who wishes to appraise forecasts is confronted by the question, What makes one forecast better than another? The principal criterion is not accuracy but usefulness in promoting wise policy choices. More specifically, the worth of a forecast depends significantly on the extent to which it both manifests and evokes creative imagination in ways that enlarge planners' and decision makers' feasible options. A forecast should, therefore, convey interesting new information that makes some possible responses more appropriate than others.

A forecast that happens to be proved correct may have been based on faulty data, untenable assumptions, and dubious inferences. Such a forecast is inferior to an incorrect one derived from better data, assumptions, and inferences, since well-reasoned forecasts are generally more likely to enhance the quality of policy formulation. Furthermore, the primary purpose of a forecast of possible disaster is to become self-negating. A forecast of this sort may be extremely useful to decision makers who take steps to make it incorrect. Thus, a negative outcome does not necessarily invalidate a forecast.

Because of such considerations, some futurists minimize the importance of careful estimates of the differential likelihood of alternative futures. They maintain that what really matters is whether decision makers remain sufficiently aware and flexible to change their policies as forecasts go awry. In other words, organizational responses are much more important than the reliability of estimates of likelihood or even than the quality of forecasts.

However, this approach, though often workable in the short run for small and medium-sized organizations, cannot provide a firm foundation for large-scale planning aimed at coping with long-term, interrelated global problems. Provisional catastrophist forecasts assert that catastrophes will probably or possibly occur if preventive steps are not taken. The credibility of these forecasts depends on whether, in the light of current evidence, the risk of disasters is sufficient to warrant the recommended efforts to avoid them. Moreover, normative forecasters are obliged to show that their preferred futures can be made likely enough to justify being selected as goals for planned change. Thus, well-founded, tentative estimates of likelihood (that is, subjective probability) are needed for intelligent planning.

More generally, useful forecasts issue from careful analysis of the best available data and theories. In other words, a good forecast projects from the available information on the relevant subject in ways fitted to enhance the quality of decision making. One of the important features of such a forecast is that it accurately conveys the appropriate degree of confidence concerning the subject.

Two further comments are pertinent at this point. The first clarifies terminology used in the subsequent analysis of forecasts and the second guards against a possible misunderstanding.

For the sake of brevity and stylistic variety, I employ several nontechnical terms—*adequate, dependable, trustworthy, reliable*—to evaluate forecasts favorably. They do not mean "accurately describes what is going to happen" but, rather, imply that the forecasts are useful for decision making. This in turn presupposes that the data, assumptions, and inferences of the forecasts can be justified by the best available information.

The insistence that forecasters should seek to make optimal use of the best available factual and theoretical information does not presuppose that all the aspects of the future other than major policy decisions are predictable in theory.

Most professional futurists assign to unexpected occurrences and intrinsically unknowable factors a role equal to or greater than human choice in determining which future will come about.

A Formal Set of Criteria?

We can formulate various criteria for assessing the quality of forecasts by detecting the factors that make forecasts useful for policy making. For instance, a forecast should creatively convey available, interesting, new information. Moreover, the appropriate degree of confidence, which sometimes precludes judgment concerning which future is most likely, needs to be expressed. Roy Amara, president of the Institute for the Future, and Gerald Selancik (1972) have proposed six indicators of forecast quality:

Specificity: stated specifically enough to permit unambiguous determination of fulfillment or nonfulfillment;

Uncertainty: estimate of probability of occurrence;

Time relatedness: embeddedness of stages of change in accurate knowledge of present conditions and development;

Intrafield relatedness: knowledgeable appraisal of the manner in which developments in the same field as the forecasted event will affect it;

Interfield relatedness: assessment of how developments in other fields may influence the event in question; and

Recognition of costs and benefits: incorporation of perceptive judgments about economic and social benefits, costs, and trade-offs (pp. 112-13).

These indicators were selected to help fomulators and users of forecasts ascertain whether a particular forecast is:

Reproducible from the given state of information,

Internally consistent and proximately validated (judged by monitoring forecasted states as events unfold), and

Explicit about the value system of the forecaster (p. 116).

This analysis by Amara and Selancik constitutes a promising beginning but does little to accomplish their ambitious goal of moving forecasting from "conjectural art toward science" (p. 112). I seriously considered evaluating forecasts on the basis of such an explicitly stated set of criteria. However, this approach is rendered questionable by omissions in current lists of criteria, lack of knowledge as to how the criteria should be weighted, the sometimes implausible results of applying the criteria, and the many respects in which forecasts differ. As Amara and Selancik recognize, it is by no means easy to formulate a nonarbitrary set of weighted criteria applicable to all forecasts. One precondition appears to be careful analysis of strengths and weaknesses of various forecasts. Even then, the extent to which this set of criteria would prove useful for further analysis remains problematic. Although I employ the Amara-Selancik criteria where appropriate and other criteria as well, I make no attempt to evaluate each forecast on the basis of such a set of criteria or to derive a formal set of weighted criteria from the evaluation.

Need for Analysis of Assumptions

What we require is a comparative analysis of the ways in which *incompatible assumptions* tend to *produce conflicting forecasts*. Moreover, we need to evaluate these assumptions. This will place us in a much better position to judge the extent to which various forecasts are suitable as guides to policy makers and to people generally.

Images of the future as continuous with current trends are typically associated with the use of the method of trend extrapolation as discontinuous, with modeling and normative forecasting. For instance, Kahn and Wiener (1967) depend primarily on qualified trend extrapolation; Meadows (1972), on computerized global modeling that involves both exploratory and normative forecasting. Such methodological assumptions tend to bias the resulting forecasts in specific directions. Forecasting methods function like different kinds of fishing nets: the varieties of fish caught depend in part on the kind of net employed. Since different methodological nets tend to catch different batches of factual fish, methodological assumptions affect the collection as well as the interpretation of data.

From his examination of various forecasts of national trends in population, economics, energy, transportation, and technology during a 50-year period, Ascher (1978) concludes that core assumptions concerning the broad context of a trend tend to affect the character of a forecast more than does the degree of methodological sophistication. Clearly, various assumptions that are not inherent in the methodology employed also shape the divergent images that emerge full-blown in forecasts. A forecaster's implicit preferences and beliefs can unwittingly "anchor" a forecast, thus subverting the presumed commitment to objectivity, influencing the purpose in forecasting, and biasing the consequent choice of method, the selection and interpretation of data, and the resulting forecast. Thus, "nonmethodological assumptions," which so far have received relatively little attention, play crucial roles in distorting forecasts. For instance, they can subtly influence forecasters' judgments concerning such factors as the likely trajectories of current trends (including the revolution in science-based technology); the capacity to use extensive planned change to cope with global problems; and the relative worth of various alternative futures.

My primary aim is to provide *a comparative analysis of representative policy-oriented forecasts in terms of their methodological and nonmethodological assumptions*. This involves intensive, systematic investigation of which forecasts are better than others and exploration of ways in which the forecasts could be improved. To keep the description of forecasts from becoming quickly outdated, I have made a special effort to select representative types of forecasts. Moreover, much of the evaluation pertains not merely to the specific forecasts but to types of forecasts and even to forecasts generally. Hence, the reader who wishes to evaluate new forecasts as they are formulated can fruitfully employ many points raised by the present analysis. Its ultimate goal is to enhance the quality of action-oriented thought about options for the future.

Though this study employs an interdisciplinary approach in explicating and evaluating assumptions, sociology plays a leading role. Knowledge of historically derived sociocultural structures and processes is valuable not only for criticizing assumptions but for improving them and the forecasts based upon them. Admittedly, sociology is by no means a mature science. Yet, one can plausibly argue, for instance, that the usual deficiency in forecasting changes in value-priorities (a deficiency of which many futurists are painfully aware) stems in part from lack of knowledge of much of the best work in historical sociology.

Criteria for evaluating forecasts on the basis of their underlying assumptions about sociocultural change emerge gradually in the course of the comparative evaluation. I have sought to use theories that are mutually consistent and justifiable. My theoretical approach comes closer to Benjamin Nelson's (1969) than to that of any other well-known analyst of sociocultural processes.

Do my own assumptions subtly bias my analysis of assumptions of forecasts? Though, subsequently, I propose a method for systematically eliciting implicit assumptions (see Chapter 9), it is still in its infancy. Rather than attempting to list my assumptions hierarchically, I have sought to make them easily detectable and to provide plausible evidence to support debatable ones.

Obviously, an evaluation of forecasts cannot be value free. Analysts can, however, explicate and assess their own normative assumptions. I have made a concerted effort to prevent my implicit preferences from issuing in an unfair comparative analysis of forecasts. By assessing ways in which questionable assumptions distort forecasts, I have become acutely aware of the obstacles that frustrate attempts to articulate and justify all of one's own assumptions. The reader is invited to help me search for any unjustifiable assumptions that still bias my analysis.

Probably the strongest objection to my comparative evaluation of forecasts is that the intensity of the critique is not entirely evenhanded. Although I have sought to reduce this unevenness, I cannot eliminate it completely and still argue for specific positions on issues that I regard as important. For instance, my focus in Chapter 8 on the ways in which the Kahn-Brown-Martel forecast (*The Next 200 Years* [1976]) seriously shortchanges sociocultural limits to growth allows me to set forth my position on a crucial issue in the growth controversy. To devote equal attention to the commendable features of the forecast would disrupt the continuity of the argument. I think that the reader who makes allowance for my efforts to advance argumentation on key issues will find the treatment quite fair.

The selected forecasts are appraised not only in terms of their theoretical assumptions but also in regard to their inferences from these assumptions and their use of data. Divergent forecasts would be easier to compare and assess if they were all rooted in the same explicit data base. However, the forecasts do not have identical data bases. Since the data bases are usually insufficiently specified, their degrees of overlap are somewhat obscure.

Selection of Forecasts

Futurists acknowledge that specialized, short-range forecasts, though usually easier to make, fail to provide the perspective necessary for satisfactorily coping with long-range, interrelated global problems. The field of inquiry is restricted here to comprehensive, long-range forecasts. To promote clarity, *comprehensive* may be stipulatively defined as global in extent, or at least covering diverse features of a nation's future and having global ramifications; *long-range*, as extending at least 20 years into the future. Of paramount importance for our purposes are forecasts of the year 2000 and of the period between 2000 and 2100.

A number of important forecasts formulated in the United States during the past 15 years are long-range and comprehensive, based on the use of different forecasting methods, characterized by incompatible images of the kind of future that is deemed most likely, and representative of divergent positions in the growth and participation controversies. This study describes, compares, and evaluates selected forecasts in this limited context. Thereby, it secondarily treats the development of U.S. futurism in terms of the responses of leading futurists to consequences of the revolution in science-based technology, the forecasts of other futurists, and objections raised by adversaries of futurism.

From the establishment strand of U.S. futurism, forecasts by the RAND Delphi panels (a study conducted by Olaf Helmer [1966] and Theodore J. Gordon), Zbigniew Brzezinski (1968), Herman Kahn and Anthony J. Wiener (1967) (updated by Kahn and B. Bruce-Briggs 1972), Daniel Bell (1973a), and Herman Kahn, William Brown, and Leon Martel (1976b) are selected for careful examination in Chapters 2, 3, 4, 5 and 8, respectively. These forecasts of relatively continuous development to a prosperous postindustrial era exhibit significant differences as well as similarities. Though the Kahn-Brown-Martel forecast sets forth a turning-point future, analysis discloses that it really belongs to this strand. Bell's (1976) new forecast (see Chapter 5) projects a much sharper departure from trends that have characterized the recent past. Objections that both futurists and opponents of futurists have raised against these forecasts are assessed.

The participatory strand displays a general lack of sophisticated forecasts, partly because discontinuous social futures are more difficult to conceptualize than continuous ones. Nevertheless, criticisms set forth by participatory futurists such as Robert Theobald are considered during the evaluation of the forecasts made by Brzezinski and Bell.

Since this study is primarily concerned with what is commonly termed *social* rather than *technological* forecasting, it provides no detailed analysis of forecasts from the ecologically optimistic strand. Yet it mentions a few during the examination of the growth controversy in Chapters 7 and 8. The forecasts that emerged from the Gordon-Helmer Delphi poll and the Kahn-Brown-Martel forecast, here analyzed in conjunction with the establishment strand, display such similarities to some forecasts of the ecologically optimistic strand that they could even be treated as one of its segments.

Chapters 6 and 7 evaluate representative forecasts chosen from the ecological provisional catastrophist strand: those made by Willis Harman (1970a, 1976) and others at the EPRC of Stanford Research Institute and by Dennis Meadows's (Meadows et al. 1972) international team that was sponsored by the Club of Rome and worked at the Massachusetts Institute of Technology. Despite agreement on certain general points, these forecasts of turning-point futures differ markedly. Both were formulated in contradistinction to forecasts of developmental futures. The Kahn-Brown-Martel forecast, though assigned to the establishment strand, is not analyzed until Chapter 8 because it presents a gradual turning-point future as a critique of the Meadows forecast. My extensive evaluation of these two forecasts is designed to yield an assessment of the growth controversy.

Admittedly, none of the forecasts that are most representative of the second and third strands is among those examined in detail. Yet the forecasts selected are important, fairly representative, and appropriate to the primary purpose of this analysis. They are formulated by professional futurists (that is, full-time forecasters) and by professors who are very concerned with forecasting. This does not reduce futurism to an elite enterprise that excludes public participation in choices between alternative futures. Nor does it minimize the contributions of perceptive science-fiction writers who, having their imaginations unfettered by institutional constraints, have often sketched more accurate pictures of the future than forecasters employed by establishment institutions. However, the forecasts formulated by Isaac Asimov, Arthur Clarke, and other writers of this genre tend to be more technologically oriented, less comprehensive, less policy relevant, or longer-range than the forecasts just selected.

Chapter 9 briefly summarizes salient weaknesses of current forecasts and prospects for improved forecasting.

Thus this study presents a comparative evaluation of selected long-range, comprehensive forecasts that are both important and representative of different orientations in U.S. futurism. Table 1.2 provides a preliminary overview of salient features of these forecasts.

TABLE 1.2

Chart of Forecasts

Forecasters	Institutional Affiliation	Method	Scope of Forecast	Focus of Forecast	Forecast
Poll of experts conducted by T. Gordon and O. Helmer, 1963/4	RAND Corporation	Delphi technique	World until the years 1984, 2000, and 2100	Beneficial consequences of probable technological breakthroughs; little concern about ecological problems	Rapid technological progress that is likely to lead to an affluent, automated world: (1) chief problem—danger of nuclear war; (2) still, confidence in the human ability to reduce greatly the probability of such war; (3) more emphasis on consensus concerning the future than on alternative futures
Z. Brzezinski, forecast made in 1968	Member of Commission the Year 2000 (unsponsored forecast); professor at Columbia University	Simple trend extrapolation and genius forecasting (methodology basically implicit)	United States (as the leader of the world)	Almost exclusive attention to the impact of breakthroughs in electronic information technology	Continuous progress to an affluent, automated technetronic age: (1) close to technological determinism; (2) society governed by a meritocratic elite, which controls the information; (3) very narrow range of alternative futures

TABLE 1.2 (continued)

Forecasters	Institutional Affiliation	Method	Scope of Forecast	Focus of Forecast	Forecast
H. Kahn and A. Wiener 1967 (also Kahn and B. Bruce-Briggs, 1972)	Hudson Institute (Kahn and Wiener are also members of the Commission on the Year 2000)	Qualified trend extrapolation; also, other methods, including scenario writing	World until the year 2000; also the early twenty-first century	Wide; many technologies, cultures, and so forth; emphasis on increasing global affluence, not on ecological problems	Probably, relatively continuous progress to affluent postindustrial society and culture: (1) continuation of the multifold trend; (2) in the twenty-first century, posteconomic society; (3) many alternative futures, but not covering a very wide range
D. Bell, 1973	Chairman of the Commission on the Year 2000 (unsponsored forecast); professor at Harvard University	"Axial principles and structures" (protomodeling; reliance on trends; importance of societal disjunctions)	United States (minimal reference to the world)	Codification and application of theoretical knowledge; change in the social structure; only minor attention to ecological and international problems (compensated for by Bell's 1976 forecast)	Relatively continuous progress to a mature, affluent, postindustrial (but not posteconomic) society: (1) primarily, a change in the social structure: rise of a professional-technical class, key members of which use intellectual technology; (2) centrality of codified knowledge; (3) rule by meritocratic elite (though not a pure technocracy); (4) absence of basically different alternative futures
W. Harman, from 1970 on (also, O.W. Markley and others, 1971 on; updated by	Educational Policy Research Center of Stanford Research Institute (contract with U.S.	FAR morphological modeling (nonmathematical); also, a problem-oriented intuitive method	United States (though the world macroproblem is important for its future) until the	Broad: combines social ecological forecasting, though little emphasis on electronic information technology	Wide range of fundamentally different alternative futures: (1) stress on futures that are discontinuous with present trends; (2) to attain a desirable future ("New Society"), need to ameliorate the world macroproblem

cultural beliefs, operative values, and institutions

to the middle of the twenty-first century)

D. Meadows et al 1972 (also J. Forrester 1971)	Professor at Massachusetts Institute of Technology (Meadows's international team sponsored by the Club of Rome)	System Dynamics—computer simulation (mathematical modeling)	World till the year 2100	Stresses ecological problems, not beneficial consequences of prospective technologies or sociocultural constraints on growth	Probable consequence of a continuation of the exponential growth of industry and population—counterintuitive overshoots, followed by disastrous collapses of both during twenty-first century: (1) depletion of nonrenewable natural resources, pollution and exhaustion of arable land: principal limits to growth; (2) to avoid catastrophe, need to achieve global equilibrium in which growth is stabilized
H. Kahn, W. Brown, and L. Martel 1976b	Hudson Institute	Scenario-writing (heavily dependent on trends)	World till the year 2176	Answer to ecological pessimists: naturally occurring, adaptive value change leading to gradual decreases in the growth rates of population and industrialization; also, harnessing of abundant, clean, inexpensive energy; little attention to limits to technological progress and to disaster-prone sociocultural contraints	Historical turningpoint to slower growth—decline so gradual that it makes feasible by 2176 a world of 15 billion people with an annual per capita income of $20,000: (1) normative changes: induced by rising per capita income; (2) global post-industrial superaffluence attained not by planned intervention to rectify global problems but by moderate technological advance and reasonably good management

Source: Compiled by the author.

PART I

FORECASTS OF DEVELOPMENTAL FUTURES

INTRODUCTION
TO PART I

In today already walks tomorrow.
Coleridge

Anticipated impacts of information technology play a crucial role in most forecasts of relatively continuous progress to mature postindustrial society. The term *information technology* refers to the techniques employed in the collection, storage, processing, dissemination, and use of information. The revolution in information technology stems from the introduction of computers and televisions, as well as from the development since 1940 of cybernetics, information theory, game theory, decision theory, and other techniques for managing complex systems to attain specific goals. Decisive innovations between 1954 and 1963 fused two lines of development: computer technology and telecommunications technology (McHale 1976). Mass production coupled with expected progress in space age miniaturization may enable many U.S. families to acquire computerized telecommunications consoles for their homes long before the turn of the century. Numerous activities that now require transportation (such as executive board meetings) could be carried out by electronic communication. The use of computerized data in the policy-formulation and decision-making processes will very probably continue to increase.

Electronic data processing has already begun to transform the information environment, thus reshaping the information content and perception of society in ways that seem likely to induce profound changes in wealth, power, and value-priorities. Knowledge, as the organized information that programs and governs the performance of machines, may become the most valuable "property" (McHale 1976, pp. 185-238). An example of the increasing importance of knowledge is the computerized calculation without which Project Apollo could not have been successful.

Advances in computer technology have created the opportunity for extensive automation of industrial production. *Cybernation*, a term that Michael coined, refers to this combination of the computer and the automated self-regulating machine. Accompanying the ongoing trend of automation in the United States has been the movement of a growing percentage of the labor force into the service sectors of the economy. Affluence and leisure time have also increased.

A number of forecasters interpret these changes as the beginning of a transition to a postindustrial age. The various expressions offered to christen the projected results of this transition include "postindustrial society," "post-industrial culture," and "technetronic age." Since *postindustrial* might be misconstrued as *nonindustrial* and does not suggest the increasingly important societal functions of information and knowledge, "information society" and "knowledge society" constitute more appropriate names. In particular, the new ways of handling information prompt visions of a wealthy computerized society guided by intelligent analysts who coordinate the information.

Policies needed to attain a postindustrial age accelerate the increasing "rationalization" of thought and action: the tendency to become more rational in the selection of strategies to attain goals. An integral aspect of rationalization is the policy-oriented projection of alternative futures by means of objective methods. Some analysts of postindustrial society emphasize such problem-solving techniques, known as "intellectual technology," more than the spectrum of electronic information technologies. Accordingly, they expect theoretical knowledge to become the chief source of policy formulation and innovation. Regardless of whether expected consequences of intellectual technology or electronic information technology predominate in a given forecast, it treats information as central to the structure and development of society.

An enlightening starting point for examining forecasts of a postindustrial age is the ambitious, wide-ranging Delphi inquiry conducted by Theodore Gordon and Olaf Helmer at RAND in 1963/64. Though deeply flawed, this daring venture remains a bench-mark study because of its methodological innovations, its stimulus to the burgeoning discipline of forecasting, and its embryonic conception of what came to be known as postindustrial society. The panelists' projections display their awareness of consequential ongoing breakthroughs in automation, electronic communication, and computerization, as well as problems engendered by the need for only the most talented people to manage the automated economy. Hence, this forecast paved the way for subsequent forecasts of a postindustrial age.

Primarily on the basis of explicit or implicit extrapolation from present trends, such U.S. forecasters as Zbigniew Brzezinski, Herman Kahn, Anthony Wiener, and Daniel Bell have projected the full emergence of a desirable postindustrial age. The forecasts of these technological optimists manifest considerable faith in human ability to take advantage of trends and to rectify chaotic conditions caused by reactions against trends but not to counteract trends. Thus, these futurists generally stop short of the utopian extreme at which R. Buckminster Fuller (1969) arrives when he contemplates the proper utilization of information. They also deem it unnecessary, unrealistic, and dangerous to adopt the provisional catastrophism of Fuller, who calls on engineers to make many of the required changes by "designing around" hopelessly outmoded politics. Likewise, they reject the provisional catastrophist approach of Robert Theobald (1976a), who opts for the participatory use of electronic information technology to prevent its abuse by elites. Interestingly, the nonutopian, nonradical stance of these optimists correlates with the respectable establishment positions that they typically occupy. Among the members of the American Academy of Arts and Sciences' "Commission on the Year 2000" are Brzezinski, Kahn, A. Wiener, and Bell.

Brzezinski's forecast stresses the importance of electronic information technology; Bell's, the importance of intellectual technology. Brzezinski implicitly uses the method of simple trend extrapolation mixed with a large amount of intuitive genius forecasting. Kahn and Wiener rely primarily on qualified trend extrapolation, though they also employ other methods. Bell employs his new theory of societal development to help formulate a forecast that ranks as the most sophisticated from a sociological point of view. The scope of the forecast by Kahn and Wiener is the broadest; its range of alternative futures, the widest. Because the forecasts by Kahn and Wiener and by Bell are especially important, we analyze them in detail.

2

DELPHI PANELISTS'
TECHNOLOGICAL "ABUNDANCE"

The world has become too dangerous for anything less than utopia.
John Platt

THE DELPHI TECHNIQUE

Judged from a methodological standpoint, most forecasts made throughout history may be lumped together as "genius forecasts." The category of genius forecasting embraces a multitude of intuitive methods. Genius forecasters somehow integrate possibilities that they regard as important, draw from their relevant experiences, and articulate their expectations (T. Gordon 1972, p. 166). Because of the central role played by luck and insight, the failures of genius forecasting have been more spectacular than its successes.

Despite its drawbacks, genius forecasting can take into account factors that more formalized forecasting methods sometimes exclude systematically. A creative forecaster may devise plausible alternative futures that diverge strikingly from present realities. Among the most imaginative genius forecasters have been utopian writers of science fiction, some of whom at times have anticipated the future with remarkable accuracy. Moreover, the future-oriented intuitive opinions of experts constitute an important ingredient in planning. Hence, some leading futurists argue that efforts should be made to obtain such information as effectively as possible from recognized experts in relevant areas (Helmer 1966, pp. 47–48). They also attach special importance to group forecasting because, given no other information, a group estimate is at least as reliable as that of a randomly chosen expert (T. Gordon 1972, p. 170). The relevance of this claim is disputed by critics who argue that experts are not picked at random to formulate forecasts.

At any rate, information about the relevant expectations of a well-chosen group of experts can be useful to a planner or a decision maker. Yet reliance on experts who are at loggerheads can stymie planning and precipitate haphazard decisions. To secure increased agreement among experts, if not to resolve dead-locks brought about by their incompatible intuitive forecasts, "consensus meth-ods" are frequently employed. The most sophisticated and popular of these methods is the "Delphi technique" (now supplemented by the "cross-impact matrix method," which is described in Chapter 1 and later in this chapter).

The Delphi technique was a brainchild of Olaf Helmer (1966) and Norman Dalkey at the RAND Corporation in the late 1950s. Delphi systematically elicits and compares the opinions of experts concerning specific events, trends, prob-lems, or other aspects of the future. Panel members, who are not known to each other, respond to questionnaires in a series of rounds. After a round, each panelist may be supplied with information about the forecasts made by the others. In view of this information, panelists may decide to change their own forecasts. Thus Delphi, which proceeds through rounds of feedback to panelists and is conducted by interlocutors who serve as editors, blends genius forecasting with a more rigorous, formalized approach.

Delphi usually accomplishes the aim of generating increased group consen-sus. Occasionally, the consensus centers on the uncertainty of the future, in which case a crystallizing of disparate positions generally becomes apparent. Theodore Gordon (1972) convincingly argues that Delphi is superior to face-to-face methods of synthesizing opinion, which have the following potential hazards:

Dominant individuals may carry the discussion by weight of their personality rather than force of argument.
The psychology of the group may lead to consensus through "bandwagon dynamics."
Time may be lost in the establishment of an intellectual "pecking order" (p. 170).

THE GORDON-HELMER DELPHI FORECAST

Methodology

Probably the best known of hundreds of Delphi inquiries is the one conducted by Theodore J. Gordon and Olaf Helmer at the RAND Corporation in 1963/64 (Helmer 1966, app. I, pp. 44-95). Gordon and Helmer sought to obtain a judicious intuitive assessment of the direction of certain long-range trends. They selected six basic features of the future world for detailed projec-tive examination. The combination of these features was intended to provide a broad but not exhaustive coverage of some of the most important determinants of future society. These features, also termed *areas* and *topics*, are scientific breakthroughs, population control, automation, space progress, war prevention, and weapons systems.

TABLE 2.1

Sample Follow-Up Questionnaire

Description of potential breakthrough	Consensus or dissensus to date	In your opinion, by what year does the probability of occurrence reach		If your 50% estimate falls within either the earlier or the later period indicated, briefly state your reason for this opinion
		50%	90%	
B1 Feasibility of chemical control over hereditary defects through molecular engineering	Consensus that it will occur; disagreement as to when			Why before 1987 *or* after 2013?
S8 Widespread socially accepted use of nonnarcotic personality control drugs producing specific psychological reactions	Divergent opinions, possibly owing to differing interpretations of the original question			Why before 1987 *or* after 2013 (or never)?

Source: Helmer 1966, p. 51. (Reprinted, by permission, from SOCIAL TECHNOLOGY, by Olaf Helmer, © 1966 by Olaf Helmer, Basic Books, Inc., Publishers, New York.)

A special panel was selected to survey each of these features. Of the 150 experts invited to participate, 82 responded to one or more of four sequential questionnaires (see Table 2.1). Copies of the questionnaires for the six panels were sent to all participants, some of whom volunteered to respond to questionnaires besides those addressed specifically to their panels. Feedback of the results of each previous questionnaire gave panel members the opportunity to revise their earlier surmises. As is usually the case in Delphi inquiries, succeeding rounds bolstered consensus.

Of these panelists, 35 were members of RAND and 7 others were RAND consultants. The remaining 40 included 6 Europeans. Twenty of the panelists were engineers; 17, physical scientists; 5, writers; 4, operations analysts; and 1, a military officer.

Although the panelists' forecasts are presented as *"predictions,"* their estimates of dates by which certain developments would have occurred are more probabilistic than the term suggests. Panelists were instructed to indicate the year by which the probability of the actualization of a particular item equaled 50 percent. Their responses were then scaled along numerical or linearly ordered axes, and the median response was designated the prediction. Thus, such a prediction amounts to the median value along two probability ranges. The meaning, then, of a forecast that a permanent base on the moon will be established by 1982 is the median prediction of the panelists' various predictions concerning when such a base would have become 50 percent likely.

Global Forecasts of 1984, 2000, and 2100

The detailed forecasts of the panels predicted specific items by year (see Figure 2.1). By abstracting the most significant items from the forecasts of the six panels, Gordon and Helmer (1966) paint portraits of the world in the years 1984, 2000, and 2100 (pp. 78-80). These portraits convey a reasonably accurate impression of the overall forecast. Hence by focusing on them, one can make a fair evaluation that centers on crucial issues.

Although the emphasis of this book is on long-range forecasts, the forecast of the year 1984 is analyzed for three reasons:

It is integral to the forecasts of later periods, since it indicates how the long-range future could begin to unfold;
It was a 20-year forecast when formulated; and
At this writing over two-thirds of the time between 1963/64 and 1984 has elapsed, providing an opportunity to investigate the extent to which the panelists' sensitivity to trends molded their expectations in ways that have proved to be insightful.

The Gordon-Helmer item-by-item presentation is summarized below.

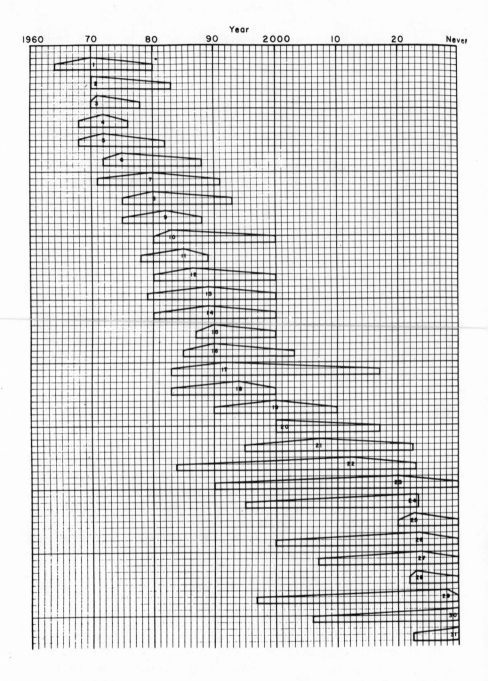

Figure 2.1. Consensus of Panel 1 on scientific breakthroughs (medians and quartiles). The interquartile range specifies the amount of dissensus (Helmer 1966, pp. 56–57). (Reprinted, by permission, from SOCIAL TECHNOLOGY, by Olaf Helmer, © 1966 by Olaf Helmer, Basic Books, Inc., Publishers, New York.)

1. Economically useful desalination of sea water

2. Effective fertility control by oral contraceptive or other simple and inexpensive means

3. Development of new synthetic materials for ultra-light construction

4. Automated language translators

5. New organs through transplanting or prosthesis

6. Reliable weather forecasts

7. Operation of a central data storage facility with wide access for general or specialized information retrieval

8. Reformation of physical theory, eliminating confusion in quantum-relativity and simplifying particle theory

9. Implanted artificial organs made of plastic and electronic components

10. Widespread and socially widely accepted use of nonnarcotic drugs (other than alcohol) for the purpose of producing specific changes in personality characteristics

11. Stimulated emission ("lasers") in X and Gamma ray region of the spectrum

12. Controlled thermo-nuclear power

13. Creation of a primitive form of artificial life (at least in the form of self-replicating molecules)

14. Economically useful exploitation of the ocean bottom through mining (other than off-shore oil drilling)

15. Feasibility of limited weather control, in the sense of substantially affecting regional weather at acceptable cost

16. Economic feasibility of commercial generation of synthetic protein for food

17. Increase by an order of magnitude in the relative number of psychotic cases amenable to physical or chemical therapy

18. Biochemical general immunization against bacterial and viral diseases

19. Feasibility (not necessarily acceptance) of chemical control over some hereditary defects by modification of genes through molecular engineering

20. Economically useful exploitation of the ocean through farming, with the effect of producing at least 20% of the world's food

21. Biochemicals to stimulate growth of new organs and limbs

22. Feasibility of using drugs to raise the level of intelligence (other than as dietary supplements and not in the sense of just temporarily raising the level of apperception)

23. Man-machine symbiosis, enabling man to extend his intelligence by direct electromechanical interaction between his brain and a computing machine

24. Chemical control of the aging process, permitting extension of life span by 50 years

25. Breeding of intelligent animals (apes, cetaceans, etc) for low-grade labor

26. Two-way communication with extra-terrestrials

27. Economic feasibility of commercial manufacture of many chemical elements from subatomic building blocks.

28. Control of gravity through some form of modification of the gravitational field

29. Feasibility of education by direct information recording on the brain

30. Long-duration coma to permit a form of time travel

31. Use of telepathy and ESP in communications

The World of 1984

World War III is 15 to 20 percent likely if present trends continue, though appropriate policy measures could reduce this probability to 5 percent.

Automation and desalinated seawater will aid agriculture in providing the increased food needed for the world's 4.3 billion people (assuming no world war).

Effective fertility control will cause the birthrate to continue to decrease.

Transplantation of natural organs and implementation of artificial (electronic and plastic) organs will be common.

Personality-control drugs will be widely accepted and used.

Sophisticated teaching machines will be in general use; automated libraries will aid research by looking up and reproducing relevant materials.

A universal satellite relay system and automatic translation machines will enhance worldwide communication.

Many service operations and some types of decision making at the management level will be automated.

A permanent lunar base will have been established; manned Mars and Venus fly-bys will have been accomplished; deep-space laboratories will be operating.

The gamut of new weapons will include quite effective anti-ICBM (intercontinental ballistic missile) missiles, small tactical nuclear bombs, and nonlethal biological devices; ground warfare will be characterized by rapid mobility and a highly automated tactical capability.

The World of 2000

The global population will have increased to about 5.1 billion people.

Large-scale ocean farming and fabrication of synthetic protein will constitute new food sources.

Controlled thermonuclear power will provide a new source of energy.

New mineral raw materials will be extracted from the oceans.

Regional weather control will have passed the experimental stage.

Primitive forms of life will have been generated in the laboratory.

The use of molecular engineering to correct genetic defects will be possible.

Automation will have advanced from menial robot services to sophisticated, high IQ machines.

A universal language will have evolved through automated communication.

Astronauts will have landed on Mars; on the moon, the mining and manufacturing of propellant materials will be progressing.

On earth, commercial ballistic transport will have been instituted.

Effective anti-ICBM air-launched missiles and directed energy beams will have been developed; weather manipulation for military purposes will be possible.

The World of 2100: Conceivable Features

Gordon and Helmer, who make no pretense of consensus among the panelists, merely present "an indication of what a number of thoughtful people think is conceivable during the next few generations to come" (p. 79).

The world population perhaps may grow to about 8 billion people.

Life expectancy may exceed 100 years, since chemical control of the aging process may have been achieved.

The growth of new limbs and organs through biochemical stimulation may be possible.

Man-machine symbiosis, enabling persons to increase their intelligence through direct electromechanical tie-in of the brain with a computing machine is clearly possible.

Automation will continue toward its zenith: household robots, completely automated highway transportation, remote facsimile reproduction of magazines and newspapers in the home, and so on.

It is even possible that elaborate differential mining processes will be abandoned in favor of commercially efficient transmutation of elements.

Presumably, international agreements will be enacted for distributing the abundance of new sources of energy and raw materials to provide the necessities of life for all people.

Gravity control, a possibility, might make revolutionary development feasible.

Among the likely achievements of the space program are regularly scheduled commercial traffic to a permanent lunar colony, a permanent base on Mars, landings on Jupiter's moons, and manned fly-bys past Pluto; among the possible achievements is a multigenerational mission to other solar systems, perhaps aided by long-duration coma.

Two-way communication with extraterrestrials is a distinct possibility.

Four Problem Areas Anticipated

The Gordon-Helmer analysis of the panelists' responses disclosed the need for major efforts in four areas to avert possible disasters (pp. 81–82).

War Prevention

The most ominous fly in the utopian ointment is the danger of large-scale nuclear war. Since the median prediction of another major war within the next generation was 20 percent, ways of forestalling such catastrophe had to be sought. Respondents were confident that vigorous pursuit of their proposals could lead to a 75 percent reduction in the median probability for 10 years and 70 percent for 25 years.

Equitable Distribution of Resources

"Although there is a consensus that eventually there will be an abundance of resources in energy, food, and raw materials, it is not at all a foregone conclusion that they will be plentifully available in time to keep ahead of the increasing world population, or that effective means of an equitable distribution of such assets will be found and agreed on" (p. 81). Timely solutions to these problems would contribute to the prevention of wars.

Social Reorganization

Industrial societies will be reshaped by extensive automation. Although automated education will make the acquisition of technical skills available to a large percentage of the population, only the most able people will probably be needed to manage the new automated economy. Inasmuch as many services will probably be taken over by robots, large segments of the population may be left without suitable employment in an economy of potential abundance. Accordingly, Gordon and Helmer conclude:

> Far-sighted and profoundly revolutionary measures may have to be taken to cope with this situation and to create new patterns within which a democratic form of society can continue to flourish. Earning a living may no longer be a necessity but a privilege; services may have to be protected from automation and given certain social status; leisure time activities may have to be invented in order to give new meaning to a mode of life that may have become economically useless for a majority of the populace. [Pp. 81–82]

Eugenics

The possibility of selective eugenic control through molecular genetic engineering poses knotty problems that will call for much forethought and wisdom. So does the possibility of extending an individual person's life-span through biochemical methods. Judged likely to become realities within the next generation or two, such capabilities could be dangerously mismanaged.

General Tone

Thus, the panelists were decidedly optimistic concerning both the direction of trends and the human ability to manage change wisely. They viewed the probable continuation of scientific and technological trends as promoting the transition from current industrial society into an age of global abundance. The admittedly speculative forecast for the year 2100 presents the image of a near-utopia.

Although other kinds of possible pitfalls were considered, global nuclear war received the most attention. Such war was deemed quite unlikely if adequate preventive measures were taken.

EVALUATION OF ASSUMPTIONS

Gordon and Helmer acknowledge that no claims are made, or can be made, for the reliability of the predictions obtained. Still, they argue that these predictions should lessen the chance of surprise and provide a sounder basis for long-range decision making than do purely implicit, unarticulated, intuitive judgments. All criticism should take into account this limited objective and should be tempered by an appreciation of the pioneering nature of this study.

The methodological assumptions of this Delphi forecast need to be examined. Furthermore, assumptions not inherent in the Delphi technique must be elicited and assessed. The task of pinpointing assumptions of the latter sort is made more difficult by lack of information about the explicit methods, if any, that the experts used to derive their individual forecasts. The chief method appears to be genius forecasting, which is hardly methodical. Hence, intuitive nonmethodological assumptions assume paramount importance in shaping this forecast as well as other Delphi forecasts. Assumptions will be uncovered as the panelists' predictions are evaluated.

Accuracy of Short-Term Predictions

From the perspective of the present, one can look backward to ascertain which of the panelists' predictions for the period from 1964 till now have been fulfilled and which have not. Such an investigation need not be based on the faulty judgment that accuracy constitutes the chief criterion for evaluating the forecast. Yet accuracy must not be dismissed as irrelevant. Since this time-dated forecast presupposes that the events it predicts as likely are aspects of ongoing trends, the extent to which events have unfolded as predicted affects the dependability of the longer-range predictions.

Robert Ament (1970) of the Institute for the Future (IFF) examined the 22 events forecasted as at least 50 percent likely by 1970 to see which had in fact occurred. His opinion poll among the staff of IFF indicated that 15 of the events had occurred, 5 had not, and 2 were uncertain because they were not described specifically enough (T. Gordon 1972, pp. 172–74). All eight of the predicted weapons systems had been actualized, suggesting which research and development (R&D) priorities had taken precedence (see Table 2.2).

Forecasts of 1984, 2000, and 2100

In the light of what has happened since 1964, how should the forecasts of the world in the years 1984, 2000, and 2100 be evaluated? Any adequate answer to this question must flow from an examination of why certain predictions have been rendered quite unlikely, how several crucial developments were overlooked, and how both of these shortcomings can be partially traced to unwarranted

TABLE 2.2

Robert Ament's Poll at IFF Evaluating the 1963/64 RAND Delphi Forecast

Near Term Forecasts of 1964 RAND Report	50 percent occurrence probability			Has the development occurred?		
	LQ	median	UQ	yes	no	partly or uncertain
Scientific breakthroughs						
Economically useful desalination of sea water	1964	1970				*
Feasibility of effective large-scale fertility control by oral contraceptive or other simple and inexpensive means	1970	1970	1983	*		
Progress in space						
USSR orbital rendezvous	1964	1964	1966	*		
USA orbital rendezvous	1965	1967	1967	*		
Increased use of near-Earth satellites for weather prediction and control	1967	1967	1970	*		
Unmanned inspections and capability for destruction of satellites	1967	1967	1970		*	
USSR manned lunar fly-by	1967	1967	1970		*	
Establishment of global communications system	1967	1968	1970	*		
USA manned lunar fly-by	1967	1970	1970	*		
Manned lunar landing and return	1969	1969	1970	*		
Rescue of astronauts stranded in orbit	1968	1970	1975		*	
Operational readiness of laser for space communications	1968	1970	1975			*
Manned co-orbital inspection of satellites	1970	1970	1974		*	
Manned scientific orbital station—ten men	1970	1970	1975		*	

Future weapon systems

Tactical kiloton nuclear weapons for use by ground troops	1964	1965	1967	*
Extensive uses of devices that persuade without killing (water cannons, tear gas, etc.)	1968	1968	1970	*
Miniature improved sensors and transmitters for snooping, reconnaissance, arms control	1968	1968	1970	*
Rapid mobility of men and light weapons to any point on Earth for police action	1966	1969	1973	*
Incapacitating chemical (as opposed to biological) agents	1965	1970	1975	*
Use of lasers for radar-type sensors, illuminators, communications	1968	1970	1975	*
Incapacitating biological agents	1968	1970	1976	*
Lethal biological agents	1967	1970	1980	*

LQ and UQ—lower and upper quartile

Note: Results of Robert Ament's poll at IFF concerning whether 22 events forecast in the 1963/64 RAND Delphi study as at least 50 percent likely by 1970 had actually occurred. This chart does not answer the question of whether a given event occurred in the median year predicted.

Source: T. Gordon 1972, pp. 172–73. (Courtesy of Theodore J. Gordon, "The Current Methods of Futures Research," *The Futurists,* ed. Alvin Toffler, 1972, pp. 172–73.)

assumptions. Hence the inquiry about accuracy leads to an assessment of the extent to which the panelists accurately conveyed the appropriate degree of confidence concerning the predicted items. To facilitate this assessment, the forecasts—especially the forecast of 1984—are analyzed under the headings that follow.

Technological Accomplishments

Several predictions about the development and use of new technologies reveal the panelists' insightfulness. For instance, worldwide communication has already been greatly accelerated and enhanced by communications satellites. Measured by volume consumed and prescriptions written, personality-control drugs such as tranquilizers have become the world's leading prescription drugs. More effective ones are in the offing. Artificial organs are being developed.

A change in political and economic priorities, however, makes it extremely doubtful that a permanent lunar base will have been established by 1984 or that manned Mars and Venus fly-bys will have been achieved. Not expecting cuts in the National Aeronautics and Space Administration's (NASA) budget, the panelists were far too optimistic in their timetable for development of space technology beyond 1970. Generally speaking, the median dates for new nonmilitary technologies appear to have been underestimated by the panelists. A major reason for this is the current insufficient funding of R&D for these technologies.

Anti-ICBMs (or antiballistic missiles [ABMs]) will probably not be "quite effective" by 1984. Antiballistic missile research and development programs have encountered serious difficulties unanticipated by the Delphi panelists. Besides, a SALT agreement that limits the implementation of ABMs has downgraded the value of R&D. Yet the unlikely possibility that powerful satellite-mounted lasers will provide such a defense by that deadline cannot be excluded.

Danger of Nuclear War

What about panelists' estimates of the likelihood of global thermonuclear war? Dependable estimates of this sort are by no means easy to make. The political decisions triggering or preventing nuclear war could be a function of the personality characteristics of decision makers as well as of the behavior of complex sociocultural systems.

Nevertheless, forecasters like Herman Kahn have sketched illuminating scenarios of various series of events and decisions that could lead to a global nuclear war. Moreover, some analysts argue plausibly that such a war becomes less likely as the perceived costs of starting it rise and the benefits diminish, though politicians are not always as rational in their decision making as this approach presupposes. Other changes, such as treaties and the development of alternative weapons, may also increase or decrease the danger of global or nuclear war. These changes can be taken into account in an estimate of the overall costs and benefits of war as perceived by each of the possible participants.

Détente and the Strategic Arms Limitation Treaty (SALT) agreements appear to have reduced the likelihood of nuclear holocaust by 1984. The panelists recognized that major policy changes could lead to such a reduction. However, they failed to anticipate the threatened rise in the likelihood of small nuclear wars, particularly after the middle 1980s. Such wars could spill over into global conflicts. Among the main factors expected to increase the chances of nuclear war are:

Continued nuclear weapons proliferation;
Spread of nuclear power facilities to many developing nations;
Implementation of additional breeder reactors and nuclear fuel reprocessing plants, with the accompanying availability of plutonium for the construction of inexpensive bombs;
The willingness in some advanced industrialized nations to sell nuclear technology, including reprocessing plants, to other nations;
Spread of the knowledge of bomb technology to various groups;
Use of lasers for isotope separation, making it much easier to build bombs even if a moratorium on breeder reactors were put into effect; and
The increasingly desperate situation of resource-poor developing countries.

Left unstemmed, the surging tide of present trends would engulf all efforts to avoid the development of an increasingly nuclearized, dangerous world. Since several of these trends were at least embryonic in 1963/64, should the panelists have recognized them? If so, they might have perceived that a much safer world could be created by effective international agreements to:

Forgo further implementation of the more dangerous fission technologies;
Facilitate the research, development, and implementation of alternative energy technologies;
Prevent nuclear proliferation, or at least greatly reduce its rate;
Enter into a phased mutual reduction of nuclear armaments; and
Meet the basic human needs of impoverished people in developing countries.

Population Growth and Food Production

The Delphi panelists grossly underestimated the increase in the world's population. Already well above the 4 billion mark, population will probably surpass the 4.3 billion of the forecast long before 1984. Many demographers now project a global population of about 7 billion—not 5.1 billion—by the year 2000 and at least 10 to 14 billion—not 8—during the next century.

These estimates may be too high but primarily for a reason that is inconsistent with the forecast. The estimates may not adequately take into account limits to population growth resulting from likely famines. Lester Brown (1966), founder of the Worldwatch Institute, has argued that much of the significant reduction in the 1974 global population growth rate was probably due to increased death rates in famished areas. Conversely, the panelists assumed that food production would far outstrip population growth.

The panelists were far too optimistic about both voluntary population control and food production. The development of better contraceptives and food production techniques by no means guarantees that they will be used to optimum advantage.

Pollution, Raw Materials, and Energy

The panelists also neglected other interlinked ecological problems that have caused much concern since the late 1960s. Although the Delphi study was designed to assess the direction of long-range trends, the panelists overlooked the dangerous trends of pollution and depletion of nonrenewable natural resources. They assumed that petroleum and other energy sources would supply plenty of reasonably priced energy until technological breakthroughs had made available an "abundance of new sources of energy and raw materials" (Gordon and Helmer 1966, p. 80). No adequate assessment was made of the feasibility, lead times, environmental impact, and economic costs of possible energy technologies. Whereas the panelists could not be expected to predict political decisions, the forecast does not even hint of such events as the Arabs' use of oil as a political weapon, the fourfold increase in the price of oil, the energy crisis, and consequent dislocations in the world economy.

To these experts, nuclear war seemed to be the only substantial threat to the continued global exponential growth of industrialization. Yet such forces as the rising price of Middle Eastern oil have at least temporarily applied the brakes to the world's exponential industrial growth. More generally, problems that could bring about undesirable futures by means of discontinuous changes are not limited to the four kinds of problems singled out by the Gordon-Helmer study.

Thus, factors omitted by a forecast can be responsible for its projection of a misleading image of the future. The factors minimized or ignored by this Delphi forecast can be traced in part to topics not covered by the six panels. Gordon and Helmer admit that the forecast could have been broadened by adding a panel on international relations. Panels on such topics as ecological problems, changes in value-priorities, the relevance of historical data, and sociocultural change would also have made the forecast more comprehensive and useful. Consider, for instance, the importance of value change, particularly with regard to its influence on political decisions that affect technological advance, pollution control, and economic growth.

Value Change and Political Decisions

Knowledge of science and technology, of research efforts being conducted, of the present financial and organizational potentiality for R&D programs, of expected costs of new technologies, and of societal value-priorities that can affect political decisions—all this savvy does establish a foundation for reasonable conjectures about the times when specific feasible technologies may be developed and adopted. The Gordon-Helmer panelists presumably took into account the first three factors. However, it is not at all clear that they paid enough attention to the fourth, and they may have overlooked the fifth. A shift in societal priorities and political decisions punctured NASA's expanding financial balloon and threw askew the panelists' predicted timetable for technological progress in space. The specific time when a major technology is developed has come to depend increasingly on R&D programs. These programs can be instituted by political decisions—as illustrated by the Manhattan Project—and can also be abrogated by such decisions—as in the case of the supersonic transport (SST). Political decisions by their very nature are generally difficult and often impossible to forecast. Therefore, the time at which a prospective technology will be developed is often difficult to anticipate.

Shifts in value-priorities often influence political decisions. These shifts, though typically much harder to forecast than possible technologies, tend to be less inscrutable than future political decisions considered apart from them. If, for instance, the panelists had anticipated the upgrading of ecological values in the United States during the early 1970s, they would have had evidence for forecasting a corresponding reordering of political decisions. Some of these decisions earmarked funds for the development of recycling technologies.

Shifts in priorities can be occasioned by unanticipated consequences of a trend that trigger a reaction against it. An example is the way that the maximization of industrial growth, promoted since World War II by new polluting technologies, increased pollution to dangerous levels in the late 1960s. This generated an ecological protest movement, which spearheaded a switch from the dirtiest technologies to cleaner ones. The neglected values of clean air and clean water were upgraded, and the prized value of maximum industrial growth was downgraded. Since the 1973/74 energy crisis, the quadrupling of oil prices, and inflation combined with recession, this new trend of priority change has been slowed.

Nonmilitary R&D will continue to concentrate on alternative energy technologies. Although pollution control is still emphasized, energy generation is taking precedence over it in an epoch of escalated energy prices and threatened shortages.

Technological and Sociocultural Optimism

Many of the Gordon-Helmer panelists appear to have shared two primary nonmethodological assumptions that shaped the forecast and deserve additional attention. The first, which may be dubbed "technological optimism," is optimism about which technologies appear feasible and about what could be done with them in principle. The second, "sociocultural optimism," consists of the expectation that human beings will promptly devise and implement beneficial technologies, will use them to resolve sociocultural problems, and also will adequately cope with those sociocultural problems that are not amenable to strictly technological solutions. This second assumption supplies the basis for a kind of technological determinism. Underlying the claim that technology constitutes the leading edge of change is an implicit model of human nature rationally using technology to resolve sociocultural problems.

Insofar as the forecast specifies technologies that probably will become feasible, it seems to be reasonably accurate and informative though perhaps a bit too optimistic. However, the estimates of lead times for the research, development, and implementation of these technologies tend to be too short. Even more important, much uncertainty surrounds the issue of whether the cost of many feasible technologies will be low enough to permit widespread implementation. The panelists' implicit presupposition that these technologies will generally be reasonably priced seriously weakens the forecast.

The extreme sociocultural optimism of the panelists is rendered dubious by still other sociocultural constraints. Frequently, the technologies selected for research, development, and implementation are those best suited to benefit special interest groups rather than the human species. Not only do applications of technologies often exacerbate sociocultural problems, many of these problems prove to be surprisingly resistant to purely technological solutions. Nor are these problems generally easy to resolve by nontechnological strategies. Thus, a technologically determined near-utopia appears to be a chimera.

Selection of Panelists

Forecasts often convey better information about the present than about the future. Obviously, the Gordon-Helmer Delphi forecast envisions the likelihood of a relatively continuous development of the perceived present, possibly interrupted by global nuclear war. The outlooks of the panelists were significantly shaped by their technological optimism and the cold war.

Does the forecast accurately reflect the collective expert opinion of the times? Were the experts who were selected as panelists truly representative of various viewpoints?

RAND was a center of technological optimism, whereas the European climate of opinion was decidedly less optimistic. Since 42 of the 82 respondents were affiliated with RAND and only 6 were from Europe, the technological optimism of the forecast was almost guaranteed by the selection of panelists. Even the choice of features of the world may have been influenced by the orientations and occupations of Gordon and Helmer. Gordon's participation in Project Apollo and RAND's government contracts to forecast space technology, nuclear technology, and consequences of their possible uses correspond to topics of the forecast. Thus, the forecast was affected by implicit biases that should be uncovered and evaluated to discover whether they can be justified.

A high degree of consensus may be relatively easy to achieve if the experts have basic unquestioned assumptions in common. The type of consensus depends largely on the type of assumptions. For instance, a quite different forecast would have resulted had the panelists been chosen from among such competent experts as Harrison Brown who criticize the extrapolation of trends to a technological near-utopian age. If the panel had combined both types of experts, much disagreement would have remained. On certain basic issues, the forecast might have boiled down to two incompatible forecasts.

A comparison of the results of the Gordon-Helmer forecast with a Delphi forecast conducted by Major Joseph Martino (1967) reveals the influence of the type of experts selected on the sort of forecast formulated. The Air Force Office of Scientific Research sponsored this long-range forecast of the international situation as an experiment to determine the problems associated with Delphi's use. The panelists who authorized use of their names were university professors. As one might expect, the forecast reflects their overall orientation (not one of ecological pessimism, which had not yet become common). Lacking the technological enthusiasm of typical Gordon-Helmer panelists, these experts appear to temper their technological optimism with awareness of some of the forces that hinder the rapid development and effective implementation of revolutionary technological innovations. Their optimism seems to center more on the human ability to solve nontechnological problems than on feasible technology. For instance, they predict an internationalized redistribution of income and, by the year 2015, limited world government. Yet they do voice doubts about the effectiveness of large-scale population control measures that will have been instituted by 1990.

Such findings dramatize the need to choose as panelists experts who, on debatable matters, represent a variety of backgrounds and defendable orientations. Although this procedure will usually produce less consensus, the measurement of disagreement can provide valuable information. The Delphi technique has more productive uses than that of unifying the anticipations of those who are already predisposed toward similar beliefs and values.

Need for a Holistic Systems Approach

Even if panels were selected optimally, Delphi forecasts, as exemplified by the Helmer-Gordon forecast, would still suffer from methodological weaknesses. A crucial deficiency of the Delphi technique stems from its requests for brief opinions about a plurality of specific future possibilities. The respondents are typically specialists whose expert opinions are derived more from intuition than from relatively objective methodology. The separate predictions that are elicited are inadequately related to each other and to possible changes in contexts. Such changes may alter the likelihood of whole sets of forecasted events. As Daniel Bell (1965) recognizes, a Delphi forecast does not anticipate how, if at all, technological possibilities will be realized within a systems context that specifies the major social, political, and economic relationships that will obtain at any given time (p. 130). The changes in such sociocultural systems and in the relationships among them, more than the technical feasibility of any of the breakthroughs, will determine the possibility of these breakthroughs being realized within a given time frame. These abstract observations can be given "cash value" by reconsidering, for instance, the previous analysis of how societal value change can lead to political R&D decisions, thus influencing the kind of technologies developed and the time of their development.

Systems-oriented forecasting and planning constitute necessary conditions for perceptive societal guidance. Societies and cultures are historically grounded, interrelated systems. Attempts to change aspects of these complex systems often produce "counterintuitive" consequences that were unanticipated by expert specialists (Forrester 1970). These consequences include some of the changes that are discontinuous with prior trends.

To be sure, the concept of counterintuitive consequences is highly subjective. The intuitive judgments of various experts and of the same expert at different times display more or less understanding of the behavior of complex sociocultural systems. Outcomes that run contrary to the intuitive expectations of most experts may be labeled as counterintuitive. Yet these experts may then correct their expectations so that future outcomes of a similar kind are no longer counterintuitive to them. Nonetheless, policy planners and decision makers are frequently misled by intuitive judgments that fail to take into account the many interactive, time-delayed relationships that condition outcomes in complex systems.

Admittedly, Delphi can produce counterintuitive results. Gordon and Helmer list a number of predictions by which they were surprised, including the likelihood of the very widespread use of personality-control drugs in the relatively near future. However, the Delphi technique, with its item-by-item requests for information that is usually of a specialized nature, is scarcely suitable for systemic analysis of dynamic, interrelated sociocultural processes.

The sociocultural systems in which forecast developments are embedded are typically shortchanged by a methodological bias of Delphi. Can this technique be modified to provide the required structural, holistic analysis? T. Gordon (1972) and other analysts developed the "cross-impact matrix method," which can be used to estimate the potential causal relationships between items that have been independently predicted. Presented with a two-entry table, experts are asked how the probability of any item would be affected by the occurrence or nonoccurrence of other items (see Figure 2.2).

The cross-impact method has proved to be quite useful in future-oriented policy analysis. Its definite worth in making Delphi forcasts more dependable is indisputable. Yet it employs an intuitive, atomistic approach, which seems somewhat inappropriate for forecasting both the effects of structural contexts on individual items and the emergence of holistic properties that cannot be reduced to the sum of their parts. The "melodies" of sociocultural processes are organized

Development D,	Probability P,
1. One-month reliable weather forecasts	.4
2. Feasibility of limited weather control	.2
3. General biochemical immunization	.5
4. Elimination of crop damage from adverse weather	.5

These events might then be arranged in matrix form:

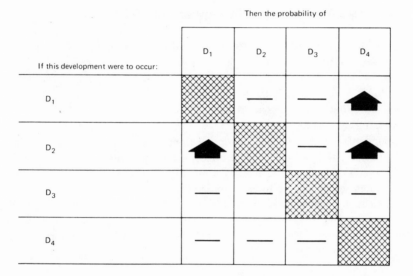

Figure 2.2. Simplified illustration of the cross-impact matrix method. Suppose that the listed developments and probabilities were forecast for a given year (T. Gordon 1972, p. 181). (Courtesy of Theodore J. Gordon, "The Current Methods of Futures Research," *The Futurists*, ed. Alvin Toffler, 1972, p. 181.)

configurations that are often difficult, if not impossible, to anticipate from an awareness of their separate "tones."

This methodological bias is reinforced by the usual use of the opinions of specialists, many of whom are not proficient forecasters. Suppose, for instance, that typical specialists are asked in a Delphi inquiry, What are the odds of achieving artificial intelligence by 1990? Their answers will probably be based on the potential of the technology and will assume no major change in the present research environment or, alternatively, a significant enhancement of it. After all, they are experts on computers, which they regard as particularly important. They have little opportunity to pursue issues outside their discipline. Hence they are likely to minimize or ignore forces that could retard the development of artificial intelligence, such as a conservative religious revival or a diversion of expected research funds to programs aimed at coping with intensified social problems. Unless the designers of cross-impact questionnaires make a concerted effort to ask questions likely to counteract this propensity of specialists, the questionnaires can easily confirm it.

Clearly, the Delphi technique coupled with the cross-impact method can be improved by treating contexts as forecast items and by including generalists among the panelists. Yet even then intuitive judgment seems less likely than modeling to disclose counterintuitive consequences of systems behavior.

Weaknesses Acknowledged by Gordon and Helmer

Finally, it should be noted that Gordon and Helmer (1966) themselves assess seven types of methodological and procedural objections to their report:

Instability of panel membership,
Time lapses between successive rounds,
Ambiguous questions,
Respondents' competence to answer questions outside their specialized fields,
Self-fulfilling and self-defeating prophecies (the possibility that a respondent's predictions might be biased by his expectation that their announcement might contribute to their becoming true or false,
Consensus by undue averaging, thus discriminating against the far-out forecaster, and
Insufficient substantive breadth resulting from failure to cover important aspects of the world (pp. 90–93).

Gordon and Helmer suggest that immediate improvements could be made by ensuring that:

The panel membership remain reasonably stable,
The time between questionnaires be held within more acceptable limits,
Questions be phrased with greater care to avoid unnecessary ambiguity, and
Enough cycles be allowed for adequate feedback, not only of the primary reasons for opinions but also for a critique of such reasons (p. 95).

Furthermore, the authors present an extended list of potential improvements through further methodological research. Of special importance are the detection of better ways of systematically selecting experts and the development of techniques for the formulation of sequential questions that would probe more systematically into the underlying reasons for the respondents' opinions, in a deliberate effort to construct a theoretical foundation for the phenomenon under inquiry" (p. 95).

Gordon and Helmer consider the plausible objection that their emphasis "on the median as a descriptor of the group opinion and on the quartile range as a measure of the degree of consensus biases the outcome unduly against the far-out predictor, whose judgment may prove to be right . . . while the majority opinion may be wrong" (p. 93). They regard this objection as not entirely unjustified in regard to their present study but as an invalid criticism of Delphi in general. Since a dissenting respondent is invited to state his reasons for disagreement to all members of the panel for evaluation, a far-out opinion is rejected only if its proponent fails to justify it before the rest of the panel.

However, if panel members are chosen to represent various orientations and theoretical assumptions, fair evaluation of a dissenter's reasons can hardly be made on the basis of a short statement that is submitted to other panelists for evaluation. How, if at all, could Delphi be modified in practice to ensure that a dissenting expert with superior reasons will generally succeed in changing the consensus of opinion? It is important to remember that one correct opinion is worth more than many incorrect ones. Since actual events often violate widely shared expectations, we should not be surprised if a consensus, especially when founded on intuitive extrapolations of trends, proves to be mistaken as compared with the forecast of a dissenter. And we should not necessarily expect a correct dissenter to be able to persuade the majority of panelists prior to being vindicated by the actualization of the future history that the dissenter has anticipated.

At the heart of this objection is the perception that a dissenter's forecast based on a superior data base and theoretical framework is more dependable than a forecast that reflects the consensus of authorities. Forecasts derived from Delphi inquiries are theoretically unsatisfactory in principle. Whereas a theory should be explicit and consistent, a Delphi forecast is constructed by piecing together forecasts stemming from the implicit use of sometimes-incompatible theories. Still, one cannot always tell whether a given theory is better than others. When recognizing justifiable opinions is difficult, Delphi provides a useful, though limited, instrument.

Unfortunately, Gordon and Helmer leave "aside the implication—to which we emphatically do not subscribe—that the publication of answers to some of our questions might in fact affect the future course of history with regard to the subject of the questions" (pp. 91-92). However, images of the future have often become self-fulfilling or self-defeating. The widespread publication of the consensus of respected experts could indeed contribute to shaping the future, as embarrassing as this might be to those who aspire to make objective forecasts. A forecast can be revised to allow for the estimated impact of the original forecast on the likelihood of the projected events.

Helmer's Subsequent Observations

Since the Gordon-Helmer study was published in 1966, many further Delphi forecasts have been formulated. Less emphasis is now placed on achieving consensus. Some Delphi inquiries have been conducted more rapidly and efficiently by means of telecommunications media and computers.

Although the methodology has been improved, it has also been forcefully criticized by researchers at RAND and elsewhere. Helmer moved from the Institute for the Future to the University of Southern California, where he headed a futures program that conducted an extensive survey of the strengths and weaknesses of Delphi. Writing in 1976, he noted that this method still lacks a sound theoretical base. A principal reason for this deficiency is that experts are rarely available as experimental laboratory subjects. Consequently, most Delphi studies are either carried out without proper experimental controls or require the use of students as surrogate experts in controlled experiments. Whether many of the results obtained by the latter kind of experimentation carry over to the former is still an open question. Recognition of this drawback does not keep Helmer (1976) from maintaining that two of Delphi's potential applications are of great potential importance: providing judgmental inputs for studies in the social-science area when "hard" data are unavailable or too costly to obtain and gathering expert opinions from the nationwide "advice community" on which government decision makers frequently depend.

From Intuitive Prediction toward Formalized Projection

Despite the foregoing objections, the Gordon-Helmer Delphi forecast provides valuable information about the kind of consensus achieved among the experts surveyed. The formalization of collective genius forecasting constitutes a genuine methodological contribution. Yet the question arises, By what methods did the experts themselves formulate their forecasts? This question underlines the need for explicit forecasting methods that can be made more dependable than intuitive forecasting as refined by the Delphi technique and the cross-impact method. When the intuitive assumptions of forecasters are objectified in the form of more explicit methodologies, these assumptions can be tested and, if proved inadequate, revised. Thus, public procedures that can be improved supplant an appeal to the authority of experts.

Hence the shift from genius forecasting (even as enhanced by Delphi) toward more formalized methods needs to continue. A long-term goal of forecasters might be to replace, insofar as feasible, the use of the intuitive judgments with judgments derived from relatively objective methods. This does not imply, however, that forecasts based on formalized methodology are always superior to genius forecasts, that eventually genius forecasting ought to be eliminated, or that formalized methodology will ever become genuinely scientific.

Accompanying this shift from intuitive methods toward formalized ones is the general shift from the prediction of specific events toward the policy-oriented projection of representative lines of development leading to alternative future contexts. Although the rationale for the latter shift was explained in Chapter 1, a few comments about the difficulty of predicting sociocultural occurrences are now in order.

To be acceptably "scientific," prediction would have to fulfill the requirements of the scientific paradigm of prediction. A scientific prediction is a conditional statement of what will happen, assuming the validity of the relevant set of scientific laws and given observations that define the initial or exogenous conditions under which these laws are expected to operate in a given instance. The predictions of forecasters typically fall far short of the requirements of this paradigm. Little is known about many relevant natural laws, the conditions under which these laws operate in particular instances, and the various exogenous conditions that may, by interference, cause different results. This is especially true of human decisions that can shape the future in alternative ways. Hence, a forecast issues only partially, if at all, from a set of specified scientific laws and observations. Since typical forecasts make assumptions about the future behavior of complex social systems, genuinely scientific prediction is clearly impossible.

The use of Delphi and other methods sometimes enables forecasters to make useful short-term, probabilistic predictions about certain features of relatively isolated systems. Yet the admittedly problematic nature of such predictions and the need for longer-range, broader forecasts open the door to the projection of alternative futures.

Delphi supplemented by the cross-impact method is generally best used in conjunction with projective methods that are relatively formalized. These methods—especially modeling—are more suitable for anticipating a variety of counterintuitive discontinuous changes that may arise from the behavior of complex sociocultural systems. As explicit projective methods become more dependable, they will also increase the dependability of the Delphi technique by improving the forecasts of those participants who use these methods.

3

BRZEZINSKI'S "TECHNETRONIC AGE"

The wave of the future is coming and there is no fighting it.
Ann M. Lindberg

The Gordon-Helmer Delphi study blazed the trail for subsequent forecasts of a postindustrial age. Zbigniew Brzezinski (1968b), who now serves as National Security Adviser in the Carter administration, dramatized the imminent arrival of this age in his essay, "America in the Technetronic Age." His forecast supplies an excellent starting point for three reasons:

1. His sketch of the sociocultural metamorphosis being wrought by electronic technology is quite enlightening.
2. For heuristic reasons, a forecast formulated by the method of simple trend extrapolation is best evaluated before looking into forecasts made by qualified trend extrapolation or modeling.
3. Brzezinski's article and the critiques it elicited provide a representative context for examining the kinds of objections raised by participatory futurists against projected elite control as well as by neo-Marxists and Marxists against U.S. projections of a postindustrial age.

In fairness to Brzezinski, it should be noted that *Between Two Ages* (1970) presents a more thorough, sophisticated analysis than does "America in the Technetronic Age." Yet he acknowledges that his book "is not an exercise in 'futurology'; it is an effort to make sense of present trends" (p. xv). In regard to the article he states: "I have significantly revised some of my views in the light of constructive criticisms made by my colleages" (p. xvi). Our treatment focuses on his article but also briefly lists major changes in his book.

BRZEZINSKI'S FORECAST

Brzezinski proclaims that the world is on the eve of a transformation that will radically alter the essence of individual and social existence. In Brzezinski's (1968b) words, "America is already beginning to experience these changes and in the course of so doing it is becoming a 'technetronic' society: a society that is shaped culturally, psychologically, socially, and economically by the impact of technology and electronics, particularly computers and communications" (p. 16).

Brzezinski identifies the revolution in technology and electronics (especially, computers and communications media) as the primary cause of the technetronic age and other aspects of applied science as a secondary cause (see Figure 3.1). Computers facilitate calculation and encourage a pragmatic, problem-solving approach. Modern communications media create an interwoven society with an impressionistic, cosmopolitan involvement in the world's problems. Such inventions of applied science exert so much impact on life-styles that our descendants will be shaped almost entirely by what they themselves create and control (p. 17). (See Table 3.1.)

To manage the rapid transition from the industrial age to the technetronic age, societies will require intelligent leadership by "a new breed of politicians-intellectuals." This paradoxical mutation may strike us as being nonadaptive. Yet Brzezinski argues that the new knowledge is becoming a tool of power, making social control possible and, in some cases, mandatory. Overcoming the traditional suspicion of change, a "meritocratic elite" will plan change to ensure rapid development. Instead of waiting for crises to arise before acting, members of this elite will direct society by "pre-crisis management." They will identify social crises in advance and devise appropriate ameliorative programs. This task is so crucial that the key to the successful adaptation to the new conditons is the effective selection and utilization of social talent (pp. 18, 22).

Thus, "power will gravitate into the hands of those who control the information, and can control it most rapidly" (p. 21). Distinguished from the hard-working, achievement-oriented few will be the intellectually inferior, leisurely, perhaps amusement-oriented many. A hierarchical restructuring of leaders and followers, therefore, will alter access to status positions and create a gap between the ascendant elite and the great majority of citizens.

Brzezinski expects such changes to interweave the educational, scientific, military, economic, and political institutional spheres. Intellectual institutions will emerge as the major institutions of this information society, with the university becoming the source of social planning. Periodic elite retraining will supplement universal education.

Politically, the United States will move toward a "meritocratic democracy" that affords special opportunities to the talented few. Since the leaders

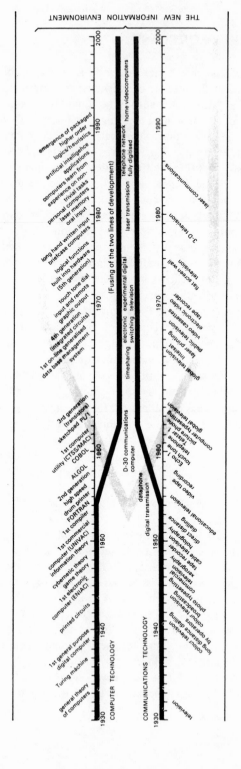

Figure 3.1. Parallel developments in computer technology and communications technology have intermeshed to produce quantum leaps in the speed and quality of information processing. (McHale 1976, p. 117). (Adaptation courtesy of THE FUTURIST, published by the World Future Society, 4916 St. Elmo Avenue, Washington, D.C. 20014.)

will be able "to impose well-nigh total political surveillance on every citizen," meritocracy could eventuate in "a technocratic dictatorship, leaving less and less room for political procedures as we know them" (pp. 17, 21). On the other hand, the rapid widespread availability of computer data will also make national coordination consonant with increased local participation in governmental decision making.

A postindustrial economy with its enlarged service section will constitute an integral aspect of a technetronic society. The closer interdependence of military, scientific, and industrial institutions will bring a depersonalization of economic power. Thus independent business tycoons will lose more and more of their power.

The domestic transition to a technetronic society has already begun to exacerbate problems of unequal distribution between nations. Rapid scientific and technological progress keeps widening the gap between the United States, which is now the "creative society," and the "underdeveloped" nations (p. 23).

The revolutions in transportation and communication make developing nations increasingly aware of their relative deprivation. Differences that seemed tolerable when slower, less extensive methods of transportation and communication separated the peoples of the world have come to engender severe tensions. "With the widening gap dooming any hope of imitation, the more likely development is an ideology of rejection of the developed world" (p. 24). Brzezinski expects that this ideology will combine nationalism and racism.

Far from being limited to economic inequality, the gap between the United States and the developing nations is widened by radically different ways of life. A culture permeated by sophisticated computer language differs profoundly from one that lacks it. Such divergent cultural orientations that reflect different eras can easily frustrate attempts to communicate and cooperate. This poses what will become the underlying problem in international relations: how to find a way of avoiding the widening of the cultural and psychosocial gap inherent in the growing differentiation of the world (p. 25).

Brzezinski regards youthful revolutionaries as the last spasm of the past. He expects that they will experience no more success in attempting to deter movement to the technetronic age than did the Luddites in their opposition to the industrial revolution. Nor does he cite any forces that might redirect the transition that he forecasts. He seems convinced that revolutionary developments in computer technology, communications technology, and, secondarily, other technologies will constitute a virtually overpowering cause of the technetronic age. At any rate, he writes as if most of the general features of the technetronic age in the United States will follow a relatively unalterable, unidirectional pattern.

TABLE 3.1

Simplified Table of Time Developments in Computer Technology

Computer Costs	In 1945 it cost about $1,000 to do a million operations on a keyboard and took at least a month	In 1952 it cost about $300 to do a million operations and took ten minutes	In 1960 it cost $.75 to do a million operations and took a second
Computer Speed		In 1954 computers have a speed of 2000 operations per second	From 1955–1965 internal speeds have increased by a factor of 200

Computer speed is up to 150,000 operations per second |
| Computer Size | | Computers have capacity of 40,000 characters | From 1955–1965 the physical size of the central processing unit decreased by a factor of 10

Computer capacity is up to 200,000 characters |

Computer Costs	Computers can do a million operations for less than 6 cents in about 1/2 a second	Computers can do a million operations for 1/10 a cent in 1/10 a second	Between 1983 and 1997 computer cost to decrease by a factor of 100
Computer Speed	From 1965–1975 internal speeds have increased by a factor of 200 Computer speeds are up to 4,000,000 operations per second		
Computer Size	By 1975 fully integrated circuits begin to reduce the size by a factor of about 100 Computer capacity is up to 15,000,000 characters		

Source: McHale 1972 ©, p. 193. (Courtesy of the Conference Board.)

EVALUATION OF ASSUMPTIONS

Importance of Computers and Communications Technologies

Brzezinski deserves commendation for his insight into the impact of changes in electronic information technology on society and culture, the importance of competent advice from intellectuals to aid governmental policy making, and the sociocultural transformation that the United States is undergoing. In addition, he perceives the necessity of formulating value systems appropriate to life in the new man-made environment.

The decade since Brzezinski published his article has witnesssed major advances in computerized information processing and communications media (see Figure 3.1). Electronic information technology is creating a new form of power and wealth: access to information and knowledge (that is, information organized for a specific purpose). What one knows rather than what one has is becoming the new basis for economic, political, and social power. Service- and knowledge-oriented enterprises are increasingly the core activities of U.S. society. Included in John McHale's (1976) inventory of potential impacts of computers and electronic communications media are:

A growing interdependence of human and machine intelligence in all areas of personal and social life,

Greatly expanded capabilities for personal development and sense experience, and

Dangers of information overload, lessened social cohesion, and the tendency to abdicate personal responsibility for decision making and to rely more on machine-readable quantitative data.

Prototypical of corporations that have decided to develop geographically vast communications networks is Goodyear Tire and Rubber Company, which by 1981 intends to have installed a computer-connected network that links some 1,700 retail stores with 2,100 computer terminals, 300 area computers, and 25,000 miles of leased connecting lines. This system, which will substitute communications for travel, will transmit data almost instantaneously and permit rapid data processing, analysis, and communications.

At least among more affluent people, home computer systems will probably be widespread by the early 1990s. Even before 1990, 10 to 20 percent of the U.S. population may have acquired computers that will send electronic letters, receive and store information, control home temperature and lighting for comfort and security, and so on.

Granted that Brzezinski's forecast highlights new developments in computers and communications technology, just how reliable does it appear to be when assessed in terms of its assumptions?

Inadequate Methodology

Brzezinski, who fails to mention any methods he may have employed, seems to have formulated his forecast on the basis of very little objective methodology. Still, his dependence on intuitive genius forecasting did not keep him from implicitly using the method of simple trend extrapolation. He derived his forecast primarily by extrapolating two beginning interrelated trends (also termed *revolutions*) that are pregnant with consequences. In other words, he extended the reinforcing trends of advances in computers and communications technology, predicting the future almost entirely in terms of their anticipated effects and human responses to these effects.

However, to formulate a dependable long-range, comprehensive forecast, a futurist must take into account many interacting forces in the complex world system. Brzezinski totally overlooked the impact of such ecological problems as pollution and shortages of energy. He did not foresee the problems engendered by the increased dependence of the U.S. economy on high-priced Arab oil. Yet forces of this sort will not only continue to affect U.S. society; they will probably even accelerate the rate of development of electronic information technology, which is relatively nonpolluting and energy efficient. Other types of technology, such as alternative energy technologies, will significantly mold the U.S. future. So will nontechnological forces. The U.S. decisions to suspend development of the SST and the breeder reactor show how value change can affect the development of technologies, instead of just being a consequence of their implementation.

The consequences of a new technology are often much more difficult to anticipate than Brzezinski's forecast might lead one to believe. Moreover, different responses to impacts of the same technology can shape the future in different ways. In short, the task of forecasting sociocultural change resulting from the introduction of new technologies is by no means easy. Hence, a forecaster's attention should be directed toward various possible futures that seem more or less likely.

A long-term trend that has established a growth trajectory despite contrary forces is generally less risky to extrapolate than a new trend. Long-range, comprehensive forecasts should take into account long-term trends, as well as all relevant trends, their interactions, and the forces most likely to influence their rates of growth and directions. Simple trend extrapolation is at best only reliable for short-range, probabilistic forecasting of trends whose causes seem unlikely to change. One requirement for this is that the trends must be quite isolated from, or impervious to, outside forces. Hence, simple trend extrapolation, particularly from only two beginning trends, is an unreliable methods for forecasting long-range, comprehensive futures.*

---

*In *The Next 200 Years*, Burnham Beckwith (1968) formulated a utopian forecast

In summary, Brzezinski's forecast is excessively:

Monocausal—focusing on the impact of only two interrelated trends that amount to a single set of causes,

Unidirectional—presupposing that this set constitutes an overpowering cause that will rapidly propel developments toward one type of future,

Technologically deterministic—neglecting the causal roles of nontechnological forces, and

Ahistorical—centering attention on two beginning trends.

Thus, Brzezinski presents more of a confident prediction than a probabilistic projection of a wide range of alternative futures. The range he considers is extremely constricted. His fixation on two new trends keeps him from taking into account the complexities of sociocultural change, including its frequent action-reaction pattern that runs contrary to the smooth extrapolation of trends. His neglect of many interrelated forces that might impact upon the trends casts serious doubt on his excessively monocausal, unidirectional prediction, as well as on its supposed comprehensiveness.

Clearly, the methodology that Brzezinski employed in 1968 is not characteristic of futurism but more akin to older breeds of forecasting. Despite its salutary features, his forecast brings to mind Paul Starr's (1978) observation:

> Images of the future are usually caricatures of the present. They inflate some recognizable features of contemporary life to extravagant proportions, and out of fear or hope respond to every vagary of historical experience, as if it were a sign of destiny.

If Brzezinski were to paint the future with a full palette, he would have to revise certain features of the portrait he here exhibits. To an appreciable but limited extent, he has accomplished this revision in *Between Two Ages*. Brzezinski (1970) still maintains that the United States is "entering an age in which technology and electronics . . . are increasingly becoming the principal determinants of social change" (p. xiv). Accordingly, "the post-industrial society is becoming a 'technetronic' society" (p. 9). The major changes from the article seem to be: (1) Brzezinski presents much more of a description of what is happening now than a forecast; (2) although "the essential problem" is still "to discover the most effective techniques for the rational exploitation of social talent" (p. 11), the meritocratic elite is not even mentioned; instead, Brzezinski comments, "The question is increasingly one of ensuring real participation in decisions that seem too complex and too far removed from the average citizen"

---

primarily by using the method of simple trend extrapolation. Anthony Wiener (1969) raised cogent objections against it in "The Rocky Road to Utopia."

(pp. 12, 13); and (3) locating the United States in the volatile international context, he seems more aware of the possibility that forces might interfere with a smooth, rapid development of the technetronic age.

A Threatening Structural Gap

The tone of "America in the Technetronic Age" conveys the impression that Brzezinski is trumpeting the arrival of a revolutionary new age in history. Might this touted age turn out to be more of a curse than a blessing? Brzezinski concedes that the coming changes will produce traumatic confrontations that could precipitate bitter struggles. His honesty reveals itself when the acknowledges the possibility of a "technocratic dictatorship," the need to counter excessive fragmentation by social controls, and widespread feelings of inferiority and helplessness among individuals who comprise the unequal masses. He admits that feelings of alienation will probably increase, because the social structure may engender a sense of nonparticipation in politics; futility concerning prospects of escaping from domination by depersonalized, invisible economic power; and insufficient identity in an increasingly atomized social life.

Members of the meritocratic elite would secure noble identities from their positions in the new society, but for ordinary people satisfactory identities would be a scarce commodity. The lost feeling of group intimacy could not be fully restored by watching television or taking psychedelic drugs. Brzezinski (1968b) tells us that there may be "millions of potentially aimless lower-middle-class blue-collar workers" (p. 18). Clearly, the structural gap between the talented few and the purposeless masses would constitute a major source of strain in the society that Brzezinski envisages.

Frequently, sociocultural change proceeds not merely by action but also by reaction that may alter the impact of the instigating force. Such reaction may, for instance, challenge policies that are felt to be oppressive. Assuming that the United States will still have free speech and anomic, impressionable television audiences, charismatic leaders might exert powerful opposition to the coming scientific-technological metamorphosis. Yet Brzezinski forecasts the decline of charismatic leadership.

Brzezinski presents political, economic, and social alienation as a consequence of the upsetting changes wrought by revolutionary scientific and technological progress. However, this alienation could also easily affect the rates of change and might lead to the redirection, or possibly even the reversal, of the two trends he projects.

One wonders whether the institutions and trends that Brzezinski foresees would produce so many alienated, anomic people that authorities would impose external controls to stem the tide of fragmentation. Might not authoritarian oppression eventuate in perpetual dehumanization or perhaps even in a revolution? At any rate, pent-up tensions could give rise to major eruptions. How can we keep from inquiring: Is this the technetronic age coming to fruition or has it merely gone to seed?

Possibility of Increased Participation

Brzezinski's "politicians-intellectuals" are reminiscent of Plato's "philosopher-king." Brzezinski, like Plato, provides no convincing evidence that intellectuals will achieve such prominence in politics. Is Brzezinski indulging in wish-fulfillment? Perhaps so, though the need for expert interpretation of computer data requires talented, trained personnel whose interpretations could be politically influential.

Brzezinski's merging of the institutionally differentiated roles of forecasting and shaping the future, coupled with his sharp dichotomy between the merito-cratic elite and the masses, delineates only one type of social structure in which intellectuals could acquire more political power. Their increased power need not be incompatible with the polity remaining the societal decision-making body and with extensive public participation in the selection of future-oriented policies.

Alvin Toffler (1976) argues that high-speed change in a democracy makes planning mandatory for survival and that anticipatory government control without effective citizen participation might be no less lethal. Hence, he concludes that the future must neither be ignored nor captured by an elite. What is needed is a new kind of planning that is not the work of central office bureaucrats but which incorporates the originality, energy, intelligence, and innovative drive of ordinary people. Thus planning should become more decentralized and partici-patory, involving ordinary people in setting the long-range goals of the system.

Toffler points to the slogan that the planning office in the state of Wash-ington used in its experiment in citizen futurism: "You don't have to be an expert to know what you want." At a recent hearing before a Senate committee, he urged senators to investigate this experiment as well as Iowa 2000, Hawaii 2000, and the various statewide and local activities that have sprung up from these programs. Toffler, who helped organize the Committee on Anticipatory Democracy in 1975, concludes that "anticipatory democracy is the only kind of democracy possible in a period of high speed social, technological, and political change" (p. 106).

Robert Theobald, another participatory futurist, has repeatedly advocated increased citizen participation in decision making, as well as planning that is done with people rather than for them by well-meaning but frequently isolated bureaucrats. He interprets violence and civil disobedience as protests against the powerlessness that U.S. citizens feel. Establishment responses of repression could lead to a police state.

In *An Alternative Future for America's Third Century* (1976a), Theobald champions decentralized government. Because of an information overload and a deepening distrust of the messages received from those in power, people are looking for ways to return power and responsibility to the individual, the family, the group, and the community. The government needs to provide citizens with accurate, understandable information on the energy crisis and to challenge them to act responsibly on it. Theobald argues that attempts at voluntarism on energy issues have failed, not because citizens are stupid or irresponsible but because they have been given such conflicting signals as: "Save energy but buy more and more goods and services that use more energy."

To construct plausible scenarios for forecasts that assume successful large-scale increases in citizen participation in policy making, one must assume that the electorate is interested, educated, and not dominated by narrowly perceived short-term self-interest. The problem of how such responsible participation could be achieved by voluntary means deserves much further investigation.

Increased participation in business policy making appears to be quite feasible. John McHale (1976) argues that the emergence of knowledge as the principal commodity in postindustrial society will tend to break down rigidly hierarchical forms of management organization. They will be replaced by relatively participatory processes in which user feedback takes on increased importance in determining company policy. McHale stresses the need to ensure wide public access to communications and computing equipment and to promote understanding of the uses to which individuals as well as government agencies and businesses can put this equipment. Otherwise, most people may actively reject the new technology or regard it solely as a threat, since they lack any way of participating effectively in its use.

Implicit Normative Bias

Sharply distinguished from the high value that Brzezinski places on expected consequences of advances in electronic information technology is the critique of technology set forth by the French forecaster, Jacques Ellul. Although Ellul (1964) did not employ the term *postindustrial society* in *The Technological Society*, we can characterize his position as postindustrial pessimism. Unlike those ecological or nuclear pessimists who fear that undesirable consequences of the revolution in science-based technology will abort the evolution of a worthwhile postindustrial age, he perceives the trend toward increasing technique as apparently inevitable as well as downright undesirable. Thus Ellul, manifesting an attitude more prevalent among European dissenters than among their U.S. analogues, expresses hostility toward the onward march of technological "progress." For him the chief failure of the revolution in science-based technology lies in its continued success.

Ellul's critique of the increasingly technological society penetrates far deeper than an attack on machines. By *technique*, he means "the *totality of methods rationally arrived at and having absolute efficiency* (for a given stage of development) in *every* field of human endeavor" (p. xxv). His analysis of the history of the technical orientation leads to the conclusion that the government, the economy, and other aspects of modern life will continue to become increasingly dominated by the technical orientation. This trend, he believes, will culminate in a dictatorship of technocrats more oppressive than ever before. Freedom, creativity, and spontaneity will be stifled as human beings become totally subservient to the dictates of rationality and efficiency.

Even though Ellul and Brzezinski agree to a fairly large extent about the general characteristics of future society, they evaluate it in diametrically opposed ways. Some of Ellul's objections to technique, though emanating from a one-sided approach, appear to supply a valuable corrective to Brzezinski's whole-hearted devotion to technique. At any rate, forecasters need to articulate their own preferences, especially when they differ from those of other forecasters, and to assess the extent to which they are warranted.

To a limited, but nonetheless significant, extent, Victor Ferkiss (1969) presents such an analysis in his *Technological Man: The Myth and the Reality*. Ferkiss, who seeks to answer Ellul's claim that technique necessarily dehumanizes people, contends that the human species will soon reach the threshold of self-transformation, having attained power over itself and its environment. Although some analysts view technology as catapulting us toward doom, the dangers reside primarily in the failure of the predominant "bourgeois man" to understand the nature of the modern world. Instead, he employs technologies to attain limited, selfish goals. What is needed to create a world society aligned to ever-higher levels of human achievement is the dominance of "technological man": a wise, perceptive world citizen who has a grasp of science and technology and treats the global environment as a system of interacting parts. Society must be reshaped to facilitate the emergence of a new philosophy established on three tenets:

The "new naturalism": Man as part of nature must live in harmony with it.
The "new holism": Everything in the universe is interconnected.
The "new immanentism": The whole is created from within (pp. 206, 207).

For the most part, technological man will not constitute a new political ruling class but will leaven all the leadership echelons of society as an ecologist-engineer who deliberately plans the constructive evolution of human civilization. Guided by a meaningful philosophy of the role of technology, technological man will not be a mere passenger but a driver of the chariot of evolution (pp. 202, 203).

Thus, the values that Ferkiss espouses conflict not merely with Ellul's but with Brzezinski's as well. If critics can properly call Ferkiss a technocrat, his reformist, ecologically oriented technological man in various societal spheres differs markedly from Brzezinski's meritocratic elite.

Although Ferkiss's overall normative orientation seems more satisfactory than those of Brzezinski and Ellul, this should not be taken for granted. Instead, forecasters and other analysts need to make such disagreements explicit and subject them to rational argumentation. Another crucial issue that pertains to exploratory forecasts such as Brzezinski's and Ellul's is the extent to which forecasters' preferences, especially when left implicit, may have subtly biased their forecasts.

Marxist and Neo-Marxist Objections

Objections raised by Marxists and neo-Marxists, whose ideological orientations clash with that of Brzezinski, disclose further concealed assumptions in his forecasts. In addition, their criticisms reflect the distinctive character of their own assumptions that, like Brzezinski's, are value laden.

Bestuzhev-Lada's Critique

On the basis of "critical theory" that yields a dialectical analysis of crisis, Marxists and neo-Marxists argue that the ruling class in capitalist society promulgates ideology to perpetuate its own interests. For instance, Igor Bestuzhev-Lada (1970), a Russian futurist and an orthodox Marxist, relegates Western forecasts of capitalist postindustrial society to the status of bourgeois ideology. Instead of achieving an affluent capitalistic utopia, capitalist societies will be plagued by intensified class struggles.

Regardless of whether he can justify this claim, Bestuzhev-Lada shows that Brzezinski's forecast is conditioned by an implicit ideology that needs to be explicated and evaluated. Paradoxically, Bestuzhev-Lada himself is ideologically restricted by the orthodox straitjacket so easily detected in his "Utopias of Bourgeois Futurology" (1970).

As distinguished from Bestuzhev-Lada and other Marxists, typical neo-Marxists advocate a much more democratic form of socialism than that which prevails in the Soviet Union. They normally claim that the revolution in science-based technology has led to systems of control that interfere with public participation in decision making, perpetuate inequalities, decrease individual freedom, and arouse alienation.

Touraine's Critique

Whether we classify the French sociologist Alain Touraine as a bona fide neo-Marxist, he does tend to view change through neo-Marxist lenses. His analyses concentrate on inequalities, class conflict, and ideology. In *The Post-Industrial Society* (1971), he portrays a society that differs in certain respects from that projected by Brzezinski and most other U.S. postindustrial theorists, who tend to play down the role of ideology.

Touraine contends that class conflict will remain fundamental in postindustrial society but will change its nature. The new dominant class, rather than being defined by possession of property, will be a meritocracy that establishes its technocratic control on knowledge of information. Meritocrats will employ information to control change rationally, thereby creating a consciously "programmed society." Hence, information will constitute a particularly valuable resource in postindustrial society. By denying ordinary people access to the information necessary to participate in decision making, the meritocracy will restrict access to its ranks. This will create new forms of privileges and inequalities, breeding alienation and, consequently, conflict (pp. 49-62).

Notice the contrast between Touraine's approach and the "end of ideology" approach that Daniel Bell propounded in the 1950s. Although Bell did not forecast the death of all ideological challenges by countercultures, he failed to anticipate the severity of the ideological conflicts of the late 1960s. The dissent of U.S. youth has persuaded Brzezinski to consider ideological resistances somewhat more seriously, but he still dismisses them as relatively ineffective, anachronistic outbursts. Yet viewed from Touraine's perspective, Brzezinski champions a class society remarkably similar to alienating, crisis-prone capitalist society as Marx analyzed it. The meritocratic elite would possess superior political power, social status, and, presumably, economic reward. The ruling ideas would be the ideas of the ruling class. How ironic that Brzezinski should construct so tempting a target, a potentially oppressive class system, for Marxist and neo-Marxist revolutionists.

Once semantic differences are eliminated, the descriptions of postindustrial society presented by Brzezinski and Touraine display remarkable similarities. The most crucial differences consist of their conflicting evaluations of this society and of their disagreement concerning the importance of class conflict and ideology. Touraine values equality, freedom, and political participation more than Brzezinski, and technological progress and rational control less. Notice the extent to which differences in priorities among values can sometimes distinguish policy-oriented forecasts from each other.

Mendel's Critique

Neo-Marxist Arthur Mendel, a basically nonviolent utopian revolutionist, stages a literary assault on Brzezinski's forecast in "Robots and Rebels" (1969). Revolting against the "totalitarian ambition" of Brzezinski's "robots," Mendel's humanistically oriented rebels participate in the "Great Refusal." They attack modern "false-consciousness," which hypostatizes technology and perpetuates the reduction of a human being to a one-dimensional "economic man." Thereby, the rebels speak for the future, taking the leap to freedom that utopians have envisioned (pp. 17, 18).

Surprisingly, Mendel claims that rebels are creating utopia gradually without a cataclysmic confrontation (p. 19). While we may admire the humaneness of his rejection of Marcuse's projected violent confrontation, can we help but wonder whether Mendel's romantic optimism betrays his kinship to Pollyanna? Not only does his utopia seem implausible in itself; the means for achieving it are quite unrealistic.

Mendel caricatures Brzezinski's position and repeatedly castigates him with ad hominem arguments. Nonetheless, some of Mendel's criticisms make inroads on Brzezinski's forecast. For instance, Mendel perceives that human well-being is excessively identified with technological progress rather than with genuine satisfaction (p. 17).

Mendel directs two particularly incisive, though overstated, objections against Brzezinski's forecast. First, achievement of the affluent society constitutes a qualitative change that radically alters the struggle for securing the material basis for social existence. Contemporary dissatisfaction displays a salutary concern with neglected fundamental values. Feelings of alienation arise from overattachment to relatively unimportant technological and economic values and from underattachment to the humane values that most affect the long-term overall satisfaction of human beings. We may agree with Mendel that devotion to human well-being should not be subordinated to "absurd production," "aggressive militarism," and "impersonal organization" (p. 18). Moreover, we can sketch scenarios in which alienation leads to normative changes that promote a peaceful, desirable redirection of economic and technological developments, though hardly the utopia ushered in by Mendel's rebellious angels.

Mendel alleges that "the opposing forces are in fact acquiring, through the very processes of the system they oppose, the power to dethrone economic man, to . . . dissolve the taut constraints, the repressions and obligations that welded generations of mankind with the 'factors of production'" (p. 18). However, it is extremely doubtful that the emerging affluent society necessarily contains within itself the seeds of its transformation into a utopia. Is a large-scale utopia with so few controls a workable form of social organization?

Second, Mendel argues that the independence of youthful rebels enables them to stand outside their society and its image in them and to judge them both. Being freer of commitments to society, they may experiment in ways that enable them to envision and help create a better future. Universities, which encourage critical evaluation of society, often function as sites of revisualizations of sociocultural reality. Rather than automatically branding rebels as anachronistic, Brzezinski might benefit by listening to their grievances and suggestions for change.

Comparative Evaluation of Mendel's and Brzezinski's Forecasts

What further criticisms can be leveled against both Mendel's and Brzezinski's forecasts? Mendel apparently engages in simple trend extrapolation that presupposes economic determinism. By neglecting many other relevant forces, including countervailing ones, he exposes his forecast to severe objections. How similar, from a formal viewpoint, to Brzezinski's excessively monocausal, unidirectional determinism!

Mendel contends that "it is . . . to Brzezinski himself, and not his New Left opponents that . . . 'counter-revolutionary' applies . . . for the dramatic revolution in process in the advanced societies today is exactly the opposite of that which Brzezinski proclaims" (pp. 17-19). Thus, Brzezinski views himself as associated with a progressive historical movement that will triumph; Mendel pictures himself in the same way, but in relation to an opposing movement. Perhaps we could introduce some clarity into this value-laden dispute by defining *revolution* as "rapid fundamental change" (which is not necessarily progressive) and *counterrevolution* as "movement opposing the original revolution" (which need not be regressive). Then we could analyze both kinds of movements in their conflicting interrelation and delineate various possible outcomes, not just the one sort of outcome that we favor most.

Upshot of the Investigation

Our investigation of criticisms raised by Marxists and neo-Marxists, as well as of arguments set forth by Ellul and non-Marxist participatory futurists, has revealed that implicit values and ideology play important roles in Brzezinski's forecast. Such assumptions must be uncovered and either justified or corrected. If, as I have argued, the forecast is shaped by unwarranted assumptions, it is untrustworthy and needs to be revised.

4

KAHN AND WIENER'S "POST-INDUSTRIAL CULTURE"

> Time present and time past are both perhaps present in time future,
> and time future contained in time past.
>
> T. S. Elliot

IMPORTANCE OF THE KAHN-WIENER FORECAST

The publication of *The Year 2000* (1967), a treatise by Herman Kahn and Anthony J. Wiener of the Hudson Institute, laid down a milestone in the development of the study of the future. The Kahn-Wiener forecast ranked as the broadest, most sophisticated large-scale effort that futurists had made to project the relatively distant future. Not only did this forecast provide a foundation for similar efforts; it stimulated strong contrary reactions, including some that warn of impending limits to growth. With the possible exception of the forecast by Dennis Meadows's team (*The Limits to Growth*, 1972), no other forecast has exerted more influence on the character of subsequent futures research in the United States.*

The Kahn-Wiener forecast was updated by Kahn and B. Bruce-Briggs in the relatively short, popularly written *Things to Come* (1972) and, more recently, by Kahn, William Brown, and Leon Martel in the paperback *The Next 200 Years* (1976b). Kahn and Bruce-Briggs compared their book with *The Year 2000*:

---

*In a Delphi poll conducted by Michael Marien, *The Year 2000* was the only book unanimously judged to be "essential (exemplary, very important)" by the panel of futurists (Marien 1972, p. vi). Yet *The Limits to Growth* (Meadows et al 1972) has been more influential when judged by these criteria: it attracted more popular attention, played a leading role in shaping the growth controversy, and stimulated a host of direct and indirect responses, many of them negative.

In many ways this book [*Things to Come*] overlaps and continues the argument of *The Year 2000*. In fact, we are pleased that *The Year 2000* holds up remarkably well six years after it was written. As a result, any discussion of the 1970's and 1980's by us will, on the whole, elaborate and develop the discussion of that book rather than contradict it. . . . Whereas *The Year 2000* is concerned with long-range prospects of mankind, *Things to Come* looks toward the 1970's and 1980's, or in what we would call the "short" and "middle-range" prospects of mankind. [P. 3]

In my judgment, this comparison neglects salient differences between the two books. *The Year 2000* is concerned with methodological issues of long-range forecasting and planning. It stresses the importance of historical data and theories for forecasting and extrapolates to a large number of alternative futures. Although *Things to Come* also projects alternative futures, it is much more predictive and places decidedly less emphasis on methodology and history. Moreover, *Things to Come* expresses a much more conservative outlook.

This chapter focuses on *The Year 2000*, which sets forth the more technical, sophisticated, and influential forecast. Implicit normative assumptions in *Things to Come* will also be examined. In Chapter 8 we will look at *The Next 200 Years*, which marshals an exceptionally optimistic attack on claims made by limits-to-growth pessimists.

DESCRIPTION OF THE FORECAST

The "Multifold Trend"

Long-term trends, Kahn contends, constitute the most basic device for forecasting. Inasmuch as trends do not always move in straight lines, qualified trend extrapolation is the primary method used to formulate this exploratory forecast. We should note, however, that Kahn and Wiener also use genius forecasting, scenario writing, some nonformalized modeling (for example, use of Sorokin's theory), and historical analogy.

Kahn and Wiener note that the basic trends of Western society can be traced back as far as the eleventh or twelfth centuries and may be viewed as parts of a "basic, long-term, multifold trend." They argue that the interacting elements of this common trend seem likely to continue at least until the year 2000, though some may saturate or begin to recede beyond that time. For analytic purposes, they have separated these elements—admittedly in a somewhat arbitrary fashion—into 13 "rubrics" from which they extrapolate to the future. These rubrics are:

1. Increasingly Sensate (empirical, this-worldly, secular, humanistic, pragmatic, utilitarian, contractual, epicurean or hedonistic, and the like) cultures

2. Bourgeois, bureaucratic, "meritocratic," democratic (and nationalistic?) elites
3. Accumulation of scientific and technological knowledge
4. Institutionalization of change, especially research, development, innovation, and diffusion
5. Worldwide industrialization and modernization
6. Increasing affluence and (recently) leisure
7. Population growth
8. Urbanization and (soon) the growth of megalopolises
9. Decreasing importance of primary and (recently) secondary occupations
10. Literacy and education
11. Increasing capability for mass destruction
12. Increasing tempo of change
13. Increasing universality of the multifold trend. [P. 7]

In slightly revised lists formulated since 1967, other elements that have been added include two presented in *Things to Come* (pp. 8, 9): (1) centralization and concentration of economic and political power and (2) innovative and manipulative social engineering—that is, rationality increasingly applied to the social, political, cultural, and economic worlds as well as to shaping and exploiting the material world—increasing problem of ritualistic, incomplete, or pseudo rationality.

The first of these elements calls for special explanation, as do the eighth and ninth. Although the trend toward increasingly Sensate cultures has been interrupted at times since its origin seven or eight centuries ago, it appears to have expanded from the West to virtually cover the globe (Kahn and Wiener 1967b, pp. 39-44). The term *Sensate* culture is borrowed from Pitirim Sorokin (1962), a Harvard sociologist, who used it to mean worldly, empirical, humanistic, and the like. He contrasted Sensate culture with "Integrated" (idealistic, moralistic, reasoning, heroic) and "Ideational" (transcendental, religious, traditional) culture.

Kahn and Wiener "are for the most part committed to the dominant Sensate (or better, Early Sensate) assumptions of our society, but are concerned about some already visible social changes that may lead in the direction of an excessively 'Late Sensate society'" (Kahn and Wiener 1967, p. 44). The contrast between these two types of Sensate culture is expressed by the ways in which they are characterized. Sensate art is described as worldly, naturalistic, realistic, visual, illusionistic, everyday, amusing, interesting, erotic, satirical, novel, eclectic, syncretic, fashionable, superb technique, impressionistic, materialistic, commercial, and professional. Conversely, Late Sensate art is depicted as underworldly, protest, revolt, overripe, extreme, sensation seeking, titillating, depraved, faddish, violently novel, exhibitionist, debased, vulgar, ugly, debunking, nihilistic, pornographic, sarcastic, and sadistic. Similar distinctions can be drawn between Sensate and Late Sensate systems of truth, architecture, music, law, economics, family relationships, civic relationships, literature, ethics, education, government, and the like. The authors do not believe that "increasingly Sensate" culture necessarily leads toward Late Sensate culture (pp. 39-44).

Kahn and Wiener expect that at least three gargantuan megalopolises will have developed in the United States by the year 2000: "Boswash" (the area between Boston and Washington), "Chipitts" (between Chicago and Pittsburgh), and "Sansan" (between San Diego and Santa Barbara and, ultimately, San Francisco). These three megalopolises should contain about half of the total U.S. population, including the overwhelming majority of the most technologically and scientifically advanced, prosperous, intellectual, and creative elements (pp. 61, 62).

The primary occupations mentioned in the ninth rubric are fishing, forestry, hunting, agriculture, and mining. Secondary occupations of manufacturing and construction process products of primary occupations. Tertiary occupations are services that support primary and secondary occupations. Among these services are transportation, insurance, finance, and management. Quaternary occupations are services rendered to tertiary occupations or to each other. Kahn and Wiener state that there will undoubtedly be a large shift to quaternary occupations, which are heavily concentrated among various levels and agencies of the government, the professions, the nonprofit private groups, and so on. This will contribute to a shift away from the private business enterprise as the major source of innovation, attention, prominence, and reward in society (pp. 62, 63).

"Surprise-Free" Projection to the Year 2000

Basic Features

The Year 2000, appropriately subtitled *A Framework for Speculation on the Next Thirty-Three Years*, calls attention to the conjectural nature of forecasts. Acknowledging that new crises or unexpected events may divert current trends and alter expectations, Kahn and Wiener set forth a relatively apolitical and "surprise-free" projection to the year 2000. This projection, formulated primarily by extending the multifold trend, is summarized by Kahn and Wiener as follows:

1. Continuation of basic, long-term "multifold trend"
2. Emergence of "post-industrial" culture
3. Worldwide capability for modern technology
4. Very small world: increasing need for regional or worldwide "zoning ordinances" for control of arms, technology, pollution, trade, transportation, population, resource utilization, and the like
5. High (1 to 10 percent) growth rates in GNP per capita
6. Increasing emphasis on "meaning and purpose"

7. Much turmoil in the "new" and possibly in the industrializing nations
8. Some possibility for sustaining "nativist," messianic, or other mass movements
9. Second rise of Japan (to being potentially, nominally, or perhaps actually, the third largest power)
10. Some further rise of Europe and China
11. Emergence of new intermediate powers, such as Brazil, Mexico, Pakistan, Indonesia, E. Germany, and Egypt
12. Some decline (relative) of the U.S. and the U.S.S.R.
13. A possible absence of stark "life and death" political and economic issues in the old nations. [P. 23]

Kahn and Wiener list 100 technological innovations that they consider very likely by the year 2000 (pp. 51–55). Some of them will probably introduce sweeping changes, as will other new technologies during the early part of the twenty-first century. Several areas in which the authors forecast major progress are nuclear power; electronics, computers, information processing, and automation; lasers; the biological manipulation of man; holography, and the art of strategic warfare (see Table 4.1).

Kahn and Wiener anticipate a continuation of the marked economic growth that began with the industrial revolution and accelerated during the 1950s and 1960s. Prior to the last three centuries, no large society produced more than the equivalent of some $200 per capita annually. While the authors project rapid worldwide growth during the rest of this century, this growth will stretch the income gap that separates the extremely rich from the poor. Five levels of industrial development and income in the year 2000 are distinguished by Kahn and Wiener (p. 58):

1. Preindustrial	$50 to $200 per capita
2. Partially industrialized or transitional	$200 to $600 per capita
3. Industrial	$600 to perhaps $1500 per capita
4. Mass consumption or advanced industrial	Perhaps $1500 to something more
5. Postindustrial	Something over $4000 per capita to perhaps $20,000 per capita

Emergence of Postindustrial Society and Culture

Of special importance in the surprise-free projection for the year 2000 is the possible emergence of postindustrial society and culture. Kahn and Wiener outline this new type of society and culture, which the United States is on the road to becoming:

1. Per capita income about fifty times the preindustrial

TABLE 4.1

Technological Innovations likely in the Last Third of the Twentieth Century

- General use of automation and cybernation in management and production
- Extensive use of robots and machines "slaved" to humans
- Automated universal (real time) credit, audit and banking systems
- Pervasive business use of computers for the storage, processing, and retrieval of information
- Shared time (public and interconnected?) computers generally available to home and business on a metered basis
- Other widespread use of computers for intellectual and professional assistance (translation, teaching, literature search, medical diagnosis, traffic control, crime detection, computation, design, analysis and to some degree as intellectual collaborator generally)
- Extensive and intensive centralization (or automatic interconnection) of current and past personal and business information in high-speed data processors
- Other new and possibly pervasive techniques for surveillance, monitoring, and control of individuals and organizations
- Home computers to "run" household and communicate with outside world
- Home education via video and computerized and programmed learning
- Inexpensive high-capacity, worldwide, regional, and local (home and business) communication (perhaps using satellites, lasers, and light pipes)
- Practical home and business use of "wired" video communication for both telephone and TV (possibly including retrieval of taped material from libraries or other sources) and rapid transmission and reception of facsimiles (possibly including news, library material, commercial announcements, instantaneous mail delivery, other printouts, and so on)
- Direct broadcasts from satellites to home receivers
- Inexpensive worldwide transportation of humans and cargo
- Multiple applications of lasers and masers for sensing, measuring, communication, cutting, heating, welding, power transmission, illumination, destructive (defensive), and other purposes
- Artificial moons and other methods for lighting large areas at night
- New or improved uses of the oceans (mining, extraction of minerals, controlled "farming," source of energy, and the like)
- Permanent inhabited undersea installations and perhaps even colonies
- Generally acceptable and competitive synthetic foods and beverages (e.g., carbohydrates, fats, proteins, enzymes, vitamins, coffee, tea, cocoa, and alcoholic liquor)
- Practical large-scale desalinization

TABLE 4.1, continued

- New techniques for very cheap, convenient, and reliable birth control
- "High quality" medical care for undeveloped areas (e.g., use of medical aides and technicians, referral hospitals, broad spectrum antibiotics, and artificial blood plasma)
- General and substantial increase in life expectancy, postponement of aging, and limited rejuvenation.
- Human hibernation for relatively extensive periods (months to years)
- Practical use of direct electronic communication with and stimulation of the brain
- Stimulated and planned and perhaps programmed dreams
- Mechanical and chemical methods for improving human analytical ability more or less directly
- New, more varied, and more reliable drugs for control of fatigue, relaxation, alertness, mood, personality, perceptions, fantasies, and other psychobiological states
- Simple techniques for extensive and "permanent" cosmetological changes (features, "figures," perhaps complexion and even skin color, and even physique)
- Major reduction in hereditary and congenital defects
- Other genetic control and/or influence over the "basic constitution" of an individual
- Extensive use of cyborg techniques (mechanical aids or substitutes for human organs, senses, limbs, or other components)
- Commercial extraction of oil from shale
- Cheap and widely available central war weapons and weapon systems
- Permanent manned satellite and lunar installations—interplanetary travel

Note: These are representative items selected from the list of 100 technical innovations that Kahn and Wiener deem very likely in the last third of the twentieth century.

Source: Kahn and Wiener 1967, pp. 51–55. (Reprinted from THE YEAR 2000 by Herman Kahn and Anthony J. Wiener, courtesy of Macmillan Publishing Co., Inc. Copyright © 1967 by The Hudson Institute, Inc.)

2. Most "economic" activities are tertiary and quaternary (service-oriented), rather than primary or secondary (production-oriented),
3. Business firms no longer the major source of innovation
4. There may be more "consentives" (vs. "marketives")
5. Effective floor on income and welfare
6. Efficiency no longer primary
7. Market plays diminished role compared to the public sector and "social accounts"
8. Widespread "cybernation"
9. "Small world"
10. Typical "doubling time" between three and thirty years
11. Learning society
12. Rapid improvement of educational institutions and techniques
13. Erosion (in middle class) of work-oriented, achievement-oriented values
14. Erosion of "national interest" values
15. Sensate, secular, humanistic, perhaps self-indulgent criteria become central. [P. 25]

The postindustrial era will be "cybernated" in the sense that computers will regulate automatic systems in ways that basically eliminate the role of people as supervisors. Yet as monitors people will be able to override a system when necessary (p. 92). The United States is already undergoing computerized automation of productive processes.

The development of a "learning society" is being stimulated in part by the information explosion but mostly by the rapidity of change. Many of the new concepts that must be devised to deal adequately with today's potentialities—for instance, concepts of appropriate computer functions—are very different from those of two or three years ago (p. 188).

Early Twenty-First Century

Kahn and Wiener also provide a table for a relatively surprise-free early twenty-first century (p. 25). Whereas their book and this chapter center attention on the surprise-free projection for the year 2000, features of this more remote projection are worth noticing:

The rise of new great powers—perhaps Japan, China, a European complex, Brazil, Mexico, or India;
New political, perhaps even "philosophical" issues;
A leveling off or diminishing of some aspects of the basic, long-term multifold trend, such as urbanization;
Realization, to a large extent, of the postindustrial and industrial worlds;
Probably some success in population control and arms control and some kind

of moderately stable international security arrangements, though probably not a world government;

Some disruptions from ideology and irrational movements in the industrializing world; and

Presumably either a return to Hellenic or older European concepts of the good life or intensified alienation and a search for identity, values, meaning, and purpose in the affluent, permissive United States and Europe.

The economic optimism that pervades this forecast is particularly evident in these quantitative estimates:

> World population in the twenty years ending in 2020 is assumed to grow about as fast as in 1965–2000, to reach 9.0 billion. Over half will live in Asia. . . . In the same period, Gross World Product will rise 5 per cent a year. The share of Asia will reach one-fourth of the total compared with the present one-eighth share, largely because of the 7.5 per cent GNP growth rate assumed for Japan.
>
> Per capita world output will nearly double in the twenty years ending in 2020, reaching then about five times the world 1965 figure. Japan leads with $33 thousand (compared with only $3.6 thousand for the United States in 1965). The United States and West Germany follow with $19 and $18 thousand, respectively. . . . The Soviet Union, with 9.7 thousand, trails the major developed countries. [Pp. 140, 141]

"Canonical Variations"

Except for the appearance of a postindustrial culture, the foregoing projection for the year 2000 is surprise free. "It assumes the continuation of the multifold trend, but excludes precisely the kinds of dramatic and/or surprising events that dominated the first two-thirds of the century" (p. 23). To allow for the effects of surprises, Kahn and Wiener list eight "canonical variations" from the "standard world" of the surprise-free projection and some possible causes of surprising changes in the old nations (p. 9). These causes include invasion and war, civil strife and revolution, famine, pestilence, despotism (persecution), natural disaster, depression or economic stagnation, development of "inexpensive" doomsday or near-doomsday machines, disruptive polarization (racial, North-South, East-West, and so forth), and new religious philosophies or other worldwide organizations (p. 24). The canonical variations are:

A. More integrated world
   1. Stability-oriented
   2. Development-oriented
B. More inward-looking worlds
   1. With an eroded Communist movement

2. With an eroded Democratic morale and some Communist dynamism
3. With a dynamic Europe and/or Japan
C. Greater disarray worlds
1. With an eroded Communist movement
2. With a dynamic Communist movement and some erosion of
democratic morale
3. With a dynamic Europe and/or Japan. [P. 9]

Characterized by a high degree of cooperation among nations, more "integrated" worlds are relatively prosperous, peaceful, and arms controlled. More
inward-looking worlds have little general coordination or arms control but are
almost as prosperous and peaceful. Greater "disarray" worlds are relatively troubled and violent, though no large central wars have occurred. The last two types
of worlds are considered likely if the democratic movement or the Communist
movement declines, or if Japan or Europe become exceptionally dynamic powers
(p. 9).

The detailed description of these canonical variations presupposes the
accuracy of the Kahn-Wiener analysis of the multifold trend, since they represent divergencies from it. These divergencies are typically more moderate than
the alternative futures on which a number of other forecasters, such as Harman
and Meadows, concentrate. Kahn and Wiener apparently assume that the extent
and character of the divergencies will generally be significantly influenced by the
multifold trend.

Despite shortcomings inherent in the neglect of alternative futures that are
radically different from the present, Kahn and Wiener anticipate alternative
futures much more prolifically and insightfully than did Brzezinski in his forecast. Kahn has commented that he could easily think of 25 different projections
for the year 2000, any of which might be actualized.

Likelihood of the Surprise-Free Projection

Although a surprise-free projection is regarded as *more likely* than any
other particular projection, "there is no implication that a *surprise-free* projection is *likely*" (p. 38). Indeed, "it would be very surprising if in any thirty-three
year period the real world did not produce many political and technological
surprises" (p. 8). However, Kahn has stated that he would be willing to place a
small bet at even odds that the surprise-free projection will be proved to be
fundamentally correct. (Wiener has responded that he would accept this wager
and double the stakes.) Surprises there will be, but the multifold trend will
probably prevail against obstacles. Like the period 1815–1914, the rest of this
century may well be a time of relatively stable growth.

Wiener, on the other hand, has acknowledged that probable surprises
preclude a confident forecast of the year 2000. His main aim in using qualified

trend extrapolation was to gain enough knowledge of the directions in which trends are headed to improve the quality of present policy making, thus promoting efforts to avert potential disasters and to take advantage of opportunities. His present attitude toward long-term projections is epitomized by the remark, "Perhaps the most surprising thing that could actually happen would be an absence of surprises."

When both the surprise-free projection and the canonical variations are taken into account, the prospects for the United States are indeed encouraging. The portrait of the likely U.S. society as painted by Kahn, if not by Wiener, displays the following lustrous features. As the leading postindustrial society, the United States will have an economy in which service-oriented activities predominate. By the year 2020, the standard of living will be three to six times as high as it was in 1965. Leisure time will have increased and the culture will have become more "Sensate." Political processes will remain quite democratic. Although international relations will still be shaped by coexistence, détente between the United States and the Soviet Union will have persisted. Politically, economically, and militarily, the United States will be in a relatively secure position. Japan, however, is eventually likely to exceed the United States in per capita income and may be the leader in certain other features of postindustrial society.

EVALUATION OF ASSUMPTIONS

Dependence of the Forecast on the Multifold Trend

A methodological bias inherent in the use of qualified trend extrapolation is its tendency to produce forecasts of relatively continuous futures. The usual presupposition is that the main causes that shape an established trend will probably change only gradually, if at all. In the Kahn-Wiener version of this method, the likelihood of a developmental future is substantially dependent on the units of the multifold trend. This is because mutually reinforcing growth trends are more likely to generate continued growth than trends that interfere with each other. Interference effects, which sometimes stem unanticipated consequences of trends, might fundamentally alter the growth rates and even the directions of long-term trends.

Do historical and contemporary data justify the assumption that the multifold trend is unified? This question is part of a broader question: How defensible is the Kahn-Wiener analysis of this trend? Answers to these questions are of crucial significance for assessing the dependability of qualified extrapolation from the multifold trend. Hence, this evaluation focuses more on the multifold trend than directly on the forecast.

If the multifold trend is to furnish a trustworthy foundation for forecasting, it must be more than an unanalyzed list of tends. That is, it needs to have been derived from an accurate, sensitive analysis of historical and contemporary sociocultural processes. The most important trends in Western society should have been selected and then properly described and classified. Description ought to be perceptive of the most relevant features of the trends. Classification encompasses differentiation of trends from one another and specification of their interrelations. The task of assessing the multifold trend would be easier if Kahn and Wiener had clearly articulated and justified whatever criteria they may have used to select, describe, and classify the component trends.

Omission of Important Trends

The multifold trend is not as comprehensive as one might expect. It neglects a number of important trends, including sociocultural "revolutions" that consist of extremely rapid, extensive departures from past orientations. Consider, for instance, the Kahn-Wiener treatment of the emergence of early modern culture in Europe.

To dub present culture as "Sensate" and locate its beginning in the Renaissance (p. 65) is to place insufficient emphasis on the lifeways derived from the "Protestant ethic," which the authors do not discuss until chapter 4. The Renaissance sprang up primarily in the Catholic culture area of Italy, whereas the Reformation flourished in a number of regions north of the Alps. Protestant ethic lifeways were more influential than Renaissance sensate culture in promoting rational bourgeois capitalism and the industrial revolution. Max Weber (1958a) shows how the success of capitalism was an unintended consequence of the Reformation. The ethic of ascetic Protestantism sanctioned discipline, hard work, profit making as a sign of God's blessing, and reinvestment rather than conspicuous consumption. Moreover, this ethic encouraged systematic rational planning. Thus, lifeways derived from the Protestant ethic are oriented toward mastering this world through discipline and organization.

Kahn and Wiener do cite the production of bourgeois elites by the Reformation (p. 65), but the failure to mention Protestant ethic culture might lead one to suppose that a Protestant social structure was imposed on a Catholic sensate culture. The authors make this problem more acute for themselves by their admission that the trend toward increasingly sensate culture was interrupted by the Reformation, which represented a contradiction to it (p. 44). If the two cultures were contradictory, could one of the cultures mix harmoniously with the other culture's social structure? The possibility of such a combination of Protestant social structure and Catholic sensate culture must not be excluded, because the former displayed sensate as well as nonsensate motifs. Yet this combination appears to violate the alleged unity of the multifold trend and, therefore, needs to be explained.

The presentation of the multifold trend creates the impression that culture and social structure are less intimately related than Kahn and Wiener actually believe. The list skips from sensate cultures to bourgeois elites without mentioning the intervening Reformation, which is treated later.

Granted a closer relation between culture and social structure, Sorokin's claim that Catholic early sensate culture of the Renaissance led to Protestant early sensate culture is still rather suspect. Historical evidence, as analyzed by Bernard Groethuysen (1968) and others, indicates that modernization and industrialization proceeded in significantly different ways in Catholic and Protestant culture areas. Although Protestant culture areas were somewhat influenced by the Renaissance, the cultural dynamics of these areas (even up to the last part of the nineteenth century) were typically more independent of it than the Kahn-Wiener account suggests.

Innovative and manipulative social engineering, a crucial addition to the multifold trend, significantly overlaps lifeways derived from the Protestant ethic. In this vein, Wiener has stated that the primary source of change in Western society is a distinguishing cultural trait: manipulative rationality. This trait involves the Faustian motivation and ability of Westerners to change their environments and themselves in rational ways, thus obtaining desired ends.

Other important trends that began during early modern times are omitted from the multifold trend. Conspicuously absent is the scientific-mathematical-philosophical revolution of the sixteenth and seventeenth centuries, together with its aftereffects on our culture. Also missing is the significant movement from "tribal brotherhood" to "universal otherhood" (Nelson 1969): a shift from parochial standards that discriminate against outsiders toward increased universalization of systems of economic exchange and credit and the like.

Further trends that were overlooked include the "revolution of rising expectations" and the revolution for racial equality. The latter revolution is related to other egalitarian revolutions, such as the revolution for women's equality. These historically rooted egalitarian revolutions, so evident today in movements for social justice and equality, are not even represented in the multifold trend. Also bypassed by this trend as presented in *The Year 2000* and *Things to Come* are some of the interrelated ecological trends that have become the source of so much current concern. Consonant with the general climate of opinion when *The Year 2000* was written, pollution received little attention and was not even listed in the index.

The Kahn-Wiener surprise-free forecast is presented as a moderately qualified extrapolation of the basic trends in Western society. Hence, the forecast's neglect of several important trends renders it quite misleading, especially since some of them clash with components of the multifold trend.

Differentiation and Interrelation of Trends

In differentiating and interrelating trends, Kahn and Wiener could have cut the categorical cake more elegantly. For instance, industrialization/modernization and urbanization, two trends of the multifold trend, are closely interconnected. The trends of urbanization and population growth in the contemporary world are best analyzed as aspects of what Philip Hauser (1968), a sociologist, has christened "the social morphological revolution." Population explosion and population implosion are interrelated demographic trends.

Increasing affluence/leisure and decreasing importance of primary/secondary occupations are advanced stages of worldwide industrialization and modernization. The accumulation of scientific/technological knowledge and literacy/ education are both parts of "the knowledge industry," of which the increasing capability for mass destruction is a product. One would expect to find these sets of trends more closely interrelated in the Kahn-Wiener list.

Unanticipated Consequences and Conflicting Trends

Qualified trend extrapolation assumes that the key causes of trends in the past will generally continue to operate in similar ways, though some variation may occur. Kahn and Wiener recognize that trends need not continue their linear growth indefinitely but may gradually "top out" or diminish. However, a trend can also produce consequences that eventuate in its sudden, catastrophic collapse. Especially important are unanticipated consequences that may touch off unexpected reactions against the trend itself or some related trend.

A number of forecasters have argued that such ecological trends as the depletion of nonrenewable energy resources and pollution threaten to undermine increasing industrialization, the very trend that has done so much to produce them. The trend of rapid population growth in many developing countries hinders two other trends: increasing industrialization and education. While birthrates do tend to decline as the per capita income rises toward $1,000 per annum, this "demographic transition" typically occurs too slowly to prevent this interference of trends. Accelerating costs and pressures of increasing urbanization and population growth might induce national leaders and citizens to make decisions that would significantly slow these two trends.

The interrelated problems that concern energy generation, raw materials availability, pollution, and food production have already contributed to such shifts in trends as a decline in the rate of global economic growth. These ecological problems, in large measure consequences of the trends of industrial and population growth, could induce major, enduring changes in trends. Yet these problems were largely neglected or discounted by Kahn and Wiener. Admittedly, the increasing need for "zoning ordinances" for control of pollution, population, resource utilization, and the like is mentioned in the surprise-free projection. At times Kahn and Wiener have responded to the recent emphasis on ecological problems by acknowledging a new element in the multifold trend: increasing attention to amelioration of the macroecological problems generated by unwanted by-products of technology. This trend, largely a reaction against unanticipated consequences of technological development, interferes with the previous direction of such development and—at least temporarily—with the trend of increasing affluence.

The trend of innovative and manipulative social engineering may also produce consequences retarding itself and other trends. One reason is that it typically eventuates in a rationalization of taboos. According to Kahn's own analysis, this erosion of taboos tends to bring decreased work motivation and increased alienation, impulsiveness, and hedonism. Taboos, Kahn argues, may be a prerequisite for a stable, progressive society.

Another reason can be inferred from remarks made by William Pfaff, a Hudson Institute researcher. He claims that liberalism in Europe and North America created expectations of both representative democracy and increased efficiency. Yet the rationalized centralization required for the latter leads to disappointments regarding the former. Since the trend of innovative and manipulative social engineering both promotes economic progress and occasions serious problems of political participation, might this cast some doubt upon the economically encouraging, apolitical surprise-free projection?

In some cases, a collision of incompatible trends can radically change the course of either or both. The trend of increasing capability for mass destruction, for instance, could lead to a global nuclear war that would reverse industrial growth, as is evident from chapter 7 of *The Year 2000*. The danger of such an explosive encounter of trends leads one to question how unified the multifold trend really is.

Thus Kahn and Wiener do not sufficiently take into account the consequences of trends and the interference of some trends with others. The key word in this sentence is *sufficiently*. The canonical variations allow for certain interference effects, as do various remarks made in *The Year 2000* after the opening chapters. Global nuclear war, for example, is regarded as capable of upsetting the multifold trend. Moreover, rejection of established economic and political systems by affluent parents' children could spread to other groups in society and influence the trajectories of trends. Yet the totality of the comments about interference effects does not appear to be completely compatible with the earlier treatment of the multifold trend and the surprise-free projection.

Variable Stages of Trends

Kahn and Wiener state that their use of terminology derived from Sorokin and other philosophers of history does not commit them to a belief in a necessary life cycle of a civilization or culture (p. 41). Yet sometimes they convey the impression that parts of the multifold trend normally develop by relatively fixed stages. Increases in the accumulation of scientific/technological knowledge, the institutionalization of change, and innovative/manipulative social engineering lead to accelerated worldwide industrialization/modernization. This in turn promotes increasing affluence/leisure and loosens taboos, thus eventuating in increasingly sensate culture. Moreover, Kahn and Wiener seem to view world-wide industrialization/modernization as a relatively uniform trend, having stages that should culminate in postindustrial society and culture.

However, "moderator variables"—factors that affect the relations between other factors—can interfere with such stages. For instance, unanticipated consequences of a trend may trigger an effective reaction against it, thus altering previous time-and-stage expectations of how both that trend and interdependent trends will develop. Kahn and Wiener are aware of this, but it does not affect their analysis of the multifold trend and their surprise-free projection. In practice, they sometimes make such concessions. Kahn recognizes that increased industrialization in Japan may not result in certain aspects of an increasingly sensate culture, including a lessened work orientation and increased alienation. The primary reason for this is the distinctive Japanese cultural orientation, which encourages prestige motivation. In public appearances, Kahn and Wiener have stressed the importance of such cultural traits as prestige motivation and manipulative rationality. Since these cultural traits might function as moderator variables that would affect trends, extrapolation should not overlook their potential impacts.

Nationalism need not facilitate the trend of modernization and industrialization, as many theorists once supposed, but may function as a moderator variable that inhibits it. This trend has already encountered unexpected setbacks in some developing nations, including Ghana. A foreign-trained, industrially oriented, modernizing elite may be viewed by the populace as unrepresentative of a truly nationalistic orientation and, therefore, as "undemocratic" (in the Kahn-Wiener sense of not having a popular political base, p. 48). Thus reactionary movements in certain developing nations have demonstrated that bourgeois, bureaucratic, and meritocratic elites can be ousted by elites that are more nationalistic and democratic. Yet Kahn and Wiener lump these elites together in the same ongoing trend that reinforces the trend of industrialization and modernization.

An historical parallel to present modernization is that of modern European nations. Despite their possession of lifeways conducive to modernization—lifeways that are lacking in many developing nations today—they experienced periods of turmoil. In an extended discussion that presents canonical variations, Kahn and Wiener admit that the developing countries will undergo instability and turbulence (Kahn and Wiener 1967, chap. 7). Yet they consider this admission to be compatible with their projection that, by the year 2000, 90 percent of the world's population will be living in countries that have boken through the subsistence barrier (p. 60). However, some kinds of possible instability and turbulence are incompatible with this projection. Might not hungry, frustrated nations formulate anti-Western ideologies that would both rationalize their failures and put a damper on their rising expectations?

Countercultural Attempts to Counteract Trends

Attempts to counteract trends warrant a closer examination. A relatively small group within a society sometimes rebels against a trend favored by the society as a whole. Max Weber, Arnold Toynbee, and other analysts of societal and civilizational history have furnished convincing evidence that many basic sociocultural changes have originated in the activities of dissenting groups. Even the United States' relatively successful societal effort—at least until the energy crisis of 1973/74—to reverse the national trends of air and water pollution began in this way and encountered stiff opposition.

However, questionable assumptions that Kahn and Wiener make about culture and change minimize the efficacy of countercultural resistance to a trend. Their forecast assumes that the components of the multifold trend are likely to unfold in a manner resembling past trajectories, regardless of any countercultural opposition. Yet both countercultural movements and reactions against them may change the rate or direction of a trend. The authors admit this in practice. An example is their recognition that the U.S. lower-middle-class reaction against violence and "Late Sensate" culture is highly significant. Still, the necessity of making such admissions indicates that their theoretical framework requires revision. Since the action-reaction pattern so pervades sociocultural change, any analysis of trends that neglects it is suspect. This neglect is only partially rectified by *Things to Come*, in which the degree to which reactions can influence trends seems unduly limited.

Kahn and Wiener proceed on these assumptions: (1) the "high culture," an educated dominant middle- and upper-class group, is of paramount significance; (2) "as go the fine arts, so goes the culture"; and (3) cultural uniformity is quite prevalent (pp. 42, 43). The first assumption is correct when a high culture is a virtually unopposed pacesetter of a new orientation. Yet this assumption should not rule out the importance of various subcultures or of a general societal culture. The U.S. lower-middle-class reaction against an increasingly sensate culture is a powerful, partially religious challenge to this trend, which is a high-culture phenomenon. This challenge is spearheaded by a so-called class that does not qualify as a high culture.

The second assumption treats changes in the fine arts as the most important lead indicators of the directions in which a culture will move. This assumption, derived from Sorokin and others despite the Kahn-Wiener endeavor to remain uncommitted to historical theories, overstates the undeniable significance that changes in the fine arts have for forecasting. Unlike universal mathematics and science, the fine arts manifest an idiosyncratic nature, which makes them somewhat difficult to use as lead indicators. They constitute only one of several indexes to the ongoing culture.

The third assumption refers to the presence of the same characteristics in different sorts of cultural activities. Kahn and Wiener "accept, with reservations, the assumption that there is, by and large, a considerable congruence or convergence among the various sectors of high culture, or perhaps of any widely held culture" (p. 43). An example would be utilitarian, hedonistic, and empirical characteristics in the arts, government, and science.

True, there is considerable conguence, particularly among the sectors of high culture. Yet the societal culture of the United States is composed of manifold layers derived from different historical sources. Many domestic problems involve clashes between the divergent cultural heritages in this melting pot culture. Not only do dissonances often emerge from contacts of such cultural activities as religion and science; even within some activities, such as religion, cultural contrasts abound. The outcomes of some cultural conflicts can affect the behavior of trends. For instance, upper classes in the United States assign a higher priority to pollution control than do growth-oriented lower middle classes, which tend to place more value on increased energy generation. The rates of the trends of energy generation and pollution control hang in the balance. Yet Kahn and Wiener circumvent numerous trend-altering factors by abstracting them from their theoretical framework.

Many of the interrelated characteristics that Kahn and Wiener assign to sensate culture have definitely increased and spread quite widely. The clash of cultural styles in the United States as well as in the world, however, necessitates qualification of their claim that an increasingly sensate culture has spread from the West to the rest of the world. The cultural uniformity of this trend is dubious. For instance, Western culture is much more permeated by lifeways derived from the Protestant ethic than is suggested by the Kahn-Wiener treatment of sensate culture. When exported to other countries, Western culture, like a chameleon, takes on new shades.

The Multifold Trend: Inadequately Analyzed and Disunified

Basic Requirements for Satisfactory Trend Analysis

Any adequate overview of the long-term, ongoing trends of modern Western civilization and the world needs to be based on the best available information about:

The extent to which each trend is quantifiable and, therefore, statistically measurable,
When, where, and how each trend originated,
How each has been diffused,
The various stages it has passed through,
Its growth rate and fluctuations,
The principle causes that produce it and whether they seem likely to change,

Its causal relations with other trends and with factors that are not trends, and
Its relative importance in producing historically significant changes.

The Year 2000 and *Things to Come* present only a moderate amount of such
information, some of which is problematic.

Justifiable projection of trends requires knowledge of the causal processes
that shape their trajectories. Factors on which the continuation, acceleration,
deceleration, topping out, redirection, and reversal of trends depend need to be
isolated and analyzed. Hence, historical knowledge of trends is indispensable, as
is knowledge of their contemporary status. Among the factors that should be
taken into account are:

Alternatives as well as limitations set by the ecological context;
Feasible technological innovations, together with their far-reaching consequences;
Societal images of the future and individual and group self-images;
Present and feasible societal and subsocietal goals; incompatible goals both with-
    in and between societies; possibility of shattered expectations and their
    consequences;
Conflicts between various groups that make incompatible demands; strength of
    countercultural movements;
Degree of perceived adequacy of current policies, institutions, and leadership, as
    well as prospects for improvements;
Possible ideological and value changes, coupled with their potential impacts;
Cultural traits, motivational patterns, and the symbolic guidance systems that
    they reflect; and
Potential range of impact of surprises.

Deficiencies of the Multifold Trend Analysis and the Forecast

Now some conclusions can be drawn. Methodologically, qualified trend
extrapolation does not take into account the interaction of enough of the relevant causes, as modeling can do (at least in principle). Substantively, the concept
of the multifold trend is the outcome of an inadequate analysis of historical and
contemporary sociocultural processes. Not only are several important trends
missing; a number of the constituent trends are inadequately described, differentiated, or interrelated. Since some of them seriously interfere with others,
the supposed unity of the multifold trend dissolves. Clearly, the multifold trend
requires extensive revision. What is called for is not the piecemeal type of
improvement accomplished in *Things to Come* but an overhaul of the general
theoretical framework. One can argue that, as an analytical tool, the multifold
trend should be replaced by a series of "revolutions"—rapid, directional sociocultural changes in relatively short time-spans, constituting perspectival breakthroughs—and trends in various stages and in both reinforcing and inhibiting
relationships (Nelson 1969).

Since the surprise-free projection is extrapolated from the multifold trend, the misleading character of the latter renders the former highly questionable. While this by no means implies that these projections are devoid of useful insights, it does cast serious doubt on the likelihood of a long-range, comprehensive future that is continuous with established trends. Thus, the Kahn-Wiener forecast, though constituting an especially important contribution to futurism, makes dubious methodological and nonmethodological assumptions that undermine its dependability.

Appraisal of Three Counterarguments

When I raised the objections presented above in conversations with Wiener, he responded in the following three ways.

First, the multifold trend is basically unified in spite of some incompatibilities within it. This reply is founded on the powerful mutually supportive relationships among several components of this trend. Yet conflictive relationships among other components and likely interference by neglected forces render smooth extrapolation from it quite dubious. Hence, Kahn's commitment to the likelihood of the surprise-free projection is difficult to defend. Wiener's supposition that one type of relatively continuous future—a surprise-free projection derived by extrapolating the multifold trend—is more likely than other types does not even commit him to the contention that continuous futures as a whole are more likely than discontinuous ones. Nonetheless, shortcomings in the analysis of the multifold trend create serious doubt that the surprise-free projection is more likely than any other kind of future.

Second, admission of the disunity of the multifold trend has different consequences for the canonical variations than for the surprise-free projection. Although this is correct, the dependability of the canonical variations is somewhat diminished by their having been conceived as departures from the surprise-free projection. Still, the major weakness appears to be one of omission: failure to include turning-point futures related to global ecological problems.

Finally, my evaluation concentrates on the early part of *The Year 2000*, whereas the later parts present richer, more detailed discussions that are less open to criticism. The beginning of the book was intended as a heuristic device, which had to be simplified to accomplish its purpose. True, the subsequent analyses of specific aspects of future-oriented problems are far superior to the excessively simplified, partially misleading overview. These analyses, which contributed to the improvement of forecasting, are indeed less vulnerable to a number of objections that score against the overview. However, it is not at all clear that the overview of the book is an adequate summary of—or is even directly derived from—the later detailed analyses and forecasts. One suspects a significant incompatibility that calls for revision of the multifold trend, the surprise-free projection, and the canonical variations that are constructed as variations from this trend and projection. Does not the burden of proof rest upon Wiener to show that the oversimplification of the multifold trend and the surprise-free projection may be dismissed as merely a presentational problem?

Implicit Normative Bias in Kahn's 1972 Forecast

A quite different kind of objection seeks to expose implicit normative biases in those exploratory forecasts that purport to be relatively "value free" or "value neutral." Assertions about these biases are often difficult to establish conclusively. Hence, analyses must be thorough and well reasoned, as is that of Marien (1973a) in his balanced review of *Things to Come* (1972).

Kahn and Bruce-Briggs state that they sought to take a "value-free" perspective, being "objective" and "descriptive" in their forecasting (p. 244). They admit that descriptive and normative forecasting cannot be completely separated and that normative aspects are present in their work (p. 245). Though Marien fails to mention this admission, his analysis reveals that they fall far short of their goal.

The tone of *Things to Come* is much more conservative than that of *The Year 2000*, which does not profess to be value free. Marien attributes this ideological difference to an ominous shift in the outlook of Kahn, who denounced the academic countercultural radicals of the late 1960s and early 1970s. Yet the chief reason for this difference appears to be the divergent orientations of the coauthors.

Marien convincingly argues that the forecasts and policy recommendations of Kahn and Bruce-Briggs were distorted by their implicit bent toward conservatism. This bias is evident in their selection and interpretation of the elements that comprise their projected futures. Marien (1973a) notes that *Things to Come*

> ignores the status of democratic participation, the state of natural resources in our throwaway society, the capacity of our institutions to cope with new realities, the mounting costs of satisfying human needs, the potentials of the multifaceted communications revolution. [P. 14]

Thus their supposedly descriptive forecast functions subtly as a normative forecast.

The bias emerges in such value-laden labels as the "Responsible Center," with which Kahn and Bruce-Briggs identify, and the "Humanist Left," which by contrast is implicitly treated as irresponsible. The outlook of the Responsible Center coincides with the established interests of government and business. The biases of the Left are repeatedly attacked by Kahn and Bruce-Briggs, whereas the biases of the Center and the Right are ignored (Marien 1973a, pp. 8, 12).

The conservative bias of Kahn and Bruce-Briggs becomes even clearer in their support of a "counter-reformation" against the threatening emergence of "late sensate culture." This bias seems to have affected their projections, as evidenced by their concentration on the faddishness and the unrealistic attempts at self-fulfilling prophecy that may cause this emergent culture to top out of its own accord. On the contrary, Willis Harman considers certain recent counter-cultural normative changes to be appropriate for coping with the world macro-problem. Thus the countercultural challenge to established premises and value-priorities appears as a threat in Kahn's and Bruce-Briggs's forecast but as a source of hope in Harman's forecast. Neither forecast is value free.

Kahn and Bruce-Briggs (1972) treat undesirable consequences of techno-logical progress under the caption, "the 1985 Technological Crisis." They take this anticipated crisis seriously enough to warn: "It is not necessary to be a 'hippie' or a hysterical academic to recognize that our much-vaunted technolog-ical advance may soon lead us to disaster" (p. 209). Yet as Marien (1973a) observes: "Not only do Kahn and Bruce-Briggs push this crisis point 13 years into the future, but they suggest that various incremental steps will be adequate to correct or alleviate these problems, and that mainstream values can and should persist" (p. 14). Conversely, forecasters such as John Platt (1969) and Richard Falk (1975) have argued that major planned changes are required to alleviate such interrelated problems.

Nisbet's Criticism: The Future as a Dice Game

Further cogent criticisms of the Kahn and Wiener and the Kahn and Bruce-Briggs forecasts will emerge implicitly and sometimes explicitly, as we explore the forecasts by Bell, Harman, and the Meadows team. This critical posture might tempt one to conclude that Kahn's forecasts, in particular, and qualified trend extrapolation, in general, are worthless and even that all forecasting is nec-essarily undependable. To reveal the inadequacy of such totalistic attempts to dismiss all forecasting as specious expertise we now turn to a typical critique of the Kahn-Wiener forecast and of futurism.

Robert Nisbet (1968), perhaps the most renowned critic of futurism, attacks "the historical-prediction business" as exemplified by the Kahn-Wiener forecast in "The Year 2000 and All That."* According to Nisbet, the claim that the future is predictable rests on these untenable assumptions:

The metapor of growth is transferable from individual organisms to social change,
Trends are causal processes, and
Significant social change often proceeds by developmental continuity (pp. 64-66).

---

*Though Nisbet's *Social Change in History* (1969) and "Has Futurology a Future?" (1971) are also relevant to evaluating the Kahn-Wiener forecast, he presents most of the important points in "The Year 2000 and All That."

The net result of these assumptions is that much social change can be predicted because it follows gradually growing trends. A prime example is the Kahn-Wiener extrapolation of the multifold trend to a surprise-free projection.

Nisbet's criticism of the first of these three assumptions is well founded but fails to establish his contrary assumption that nothing like growth occurs regularly in societies. Kahn and Wiener argue convincingly that sizable changes over a period of time—such as increases in scientific knowledge and the rate of technical innovations—often follow a more-or-less continuous pattern of development.

Inveighing against the second assumption, Nisbet correctly distinguishes between trends and causal processes. Trends are abstractions formulated on the basis of what the analyst selects as significant for understanding cumulative change. The chronological continuity of the successive features of a trend must not be confused with the specific causes involved in genetic continuity. Since particular events rather than abstractions derived from them cause change, the question arises: How can one justifiably make a forecast on the basis of abstractions?

Far from being oblivious of the abstract nature of trends, Kahn and Wiener (1967) perceive:

> The system in which worldwide changes take place is far more complicated than can be suggested by any effort to identify a limited number of abstract "trends," let alone to specify which of the abstractions "causes" the others. [P. 65]

This admission, however, does not warrant the conclusion that Nisbet draws merely from his analysis of the language involved: As an abstraction, a trend *in principle* cannot be causal in any way (p. 65). Statistical trend extrapolation based on numerical samples taken at regular intervals furnishes a fairly reliable basis for short-term forecasting, provided that key forces seem likely to remain relatively constant. For instance, the rate of population increase in a developing country may be extrapolated in this way, assuming the absence of war and mass starvation, lack of more effective birth control techniques, and so on. Moreover, awareness of such forces, coupled with cautious estimates of the likelihood of their occurrence and impacts, provides insight into how a trend can be changed. Causality is, therefore, by no means an utter foreigner in the domain of statistical trend extrapolation.

Granted that nonstatistical trends neglect many causal relations and only generalize concerning others, they may nevertheless summarize causal processes. For instance, industrialization has generally been found to be accompanied by increasing urbanization, bureaucratization, and affluence. Does one commit a logical howler by projecting these already-increasing trends as probable for a developing society that seems to have adequate resources and motivation to industrialize extensively? No. Abstractions from causal relations may remain causally relevant. By treating trend extrapolation as totally noncausal by definition, Nisbet tries to get far too much mileage out of his argument. It could be used to show that forecasters, such as Kahn and Wiener, can easily overlook trend-modifying forces or seriously misjudge the likelihood of their occurrence or the strength of their impacts.

Nisbet counters the third assumption by contending that all kinds of change "worth looking at" are "the consequence of the Random Event, the Genius, the Maniac, and the Prophet," not of developmental continuity (p. 66). Today's prognosticators as exemplified by Kahn and Wiener do not suggest that these four kinds of change can be predicted. Hence, there is no significant kind of social change left for them to predict.

Again Nisbet vitiates a plausible objection by grossly overstating it. Major changes often have been unexpected, particularly in the twentieth century. So-called great men have left their mark by introducing discontinuous changes that have diverted the stream of history from its established course. Without Lenin the 1917 Bolshevik revolution would not have occurred or succeeded and world history would have been radically different. Einstein revolutionized Newtonian physics. Hitler and Stalin engineered unprecedented totalitarian domination and killed millions of people in extermination and forced labor camps.

Surprising as these action and events were, they could not have occurred in just any historically derived sociocultural setting. *The context* may not determine the event or action but it *sets the alternatives*, however unlikely some of them may be. It not only limits the viable options open to a great leader; it also provides opportunities. Lenin did not make the 1917 revolution but took advantage of an opportunity. Einstein could not have discovered the theory of relativity in 1500. Hitler could not have succeeded without the consent of many Germans. Nor were the world wars and the depression context free. Indeed, the 100 technical innovations that Kahn and Wiener list as very likely in the last third of the twentieth century (pp. 51-55) would bring about profound changes, but a necessary condition for many of these breakthroughs is a continuation of the trends of the accumulation of scientific and technological knowledge and the institutionalization of change. Thus Nisbet fails to appreciate the extent to which unanticipated events and innovative actions depend on contexts, which are easier to forecast than events. Careful projection of a wide range of possible discontinuous social changes can aid efforts to prepare for, and sometimes even control or create, the highly uncertain future.

Kahn and Wiener plausibly maintain that the long-term, cumulative operation of the elements of the multifold trend would ultimately create differences in degree amounting to qualitative changes in some or all of the elements (p. 65, table IX). Since an accumulation of relatively minor changes—for instance, scientific and technological advance, the growth of population, and the rise in living standards—can bring about major changes, Nisbet's claim that no significant social change proceeds by developmental continuity is simply mistaken.

Nisbet sets forth a dice model of change as "much better than the models drawn from organic growth" (p. 65). Just as a gambler's hot streak exerts no influence over the outcome of the next throw of the dice, so, Nisbet contends, the previous historical trend is independent of the next event. However, history is not a dice game consisting of equipossible alternatives. Each historical event is not totally independent of all prior events. The dice game metaphor is rendered even more misleading by Nisbet's neglect of increasingly important planned change, which sometimes negates his causal priority of the random event.

Finally, Nisbet's contention that the significant future is unpredictable conceals the prediction that the future will be so novel and surprising that prediction is thereby precluded. The uncertainty of tentative forecasts does not prevent them from properly excluding many alternatives and favoring some alternative above others, thereby providing valuable information for policy formulation.

Conclusion

This critique of the Kahn-Wiener forecast would be unbalanced if it failed to end on a note of appreciation. Kahn and Wiener did contribute substantially to the progress of forecasting as a field of inquiry and exploration. Among the commendable features of their forecast are:

Recognition of both the impossibility of prediction and the importance of forecasting for the more limited purpose of improving current decisions,
Multiplicity of alternative futures,
Comprehensiveness,
Emphasis on the importance of long-term trends for forecasting, coupled with the partially successful effort to identify the major ones,
Claim that many trends must be taken into account along with the key causal factors affecting them,
Effective use of scenarios,
Stress on the relevance of cultures and cultural traits to forecasting,
Insight into certain future prospects and problems, and
Development of the concept of postindustrial society and culture.

The Kahn-Wiener forecast is best viewed as an important stepping-stone along the path to improved methodology and better forecasts. To move forward, forecasters need to formulate admittedly speculative forecasts that draw on previous advances. Then these forecasts must be subjected to rigorous criticism, on the basis of which appropriate revisions in methodology and forecasts should be made. As this cycle continues, it can assume the form of an ongoing upward spiral. Progress is furthered if creative pioneers do not become so overcommitted to their previous forecasts that they fail to make major changes required to correct weaknesses that objections have revealed.

Reliance on trend extrapolation alone amounts to a refusal to cut the umbilical cord that binds the future to the past. Although the past must be carefully analyzed, the aim is not to repeat its mistakes but rather to build constructively out of it. While Kahn and Wiener do engage in normative forecasting when they suggest ways of avoiding nuclear wars and other twenty-first century nightmares, such forecasting is also needed to open up a wider range of desirable futures than they have presented. Kahn himself has recently expressed hope that "descriptive" and normative forecasting will be used productively in tandem. The contrast between confinement to trend extrapolation alone and the use of normative forecasting is epitomized by George Bernard Shaw's remark:

> Some see things as they are and say, Why?
> I dream things that never were and say, Why not?

5

BELL'S "POST-INDUSTRIAL SOCIETY"

> Twixt the optimist and the pessimist
> The difference is droll.
> The optimist sees the doughnut,
> But the pessimist sees the hole.
> McLandburgh Wilson

BELL'S FORECAST

Hailed by some reviewers as one of the most insightful, seminal works of our time and castigated by others as unimaginative and conducive to elite domination, Daniel Bell's *The Coming of Post-Industrial Society* (1973a) has generated a tidal wave of controversy. Bell's treatise has become the principal locus of the participation controversy. Participatory futurists contend that his forecast of postindustrial society, like Brzezinski's forecast of a technetronic age, endangers democracy by lending support to the development of an authoritarian technocracy. Both forecasts sketch futures in which the influence of small elites of technically oriented experts on societal policies has skyrocketed.

Bell's position is less extreme than Brzezinski's, whose projected meritocracy is more technocratic. Not only do these two forecasters present somewhat different images of a relatively continuous future; Brzezinski appears to enthusiastically endorse a form of technocracy, while Bell admits that a technocratic society is not ennobling (p. 180).

For such reasons as the following, any simple summary or assessment of Bell's forecast is prone to distortions. His lengthy volume about a projected change in the social framework of Western society consists of six chapters and a coda that perceptively explore diverse themes, but are quite repetitious and sometimes difficult to correlate precisely. Further interpretive problems are posed by his rather esoteric terminology. Even though his book purports to be an essay in social forecasting, much of it turns out to be about the present

111

condition of U.S. society and the trends at work in it. Moreover, from the book's concentration on just one basic type of alternative future, the casual reader might get the mistaken impression that Bell denies the openness of history.

These considerations underline the need to engage in a careful, detailed analysis that avoids the misrepresentations that Bell has justifiably accused many of his critics of making. Our analysis focuses on the comprehensive forecast that Bell presented in 1973 but concludes by observing the subsequent shift in his outlook from moderate optimism to the unmistakable pessimism, manifested in *The Cultural Contradictions of Capitalism* (1976).

Methodology

Bell's concept of postindustrial society, an "ideal type," is an analytical construct of diverse changes in society rather than a picture of a specific society (pp. 483, 487). His projection is a scenario, a logical construction of what could be (p. 14). Its purpose is to explore the meaning and consequences of the full development of beginning changes in the social structure. As he acknowledges, there is no guarantee that these changes will unfold in this way. Employing his analytical theory of social development, he forecasts a structurally changed context on the basis of the current context, trends, and an axial principle.

What is an "axial" principle? Although Bell's abstract methodology may seem enigmatic at first glance, it is integral to his forecast and well worth the considerable effort required to decipher it. Bell engages in multiperspective conceptual analysis to bring order into the bewildering number of possible perspectives from which macrohistorical change can be interpreted (p. xi). He regards the task as twofold: methodologically, to analyze conceptually by means of axial principles and structures and, empirically, to indentify the substantive character and sources of structural changes in society.

Thus Bell seeks to make sense out of a complex conceptual framework or schema such as postindustrial society, by viewing it as resting on an *axial principle* that *energizes* it and as having an *axial structure* that *organizes* it (p. 10). Just as an axis, the line around which a body turns, is central to that body, so axial principles and sturctures are central to conceptual schemes. For instance, Alexis de Tocqueville (1966) explained that the spread of democratic feeling in U.S. society in terms of the axial principle of equality. Max Weber (1958a) interpreted the transformation of the Western world from a traditional to a modern society by means of the axial principle of rationalization.

Axial analysis, which makes conceptual schemes easier to understand, seeks to specify centrality, not causation. Hence, it does not construct causal models but rather paradigms (in Thomas Kuhn's [1967] sense) from which models could be generated (Bell 1973a, p. 112).

Analytically, Bell distinguishes preindustrial, industrial, and postindustrial society (see Table 5.1). Each of these three basic types of society is organized

TABLE 5.1

General Schema of Social Change from Industrial to Postindustrial Society

	Preindustrial	Industrial	Postindustrial	
Regions:	Asia Africa Latin America	Western Europe Soviet Union Japan	United States	
Economic sector:	Primary Extractive: Agriculture Mining Fishing Timber	Secondary Goods producing: Manufacturing Processing	Tertiary: Transport Recreation	Quaternary: Trade Finance Insurance Real estate Quinary: Health Education Research Government
Occupational slope:	Farmer Miner Fisherman Unskilled worker	Semi-skilled worker Engineer	Professional and technical Scientists	
Technology:	Raw materials	Energy	Information	
Design:	Game against nature	Game against fabricated nature	Game between persons	
Methodology:	Common sense experience	Empiricism Experimentation	Abstract theory: models, simulation, decision theory, systems analysis	
Time perspective:	Orientation to the past Ad hoc responses	Ad hoc adaptive- ness Projections	Future orientation Forecasting	
Axial principle:	Traditionalism: Land/resource limitation	Economic growth: State or private control of invest- ment decisions	Centrality of and codi- fication of theoretical knowledge	

Source: Bell 1973a, p. 117. (Reprinted, by permission, from THE COMING OF POST-INDUSTRIAL SOCIETY: A Venture in Social Forecasting, by Daniel Bell, ©1973 by Daniel Bell, Basic Books, Inc., Publishers, New York.)

around a different axial principle: traditionalism, economic growth, and the centrality of codified theoretical knowledge as the source of social innovation and policy formulation (p. 14). Similarly, he differentiates society into the social structure, the polity, and the culture. Each of these parts is ruled by a different axial principle—efficient *economizing, participation,* and the desire for *self-enhancement*—that conflicts with at least one of the two other principles. He draws a further distinction between three aspects of the social structure: technology, the economy, and the occupational system (p. 12).

Changes in the Social Structure

Bell states that "the concept of the post-industrial society deals primarily with changes in the social structure, the way in which the economy is being transformed and the occupational system reworked, and with the new relations between theory and empiricism, particularly science and technology." (p. 13). He specifies five significant respects ("dimensions" or "components") in which the concept of postindustrial society differs from that of industrial society:

1. Economic sector: the change from a goods-producing to a service economy
2. Occupational distribution: the pre-eminence of the professional and technical class
3. Axial principle: the centrality of theoretical knowledge as the source of innovation and of policy formulation for the society
4. Future orientation: the control of technology and technology assessment
5. Decision-making: the creation of a new "intellectual technology."
   [P. 14]

Bell forecasts the full emergence of postindustrial society within the next 30 to 50 years (p. x). In the social structures of the United States, Japan, the Soviet Union, and Western Europe, it will constitute a major feature of the twenty-first century. The development Of post-industrial society, which consists principally of changes in the social structure, will have varied consequences in societies with different political and cultural configurations (pp. x, 13). Yet Bell limits his illustrative analysis to the United States, in which the processes of change are more advanced and visible (p. x).

A "Knowledge Society"

Bell conceives of postindustrial society as a "knowledge society" in which theoretical knowledge plays a leading role. He maintains:

The major source of structural change in society—the change in the modes of innovation in the relation of science to technology and in public policy—is the change in the character of knowledge: the exponential growth and branching of science, the rise of the new intellectual technology, the creation of systematic research through R&D budgets, and, as the calyx of all this, the codification of theoretical knowledge.

Table 5.2 reveals how integral theoretical knowledge, knowledge workers, and knowledge institutions are to Bell's concept of postindustrial society.

TABLE 5.2

Structure and Problems of the Postindustrial Society

Axial principle:	The Centrality and Codification of Theoretical Knowledge
Primary institutions:	University
	Academy institutes
	Research corporations
Economic ground:	Science-based industries
Primary resource:	Human capital
Political problem:	Science policy
	Education policy
Structural problem:	Balance of private and public sectors
Stratification: Base—	Skill
Access—	Education
Theoretical issue:	Cohesiveness of "new class"
Sociological reactions:	The resistance to bureaucratization
	The adversary culture

Source: Bell 1973a, p. 118. (Reprinted, by permission, from THE COMING OF POST-INDUSTRIAL SOCIETY: A Venture in Social Forecasting, by Daniel Bell, © 1973 by Daniel Bell, Basic Books, Inc., Publishers, New York.)

Bell argues that Brzezinski's neologism "technetronic age" misleadingly shifts the focus of change from theoretical knowledge to the practical application of technology (p. 38). Conversely, Bell emphasizes the increasing codification of knowledge into abstract systems of symbols that can be employed to illuminate many areas of experience and to manage complex systems (p. 20). A current example of the application of theoretical knowledge to societal problems is proved by technology assessment, which is used to help decide which feasible technologies should be researched, developed, and implemented. Thus codified knowledge can constitute an "*intellectual* technology . . . :the substitution of algorithms (problem-solving rules) for intuitive judgments" (p. 29).

Since algorithms may be embodied in a computer program, intellectual technology is linked to electronic information technology. In fact, the computer is a tool of intellectual technology (p. 30).

The methodology of intellectual technology consists of modeling, simulation cybernetics, decision theory, decision-making logic that follows systems analysis, and similar techniques. What is distinctive about this methodology is its effort to define rational action and identify the means of achieving it. The goal is to realize the social alchemist's dream—the dream of "ordering" the mass society (p. 33). Bell is aware of the problem inherent in "the very idea of rationality that guides the enterprise—the definition of a function without justification of reason" (p. 33). To put it differently, intellectual technology tends to have a somewhat Sisyphean character: The very attempt to order the world rationally can be founded on arbitrary, even irrational, assumptions. Despite his awareness of this dog-chasing-tail propensity, Bell maintains that by the end of this century the new intellectual technology may have become as salient in human affairs as machine technology has been for the past century and a half (p. 28).

Codified theoretical knowledge constitutes the axis around which new technology, economic growth, and the stratification of postindustrial society will be organized. Such organization will serve "the purpose of social control and the directing of innovation and change" (p. 112). A consequence will be the origin of new social relationships and structures that have managed politically (p. 20). In summary, the emphasis on the *codification of theoretical knowledge* and its use for societal guidance *will bring about major changes in the social structure*, including a service economy and the rise of a new professional-technical class that will pose management problems for the political system (p. 13).

The primary institutions in postindustrial society will be intellectual institutions (universities, academy institutes, research corporations) where theoretical knowledge will be codified. Even more than today, educational institutions will provide the mode of access to many desirable social positions.

A Service Economy

A crucial aspect of the transition to postindustrial society is the development of an economy that concentrates primarily on providing services, as distinguished from the production of food and industrial goods. If industrial society is regarded as a goods-producing society in which the character of the labor force is chiefly shaped by manufacturing, the United States is no longer an industrial society. Bell notes that the United States is the only nation in which the service sector accounts for more than half the total employment (about 60 percent) and more than half the gross national product (see Figure 5.1). The new U.S. intelligentsia performs "quinary" services (health, education, research, and government services) that are so integral to postindustrial society (p. 15).

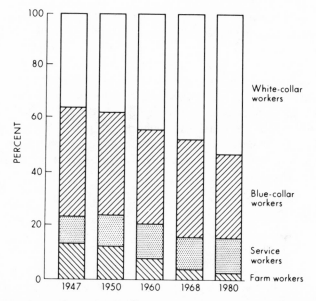

*Farm workers include farm managers.

Figure 5.1. U.S. employment among major categories, from 1948 to 1968 and projected for 1980 trends (for a service economy with 3 percent unemployment) (Bell 1973a, p. 137). (Reprinted, by permission, from THE COMING OF POST-INDUSTRIAL SOCIETY: A Venture in Social Forecasting, by Daniel Bell, ©1973 by Daniel Bell, Basic Books, Inc., Publishers, New York.)

The axial principle of the social structure is economizing: a way of allocating resources according to principles of least cost, substitutability, optimization, maximization, and the like (p. 12). Services are less productive than industry because they involve a relation between persons rather than between persons and machines. Indeed, the design of postindustrial society is "a 'game between persons' in which an 'intellectual technology,' based on information, rises alongside machine technology" (p. 116). One consequence is increased inflation, for rising costs of labor may run 70 percent or more of the total costs of services. Hence, the axial principle of the social structure is subject to definite constraints in a service-producing economy.

The Professional-Technical Class: A Meritocratic Elite

In postindustrial society, occupation is the most important determinant of social stratification (p. 15). A result of the emphasis on quinary services is the growth of a new class structure based on knowledge and dominated by such professional, technical, and scientific personnel as mathematicians, engineers, and economists. This expanding professional and technical class, "the heart of postindustrial society," is a meritocratic elite founded on knowledge rather than on property (p. 374). Thus the primary resource in postindustrial society is human capital, the most valued characteristic of which is talent.

Bell draws a major distinction between this leading professional class (or set of classes) and other classes of workers: technicians and semiprofessionals; then clerical and sales; and, finally, craftsmen and semiskilled (p. 374). He distinguishes four "estates" of the professional class. Members of the cultural estate, such as numerous literary intellectuals, can be expected to disagree frequently with members of the scientific, technological, and administrative estates. Members of the professional class are employed in various "situses" or locations of occupational activities: businesses, government, universities and research organizations, social complexes, and the military. Although the classes may be represented horizontally by *statuses*, postindustrial society is organized vertically by *situses* (p. 376). (See Table 5.3.)

The Political Order

The Primary Control System

Changes in the social structure, rather than determining corresponding changes in the polity or the culture, raise questions for the rest of society. These changes pose management problems and policy issues for the political system. Societies entering a postindustrial phase may confront a similar core of problems, but responses will be relative to their different political and cultural organizations (pp. 113, 114). While one can forecast the limits within which the future may be defined, the definition itself will depend mainly on political creativity (p. 4).

The political order has already become the primary control system of society. Bell observes that "the decisive social change taking place in our time—because of the interdependence of men and the aggregative character of economic actions, the rise of externalities and social costs, and the need to control the effects of technical change—is the subordination of the economic function to the political order" (p. 373). In a postindustrial society, the polity, which regulates the distribution of power and adjudicates the conflicting claims made by individuals and groups, will necessarily engage in more conscious decision making (p.43).

Bell objects to the primacy of technetronic factors in Brzezinski's 1970 forecast. This primacy implies a technological determinism that runs contrary to the actual subordination of economics to the political system (p. 38). The controlling agency of the new society is not the technology but the character of the political managers.

The new knowledge and its intellectual technology are essential to the formulation and analysis of issues upon which increasingly technical political decisions must be made. This will increasingly bring scientists, economists, and other experts into the decision-making process, which uses such modern techniques as systems analysis and program budgeting. Bell claims that "eventually, the entire complex of prestige and status will be rooted in the intellectual and scientific communities." (p. 43).

TABLE 5.3

Schema of the Societal Structure of Postindustrial Society, U.S. Model

I. *Statuses: Axis of Stratification—Based on Knowledge* (Horizontal Structures)
   A. The professional class: the four estates
      1. Scientific
      2. Technological (applied skills: engineering, economics, medicine)
      3. Administrative
      4. Cultural (artistic and religious)
   B. Technicians and semi-professional
   C. Clerical and sales
   D. Craftsmen and semi-skilled (blue-collar)

II. *Situses: Locations of Occupational Activities* (Vertical Structures)
   A. Economic enterprises and business firms
   B. Government (bureaucratic: judicial and administrative)
   C. Universities and research institutions
   D. Social complexes (hospitals, social-service centers, etc.)
   E. The military

III. *Control System: The Political Order*
   A. The directorate
      1. Office of the President
      2. Legislative leaders
      3. Bureaucratic chiefs
      4. Military chiefs
   B. The polities: constituencies and claimants
      1. Parties
      2. Elites (scientific, academic, business, military)
      3. Mobilized groups
         a) functional groups (business, professional, labor)
         b) Ethnic groups
         c) Special-focus groups
            (1) Functional (mayors of cities, poor, etc.)
            (2) Expressive (youth, women, homosexual, etc.)

Source: Bell 1973a, p. 375. (Reprinted, by permission from THE COMING OF POST-INDUSTRIAL SOCIETY: A Venture in Social Forecasting, by Daniel Bell, © 1973 by Daniel Bell, Basic Books, Inc., Publishers, New York.)

Nevertheless, because political decisions are central, the relation of knowledge to power is one of subservience. The power to innovate, which is rooted in specialized knowledge and professional expertise, "is not the power to say 'yes' or 'no', which is where the real power lies" (pp. 481, 482). "The political system in postindustrial society," Bell maintains, "can never be wholly technocratic" (pp. 481).

Who will manage the political order? This remains an open question, since how professionals and technicians will organize themselves is not clear. Still, their political power will be more restricted than suggested in Brzezinski's projections. Young professionals may push for drastic changes, but there appears to be little basis for the cohesion of the knowledge elite. Members of the professional class will be in various situses, which, rather than the statuses, will constitute the major political interest units in postindustrial society (p. 377).

In any case, elite leadership is integral to Bell's concept of postindustrial society. Since Bell also affirms that the axial principle of the modern Western polity is participation, he expects the movement toward a meritocratic elite to generate much tension between elitism and populism.

Continuing Changes in the U.S. Polity

Elsewhere, Bell (1971) pinpoints three kinds of ongoing structural changes in U.S. polity:

1. *Integration.* Technology-based contacts and other factors have produced such an interactive, interdependent "national society" that changes occurring in one social sector can have immediate repercussive effects in all others.

2. *Collective goods orientation* (also, collective rights of disadvantaged groups). More goods need to be purchased communally. Among these goods are rapid transit systems, adequate medical care, education, and the reduction of air pollution. Public policy that regulates behavior concerning collective goods, such as the previously free resources of clean water and air, is not based on the calculation and distribution of divisible benefits. The definition of social rights in group, rather than individual terms—for instance, by disadvantaged minorities seeking "quotas"—also leads to a "communal society" in which public, nonmarket decision-making thrives.

3. *Politicization.* The political sector has become increasingly involved in all aspects of social life, with a consequent blurring of the distinction between public and private. In *The Coming of Post-Industrial Society* Bell (1973) remarks: "Politically, the problem of a post-industrial society . . . is the growth of a non-market welfare economics and the lack of adequate mechanisms to decide the allocation of public goods" (p. 118). "The chief problem is the stipulation of social choices that accurately reflect the 'ordering' of preferences by individuals" (p. 43). Difficulties stem not only from the shortcomings of present concepts and tools for social choice and planning but also from the overload of issues that get piled on the polity.

Bell expects similar changes to occur in other societies as they begin to become postindustrial.

Antinomian Culture

As defined by Bell, "the culture is the realm of expressive symbolism and meanings" (p. 12). Because of its relative autonomy, present-day culture sometimes brings about changes in values and life-styles that do not derive from changes in the social structure (p. 39). Hence, Bell's brief treatment of culture in *The Coming of Post-Industrial Society* is integral to his forecast and needs to be examined before we turn to *The Cultural Contradictions of Capitalism*.

The axial principle of the culture of modern Western society is the desire for the fulfillment and enhancement of self (p. 12). This principle conflicts with the economizing axial principle of the social structure. In other words, the antinomian, antiinstitutional culture is hostile to the functional rationality that tends to dominate the application of knowledge by the technocratic and administrative estates (p. 376). The result is a "radical disjunction" between the social structure and the culture (p. 39).

Bell states that sources of this disjunction lie deep in the anti-bourgeois character of a modernist movement. Bourgeois society of the nineteenth century was an integrated whole in which culture, economy, and social structure were infused by a single value system. During the last 100 years, the axial thread in Western culture has been modernism with its onslaught on tradition and established institutions. Ironically, capitalism itself "destroyed the Protestant ethic by zealously promoting a hedonistic way of life" (pp. 12, 13, 477). As producers, people were encouraged to work hard and defer gratification; as consumers, to buy on credit, thus satisfying their immediate wants far beyond their current ability to pay. Thus the inherent dynamics of the capitalist system required that people behave in contrary ways. The consumption life-style that promoted hedonism came to predominate. A rising material standard of living became an end in itself. So did the relaxation of morals, thus greatly expanding the realm of personal freedom. These changes generated both an "adversary culture" and a "counter-culture" (p. 479).

Gone are the historic legitimations of bourgeois society in the realms of religion and character. Property and work, which in the past performed an important legitimizing function, have become subordinate to bureaucratic enterprises.

A transcendentalist ethic of the sort envisioned by Willis Harman might seem capable of reintegrating current Western culture, economy, and social structure into a system of "humane capitalism" (see Chapter 6). Bell, however, contends that "a post-industrial society cannot provide a transcendent ethic—except for the few who devote themselves to the temple of science" (p. 480). Although a less-metaphysical "communal ethic" would also promote this reintegration, Bell questions the extent to which such an ethic is feasible in postindustrial society (p. 483). He concludes that the disjunction between social structure and culture is bound to widen in postindustrial society (p. 480).

Problems of Postindustrial Society: Overview of Disjunctions

Bell's forecast is distinctly more problem oriented than most forecasts of postindustrial society. Changes in the social structure pose problems or issues, "an agenda of questions," for the rest of society and for the political system in particular (p. 9). Although Bell discerns many of these problems, his various lists (pp. 9, 13, 44, 118, 483, 487) are not easy to correlate, and his analysis appears to be somewhat inconsistent (pp. 43, 44, 116, 119, 482).* Now that the outlines of his concept of postindustrial society have been sketched, the problem-spawning societal "disjunctions" need to be revisited for a more systematic examination that will place them in proper perspective (see Table 5.4).

TABLE 5.4

Bell's Conception of Three Main Parts of Society, Each Ruled by a Different Axial Principle

Parts of Society	Conflicting Axial Principles	Primary Disjunctions
the social structure	economizing	between the social structure and the polity
the polity	participation	
the culture	self-enhancement	between the social structure and the culture

Note: According to Bell, each of the three main parts of society is ruled by a different axial principle that conflicts with at least one of the other two principles. The results are troublesome societal disjunctions or rifts that need to be managed.

Source: Bell 1973a. (Reprinted, by permission, from THE COMING OF POST-INDUSTRIAL SOCIETY: A Venture in Social Forecasting, by Daniel Bell, © 1973 by Daniel Bell, Basic Books, Inc., Publishers, New York.)

---

*Compare "the chief problem," pp. 43, 44, and 116 (all different); "the most besetting dilemma," p. 119: "ultimately, the most fundamental problem," p. 44; the "crucial problem for the communal society," p. 482; and "politically, the problem of post-industrial society," p. 118. Bell's presentation is quite unsystematic and confusing, though discrepancies are partly explicable in terms of the different contexts in which expressions are used.

A knowledge society must organize science and relate it to public policy. Yet its attempt to do this efficiently encounters opposition from the polity and especially from the culture. A primary source of problems is the widening of disjunctions or rifts between the new social structure, the polity, and the culture, which are governed by conflicting axial principles. The principle of meritocratic "economizing" in the application of codified theoretical knowledge is incompatible with the principles of "participation" and "fulfillment and enhancement of the self" (p. 12).

The disjunction between the social structure and the polity raises a crucial question: What probably will be, and what should be, the relationship between technocratic and political decision making (p. 475) (as well as between bureaucracies and individuals who demand full participation in the decisions that affect their lives [p. 115])? Bell contends that "the chief problem . . . is the conflict generated by a meritocracy principle which is central to the allocation of position in the knowledge society" (p. 44). This conflict makes it all the more difficult to accomplish the task of establishing political institutions that are adequate to manage postindustrial society.

The radical disjunction between the social structure and the culture generates tension that will "ultimately [prove to be] the most fundamental problem of the post-industrial society" (p. 44). Even now, advanced capitalist society faces the dilemma that "it must . . . acknowledge the triumph (albeit tempered) of an 'adversary ideology', the emergence of a new class which sustains this ideology, and the collapse of the older value system which was, ironically, undermined by the structural transformation of capitalism itself" (p. 479). Bell maintains that the lack of a rooted moral belief system constitutes the deepest challenge to the survival of postindustrial society (p. 480).

Exponential Economic Growth, but No Utopia

Bell forecasts that, at least until the year 2000, private corporations will remain the major organizing modes of capitalist societies. He expects increasing interdependence of the world economy and rise of the world business corporation by the end of the twentieth century. Manufacturing of the standardized sort will increasingly move to poorer areas of the world, while postindustrial societies will concentrate on knowledge-creating and knowledge-processing industries. In the production of technology, science-based industries will be central (pp. 118, 484, 487).

Bell seems to believe that the most likely type of future, at least for the next 100 years, is "neither Utopia nor Doomsday but the same state that has existed for the last hundred years": fairly steady exponential economic growth (p. 465). He combats the "technological euphoria" of the Kahn-Wiener forecast on the one hand; the "apocalyptic hysteria" of the Forrester-Meadows forecasts on the other (pp. 460–465). He maintains that Kahn and Wiener give the term *postindustrial society* a narrow, almost entirely economic meaning as a "post-mass-consumption society." However, the rate of increasing affluence that they forecast is so great they

> almost assume a "post-economic" society in which there is no scarcity and the only problems are how to use abundance. Yet the concept "post-economic" has no logical meaning since it implies a social situation in which there are no costs for anything (for economics is the management of costs) or the resources are endless. [p. 38]

Rather than ushering in posteconomic abundance, coutinuing economic growth will generate new types of scarcities measured in terms of relative costs. Of chief importance will be costs of information, coordination, and time (pp. 38, 466, 467).

Furthermore, affluent postindustrial society will exacerbate the clash of personal interests. This clash, arising from "each following his own whim, leads necessarily to a greater need for collective regulation and a greater degree of coercion (with a reduction of personal freedom) in order to have effective communal action" (p. 475). Thus Bell contends that postindustrial society is by no means a utopia in which people would be free to pursue their own interests. This argument is aimed against such technological utopians as Paul Goodman, Murray Bookchin, Robert Theobald (in his preecological days), R. Buckminster Fuller, and typical Marxist and neo-Marxist futurists. They assume that competitiveness and strife arise from scarcity, which can be overcome by technological abundance. Such abundance would bring what John Maynard Keynes envisioned: a postscarcity society in which the economic problem had been solved. Goodman and Bookchin argue that a plethora of goods would enable human beings to live spontaneously and joyously with each other and to experience a "free" relation to nature rather than a dependence on it (Bell 1973a, p. 456). As Fuller puts it, the way to change people is to change the environment by designing efficiently to do more with less resources. Bell would agree that a postindustrial environment will influence people's competitive behavior, but in the direction opposite to that projected by technological utopians.

EVALUATION OF ASSUMPTIONS

Ambiguities and Qualifications

Unless forecasts are sufficiently precise for analysts to specify the kind of evidence that would verify or falsify their claims, their ambiguity renders them unsuitable for use by planners. Many parts of Bell's forecast of postindustrial society display exemplary clarity. Yet his overall argument (premises, inferences, conclusions) lacks the lucidity that delights the hearts of analysts. One cause of this vagueness is his "pinwheel approach," which essentially consists of topical essays that were originally written at different times and were never woven together into an integrated futuristic pattern. At best, some of his apparently incongruous statements about the same subject pose knotty correlational problems; at worst, they are inconsistent. At any rate, his imprecision makes it somewhat difficult for an analyst to decide how to proceed.

For instance, one wonders whether Bell is concerned merely with possible or also with likely future changes: with "a fiction" that might, or with changes that "will" occur (pp. x, 14). Is he just setting forth a projection or scenario as his statements about methodology affirm or sometimes a prediction of certain changes? Some of his remarks seem to imply the latter (p. x), despite his denial.

Bell is also unclear about the relation of the definitional character of post-industrial society to its projected substantive character. On the one hand, post-industrial society is "an analytical construct, not a picture of a specific or a concrete society"; on the other, "a social form ... that will be a major feature of the twenty-first century, in the social structures of the United States, Japan." (p. x). This complicates the problem of how to evaluate Bell's claims. Different sets of criteria are appropriate for evaluating axial constructs and assertions that a possible type of future will in fact be actualized. A crucial issue concerns the extent to which Bell is making empirical claims that current evidence can strengthen or weaken and that future occurrences could confirm or disconfirm. Whereas Bell's noncausal axial analysis elucidates central structural features of the concept of postindustrial society, it also provokes such unanswered questions as : How many exceptions are required to invalidate an ideal type or structural context such as postindustrial society? Thus the criteria for assessing Bell's forecast as an analytical construct are not nearly as clear as the criteria for appraising it as an empirical hypothesis.

Less-formidable obstacles to providing a convincing evaluation of Bell's forecast stem not from his unconscious ambiguities but from his intentional, commendable effort to qualify his forecast in many respects. The uncertainty that pervades the future makes such qualifications mandatory for credibility. Still, an effort to protect a forecast against criticisms by qualifying its controversial points can make it vague and thereby reduce its usefulness. At the extreme not approached by Bell, a futurist can make a forecast so vacuous that it is compatible with anything that happens and, hence, conveys no useful information about the future. Regardless of what Bell's motives were, the numerous ways in which he cautiously hedges his bets render his forecast easier to defend but also impart to it a chameleonlike appearance. In short, much of the forecast is open to evaluation on the basis of the best available data and theories, but not as much as if it were more precise and somewhat less qualified.

A Promising Methodological Beginning

Although Bell's methodology calls for much further theoretical development and application, it constitutes a promising beginning that has already improved the methodology of social forecasting. His conceptual analysis by means of axial principles and structures provides an enlightening technique for interpreting macrohistorical change. Especially insightful is his treatment of societal disjunctions as rooted in conflicting axial principles. Similarly, Benjamin Nelson, whose approach will be presented briefly in Chapter 9, emphasizes the importance of axial principles and "symbolic guidance systems" in shaping sociocultural structures and processes.

Bell's problem-oriented methodology correctly treats societies as complex and not totally integrated. Being geared to the explication of conflicts arising from commitment to incompatible principles, it centers attention on a crucial kind of conflict sometimes overlooked by forecasters. Yet one suspects that other kinds of conflict get shortchanged. Moreover, to become suitable for anticipating some of the major discontinuous changes that could occur, Bell's concentration on societal problems needs to be expanded systematically to encompass international ecological problems.

Bell has detected three basic axial principles that are conflictually interrelated, but what about other axial principles within each of his three parts of society (such as the culture, which is not uniform)? One not only wonders whether he has properly differentiated and interrelated these parts but also whether the analysis of incompatible axial principles should be so closely tied to this specific division of society and whether the division provides a more fruitful analytic framework than any alternatives. One drawback of this division is that social and cultural processes are too closely interlaced to be relegated to relatively independent societal spheres (Nelson 1969). The analytical disadvantages of this divorce of social structure and culture, which is fundamental to Bell's axial analysis and forecast, are only partially obviated by his surprising use of *the culture* to refer merely to the realm of expressive symbolism and meaning. One strange consequence is that scientific symbols and technologies do not even qualify as cultural but are treated as aspects of the social structure.

Axial Analysis and Causality

An important set of Bell's methodological assumptions concerns the relation of axial principles and ideal types to causal models and sociocultural processes. Bell presupposes that his axial analysis, which seeks to specify centrality rather than causality, is appropriate for producing a trustworthy forecast of postindustrial society. However, certain salient features of his forecast cannot be justified by axial analysis alone. A causal model seems to be necessary to establish, for instance, his claim that certain tendencies summarized by a primary axial principle will continue to develop (p. 14). Such a model would be grounded in his axial analysis and in the study of the systemic interrelations of trends and problems. Though he could construct a formal model of this sort, he neglects to do so.

In practice, Bell (1973b) does cite causes, as is evidenced by his reply to Timothy Tilton: "My estimates are . . . [that services important for postindustrial society] will continue to grow because of the changed character of knowledge, the shift from the market to public decision-making, and the demand of the disadvantaged for more services" (p. 749). The methodology that Bell actually employs is closer to qualified trend extrapolation or to nonmathematical modeling than his statements about methodology might lead one to expect.

As Bell recognizes, the ideal types that he employs are abstractions. While ideal types can be used productively to clarify basic features, they tend to neglect complexities and do not provide a dynamic process theory of sociocultural change. The unfolding of processes is not adequately depicted by a series of snapshots, as it were, of leaps between ideal types. Nelson's (1969) methodology, for instance, is more process oriented than Bell's.

Inference from a Single Instance

An inductive inference to what is presently unobservable—in this case, to mature postindustrial society in the future—would ideally be founded on a number of representative instances that are moving in that direction. If similar processes leading toward a relatively uniform postindustrial social structure were discernible cross-culturally in all industrially advanced societies, the evidence for the likelihood of such a social structure (assuming the absence of countervailing factors) would be quite convincing. However, Bell projects this social structure on the basis of its beginnings in only one instance: the United States. Hence, the inference is quite risky.

Bell's judgment that the United States is the prime instance of a beginning postindustrial society appears to be correct. Nonetheless, U.S. social structure may not be the most advanced in all respects. Some socialists have argued, for instance, that the egalitarian nature of the Swedish social structure is more indicative of future development than is Bell's projected meritocracy. A comparative analysis of tendencies toward postindustrial society in the United States and Japan, for instance, should prove broadening and might result in a partial revision of Bell's conclusions.

In defense of Bell, it should be noted that tentative inferences from limited data can be enlightening and sometimes useful for policy formulation. Bell has undertaken an extremely difficult but worthwhile task. By analogy, Karl Marx could also be branded ethnocentric in that all his instructive examples of capitalism were drawn from one country, Great Britain.

Yet must postindustrial society have the kind of social structure that Bell delineates? If that specific social structure is taken to be part of the definition of postindustrial society, an affirmative answer amounts to an empty tautology.

This tautology does not preclude the possibility of a range of future social structures in affluent, automated information societies. These social structures could differ markedly in such respects as the kinds and amounts of services emphasized, intellectual technology employed, and inequalities present between classes.

Changes in the Social Structure: The Leading Edge?

In social forecasting, Bell comments that "sociological variables are usually the independent, or exogenous, variables which affect the behavior of the other variables" (p. 4). He makes the crucial, questionable assumption that cross-societal *changes in the social structure lead the way*, posing an agenda of questions for polities.

Bell's axial analysis, though not explicitly causal, comes close to presupposing an overpowering cause: the cluster of forces that promote the increasing centrality of ever-more codified theoretical knowledge as the source of innovation and policy formulation for the society. Inherent in this ongoing trend are major continuing changes in the social structure, such as the growth of the professional-technical class. Other projected changes in the social structure, including the ascendency of this class and its highly elitist character, can be viewed as expected consequences of this trend rather than part and parcel of it. Since the altered social structure poses the issues that call for action, it defines the range of alternative futures among which the polity and the culture are challenged to choose.

Will this trend toward the practical application of codified theoretical knowledge crush any obstacles like a steamroller in high gear, or will it subside like the pounding surf? If it prevails, will it bring about all those changes in the social structure that Bell projects? Would these changes pose the agenda of questions that he anticipates? Would the alternatives to which these questions point encompass the spectrum of feasible societal futures?

Codified Intellectual Knowledge: How Central?

To forecast changes in the social structure, Bell needs a model of the underlying causes of the current tendencies on which his axial analysis is based. Some of these causes of the increasing centrality of codified theoretical knowledge are political decisions that, he acknowledges, are difficult to forecast. An example is President Kennedy's decision to inaugurate Project Apollo. Few people expected this massive program prior to the successful flight of the first Soviet Sputnik. Even then, the specific nature of the forthcoming U.S. response was by no means obvious. The president was motivated to attain U.S. superiority, or at least equality, in space achievements, thus both preventing Soviet use of space as a trump card in the nuclear balance of terror and restoring lost U.S. prestige. He decided that the best way to achieve this general goal was to land U.S. astronauts on the moon before the end of the decade.

Thus attempts to forecast project-creating political decisions, one leading edge of the transition to postindustrial society, are quite conjectural. The tacit assumption that the impact of such decisions will accelerate weakens Bell's forecast, as does the somewhat-less-questionable assumption that the quinary services will gain momentum. The growth of these services, which are more important than others for postindustrial society, would generate greater demand for knowldge workers and their intellectual technology.

Bell is obliged to account for recent slowdowns in the growth of some quinary services in the United States. Government aid to graduate schools has decreased, thus contributing to a period of retrenchment for higher education. Government service became unpopular in the wake of the Watergate scandal. Former President Nixon eliminated the Office of Science and Technology. Despite the alarming increase in cancer victims and other signs that threaten a decline of national health, the government has been relatively unresponsive to the need for enhancing health services. The passage of "Proposition 13" has resulted in major cutbacks in quinary services in California and has sparked similar revolts of the middle class against higher taxes in many other states.

In response to Timothy Tilton's critique, Bell (1973b) admits that it is "debatable" whether the services emphasized in postindustrial society will continue to grow (p. 749). Nonetheless, he tends to regard recent setbacks as temporary aberrations. At least to a substantial extent, he appears to be correct. The number of Ph.D's and M.D.'s is still growing. The big explosion in paraprofessional health and educational workers proceeds unabated. Since a modern U.S. administration finds it difficult to dispense with a science advisory mechanism, the Office of Science and Technology has been revived. The complexity and intensity of societal problems will probably raise the demand for services that use intellectual technology.

For such reasons, the continued advance of the United States into postindustrial society seems likely. Yet the trajectory is problematic, as is the character of the society.

Bell's forecast not only assumes that appropriate political decisions will be made to meet societal needs but that typical programs based upon these decisions will successfully navigate the rapids that they will encounter. The compass used to navigate as well as to set the course originally is intellectual technology. Thus the forecast presupposes that actions by societal leaders will be quite rational. Indeed, Bell states that "forecasting is possible only where one can assume a high degree of rationality on the part of men who influence events" (p. 4).

However, leaders do not always behave rationally, especially in unexpected, emotionally charged crisis situations that require rapid responses. Nor do influential people always agree on what is rational—an example being the debate between Herman Kahn and his critics about whether nuclear war could be waged rationally. Finally, the capacity of the professional-technical class to resolve societal problems with its intellectual technology is problematic. Recent experience shows that intellectual expertise is often ignored by decision makers and is sometimes ineffective when acted upon.

To be sure, Bell admits limitations to the potentials of intellectual technology and the knowledge elite. Yet he plays this theme with the soft pedal. Kahn seems much more aware of the prevalence of what Thorstein Veblen dubbed "educated incapacity." Intellectuals have too frequently been taught to respond in ways that prove to be counterproductive when applied to the practical world of politics and business. A principal shortcoming is the frequent attempt to reduce social problems to technical problems that can be resolved by technical means.

Whether intellectual technology and its knowledge workers will become as central to society as Bell projects may depend significantly on the perceived successes and failures of its applications to public policy. Reactions against intellectual technology have been occasioned by some of its unsuccessful uses. For instance, its use by Secretary of Defense McNamara in the Vietnam war backfired, provoking criticism of his expertise. Even though this particular case may not have appreciable long-term effects, it illustrates the important role of feedback from the public and from politicians. Such feedback should be taken into account by forecasters.

Reactions against the unsuccessful elitist use of information technology could evoke changes in value priorities conducive to a social structure different from that which Bell projects. One example of such changes is the upgrading of the value of public participation in the decision-making process. Another is increased emphasis on "equality of results," which sanctions extensive redistribution of benefits to disadvantaged groups and individuals. Such equality is antithetical to meritocratic "equality of opportunity," which promotes individual advancement as a reward for talent and hard work. Widespread rejection of information technology might even preclude the maturation of postindustrial society.

Neglect of Ecological and International Problems

Bell devotes little attention to problems occasioned by shortages of energy and raw materials, pollution generation, and insufficient food production. He dismisses warnings of physical limits to growth as "apocalyptic hysteria." Although his antiutopian treatment of new types of costs and scarcities in postindustrial society is perceptive, he largely ignores an important range of sociocultural limits to nonutopian growth. For instance, he seems to be overly optimistic that corporations will adopt proper balances of the "economizing" and "sociologizing" modes, thus sacrificing appreciable amounts of profits to fulfill social and ecological responsibilities.

Bell's minimization of national and global ecological problems as well as other types of international problems is paradoxical, for these problems may stimulate much demand for intellectual technology and knowledge workers during the next three or more decades. Furthermore, one can write plausible scenarios in which such problems as energy shortages, pollution, "stagflation," and the instability of the international monetary system reshape, hinder, or prevent the development of postindustrial society. The use of information technology to cope with these problems could either facilitate this transition or provoke powerful reactions. Bell's failure to explore the relevance of these problems to postindustrial society reveals that his book, though published in 1973, is basically a product of the 1960s in its general orientation.

More generally, Bell's neglect or inadequate treatment of various interrelated global problems undermines his forecast. Future options are not confined to feasible responses to problems arising from postindustrial social structure. A much *wider* range of alternative futures comes into play *before*, as well as after, postindustrial social structure has posed an agenda of questions. Among these futures are alternative postindustrial social structures, including ones that involve more participation and less inequality.

Bell properly treats postindustrial social structure as less variable than the polity or the culture and as posing a common core of problems. Nonetheless, there will probably be more intersocietal variation in the problems than he suggests, partly because of more diversity in the social structure. Besides, the common core could hardly omit the international and ecological issues that he downplays.

The Social Structure: How Meritocratic?

How likely is the degree of meritocracy that Bell projects? Should it constitute a goal? Much of what he observes about the increasing practical importance of codified theoretical knowledge and knowledge workers is enlightening. Yet is is doubtful that "eventually, the entire complex of prestige and status will be rooted in the intellectual and scientific communities" (p. 43). Their prestige and status will probably depend largely on:

The extent to which efforts are made to meet societal needs for the codifiation and application of theoretical knowledge,
The degree to which these efforts are successful or unsuccessful, and
The ways in which individuals and groups perceive and respond to the gap that separates the knowledge elite from other members of society.

Furthermore, Bell fails to supply convincing evidence that universities will become as prestigious and central to society as he intimates. Perhaps his being "an intellectual's intellectual" has biased his expectations.

Although Bell does not forecast a bona fide technocracy, his meritocracy comes uncomfortably close to it and thereby strays from the principles of U.S. democracy. He foresees a need for increased regulation and coercion that restricts political freedom. The possible consequences are sufficiently unsavory to encourage the search for social structures that are more palatable to the public taste. Bell's image of a coercive society rests on more than a sociological analysis of the increased interaction of individuals and of groups that demand to be treated as equals. Some features of this image appear to be molded by Hobbesian assumptions about human nature. The pronounced inequalities and increased coercion in Bell's version of postindustrial society lead one to inquire: Might the social structure undergo such severe strains between the professional-technical class and classes outside it that, to avoid a fracture, it would move in a less meritocratic direction? Probably so. The contest would be unlikely to consist of uncompromising war between well-defined classes or to result in the elimination of a differential reward system. Since attachments to situses tend to be more important to members of the professional-technical class than their diffuse status identity, this class seems likely to remain quite disunified. Status identity might be significantly strengthened if this class were seriously challenged by other classes, but confrontation would probably be met by compromises before it led to violent revolution. Still, one wonders whether considerable social conflict would not be necessary to fulfill Bell's hopes that meritocrats will not obtain excessively disparate social and material advantages and that a "social minimum" will be established. Far from being Hobbesian like some of Bell's other assumptions, the assumptions underlying these hopes may be overly optimistic. The contrasting assumptions suggest that Bell expects the professional-technical class to act much more responsibly than less-talented classes.

To promote excellence within various occupations and to bolster those occupations that are most crucial for societal guidance, significant inequalities of rewards would be required. Nonetheless, postindustrial society would definitely be better for most people if some efficiency were traded off for decreased inequalities of status, wealth, and power. Equality of results and equality of opportunity need to be balanced in ways that will meet people's needs without undermining incentives.

Decision Making: How Centralized?

To cope with problems, Bell assumes a great deal of centralized political decision making is mandatory. He perceptively calls for revamping the U.S. patchwork system of overlapping political sovereignties and jurisdictions. Such inefficient decentralization impedes the rapid, effective decision making needed to prevent unresolved problems from snowballing to unmanageable proportions.

However, Bell's vision is focused so intently on these shortcomings that he overlooks both the need and the opportunities for decentralized, less bureaucratic decision making. Appropriate responses to some kinds of problems require greater amounts of centralized decision making; to other kinds, decentralized decision making. Cybernetics, an intellectual technology, teaches that adequate information flowing to competent decentralized decision makers provides more flexibility and adaptability. Of utmost importance on national issues are clear, appropriate signals emitted from a centralized source. Within this framework, decentralized decision making provides a remedy for bureaucratic stultification and an opportunity for more people to influence policies that will shape their futures. Such decentralization pertains to administration and also to policy formulation, especially on local issues. Centralized and decentralized decision making must be carefully interwoven if they are to be effective in complex societies.

Although the crucial unification of developments in computerization and telecommunications is largely neglected by Bell, its consequences could shape postindustrial society in significant ways.* For instance, techniques are being devised to facilitate widespread participation in the preference-rating and decision-making processes. Researchers at the University of Illinois have developed the "Plato System," which supplies rapidly tabulated feedback of viewers' preferences by means of teletypewriters connected to many televisionlike sets and a central computer. Experts of various political persuasions could be elected to panels that would present diverse policy options to viewers, who would express their preferences. This technology could be used to increase participation in the evaluation of national as well as local issues and options.

Within bureaucracies, enhanced participation in decision making is made possible by improved information flows and better-trained personnel. Bell fails to recognize the potential importance of the beginning shifts toward: increased decision making in the middle levels of more flexible bureaucracies and the "task force" orientation of generalists-specialists who can apply general principles to many different tasks. The latter approach represents a movement away from specialization toward holism in an era of the decreasing half-life of bits of specialized information needed to perform specialized tasks. Specialization is still necessary, but so are coordination, integration, and adaptation to changing knowledge.

"Computer conferencing" is likely to make geographically dispersed ad hoc task forces much more feasible. Similarly, widely separated executives using flip-charts will probably participate in televised board meetings. Primarily because of breakthroughs in miniaturization, computerized telecommunications consoles for the home may be available at reasonable prices within 10 to 20 years. Besides being employed for preference rating, consoles of this sort could perform many of the tasks—for instance, shopping and banking—that now require transportation. This capacity for efficient decentralization could be used to stem the tide of urbanization. The efficient coordination of centralized and

---

*Bell has recently turned his attention toward telecommunications and information processing.

decentralized decision making could provide the lubricant that would facilitate smooth interaction of the decentralized parts of an information society.

Information societies could have political orders ranging from a more participatory democracy to a basically technocratic totalitarianism. Bell's minimization of the likely and possible impacts of many prospective technological innovations serves as a corrective to forecasts by technological determinists (such as Brzezinski) and exaggerators of future shock (Toffler) but constricts his vision of alternative futures.

In summary, intelligent guidance of postindustrial society requires the advice of experts. Yet channels of communication need to be opened between them and ordinary citizens. On many aspects of numerous issues, citizens could participate intelligently in the preference-rating and decision-making processes. For such a participatory form of postindustrial society to progress satisfactorily, citizens would have to make concerted efforts to choose wisely among future options.

Assumptions Concerning the Culture

Bell's analysis of historically rooted cultural processes is interesting but questionable. Although he is partially right in tracing antinomianism to "modernism" during the last 100 years, U.S. culture has always sought freedom from constraints. He claims that capitalism has destroyed the Protestant ethic (p. 477), which, however, happens to be very much alive as a set of lifeways oriented toward mastering this world through discipline and organization.

This characterization of the *Protestant ethic* reflects Max Weber's (1958a) primary usage of the term. Although the disagreement about whether this ethic is dead or alive is in part a semantic conflict, the real issue goes far deeper. To be sure, this ethic has undergone a number of changes. Bell correctly maintains that U.S. culture has generally become less religious and less willing to accept deferred gratification. Yet his concentration on those aspects of the ethic that have changed and his conclusion that it has expired keep him from grasping how vigorously it is being asserted and, at the same time, challenged. This historically grounded set of lifeways, largely separated from its religious background, continues to prevail in such undertakings as the space program and multinational corporations and in such western states as Arizona, (Nelson 1969). It has also encountered serious challenges, including outright rejection by segments of the counterculture and demands for equality of results rather than equality of opportunity.

A definite, though limited, decrease in general work motivation testifies to the waning of the Portestant sanctification of work. Still, increasing affluence has not so much eliminated the desire to work as rechanneled it toward meaningful, relevant jobs that promote self-actualization. Workers often demand large increases in wages for the types of jobs that they regard as relatively demeaning or unconducive to self-actualization. In addition, they seek to improve their working conditions. Thus a shift has occurred from the predominance of quantitative values toward emphasis on the quality of life.

For many people, the meaning of life is still intertwined with the work they do. They are willing to work reasonably hard at rewarding jobs and to be disciplined and organized enough to perform the required tasks. Moreover, previously declining work motivation has experienced a resurgence since the 1973/74 energy crisis and the onset of stagflation. Current examples of the outpouring of directed energy in the United States include promising efforts to cope with the problems of pollution, energy shortages, and resource depletion by devising new technologies and by beginning to revise established lifeways.

Bell assumes the relative uniformity of U.S. culture, though he acknowledges diversity and regards the counterculture as here to stay. He also assumes the relative unidirectionality of the culture toward increasing antinomianism and antiinstitutionalism. However, his analysis is at best seriously oversimplified; at worst, wrongheaded. Many dyschronic, conflicting layers compose U.S. culture, even in Bell's narrow sense of *the culture*. Conflicts are evident, for instance, among organized groups within the counterculture. During the late 1960s, the establishment's orientation was challenged by such incompatible value system as those of hippies and radical members of the Students for a Democratic Society (SDS). Herman Kahn maintains that the values of the counterculture are being opposed by a powerful "counterreformation" of U.S. values.

Bell presupposes that basic values are especially resistant to change and tend to endure. Although this is generally correct for societies, major crises can induce rapid, discontinuous changes in value-priorities. For instance, the Arab oil crisis of 1973/74 led to a fundamental, though temporary, normative shift in the United States. Better U.S. leadership could have instituted incentives to bring this shift to fruition. Sociocultural changes with revolutionary impact can make new axial principles and structures appropriate for specifying energizing principles and organizing frames.

Bell's analysis is diametrically opposed to certain other analyses of contemporary changes in value-priorities, such as that presented by Willis Harman (Chapter 6). Harman views these changes not so much as a threat but as a promising movement toward the kind of changes required to resolve the "world macroproblem." He calls attention to the possible emergence of a revolutionary "transcendental" ethic. Conversely, Bell deems this type of ethic incompatible with postindustrial society and interprets the student revolts of the late 1960s as reactions against the beginnings of the new postindustrial social structure. However, the Vietnam war seems to have been a more powerful instigator of these revolts. Thus Bell's treatment of the culture, though perceptive of key problems, is quite problematic.

Assumptions about Disjunctions

Bell presents a penetrating analysis of conflicts that spring from the clash of behavior governed by incompatible principles in U.S. society. He thereby sheds considerable light on problems likely to characterize postindustrial society. However, he makes such questionable assumptions as:

Major changes in basic cultural beliefs, values, goals, and behavior—changes that would warrant a revision of fundamental axial principles—are unlikely to occur (except, perhaps, gradually over long periods of time).

The disjunctions between the social structure, the culture, and the polity are bound to widen in postindustrial society.

The only realistic way to manage disjunctions is to achieve reasonable "balances" between the conflicting axial principles.

The first assumption is implicit, and the third is partially so.

Under the pressure of such national and global ecological issues as those of energy, raw materials, pollution, food, population, and urbanization, revolutionary changes might alter basic cultural orientations. This could render new or revised axial principles more applicable and even diminish disjunctions. The three major axial principles, for instance, would become more harmonious if economic and political systems were increasingly geared to promoting human self-actualization, which includes opportunities for political participation. Inherent in a major movement in this direction would be revolutionary changes in entrenched cultural beliefs and value priorities. Although such changes can be regarded as improvements in "balances" between axial principles, the quantity and quality of change could be considerably more extensive than that involved in the balances that Bell recommends. His balances, appropriate for some situations but not for others, are more suggestive of casuistry (the adjustment of general guidance principles to individual cases) than of the revolutionary changes in principles that have sometimes occurred.

Normative Bias: An Establishment Orientation

Although Bell seeks to provide an objective analysis, his approach is somewhat distorted by certain implicit normative biases of an establishment intellectual.* For instance, he opposes the counterculture and the adversary culture. He

---

*Michael Marien (1973b), who espouses egalitarian values, detects a number of establishment biases in Bell's book, thus dramatizing the need for value-explicit forecasting (pp. 262, 268). Yet like many of Bell's critics, Marien raises a number of caustic objections that rest on emotionally charged misunderstandings.

tends to minimize adverse impacts of technologies. His selection of the authors, data, and theories that he relies on displays a distinct establishment outlook.

Furthermore, Bell presupposes that his projected meritocratic elite is likely to succeed in its use of intellectual technology to cope with societal problems. With some qualifications, he glorifies this knowledge elite and manifests belief in the efficacy of established institutions. Indeed, he perceives the anachronistic nature of the U.S. political system. Yet the major institutional changes he envisions do not constitute clear-cut departures from an establishment orientation. While he maintains that the culture of postindustrial society poses a serious long-range threat, his forecast generally lacks alternative futures that are fundamentally different from one another or discontinuous with present trends. He seems to believe that a developmental future is most likely.

FROM OPTIMISM TO PESSIMISM

The Cultural Contradictions of Capitalism (1976) was not published until three years after *The Coming of Post-Industrial Society.* Hence, Bell had ample opportunity to enlarge and revise his views. Even though the later work is billed as an extension of his earlier forecast into the domain of the culture, it manifests a turnabout in his outlook. It is also more readable, unified, and consistent.

The Cultural Contradictions of Capitalism concentrates on "culture, especially the idea of modernity, and ... the problems of managing a complex polity when the values of the society express unrestrained appetite" (p. xi). This focus on the cultural contradictions that may ultimately tear apart Western society renders the general tone of *The Cultural Contradictions of Capitalism* distinctly pessimistic. Bell's pessimism, however, is also deeply rooted in his evolving views in three other areas, none of which is explored in detail in *The Coming of Post-Industrial Society*:

The increasing dependence of the United States on the world economy, especially in regard to natural resources availability;

The United States's loss of economic and political power, resulting from such factors as the Vietnam war and the balance of payments deficit and threatening to become an "irreversible slide" (p. 206); and

· The obsolesence of the political system, which needs to undergo key revisions to acquire the ability to manage societal disjunctions successfully.

The primary reason for Bell's movement from moderate optimism to pessimism is his perception of U.S. society as enmeshed in the complex net of international problems.

Cultural Contradictions of Capitalism

The contradictions or incompatibilities that Bell discerns in contemporary capitalism stem from the unraveling of threads that once held the culture and the economy together. Hedonism, he argues, has destroyed the Protestant ethic to become the prevailing value in U.S. society (Bell 1976, pp. 21, 84). The greatest single engine that powered this destruction was the invention of the installment plan. Its instant credit impelled movement from the deferred gratification required for saving to indulgence in instant satisfaction (p. 21).

The breakup of the Protestant ethic and the Puritan temper undercut the moral system that sanctioned work and reward in U.S. society, thus depriving U.S. capitalism of its traditional source of legitimacy (pp. 55, 84). The social order was left without either a culture that symbolically expresses any vitality or a moral impulse that is a motivational force. The cultural contradiction or disjunction between the economizing axial principle of industrialism and the self-gratification principle of the modernist culture "is, in the longer run, the most fateful division in the society" (p. 84). This contradiction pits anticognitivist, antiintellectual orientations that look longingly toward a return to instinctual sources of expression against the established emphasis on efficiency, least cost, maximization, optimization, and functional rationality.

U.S. Dependence on the World Economy

Bell notes that by the early 1970s, "the structural context of decisions was becoming enlarged and ... most of the significant questions concerning the society, particularly the economic ones, were no longer within the power of America to decide" (p. 206). In other words, the shift in context from the national situs to the international arena has rendered problematic the ability of U.S. society to solve its own problems (p. 205).

The growth of a world economy and a world society, Bell observes, makes central the problems of resource management on an international scale (p. 211). The vulnerability of oil-dependent Western industrial societies was exposed by the Arab oil boycott and the quadrupling of oil prices. Moreover, a need has emerged for monitoring changes that technologies induce in the environment. The interplay of resources (food, energy, materials), population, and the environment will set the basic framework of socioeconomic policy in the next decades (p. 237).

Bell observes that "the commitment to economic growth, or even the ability of advanced economies to sustain growth, has been called into question for a host of ... reasons, among them the adequacy of resources and the spillover effects on the environment" (p. 237). He argues that the drag on economic growth for the rest of this century will not be the physical magnitudes of natural resources but the costs of extracting minerals or the payment of "monopoly" prices to producer cartels (p. 237).

Bell concludes: "Ours is a world that will require more authority and more regulation, everywhere" (p. 212). The challenge is to construct new forms appropriate to the management of increasing scale.

An "American Climacteric"?

Bell forecasts significant shifts in economic and political power during the last quarter of the twentieth century (p. 27). Already, the United States has "begun a headlong retreat from its previous role as the paramount political power in *all* parts of the world" (pp. 205, 206). For such reasons as the following, this political retreat may continue along with a decline in comparative economic advantage.

The Vietnam war unleashed a large wave of protest and discontent, a questioning of the legitimacy of the United States and its institutions of authority (p. 217). Young people experienced this war as the single most direct source of their alienation (p. 191). Whether this estrangement of a major section of the future elite can be overcome poses a basic question about the future strength and will of the United States as a great power (p. 191). Bell contends, "The test of any country . . . is its ability to survive humiliation in war, and the United States will have to grapple in the next decade with the effects of its involvement in Vietnam" (p. 217). No longer able to be the hegemonic power by forcefully imposing its will, the United States will experience difficulty enough in maintaining its own political stability (p. 218). Thus the U.S. sense of a manifest destiny has been shattered. Only hedonism remains (p. 281).

U.S. economic dominance in the world has crested. Balance of payments deficits have dethroned the dollar as the world monetary standard. Except for computers and airplanes, the United States has begun to lose its product advantage in crucial areas of technology. Whether high technology devised to create new energy sources will give the United States added advantage is uncertain. A capital shortage, derived from declining profit margins of U.S. firms and a low rate of household savings, may prove to be a real problem (p. 214).

Although Bell admits that the idea of a "climacteric" is elusive, he comments: "One thinks of an American climacteric, a critical change of life . . . carrying the implication that the U.S. economy has passed its peak, that the "aging" process is real, and that the loss of leadership is irretrievable" (p. 213). Nevertheless, the United States may continue to be the paramount global power for the foreseeable future and could attain considerable economic independence (pp. 217, 218). Much depends on contingencies.

Relevant to Bell's discussion of the American climacteric is his claim that economic growth may be the source of a contradiction of capitalism, "a contradiction that may be the cause of its economic undoing" (p. 238). Economic growth under capitalism has become inextricably linked with inflation. Double-digit inflation that wrecks the middle class needs to be banished without resorting to strong deflationary policy that creates rising unemployment among members of the working class. To accomplish this, long-lasting wage-price controls together with an income policy to adjust inequities may become mandatory. The enactment of such policy would transform the private enterprise economy into a regulated corporate society (p. 240).

Needed Revisions in the Political System

One of the most telling criticisms of *The Coming of Post-Industrial Society** was raised by the sociologist Reinhard Bendix. Bell states that the critical turning points in a society occur in a political form and that the politician rather than the technocrat ultimately holds power. Accordingly, Bendix (1974) inquires:

> What is one to make of a book of 489 pages on a new type of society, in which one half is devoted to the delineation and extrapolation of social trends, roughly one fourth to the enumeration of the questions posed by these trends, but nothing of comparable length or substance to the outlines of the political structure? As far as I can see, Professor Bell's book fails to deal with the topic he himself considers decisive: the politics of post-industrial society . . . with the notable exception of the discussion of education. [p. 101]

Bendix also argues that "perhaps it was premature . . . to talk of a new type of society when the key elements of its structure of authority cannot be specified" (p. 101). He concedes that there is an answer to this objection: Bell does not really discuss a new social structure (despite the many passages that read that way) but rather the *coming* of an unknown future (p. 101). Accordingly, Bell "is concerned to show that an extrapolation of current trends leads to a series of questions which are unprecedented in previous experience and for which no ready solutions are in sight" (p. 101). Most of these comprehensively enumerated questions pose difficult political choices. "If *The Coming of Post-Industrial Society* seems to promise too much, as an essay on 'Recent Social Trends and the Waning of Utopia' the book is well worth pondering" (p. 101).

Although Bendix's critique deserves careful consideration, this part of it is somewhat overstated. To be sure, Bell's relative neglect of the outlines of the

---

*The March 1974 issue of *Contemporary Sociology* also contains reviews of *The Coming of Post-Industrial Society* by Stephen D. Berger and Amitai Etzioni, along with Bell's responses. Another of several exchanges between Bell and his critics is presented in *Society*, May/June, 1974. The reviewer is Peter N. Stearns. Ian Miles's *The Poverty of Prediction* provides a lengthy discussion of Bell's treatment of postindustrial society.

political structure constitutes a major weakness in his 1973 projection. Various types of political decisions could contribute to the development of different kinds of postindustrial social structure. Yet Bell's forecast of the social structure, even if somewhat premature, does provide a helpful characterization of the general direction and possible result of a number of important, interrelated contemporary changes.

The last chapter of *The Cultural Contradictions of Capitalism* treats aspects of the political structure of postindustrial society and, thereby, begins to fill this crucial gap in Bell's projection. Bell maintains that the ability of the United States to cope with its problems depends on the capacity of the polity to come to some conception of a "public household" (p. 219). He uses this term to refer to the management of state revenues and expenditures or, more broadly, the agency for the satisfaction of public needs and public wants as distinguished from private wants (p. 221). As a third sector of economic activity alongside the domestic household and the market economy, the public household has come to the fore in the last 25 years. It will play an even more crucial role during the next 25 years. U.S. society must increasingly devote itself to the production of public goods at the expense of private goods and to the nurturing of a public instead of a private sector (p. 176).

Despite the growing importance of the public household, "the United States, so strongly individualistic in temper, and so bourgeois in appetite, has never wholly mastered the art of collective solutions, or of readily accepting the idea of a public interest, as against private gain" (pp. 218, 219). "Political contradictions," Bell argues, "derive from the fact that liberal society was originally set up—in its ethos, laws, and reward systems—to promote *individual ends*, yet has now become an interdependent economy that must stipulate *collective goals*" (p. 176). He proposes certain means of reconciling political liberalism, a crucial value for modern society, with the necessary communal features of societal management. Of special importance are efforts to make institutions work and to create a new public philosophy that commands respect.

Other factors besides liberal individualism make efficient operation of the public household difficult. One is the consideration that sometimes the collectivities are subgroups of the society, while at other times the collectivity is the entire society. Increasingly, the society must pay heed to group, rather than individual, rights and redress. Besides being the primary control system of society, the polity is inevitably the arena for contending parties (pp. 175, 176).

A further factor that presents problems for the public household is the projected decline of U.S. international influence and a consequent tendency for disruptions in U.S. politics (p. 216). Still another is revealed by Bell's admission that the record of U.S. social scientists on social policy is even more dismal than that of economists. "The failure of liberalism . . . is in part," Bell admits, "*a failure of knowledge*" (p. 203). Such remarks suggest that he has lost some of his faith in the ability of the professional-technical class to ameliorate societal problems by applying its intellectual technology.

Consequences for Postindustrial Society

A number of the points made by Bell in *The Cultural Contradictions of Capitalism* correspond to some of the objections raised earlier in this chapter. Seeking to explain this coincidence, I asked myself whether I had asserted claims that Bell would have found completely compatible with his forecast in 1973. With the exception of short-term deviations that he doubtless would have discounted, the answer appears to be no. Hence, significant features of Bell's new orientation are incompatible with, or at least present extremely serious problems for, his prior forecast.

Changes in Bell's position can be traced to his responses to criticisms of his forecast as well as to his experience of recent upsetting events, such as the Arab oil crisis and the atrocities of the Nixon administration, on the international and domestic scenes. In particular, his recognition of the increased dependence of the United States on the unstable world economic system seems to have made him much less confident of a relatively continuous future of exponential growth and more concerned about the current slowdown and possible breakdowns. He acknowledges that "calamity has struck, and will strike again and again" (p. 28). The whole tone of *The Cultural Contradictions of Capitalism* casts grave doubt on the exponential economic growth projected in *The Coming of Post-Industrial Society*: "Neither Utopia nor Doomsday but the same state that has existed for the last hundred years" (Bell 1973a, p. 465). In short, Bell now appears to believe that a turning-point future is more likely than a developmental future.

Despite its weaknesses and outmoded aspects, Bell's 1973 forecast of postindustrial society embodies many enlightening insights and deserves to be updated. Openness to revising one's forecasts as criticisms, events, and increasing knowledge make revisions appropriate contributes to the improvement of forecasting. Bell could perform a valuable service by comparing in detail his positions in the two books and by specifying the extent to which new considerations lead him to alter his earlier forecast. Presumably, he would now forecast a turbulent transition to a less-affluent form of postindustrial society (compare Gappert 1974). An important question for assessing the plausibility of such a forecast concerns the extent to which quinary services, which are so crucial to postindustrial society, depend on industrial growth.

Bell's new orientation displays definite improvements. The extent to which it can be supported will become clearer as we examine forecasts of other turning-point futures. From that vantage point, it can be viewed as excessively pessimistic and, except for some constructive suggestions concerning the public household, quite neglectful of desirable alternative futures. As a counterbalance to Bell's foreboding, consider Brzezinski's (1970) encouraging reflection:

> Although I do not mean to minimize the gravity of America's problems—their catalogue is long, the dilemmas are acute, and the signs of a meaningful response are at most ambivalent—I truly believe that

this society has the capacity, the talent, the wealth, and, increasingly, the will to surmount the difficulties inherent in this current historical transition. [P. xvii]

PART II

FORECASTS OF
TURNING-POINT FUTURES

INTRODUCTION
TO PART II

> To see the earth as it truly is, small and blue and beautiful . . . is to
> see ourselves as riders on the earth together, . . . brothers who know
> now they are truly brothers.
>
> Archibald MacLeish

Sharply differentiated from forecasts of the relatively continuous development of postindustrial society are typical forecasts of turning-point futures. We have seen that some provisional catastrophists brand the elitist type of postindustrial society as domineering, mechanizing, or dehumanizing in other ways. Hence, they opt for major changes designed to forestall technocratic control and facilitate participatory uses of electronic information technology. Similarly, nuclear provisional catastrophists propose fundamental reforms aimed at averting a global holocaust.

The ecologically oriented forecasters who we are now considering seriously question the likelihood, or even the possibility, of achieving a mature, enduring global postindustrial age. These "ecological provisional catastrophists" (or "realists," as some of them prfer to be called) tend to argue as follows. A continuation of rapid industrial and population growth in the limited global support system threatens to surpass ecologically or societally sustainable levels within the next century. The most likely consequence would be the traumatic reversal of growth: descent into the maelstrom of pollution, shortages of affordable energy and raw materials, insufficient food and drinking water, and crowding. Societies should, therefore, deliberately slow and then stabilize growth, or at least curtail the kinds of growth that are most disaster prone.

These forecasters do not restrict their warnings to decisive encounters with limits to growth. International tensions arising from distinctly ecological problems, gross economic inequalities among nations, and proliferation of dangerous technologies could easily erode the quality of life and precipitate regional disasters. Such tensions could even trigger global nuclear war, which might leave no future worth speculating about. Alternatively, successful planned intervention to ameliorate interrelated global problems could create desirable futures that are discontinuous with dangerous established trends. This presupposes appropriate changes in cultural beliefs and values. Failure to make these changes and to intervene effectively would abort, or at least indefinitely postpone, the arrival of a postindustrial age.

Whereas ecological provisional catastrophists are uniformly pessimistic about the directions of various ecological and sociocultural trends, they differ markedly in their assessment of prospects for mobilizing cooperative efforts that would stem the tide of these trends. More precisely, they disagree concerning the extent to which technological solutions are possible; cultural beliefs and values, institutions, and policies need to be changed; sufficient motivation can be aroused to bring about these changes; policy implementation is likely to accomplish its goals; and necessary reforms can be carried out by democratic processes.

Several of these forecasters belong to two groups, each affiliated with an established intellectual institution. Willis Harman and others work for the Educational Policy Research Center (EPRC), which has become part of the Center for the Study of Social Policy of Stanford Research Institute (SRI), now called "Sri International, Inc." Like Harman, O. W. Markley, Arnold Mitchell, and Russell Rhyne contributed substantially to the SRI forecasts. Jay Forrester and an international team headed by Dennis Meadows devised their well-known forecasts at Massachusetts Institute of Technology (MIT), though Meadows has since moved to Dartmouth College. The United States Office of Education funded the EPRC of SRI, while the Club of Rome sponsored Meadows's team.

Formulated on the basis of explicit models, the SRI and MIT forecasts estimate the consequences of a continuation of interrelated trends and problems. To investigate the kinds of policies that could beget preferable futures, the forecasters at each institution experimented with a variety of changes in their models. The SRI prognosticators used the method of nonmathematical modeling; their MIT counterparts, mathematical, computerized modeling. Both groups employed scenarios. Whereas the MIT global forecasts until the year 2100 focus almost exclusively on ecological problems, the SRI forecasts range over a much broader sociocultural spectrum. Although the basic SRI forecast concentrates on alternative futures for the United States until the year 2000, it projects them as affected by intertwined global problems and extends them to the middle of the next century.

The disproportionately long evaluation of forecasts by Meadows's team (Chapter 7) and by Herman Kahn, William Brown, and Leon Martel (Chapter 8) calls for special explanation. To make a thorough evaluation of the sophisticated, complicated SRI forecast, I would require access to extensive data concerning the results of steps in the forecasting process. Unfortunately, available SRI publications, on which my evaluation is based, mention data of this sort only minimally. Furthermore, the lucid, widely publicized forecasts by Meadows and by Kahn furnish the most representative contexts for evaluating the crucial controversy about global limits to industrial and population growth. Whereas Meadows recommends the stabilization of growth to prevent catastrophic collapses of the world's economy and population, Kahn and his coauthors set forth a growth scenario for the world until the year 2176 as a critique of forecasts made by Meadows and other ecological provisional catastrophists. Indeed, Kahn argues for an imminent turning-point in growth rates, but he expects the slowdown to be so gradual that a postindustrial era of abundance will probably evolve. My position in the growth controversy emerges from evaluations of the forecasts by Kahn and Meadows.

The clash between continuous and discontinuous images of the future currently centers in the growth controversy. At its extremes, this controversy pits zero-growth ecologists against developmental economists and technological utopians. It also encompasses a whole spectrum of intermediate positions.

Integral to the growth controversy are the energy debate and the debate about sociocultural constraints. The former debate is especially concerned with whether enough relatively nonpolluting, affordable energy can be generated to support the ongoing growth of industry and population. The latter focuses on the extent to which today's limits to sustainable growth arise from ecologically inadvisable practices and on the ways in which appropriate changes in policies, institutions, goals, and cultural beliefs and values would stretch these elastic constraints to raise the level of sustainable growth.

Intense debate will continue on such growth issues as energy generation, availability of raw materials, pollution control, food production, population control, and inequitably distributed economic growth. The growth controversy looms as a fundamental battlefield on which the industrialized and less-industrialized nations seem likely to oppose each other, as suggested by the heated responses of representatives of the latter to the Forrester-Meadows forecasts at the UN Stockholm Conference on the Human Environment (1972). In short, the growth controversy may well occupy center stage during the next decade or two. Its outcome will profoundly shape the future of the human species.

6

HARMAN'S "WORLD MACROPROBLEM"

It is the business of the future to be dangerous. . . . The major advances in civilization are processes that all but wreck the societies in which they occur.

Alfred North Whitehead

A DRAMATIC CHANGE FROM KAHN'S OUTLOOK

The basic system goals that have dominated the industrial era and that have been approached through a set of fundamental subgoals have resulted in processes and states which end up counteracting human ends. The result is a massive and growing challenge to the legitimacy of the basic goals and institutions of the present industrial system. [Harman 1977a, P. 9]

Willis Harman's startling conclusion emerged from an extensive, ongoing research program at the Educational Policy Research Center (EPRC) of Stanford Research Institute (SRI). In 1970 and 1971 the EPRC set forth a basic projection of alternative future histories for the United States until the year 2000. Willis Harman, then the director of the EPRC, further developed key motifs of this forecast in subsequent publications, including *An Incomplete Guide to the Future* (1976) and "The Coming Transformation" (*Futurist*, February 1977b, April 1977a).

The work of the EPRC constitutes an incisive though generally implicit critique of forecasts of relatively continuous business-as-usual futures by post-industrial optimists. O. W. Markley (1971, p. 6) then a principal analyst at the EPRC and now a professor at the University of Houston, recalls that he and his colleagues at first accepted the essential plausibility of such relatively optimistic forecasts as that set forth by Herman Kahn and Anthony J. Wiener in *The Year 2000.* At least in principle, any given difficulties seemed to be surmountable by conventional means. However, further research led the SRI analysts to view most contemporary problems as a network of social forces that have been brought about by a combination of proliferating knowledge, industrial development unmoderated by a larger sense of social responsibility, rising population levels (which stem from technologically reduced morality rates), and an expanding have/have-not gap (p. 6).

The SRI analysts construed the transnational, interrelated problems created by this network of forces as constituting a formidable "world macroproblem," which Harman (1970a) subdivided into three groups of problems:

Problems of the ecosystem, such as overpopulation and its consequences, resource depletion and, pollution;

An intrinsically expanding "have/have-not" gap, both domestically and between nations, resulting in internal and external dissension; and

Technological threats, including weapons of mass destruction, misuse of genetic engineering, and vulnerability of a complex society to sabotage (p. 6).

Markley (1971) added a fourth group: problems springing from the incipient crisis of specialization and rapid growth without adequate overall perspectives (p. 8). Subsequently, Harman (1972a) argued that unemployment, urban decay, crime, and alienation are also manifestations of the world macroproblem (p. 2).

Analysis of the intertwined components of the world macroproblem, Markley (1971) tells us, led the SRI team to conclude that both "the expectation of a shift from industrial to post-industrial society and [the view] that either technological or governmental interventions would be adequate to ameliorate the world macroproblem were no longer very credible" (p. 8). Although Harman has generally displayed more optimism than several other SRI researchers concerning the continuation of the shift toward postindustrial society, he, too, has maintained that the success of this continuation depends upon making basic changes in the established industrial system.

To enhance our grasp of why the SRI analysts rejected the likelihood of relatively continuous development to mature postindustrial society, we need to examine their methodology and forecast for the United States till the year 2000. Since they treat domestic problems as intermeshed with international problems, analysis of this forecast will help us to understand the changes that they deem necessary for alleviating the world macroproblem. We will also consider Harman's additions to this basic forecast.

THE HARMAN-SRI FORECASTS

Methodology

The SRI forecasters used two problem-oriented, holistic methods to construct a comprehensive set of "alternative future histories." The systems-oriented approach toward which both methods incline their users discloses systemic problems that might disrupt the continuation of beneficial trends. One method, which is quite intuitive, begins with special social problems and expands the context to reach the key metaproblems confronting the society (Markley 1971, pp. 2-3; Harman 1970b, pp. 283, 284). The other, dubbed the Field Anomaly Relaxation Method (FAR), is a more formal, morphological method of modeling (Markley 1971, pp. 2, 3; Rhyne 1971).

FAR, which derives from an approach originated during the 1960s by Robert Johnson and developed by Russell Rhyne, is akin to the relaxation methods used in mathematical physics to model complex dynamic systems. As applied by the SRI, this method permits qualitative analysis of complex fields of partly or wholly unquantifiable information. The researchers categorize U.S. society into 12 "social sectors" (such as the economic sector) within which they define 4 to 7 "societal states" (for instance, severe depression). Then they construct "futures" by provisionally selecting a societal state from each sector in such a way that the combination of these societal states could plausibly coexist in the real world. Through systematic iterations, the FAR method refines a forecast by progressively eliminating internal inconsistencies and by adding new constructs and data. One way to reduce the large number of internally consistent futures is to assess the likelihood of reaching these futures from the description of current societal states within a reasonable period of time. Thus the FAR method is holistic, stressing internal consistency and sequential continuity.

The SRI team employed the two methods to project a "tree" of alternative future histories for the United States. Team members represent the straightforward extrapolation of currently dominant trends as the trunk and each alternative line of development as a branch. They attach crucial importance to the branch points, which identify choices and other occurrences that lead to different futures.

U.S. Alternative Future Histories Till the Year 2000

Although the SRI forecasters concentrated on projecting alternative future histories for the United States until the year 2000, they did this within the context of the world system and extended the forecast to the middle of the next century. They began by identifying approximately 300 plausible alternative future histories. Yet the U.S. Office of Education, which sponsored the forecast, wanted a small set of scenarios conveying a sense of the range of possible futures and a feel for some of the key themes. To provide the widest possible balanced coverage of alternatives that would nonetheless be condensed enough to be usable for policy decisions, the SRI team distilled 5 main lines of development with secondary branches from about 40 highly plausible futures. The resulting "planning cone," which is intended to bracket the future that probably will come about, makes it easier for policy makers to test long-range plans. A planning cone representation of the year 2000 slice of the future tree shows five basic futures that differ from each other in two especially significant directions: (1) the degree to which U.S. society is adept in the Faustian sense of being both competent and motivated to attempt control of its own destiny and (2) the degree of social "openness" or "civility", characterized as flexibility, the social cohesion that comes from trust, tolerance for diversity, and the ability to sustain decentralized decision making without undue internal violence (see Figure 6.1).

Team members admit the tentative nature of their forecast of these five alternative future histories (see Figures 6.2 and 6.3):

1. A successful national effort or "war" on the ecosystem imbalance. The scenario for this future, which is discontinuous with the present, proceeds as follows. During the 1970s and early 1980s, the nation undertakes a large-scale effort to reestablish a balanced ecology, reduce pollution to acceptable levels, and redistribute wealth sufficiently to eliminate extreme domestic poverty. An unmistakable calamity could occasion such a moral equivalent of war, but continuing national effort requires both a national consensus supporting the war and a favorable combination of education and leadership. Institutions and individuals would increasingly interpret the war as a set of cultural lessons to be learned. The result of coming to view all elements of human interaction ecologically would be a *"new" society* that is both "open" and "adept" (Markley 1971, pp. 5, 10). Most other alternative futures are "closed," "inept," or both.

2. A "least-surprises" extension of the status quo. The second future, which is preferable to most others, is similar to the Kahn-Wiener surprise-free projection for the year 2000. Economic and political patterns during the next 15 years closely resemble those of preceding decades. The limitations of retraining and management cause the accelerating rates of technological and cultural change to slow down somewhat, causing a moderate decline in the high economic growth rate. Serious pollution problems are brought under control. However, urban problems increase and the international cold war reemerges. Yet this future is admittedly preferable to most others.

If this second future occurs, SRI's analysis of the "various elements that combine to form the 'world macroproblem' will prove in retrospect to have been grossly exaggerated" (p. 10). More specifically, Markley cites three impediments to the projected shift from industrial to postindustrial society: (1) the "tragedy of the commons," the longer-range depletion of collectively held resources resulting from personally profitable short-term behavior; (2) rapid technological and cultural change, which produces "future shock" and makes conventional management techniques obsolete; and (3) the refusal of youth to go along with present societal institutions. [P. 8]

3. Imprudent optimism, leading to a left-centrist recession and bureaucratic stultification. A "bad luck" version of the first scenario, the scenario for this third future depicts government controls aimed at correcting environmental and social ills as becoming quite inept. Because of social dissatisfaction with the

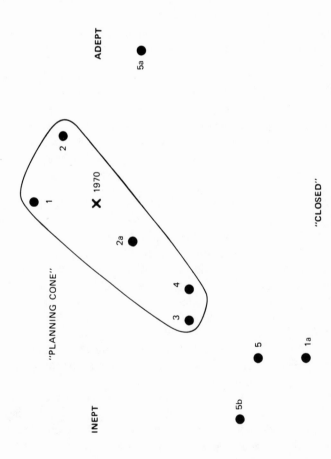

"OPEN"

"PLANNING CONE"

× 1970

ADEPT

INEPT

"CLOSED"

1 "New" Society
2 "Least Surprises" High Growth
3 Bureaucratic Stultification
4 General Recession
5 Authoritarian Order, Recession
1a "New Age" Dictatorship, Slow Growth
2a "Least Surprises" Slow Growth
5b Violent Retrograde
5a Caesarist High Growth

Figure 6.1. "Tree" of alternative future histories, year–2000 slice (Markley 1971, p. 7).

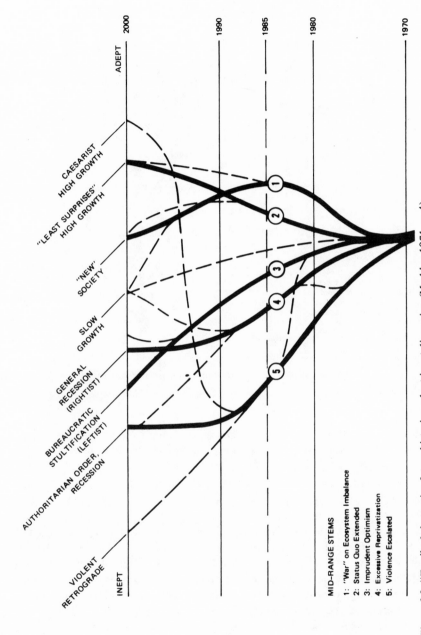

Figure 6.2. "Tree" of alternative future histories, adept-inept dimension (Markley 1971, p. 4).

The following labels appear within the figure:

ADEPT

2000
1990
1985
1980
1970

CAESARIST HIGH GROWTH
"LEAST SURPRISES" HIGH GROWTH
"NEW" SOCIETY
SLOW GROWTH
GENERAL RECESSION (RIGHTIST)
BUREAUCRATIC STULTIFICATION (LEFTIST)
AUTHORITARIAN ORDER, RECESSION
VIOLENT RETROGRADE

INEPT

MID-RANGE STEMS

1: "War" on Ecosystem Imbalance
2: Status Quo Extended
3: Imprudent Optimism
4: Excessive Reprivatization
5: Violence Escalated

155

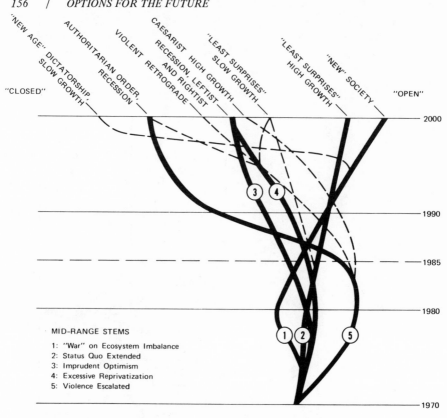

Figure 6.3. "Tree" of alternative future histories, open-closed dimension (Markley 1971, p. 5).

resulting recession, economic growth and concern for stability take precedence over a holistic resolution of the world macroproblem. Pollution worsens in this relatively stable society (pp. 10, 11).

4. Excessive reprivatization, leading to a right-centrist recession and a "garrison state." According to this scenario, a "bad luck" version of the second one, bureaucratic intervention proves ineffective for controlling the economy and dealing with social problems. Hence, emphasis shifts from centrally administered programs to a return to private enterprise via "funding of the people." After a while, initial optimism fades as the government fails to tune the economy successfully, as recession threatens, and as subcultural or "stakeholder" coalitions preemptively try to get the shares they demand. Authorities invoke increasingly severe forms of repression against those who protest violently. Late in the century, recession imposes international political disengagement of the United States and consequent economic isolation. Since the North Atlantic community

must continually defend itself against politicized violence from the chaotic Third World, an international garrison state arises in parallel to the domestic one in the United States (pp. 10, 11).

5. Violence escalated, resulting in authoritarian order and recession. An acceleration of two present trends would provoke violent behavior. One is the use of confrontation politics as a means of achieving pervasive societal reforms; the other, the institutional encouragement of the stakeholder differences by inept attempts at participatory planning. The scenario proposes that a breakdown of confidence and trust throughout society leads authorities to rely increasingly on force to maintain control. Thus power replaces consensual authority. Such authoritarianism would probably beget recessive trends, though the possibility of a high-growth Caesarist take-over remains (p. 11).

Underlying Causes of the World Macroproblem

Many variations of these alternative future histories could occur. Willis Harman (1970a) states:

> Of some 40 feasible future histories, there are very few that manage to avoid some period of serious trouble between now and 2050. The few that do appear to require a dramatic shift of values and perceptions with regard to . . . the "world macroproblem." [P. 6]

Outmoded Cultural Premises and Values

The founding of the world religions, the fall of the Roman Empire, and the end of the Middle Ages brought not merely changes in social roles and institutions but profound underlying changes in cultural premises, dominant values, and images of man-in-the-universe. Lewis Mumford notes in *The Transformation of Man* (1962) that the fundamental changes in Western society, probably no more than half a dozen since primitive society, rested upon deep stirrings and intuitions whose rationalized expression assumed the form of new pictures of the cosmos and of the nature of man. New beliefs, values, and perceptions were found to be more appropriate to altered situations. Might we be on the verge of another transformation?

The SRI team came to regard various aspects of the world macroproblem as surface manifestations of a fundamental cultural condition. Harman (1970b), for instance, interprets contemporary political, military, economic, ecological, and social crises as reflections of an underlying moral and spiritual crisis of civilization (p. 290). Analysis strongly suggests that some of the operative values that fathered industrial civilization have gone out of phase, for by their very success in ameliorating previous problems they have created new ones. For instance, industrial civilization's dominant value of material economic growth has greatly elevated living standards and expanded opportunities in many countries but increasingly encounters problems of pollution and resource depletion on our small planet as well as problems inherent in radically different rates of growth in diverse regions.

These obsolete values are incapable of promoting rectification of the problems that they now exacerbate. Problems stemming from growth cannot be sufficiently alleviated by more growth of the same kind. *Hence, attainment of a desirable future apparently requires appropriate revision of certain cultural premises and corresponding operative values.* Harman (1970a) lists nine of these premises:

The pride of families, the power of nations, and the survival of the human species should be promoted by population increase, as they have been in the past.

Crucial to progress is behavior governed by the "technological imperative": Any technology that can be developed should be developed; any knowledge that can be applied should be applied.

The summed knowledge of experts constitutes wisdom.

Science has justified the reductionist view of man (which lends sanction to dehumanizing ways of thinking about and treating man).

Men are essentially separate, so that they need not feel more than a modicum of intrinsic responsibility for the effects of their present actions on remote individuals or future generations.

Man, since separate from nature, ought to exploit and control it rather than cooperate with it.

Behavior should be guided by the "economic man" image, which supports a system of economics based on ever-increasing GNP, consumption, and expenditure of irreplaceable resources.

The future of the planet can safely be left to autonomous nation-states, operating essentially independently.

"What ought to be" does not refer to any state of affairs that can be achieved, nor does it even express a meaningful concept (pp. 9, 10).

Dilemmas Stemming from the Industrial-State Paradigm

All but the first of these "pathogenic" premises are characteristic features of what Harman christens the "industrial-state paradigm." Following Thomas Kuhn's (1970) use, Harman (1977b) defines a "dominant paradigm" as the basic way of thinking, perceiving, and doing that is associated with a particular vision of reality. As more than an ideology and less than a total culture, a societal paradigm is largely embodied in the unquestioned, tacit understanding shared by people in the society and transmitted through exemplars in daily life (p. 5).

Differing sharply from the paradigm of the medieval age, the industrial-state paradigm has promoted:

- The development and application of the scientific method, and the wedding of science to technological advance
- Industrialization through the organization and division of labor; the replacement of human labor by machines
- Acquisitive materialism as a dominant value; the work ethic; an economic image of man; belief in unlimited material progress and in technological and economic growth
- Manipulative rationality as a dominant theme; a search for control over nature; a positivistic theory of knowledge
- Pragmatic values held by the individual; individual responsibility for his own destiny; freedom and equality as fundamental rights; individual determination of what is "good"; society viewed as an aggregate of individuals pursuing their own interests. [P. 5]

Both capitalist and socialist industrial societies have achieved extraordinarily high material living standards, increased food production, and universal education. However, the pathogenic premises are generating undesirable consequences at an accelerating rate. More specifically, the paradigm's fabulous success has given rise to worsening dilemmas that inhere in industrial society. At the core of these dilemmas is *the fundamental dilemma*, which constitutes the very essence of the world macroproblem (p. 9). This dilemma is intrinsic to the industrial state and probably cannot be resolved by strategies that the paradigm governs. Harman (1976) formulates the fundamental dilemma or anomaly as follows:

> the basic paradigm that has dominated the industrial era (including emphasis on individualism, free enterprise, and material progress; with social responsibility primarily the concern of the government; and with few restraints on capital accumulation, etc.),
> - and that involves striving toward such goals as efficiency, productivity, continued growth of production and consumption, continued growth of technological and manipulative power,
> - has resulted in processes and states (e.g., extreme division of labor and specialization, cybernation, stimulated consumption, planned obsolescence and waste, exploitation of common resources, alienation of persons from community and nature, etc.),
> - which end up counteracting human ends (e.g., enriching work roles, resource conservation, environmental enhancement, equitable sharing of the earth's resources).
> The result is a cultural crisis of major proportions—*a growing and massive challenge to the legitimacy of the present industrial system.* [P. 115]

Thus the basic problem is that *microdecisions based on self-interest*, which are perfectly reasonable when judged by the criteria that have governed past decisions, *"are currently adding up to largely unsatisfactory macrodecisions"* (Harman 1976, p. 86; 1977b, p. 9). For instance, decisions to produce and buy a certain product may lead to increased air pollution and an unnecessary waste of energy.

Harman distinguishes four specific dilemmas that are rooted in the fundamental dilemma. These dilemmas, which resist collective resolution while the paradigm remains dominant, are:

The growth dilemma: We need continued economic growth but cannot live with the environmental and social costs of continued exponential growth in our use of energy and materials. Lower wages, increased unemployment, and further alienation of poor people whose "slice of the economic pie" stops expanding appear unacceptable, but so do health hazards engendered by major increases in pollution, excessive depletion of the natural resources on which industry depends, and proliferating arms races.

The control dilemma: We need to guide technological innovation but shun centralized control. The adverse consequences of such polluting but economically profitable technologies as aerosol sprays make anticipatory control of new technologies mandatory, but at the high price of jeopardizing certain basic features of the private market systems.

The distribution dilemma: The industrialized nations find it costly to share the earth's resources with less developed nations, but a failure to do so might prove even more costly. Though stability of the world order cannot be achieved when millions of people are compulsively consuming and wasting while millions of others are starving, the industrial system provides no suitable mechanism for redistribution.

The work-roles dilemma: Industrial Society is increasingly unable to supply an adequate number of meaningful social roles. Technology, so integral to the industrial system, bestows such benefits as increased production and performance of burdensome labor, but also endangers effective citizenship and self-respect by depriving many people of the privilege of performing wholesome, appreciated work. [1977b, p. 6]

The first three dilemmas can be traced to the "new scarcity," which results from our approaching the finite planetary limits of:

- Fossil fuels and other sources of energy
- Mineral and nonmineral resources
- Fresh water
- Arable land and habitable space
- Waste-absorbing capacity of the natural environment
- Resilience of the planet's life-supporting ecosystems. [1976, p. 39]

Attempts to cope with the growth dilemma by energy conservation and environmental protection sometimes cost jobs, thus intensifying the work-roles dilemma. Hence, the limits to growth exacerbate each of the dilemmas. Consequences of the pathogenic premises await only sufficiently high levels of population and industrialization to become intolerable.

A New Societal Paradigm

Need for a New Dominant Paradigm

How, in summary, are the key concepts of Harman's analysis of the world macroproblem interrelated? The pathogenic premises of the industrial-state paradigm give rise to the fundamental dilemma, in which four interrelated dilemmas—the growth dilemma, the control dilemma, the distribution dilemma, and the work-roles dilemma—are rooted. The fundamental dilemma constitutes the essence of the world macroproblem and the four dilemmas compose its core. Since the dilemmas are integral to the paradigm, they resist resolution by strategies that the paradigm governs. What is needed is a shift to a new societal paradigm that would modify the pathogenic premises in ways conducive to resolution of the dilemmas and hence amelioration of the world macroproblem. Thus the drastically revised paradigm would furnish guidance for a sweeping societal transformation (p. 135). Crucial to such a historically rare transformation would be a change in the basic perception of reality. As Harman (1972b) puts it:

> Among the "alternative future histories" . . . is one that comprises a rapid and drastic break with trends of the recent past, characterized essentially by a change in that basic vision of man-in-the-universe in which the operative values of the society have their origins. . . . The change would be in such a direction as to assist in the resolution of the society's most serious problems. [P. 50]

As far back as 1970, Harman (1970b) formulated a forecast of the "New Reformation" with "New Age" premises. He argued:

> *A set of "New Age" premises and values is emerging which is uniquely suited to preserving the planet's habitability and to creating a society conducive to the individual's achieving the highest degree of self-fulfillment.* These premises, in one sense, comprise a synthesis of aspects of the modern scientific world view, the medieval view of man, and the Eastern religious philosophies—or more accurately, a blend of emphases. [P. 287]

Suitable systemic change, comparable in importance with the industrial revolution and the Copernican revolution, would bring a metamorphosis in basic cultural premises and values, in the root image of man-in-society, and in all aspects of social roles and institutions (1977a, p. 106). *"The whole system must change,"* Harman (1976) contends, *"and nothing less than that will meet the challenge of our time"* (p. 126). The need for such change, however, does not imply that a grand design would prove to be a more effective response than well-coordinated incremental strategies (p. 110).

An Emerging Paradigm?

Harman (1977a) concedes that at best we can make only an informed guess concerning the character of the societal paradigm that will succeed the industrial-state paradigm (p. 106). Yet the plausibility of an imminent paradigm shift is enhanced by:

The urgent need to resolve the dilemmas;

The prominence during the last decade of various types of lead indicators that have preceded periods of historic cultural change (including increases in the following: alienation, the rate of social disruptions, the use of police to control behavior, public acceptance of hedonistic behavior, and interest in noninstitutionalized religious activities) (1977a, p. 107); and

The apparent emergence of a competing paradigm (as suggested by surveys and polls, such cultural indicators as themes of recent motion pictures and elements of the new-age subculture, and new scientific interest in exploring subjective and altered states of consciousness) (pp. 107, 108).

Harman maintains that these three kinds of evidence enable us to infer something about the direction in which values, and the dominant image of man-in-the-universe, are likely to move (p. 108). The key features of the new paradigm can be deduced by assuming that it will grow smoothly out of, and will be rooted in, the past and that it will provide a setting in which the basic dilemmas become resolvable (1976, p. 28). A posttransformational paradigm could display the following characteristics:

Complementarity of physical and spiritual experience; use of different noncontradictory "levels of explanation" for physical, biological, mental, and spiritual reality; recognition that all "explanation" is only metaphor;

Reorientation of science, which has been shaped by the prediction-and-control values of the industrial-state paradigm, toward guiding evolutionary development in ways that place more emphasis on understanding technology;

Sense of life and evolution as having purpose and direction, being guided by supraconscious evolutionary tendencies toward development of human spiritual potentialities;

Perception of ultimate reality as unitary, with a discoverable transcendent spiritual order against which human value choices can be assessed;

Basis for value-postulates also discoverable in an individual's inner experience of a hierarchy of "levels of consciousness"; potential for supraconscious and subconscious experience;

Goals of life: aware participation in individual growth and in the evolutionary process; integration of work, play, and growth; individual fulfillment through community; and

Goals of society: development of the transcendent and emergent capabilities of individuals, fostered by appropriate kinds of technological development, economic growth, social institutions, authority structures, work roles, and environments (1977a, p. 108; 1976, pp. 32, 33; also Markley et al. 1974, pp. 143 ff.).

Harman asserts that such a paradigm would extend rather than contradict the contemporary scientific view (1976, p. 33). This statement, paradoxical since many of today's scientists reject some of the features of the suggested paradigm, must be understood in terms of Harman's illustration: the way in which Einstein's theory extended Newtonian mechanics. Scientific data and theories would be interpreted as harmonious with Harman's transcendentalist outlook.

The most basic postulates of this burgeoning paradigm are not essentially new but have comprised a central stream of thought in the humanities, in Western political theory, and in U.S. transcendentalist movements. Yet these postulates have never formed the guiding paradigm of an entire society. Harman argues for a potentially broad acceptability of the paradigm, both in industrialized and less-industrialized countries, because of its compatibility with traditional belief systems about the world (pp. 33, 37).

An Emerging Image of Man

At the heart of the contending paradigm is a fundamental change in the currently ascendant image of man. Industrial society is pulled toward this paradigm by a newly emerging image of man and pushed toward it by the dilemmas (p. 89).

The industrial-state paradigm has promoted the image of man as activated largely by economic motivations. Other images need to be revived to balance this restrictive economic emphasis (Markley 1974). Harman (1976) maintains that man is physical as well as spiritual, both aspects being real and neither fully describable in terms of the other (p. 100). Man is a transcendental, choosing, ultimately responsible self. His potentialities are enormous, for limitations to human development are ultimately self-chosen. Thus this image, traces of which can be found throughout history, also challenges the established scientific world view that remains dominant despite recent scientific advances that seem to substantiate the image (pp. 105, 111, 115).

The new premises derived from this enriched image of man were summarized quite well by Aldous Huxley in *The Perennial Philosophy* (1945). As Harman (1970b) observes while recounting Huxley's treatment, these premises include

preeminently an image of man as a part of a Whole, potentially capable of an awareness transcending ordinary awareness in which his identity with the Whole and his role as chooser of the experiences that happen to him become apparent. Thus man is viewed as a part of Nature, partner in the adventure of evolution. . . . The "New Age" premises contain the communion with nature prerequisite to resolving the planet's ecological problems, the fraternity to fellow men without which social problems will resist solution, and the supremely meaningful task of human evolution to eliminate the anomie of our time. [P. 289]

The Ecological and Self-Realization Ethics

From the emerging image of man as transcendent, Harman derives two complementary ethics that characterize the replacement paradigm and offer the kind of guidance needed to resolve the dilemmas. The ecological ethic is based on the recognition that resources are limited. It treats man as an integral part of the natural world and, hence, as inseparable from its laws and processes. By relating self-interest to the interests of others and of future generations, this ethic fosters the total community of man and responsibility for the future of the planet (1977a, p. 110). This ethic could guide people to replace the life-style of maximum production and consumption with that of "voluntary simplicity" (1977b, p. 10).

The self-realization ethic prescribes the further development of the emergent self and of the human species as the appropriate end of all individual experience. The proper function of all social institutions is to create an environment that will foster this process. To satisfy the individual's need for full participation in society, social decision making should be highly decentralized. Furthermore, a strong free enterprise private sector should be preferred over public bureaucracy for the accomplishment of most social tasks (1977a, p. 110).

Guidance toward "Transindustrial Society"

Harman (1972a), once relatively optimistic about potential technological benefits, maintained that the new reformation would make a rewarding post-industrial age possible (pp. 2-4). He now appears to have abandoned the post-industrial perspective and instead calls attention to the possible shift to a steady-state "transindustrial society" characterized by:

The human ability to share the physical environment,
An emphasis on human development,
Concern with the inner frontiers of mind and spirit,
An orientation toward learning at all phases of life, and
Use of "frugal technology" that harmonizes with the "new scarcity" of planetary ecological constraints (1976, p. 3; 1977b, p. 10).

Examples of frugal technology include the "soft" energy technologies (such as solar, wind, hydroelectric, and bioconversion advocated by Amory Lovens (Lovens and Price 1975). Frugal technology for developing countries consists of "intermediate" technologies that are appropriate to their needs and resources (Schumacher 1973).

Because of planetary limitations, the exponential growth of population and of individual demands on the environment must level off at some point (Harman 1976, p. 4). Harman's transindustrial society would be a "frugal society," dedicated to "doing more with less." Harman describes such a society in this way:

- An ethic of frugality and ecological harmony would replace the consumption-and-waste ehtic of industrial society.
- Human energy and social resources would be devoted largely to creating meaningful individual lives and a humane society, and far less to those kinds of technological achievements that are wasteful of physical resources.
- Evolutionary change would occur, but growth in a material sense would be slow.
- Technology would be very sophisticated but would conserve energy and materials and would be small in scale.
- Production units (e.g., farms, factories) would tend to be small and relatively self-sufficient. [P. 49]

"The key to resolving the growth, work, distribution, and control dilemmas," Harman observes, "lies in the transformation to ... a transindustrial society" (p. 135). (See Figure 6.4.) Yet such a society would not automatically cure all ills. Nor is the transformation predictable or even necessarily probable (p. 4).

Harman's Forecast of the "Coming Transformation"

Three Alternative Futures

We have seen that Harman not only stresses the need for a paradigm shift but calls attention to a confluence of signs that an appropriate paradigm may be emerging (p. 236ff.). What kinds of alternative futures does he now project? How likely is a transformation and how imminent might it be? What consequences would it bring? (See Figure 6.5.)

Harman acknowledges that the industrial-state paradigm might remain dominant, promoting continued economic growth, industrialization, and technological development. Occurrence of this type of future would mean that his arguments are mistaken (pp. 34, 35).

A second future history would make a successful transformation to a transindustrial society. This radical change would profoundly alter the Kahn-Wiener basic, long-term multifold trend, particularly in regard to an increasingly

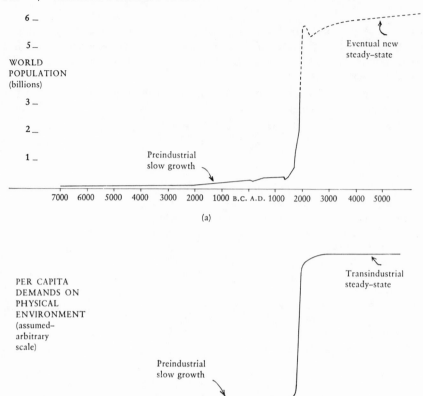

Figure 6.4. Two curves illustrating the uniqueness of the present point in history: (a) world population and (b) per capita demands on the physical environment (Harman 1976, p. 5). (Reproduced from AN INCOMPLETE GUIDE TO THE FUTURE by Willis W. Harman, by permission of W. W. Norton & Company, Inc. Copyright ©1979, 1976 by Willis W. Harman. Originally published as part of the Portable Stanford by The Stanford Alumni Association, Stanford, Ca.)

sensate (empirical, this-worldly, secular, humanistic, pragmatic, utilitarian, contractual, epicurean or hedonistic, and the like) culture and rapid industrial growth. Unless a transindustrial future is constructed on the foundation laid down by the past, the transition could easily prove to be unmanageable. Hence, most existing institutions would probably retain a similar external form. However, their operative goals may become significantly or even drastically different (pp. 34, 35), as exemplified by the overall goal of developing the transcendent and emergent capacities of people (pp. 32, 33).

During a third future history, the disruptive stress of the forces for transformation would overcome society. Before the end of the century, society would suffer a general breakdown that would include a decline of technological capabilities (p. 35). A violent confrontation between the new demands and the old rigidities could precipitate decisive destruction that would leave no promise of rebuilding to previous heights (1977a, p. 112).

Apparent Imminence of an Upsetting Transformation

Admitting the tentative nature of his forecast, Harman calls attention to the apparent imminence of a societal transformation. The magnitude of such a transformation has not been paralleled more than half a dozen times in the history of Western civilization. Harman maintains that the forces of transformation have gathered impressive momentum. The industrialized world is already experiencing both *"a conceptual revolution* as thoroughgoing in its effects as the Copernican Revolution" and *"an institutional revolution* as profound as the

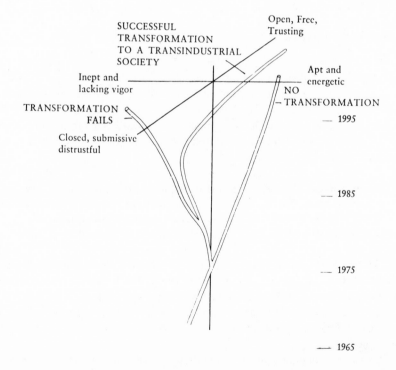

Figure 6.5. Three alternative future histories (Harman 1976, p. 35). (Reproduced from AN INCOMPLETE GUIDE TO THE FUTURE by Willis W. Harman, by permission of W. W. Norton & Company, Inc. Copyright © 1979, 1976 by Willis W. Harman. Originally published as part of the Portable Stanford by The Stanford Alumni Association, Stanford, Ca.)

Industrial Revolution" (p. 106). This overall transformation is proceeding so rapidly that it will pass through its most critical period within a decade [p. 106).

"There is nothing in history," Harman (1977a) observes, "to suggest that a social transformation of the magnitude suggested could occur without the most severe economic and social disruptions and systems breakdowns" (p. 110). A transition to transindustrial society would probably be wrenching and traumatic. "A period of chaos seems inevitable as the powerful momentum of the industrial era is turned in a new direction and the various members and institutions of the society respond at different speeds" (1976, p. 36).

Sharp shortages of various resources are likely, as is a dropping off of economic growth due to external factors. Economic decline in rich countries could easily lead to depression. As businesses are called upon to design new management structures, anticipate future costs and internalize external costs, and adopt frugal technologies, authoritarian government is likely to be invoked temporarily to maintain stability. In poor countries, famines and plagues will probably rage out of control. A high conflict level will result from such pressures as the demand for a more equitable distribution of the world's resources (p. 10).

Negotiating the Transition

If this transition is underway, the principal challenge to industrial societies is to bring it about without shaking themselves apart. Whether the social structure can withstand the strain depends largely on how well the nature and necessity of this transformation is understood while it is being under-taken (1977a, p. 106). Disruptions need to be interpreted as necessary steps in the movement toward a more workable system rather than as capricious and inherently destructive events. Harman (1976) suggests:

> If the forces are there, a transformation is probably beyond our power to stop. But if they are there and we understand them, we might be able to move with them in such a way that the transformation becomes an exhilarating ride instead of a crashing disaster. [P. 7]

Harman's treatment of the impact of interrelated world problems on the United States and his expectation of a disruptive domestic societal transition not only resembles Daniel Bell's (1976) analysis of a possible American "climacteric" but also differs from it. Harman, who projects disruptions that seem to be more severe, also offers more hope of successfully making the transition to a desirable type of society.

Instead of recommending a "grand design," Harman (1977a) contends that a global problem does not necessarily require a global solution. Rather, we now need a *radical vision with adaptive incremental strategies* that are coordinated through widespread understanding of the interrelatedness of separate actions (p. 110). To cope with the basic problem that microdecisions often add up to an unsatisfactory macrodecision, appropriate macrodecisions must first be identified. Then patterns of microdecisions required to bring about those macrodecisions should be investigated.

What means should be used to obtain the desired decisions? Harman (1977b) replies that "the only means compatible with our goals is the reeducation of people to enable them to appreciate the desired goals and to understand the microdecisions necessary for reaching them" (p. 10). Crucial to such an undertaking is the revision of outmoded cultural premises. If the SRI team is correct in its analysis of such premises, Harman (1972b) maintains, education toward changing them constitutes the paramount educational task of the nation and the world. Likewise, national policy makers should seek to make the emergent paradigm dominant (pp. 83, 92).

Since a society's image of a future frequently serves as a key to the realization of that future, we should adopt a positive, inspiring image. Such an image would provide a guiding vision of a workable future society constructed in harmony with the emerging image of man and the transindustrial paradigm. Such an image would portray a central project to which the society dedicates itself.

Harman (1977a) opts for a societal project that would encourage adoption of a self-realization ethic and undertake a major scientific investigation of the transcendental aspects of reality, including the exploration of inner experience (p. 112). (His advocacy of the systematic exploration of "inner space" contrasts with Herman Kahn's recent endorsement of large-scale immigration to space colonies [Kahn, Brown, and Martel 1976b].) Similarly, Harman (1976) elsewhere recommends a "learning and planning society" aligned to promoting individual growth (p. 125). A well-coordinated network of planning units needs to be instituted at the local, regional, national, and planetary levels. Experts would define and compare alternatives, but citizens would participate in selecting and actualizing the alternatives. Unlimited numbers of people could be employed to perform this meaningful task of designing the future (1977a, p. 112). Harman's summary of requirements for resolving the fundamental societal dilemmas is shown in Table 6.1.

While Harman admits that he can present no strategy of deliberate change for a well-ordered transition, he specifies several high-priority tasks for fostering the transition:

- Business institutions move toward synergism with societal needs through changed corporate goals as stability considerations permit.
- Take measures to foster a strong, broadly responsible voluntary/ nonprofit sector.
- All three sectors [private, public, voluntary/nonprofit] together experiment with approaches to work-roles dilemma.
- Promote social innovation, frugal technology, orderly movement toward a more frugal society.
- Implement future-oriented planning system (local, regional, national, planetary) with effective citizen participation.
- Devise incentive structures and organizations (e.g., ANCOM) to

TABLE 6.1

Interrelating Nature of Society's Fundamental Dilemmas and
Requirement of Whole-System Change for Eventual Resolution

Fundamental Dilemma	Nature of Resolution	Requires for Resolution	Resolution Would Contribute to
Growth	Movement toward a frugal society	Ecological ethic Resolution of the work dilemma	Resolution of distribution dilemma Easing of resource and environmental problems, hence of problems of technology management
Work roles	Commitment to full and valued participation as a fundamental political right Institutionalization of a learning and planning society	Self-realization ethic Meaningful "central project"	Resolution of growth dilemma Resolution of distribution dilemma
Distribution	More equitable distribution of the earth's resources Overlapping supranational institutions forming a planetary regulatory system (with important roles being played by the private and voluntary sectors)	Ecological ethic Movement toward a frugal society in the rich nations Resolution of the work dilemma	Reduction of world tensions and nuclear threat World stability Ability to deal more rationally with the growth dilemma
Control	Multi-level citizen participation network for technology assessment and management	Ecological ethic (to reduce tendency to approach problems in adversary mode)	Resolution of growth dilemma Resolution of the work dilemma
Cultural crisis (alienation, lack of agreed-upon goals, low trust in institutions)	Restructured society around a new image of man	Commitment to a new "central project"	Resolution of all four dilemmas

Source: Harman 1976, p. 137. (Reproduced from AN INCOMPLETE GUIDE TO THE FUTURE by Willis W. Harman, by permission of W. W. Norton & Company, Inc. Copyright © 1979, 1976 by Willis W. Harman. Originally published as part of the Portable Stanford by The Stanford Alumni Association, Stanford, Ca.)

make multinational corporations more effective agents of third-world development. [P. 10]

Harman states that "one cannot be too sanguine about the danger of failure to make the transformation, with the resultant danger of decline and collapse" (p. 10). Still, he appears to be generally optimistic about the human ability to negotiate the evolutionary leap to transindustrial society. He concludes:

> Our hope, our beliefs, is that it is precisely when society's future seems most beleaguered ... that it is most likely to achieve a metamorphosis in growth toward maturity, toward more truly enhancing and fulfilling the human spirit than ever before. [1976, pp. 144–45]

EVALUATION OF ASSUMPTIONS

Methodology

To our inquiring eyes, the distinctly intuitive method employed by the SRI researchers remains shrouded in mystery. However, FAR seems to be the most sophisticated method available for formulating long-range, comprehensive forecasts. This is, of course, a comparative judgment that does not warrant complacency concerning the need to improve FAR and to devise better methods.

Among the features of FAR that contribute to its relative reliability are its systematic use of scenarios and its capacity to take qualitative data into account, which forecasters too often ignore or misrepresent. Moreover, its holistic character renders it superior to most methods, including the Delphi technique, for analyzing part-whole relationships. The SRI team's acknowledgement of the tentative nature of its forecast further enhances the trustworthiness of its use of FAR. Unfortunately, the cost and complexity of this method in its complete version have prevented the SRI team from using it in subsequent research for various clients.

The formal virtues of FAR, however, provide no guarantee that forecasters using it will representatively sample and correctly interpret data or that they will make justifiable nonmethodological theoretical assumptions. The data base and assumptions of the SRI team are not as explicit as they could be. For instance, users of the forecast are not supplied with sufficiently detailed information to judge whether the team accomplished its differentiation of U.S. society into societal sectors and societal states in the most plausible way. Inasmuch as all analytic divisions of society have proved to be somewhat arbitrary, the primary question is whether a given set of categories is useful in generating feasible alternative future histories. Yet we should not dismiss the question of sound sociocultural analysis. A reliable forecast can hardly be based on misconceptions of the structural dynamics of a society.

Furthermore, FAR depends on numerous intuitive judgments as to what constitute plausible sequences of states in society (Markley 1971, p. 3). This is more of a drawback for users of FAR forecasts than for forecasters, since to a large extent these judgments are self-checking through the iterative nature of the process. Yet our lack of specific information concerning the results of each step in the forecasting process makes the forecast for the United States until the year 2000 difficult to evaluate. This difficulty is compounded by SRI's use of the minimally described intuitive method and by our uncertainty about the respective contributions of the two methods to the forecast. We do not even know the precise extent to which use of the two methods yielded compatible forecasts.

Forecast for the United States till the Year 2000

The SRI forecast presents an exceptionally wide range of carefully constructed alternative future histories. It appears to be more reliable than the forecasts made by the Gordon-Helmer Delphi panelists, Brzezinski, Kahn and Wiener, and Bell.

Still, the SRI team appears to have underestimated the enormous thrust that electronic information technology will probably exert toward a postindustrial era in the United States. Since this energy-efficient, relatively clean type of technology is less limited than many other types by depletion of natural resources or by pollution, it opens an avenue to safe economic growth. Such technology facilitates growth in the service areas, which are so integral to postindustrial society. This growth alternative should make it easier to restrict polluting industrial technologies. Hence, one wonders whether the United States might not attain a relatively desirable future by the year 2000 without mobilizing so large an effort to rectify the ecosystem imbalance that SRI's radically discontinuous new society would result.

By including the "status quo extended" as its second alternative future, the SRI team admits that Herman Kahn could be right. But is there not a range of desirable futures between the extremes of Kahn's future and SRI's new society? Fitting changes in those value-priorities that impede rapid research, development, and implementation of promising new technologies might even result, for instance, in the production of economically feasible solar photovoltaic electric energy within the next three or four decades. A transition to such abundant, ultraclean energy could alleviate ecological problems and usher in a new era of sustainable economic growth. This illustrates how a few of the most advantageous technological and nontechnological changes made quickly at appropriate points in the national or world system could appreciably improve future prospects.

Indeed, the United States would enjoy a much brighter future if it had successfully negotiated the transition to SRI's new society. Yet formidable hindrances confront attempts to make this radical change quickly. Typically, societies that have undergone successful transformations have been almost wrenched apart in the process. Although sometimes societally disruptive change is required to resolve knotty problems and achieve preferable goals, at other times its risks are too grave to justify policies designed to bring it about. A number of twentieth century political revolutions, though inspired by lofty ideals, either have failed because of the difficulty of the undertaking or have sacrificed their ideals in order to gain and maintain control. In some of these instances, efforts to implement constructive reforms would probably have produced better results. Likewise, attempts to implement utopian communities based on perfectionist goals are prone either to disruption or to disillusionment when they compromise enough to achieve relative success in this imperfect world. Imaginative projections of attractive futures need to be tempered by a sense of what can be achieved in the real world. If desirable futures (though somewhat less desirable than SRI's new society) can be achieved through less disruptive, more reliable strategies than that which the SRI team favors, regard for society's safety may warrant policies directed toward one of these futures. Toward the end of Chapter 8, we sketch a set of global goals appropriate to a future of this sort and briefly suggest a general motivational strategy for attaining it.

The SRI analysts may have devised desirable futures between the extremes of the new society and the status quo extended, for they projected some 300 alternative future histories that they then condensed to about 40. The further reduction to five fundamental futures was prompted by the consideration that the U.S. Office of Education, which sponsored the forecast, wanted a small set of scenarios conveying a sense of the range of possible futures and a feel for some of the key themes. The resulting user-oriented forecast and the accompanying analysis, however, neglects intermediate futures that seem most important as guides to policy formulation.

The team's pioneering analysis of intermeshed global problems deserves applause but nonetheless stands in need of certain improvements. For instance, societies can display more flexibility in adapting to changed situations than the published forecast might lead one to believe. To be sure, the initial projection of about 300 futures reflects the forecasters' commitment to a considerable amount of flexibility.* Yet the five basic futures that they selected as illustrative samples furnish little insight into processes by which societies sometimes appropriately revise outdated institutions and policies without making fundamental changes

---

*One of FAR's virtues is that it generates and retains some types of possible futures that any other existing methodology bypasses. The SRI team's process for excluding an overall societal state required a unanimous vote of team members coupled with strong reasons describing why such a state was implausible. Many states that displayed substantial internal incongruities were retained by the team as workable 5-to-15-year transitional phases. (Still, in light of Daniel Bell's analysis of long-enduring societal disjunctions, one wonders whether the team did not place a bit too much emphasis on major unresolved incongruities as an important source of change, thus eliminating some plausible intermediate- and long-range alternative futures.)

in underlying beliefs and values (see Nelson 1969). For instance, medieval Catholic culture areas adapted to altered conditions not so much by making revolutionary changes in guiding principles as by casuistry: the art of tailoring general principles to specific kinds of situations. Instead of being discarded, the principles were reinterpreted to apply to new situations. To a somewhat lesser but significant extent, Catholic societies during the Renaissance coped with rapid change by continued use of casuistry. As distinguished from the revolutionary Protestant Reformation, the Catholic Counter-Reformation was casuistic.

Although a casuistic approach by itself is insufficient to bring about the major normative changes that are called for today, it could supplement revolutionary value change. The resulting adjustment process might be distinctly less traumatic than that posited by the SRI team.

Major policy changes that reflect underlying changes in priorities sometimes occur without conscious intent. Indeed, such changes may proceed almost imperceptibly. For instance, the U.S. Social Security system was designed in the 1930s merely to provide supplemental income so that people forced to retire would not be destitute. Without a deliberate shift by the government or citizens, people have come to expect that Social Security will supply sufficient funds to support them. The enormous financial drain on the system has brought the basic change to our attention. Regardless of our verdict when we appraise this change from a long-range perspective, changes that occur without conscious guidance can be adaptive. This observation provides no excuse for failing to undertake programs aimed at coping with the world macroproblem but does make us aware of another kind of priority change neglected by the SRI researchers.

Despite such shortcomings, the SRI forecast seems to be relatively dependable and significant for policy formulation. The SRI team diagnoses interrelated global problems, delineates various kinds of undesirable futures to which they could lead, traces these problems to obsolete cultural beliefs and values, and detects some of the basic changes needed to actualize preferable futures.

The Coming Transformation

How should we assess Harman's forecast of the coming transformation? Certainly his projected paradigm change is more speculative and subjectively conditioned than the FAR forecast that it seeks to use as a springboard. It is not at all clear that his forecast of an imminent, traumatic societal transformation is the most appropriate extension of the forecast derived from the previous use of FAR.

To provide an alternative to the unacceptable futures to which a continuation of contemporary trends and problems points, Harman both extrapolates a possible beginning trend and engages in normative forecasting. Despite its frugality, his transindustrial society promises to be far more desirable than the present crisis-prone state of affairs. Hence, his projected future, even if shown to be only partially feasible because of near-utopian aspects, would warrant significant changes in present policies and, therefore, deserves serious consideration.

Unlike many forecasters who either neglect revolutionary sociocultural changes or treat them superficially, Harman carefully investigates such historical changes in perception, beliefs, and operative values from a historical, comparative, civilizational perspective. He observes that the very success of action governed by cultural values can render them counterproductive and, therefore, outmoded. He also analyzes lead indicators of shifts in values. For instance, he recognizes that alienation and anomie can precipitate fundamental change. Thus his approach to revolutionary value change seems at least as sophisticated as that of any other futurist.

The Two Main Forces: How Strong?

Harman's tentative forecast is indeed enlightening but by no means immune to cogent criticism. His analysis of the outmoded character of the industrial-state paradigm and of the interrelated dilemmas that it engenders is more persuasive than his projection of imminent revolutionary change that results in either the dominance of a transcendentalist paradigm or societal collapse. The *push of the dilemmas* and the *pull of the emerging image of man*, the two main forces that stimulate the projected transformation, *seem insufficiently powerful* to bring about a momentous transformation that would pass through its most critical stage during the coming decade.

The likely change-inducing impact of the new image of man appears to be distinctly less than Harman suggests. At least at present in the United States, this full-blown image has proved to be attractive primarily to some members of upper-middle classes and upper classes. Many scientists oppose its transcendental aspects. Perhaps typical blue-collar workers are somewhat more amenable to these aspects. Yet such workers will probably continue to be influenced strongly by the "economic man" image, especially if the dilemmas apply the economic squeeze that Harman expects. Under such conditions, even the affluent, who previously took their wealth for granted, tend to upgrade economic priorities. We may, however, hope that the new image will influence policy makers' decisions significantly.

The dilemmas embody more revolutionary potential than does the emerging image of man, but even they seem unlikely to become critical enough during the coming decade to propel the momentous change that Harman envisions. His forecast hinges on the assumption of upsetting *encounters with planetary limits to growth during the next few years.* Such encounters could cause the dilemmas to become critical, thus dramatizing the need for drastic change.

Planetary Limits: How Proximate?

Our analysis of the growth controversy in the next two chapters furnishes evidence that the primary limits to growth at the present time are sociocultural rather than physical. They could be pushed back safely by appropriate changes in beliefs, values, goals, institutions, and policies. These changes, though substantial, need not be as extreme, unitary, or sudden as Harman's projected paradigm shift. Such nontechnological changes coupled with the development and use of suitable technologies could apparently make feasible a fairly large amount of sustainable selective economic growth on this planet. Harman's (1977b) crucial assumption that "energy and raw materials will never again be as plentiful and cheap" (p. 8) is questionable, at least in regard to the possibility of a plentiful future supply of economically feasible raw materials and energy.

Yet if no source of abundant, relatively nonpolluting, affordable energy is harnessed, industrial growth will need to be virtually stabilized, perhaps early in the next century. Then frugal transindustrial society would become a mandatory goal. Unless energy conservation and slower rates of selective industrial growth become policy goals soon, the transition would probably be unnecessarily disruptive. Hence, Harman's concept of transindustrial society is relevant to current policy making.

Our conclusions about the growth controversy, submitted at this point as a promissory note, indicate that:

Planetary limits to growth are more distant than Harman intimates;
The dilemmas will probably induce considerable turbulence without precipitating Harman's "coming transformation" during the next decade or two; and
A number of possible futures that Harman fails to focus upon come into play.

More likely than any of his three extreme alternative futures are futures that are intermediate between them. This does not mean that revolutionary sociocultural change will not occur, for fundamental change appears necessary for reaching a desirable world future. Yet Harman probably exaggerates the imminence of large-scale revolutionary change and perhaps its likely magnitude.

A Depression in the 1980s?

Although planetary limits to growth are more remote than Harman's analysis suggests, sociocultural constraints pose the threat of a recession or even a major depression in the United States and the world during the 1980s. We will briefly consider forecasts of such a depression, because it might afford an opportunity for a turbulent transition to Harman's transindustrial society.

Jay Forrester (1978) of MIT reports that his System Dynamics National Model, a computerized econometric model of the U.S. economy, confirms the existence of a long-term (45-to-60-year) cycle in the economy. This controversial Kondratieff cycle or wave, named after the Soviet economist who claimed to detect it in the history of industrialized Western nations, manifests itself as a massive expansion of the capital sectors followed by a relatively rapid collapse in their output.

According to Forrester, forces arising from this cycle seem to explain the great depressions of the 1830s, 1800s, and 1930s. Today's economic conditions—a decline in capital investment, rising unemployment, a leveling out of labor productivity, and decreased innovation—resemble those at the peak of a long-wave cycle. Hence Forrester expects a sharp economic downturn in the near future. This depression, he contends, will correct such systemic imbalances as excessive debt and will prepare the way for major technological change and the restructuring of society (Forrester 1978).

Similarly, A. Ehud Levy-Pascal (1976) has constructed an economic model that supports the existence of the Kondratieff cycle and projects an imminent economic slump. The increased interconnectedness of the international economic system, facilitated by improved transportation and communication, has produced a high degree of synchronization in the economies of highly industrialized nations. This synchronization is evident in simultaneous recession, unemployment, inflation, and decline of popular support of government.

International interconnectedness raises the probability that economic decline will be widespread (1976). Levy-Pascal argues that the rising price of energy appears to be the main force driving industrialized countries to the brink of the Kondratieff cycle's descent (1979, p. 479). He warns that a depressionary landslide could easily give rise to political and social upheavals (pp. 479–80).

Edward Cornish (1979), president of the World Future Society, declares: "My investigation of the possibility of a depression leaves me convinced that a depression during the 1980's is not only possible, but probable" (p. 376). He reached this conclusion on the basis of both the cyclical theory as set forth by Forrester, Levy-Pascal, and others and his analysis of several intertwined symptoms of the U.S. economy: (1) lack of liquidity, (2) heavy speculation in real estate, (3) major threats to the automobile, (4) the increasing cost of energy, (5) the high cost of labor and capital, and (6) the financial disorder brought about by the severance of the dollar's tie to gold (pp. 378, 379). These worsening symptoms lead him to believe that increasingly less shock to the stiffly, erratically functioning economy will be sufficient to touch off a chain reaction of slumping sales, bankruptcies, and layoffs, marking the start of the Second Great Depression in the United States (p. 379). This depression, which Cornish thinks will be worse in many ways than the first, would probably be transmitted quickly to most capitalist countries (pp. 379–80). A global depression during the 1980s, he notes, would probably amount to the biggest economic debacle in history. Such a depression would bring about a major turning point in many of the trends that have characterized the human enterprise since World War II (p. 381).

Some forecasters, such as Herman Kahn, regard a large-scale depression during the 1980s as quite unlikely. A number of economists who are less optimistic than Kahn expect inflation and recession but not a depression. The similarities between economic conditions today and those prior to the crash in 1929 are at least partially offset by differences, such as stricter limitations on speculation, greater government control of the economy, and increased knowledge of how to manipulate the economy to prevent another depression.

To argue the pros and cons of this debate would require an extended analysis that would take us too far afield from our evaluation of Harman's forecast of the coming transformation. Yet we can agree with Cornish that, regardless of whether a full-scale depression is likely during the present decade, it would be so disastrous that concerted efforts should be made to find ways of avoiding it and of reducing its severity if it occurs (Cornish 1979, p. 380). Harman's depiction of transindustrial society and his analysis of strategies for attaining it in the midst of turbulence might prove useful in mitigating a depression and reconstructing society. Yet there is certainly no guarantee that the rather weak "pull" of the emerging image of man would become sufficiently strong to pave the road to transindustrial society. The strength of this pull is related to the manner in which people perceive the dilemmas that beset the industrial state paradigm.

Types of Responses to the Dilemmas

The potential for revolutionary change depends not merely on worsening consequences of the dilemmas but also on how people perceive these dilemmas and their consequences. It is by no means clear that during the coming decade most leaders or citizens will interpret the dilemmas as intrinsic to the industrial-state paradigm and resolvable only by switching to a radically different dominant paradigm. Modification of selected premises of the industrial-state paradigm seems more probable in the near future than a rejection of the paradigm as a whole in favor of a transcendentalist paradigm. One suspects that some problems, but not others, can be alleviated in a more-or-less piecemeal fashion without touching off harmful consequences elsewhere in either the national or world systems.

For instance, the dangers of global nuclear war and extensive pollution across national boundaries call for comprehensive international agreements. Yet much pollution occurs within specific nations and can be alleviated by effective national and local policies. The research, development, and implementation of energy technologies for meeting long-term global energy needs in environmentally acceptable ways require extensive international cooperation. Nonetheless, achievement of an increased amount of energy independence in the short term decreases the likelihood of sharing a bad fortune and being held hostage. Although Herman Kahn carries to extremes his attack on the value of global interdependence and the necessity of solving problems in a global context by concerted global action, he recognizes that organic global interdependence would increase the likelihood that a dislocation anywhere would be a dislocation everywhere (Kahn, Brown, and Martel 1976b, p. 216).

Furthermore, Harman's analysis of these dilemmas, though quite persuasive, falls short of proving that the set can be ameliorated only by radical system change. The harnessing of abundant, affordable solar energy, for instance, could greatly diminish the ecological problems that exacerbate this set of dilemmas. Moreover, increasingly selective economic growth would enable us to reap the fruits of growth without becoming impaled by its thorns. Thus we could escape between the horns of the growth dilemma.

Nonetheless, the two types of adaptation just cited would require basic, though probably not radical, system change. More generally, O. W. Markley (1976) argues persuasively that successful responses to major crises typically involve restructured images and modes of system organization. Significant change in the industrial-state paradigm, or perhaps the adoption of a new paradigm, appears requisite for coping with today's interrelated societal dilemmas.

Suitability of the Emerging Paradigm

How suitable is the emerging paradigm for attracting the widespread support necessary to become a dominant societal paradigm? The paradigm is distinguished by its transcendentalist character. In the tradition of transcendentalists, in particular, and philosophical idealists, in general, Harman relegates conflicting claims and incompatibilities to various levels and regards them as resolved in their relations to the whole. More specifically, he argues that "the scientific explanation of the level of sensory experience in no way contradicts religious, philosophical, or poetic interpretations of suprasensory experience" but rather "is complementary to them" (1977a, p. 108). "A fundamental characteristic of the paradigm that may be emerging is the complementarity that the paradigm gives to such currently troublesome opposites as spirit/body, science/religion, and determinism/free will" (p. 108). Accordingly, a "post-transformation paradigm" may be characterized by use of differing, noncontradictory "levels of explanation" for physical, biological, mental, and spiritual reality (p. 108). Harman (1969) suggests that "the typical common-sense scientific point of view of reality will be considered to be a valid but partial view . . . others, such as certain religious or metaphysical views, will be considered . . . equally valid but more appropriate for certain areas of human experience" (p. 8). Today's preliminary evidence, he maintains, indicates that a new "science of subjective experience . . . will incorporate some way of referring to the subjective experience of a unity in all things" (p. 8).

To become a dominant social paradigm, this transcendentalist orientation would presumably have to prove highly successful in resolving disagreements. Assuming that disputants accepted the paradigm, they would find some of their disagreements obviated in the way that the automobile alleviated the problem of horse beating. But how likely are they to accept it? Would most disputants in real-world situations be willing to resolve crucial disagreements by making a theoretical distinction between different levels to which incompatible claims are assigned?

Among those likely to oppose the paradigm as incompatible with their outlooks are many conservative religious people, atheists, and scientists. Most scientists, for instance, would probably object to the paradigm's departure from a number of premises that the established scientific paradigm has promoted, including:

The only way one acquires knowledge is through his physical senses and possibly memory stored in the genes.

A person's mental activity cannot exert any direct effect on the physical world outside the organism, other than through the normal functioning of his psychomotor system.

The evolution of man and the universe has come about through purely physical causes that involve random mutations and natural selection.

The concept of "the free inner person" is a prescientific illusion.

The individual does not survive the death of the organism; or if he does, we can obtain no knowledge about it (1976, pp. 95, 96).

Harman maintains that research into consciousness and psychic phenomena has produced data that challenge these premises (p. 96). Regardless of the extent to which he is correct, one wonders whether the transcendentalist paradigm would be too divisive on important issues to establish a firm foundation for the conceptual reconstruction of industrial societies. Most scientists seem quite unlikely to welcome a "new knowledge paradigm" that would support such "drastic alterations in the nature of scientific inquiry, both in the subjects examined and the methods used" (p. 123). In short, obstacles to societal acceptance of the candidate paradigm are much more formidable than Harman appears willing to concede.

Thus the emerging paradigm would be distinctly less useful for resolving disputes than might appear at first sight. People who would refuse to accept its canons for dispute resolution would thereby reject it. Although the candidate paradigm may become quite popular among some groups, the question of whether it will become societally dominant is quite problematic.

A desirable long-range future may require widespread adherence to several universal principles of a planetary ecological ethic that would nonetheless allow for great diversity on nonglobal issues. Harman's preliminary formulation of some of the appropriate principles constitutes a significant contribution. However, it is far from obvious that his transcendentalist paradigm is the *only* appropriate paradigm or that acceptance of this single metaphysic-laden paradigm is *necessary* to secure sufficient agreement on global normative principles.

In view of our knowledge of differences among individuals, the prospects of attaining general agreement on a single metaphysic (even one as geared to reconciling differences as transcendentalism is) in the near future seem quite discouraging. Moreover, reeducation, though necessary, might not produce sufficient unanimity on appropriately revised premises. In fact, education frequently increases diversity of opinion. The harmonious unanimity dreamed of by some utopian writers never gets fully implemented in the real world of multitudinous diversities. Harman's approach seems almost to presuppose the creation of a new "man" out of differing "men."

Contemporary Value Change: How Unified and Decisive?

Is the candidate paradigm emerging rapidly and decisively in a relatively unified form? Harman's analyses tend to center attention on those aspects of contemporary change that harmonize with his conception of appropriate changes and to overlook or minimize the rest. However, many recent normative changes have hardly furthered the tolerance and universal syncretism of a transcendentalist paradigm. Some of these changes, such as "do your own thing" carried to an extreme, seem more likely to exacerbate problems than to offer solutions to them. Furthermore, some of the inappropriate changes have interfered with the appropriate ones.

A hallmark of many contemporary dissenters from established cultural beliefs and values is dissent among themselves rather than the reconciliation of differences that a transcendentalist movement would be likely to promote. The establishment's normative orientation in the United States has recently been opposed by alternate sets of value priorities: those of political radicals (for instance, SDS members), cultural dropouts (hippies), crusaders for racial equality (Black Panthers), and advocates of radical religious reform (Jesus freaks), among others. Although we can discern certain agreements among these sets of value-priorities, the disagreements are in many cases enormous. The frequently observed inability of dissenting groups to work together offers convincing evidence of the mutual incompatibility of directives that flow from clashing sets of priorities. Even within such a movement as the SDS, pronounced disagreements concerning the relative priorities assigned to democratic participation versus efficient hierarchical control, as well as to freedom versus equality, produced splits.

Still, recent dissent is by no means totally fragmented. A number of groups, such as the Sierra Club and Common Cause, have been able to ally themselves with each other's causes. Particularly among many environmentalists, substantial areas of agreement have provided a basis for unified efforts to make specific reforms. Harman points to Marilyn Ferguson's (1980) claim that a leaderless but powerful network in the United States is now working from the inside to bring about radical change that would humanize institutions. This network, she argues, is composed of many small, nonhierarchical groups sharing an array of goals, the accomplishment of which would transform every aspect of contemporary life. She maintains that these linked groups, which have arisen from a turnabout in the consciousness of individuals, have come to constitute a benign "Aquarian Conspiracy" that has triggered the most radical cultural realignment in history. Although she appears to exaggerate the current power and unanimity of this network, it does exist and might become a potent force for constructive change. The question of whether mutually helpful groups will become dominant among dissenters and sufficiently influential to propel the movement toward a new societal paradigm is more problematic than Harman's forecast suggests.

The supposed unity of current value change may be no more real than the supposed unity of Kahn's multifold trend. Regardless of whether the seeds of an appropriate reconstruction of cultural premises have been sown, Harman bypasses problems engendered by the great differences among many of the normative systems that have emerged as challenges to the establishment orientation. In short, the evidence that a new transcendentalist paradigm may be emerging rapidly and decisively is at best very ambiguous.

Emergence of a Holographic Paradigm?

A paradigm shift akin to, but not identical with, that envisioned by Harman may be in the offing. Karl Pribram, head of the Neuropsychology Laboratories at Stanford University, has accumulated persuasive experimental evidence for his holographic theory of brain functioning (Pribram 1977).

In 1947 Dennis Gabor mathematically described a potential three-dimensional photography, namely, holography. The construction of holograms, achieved in 1965, awaited the discovery of laser beams. A wave field of light scattered by an object is recorded by lensless photography on a plate as an interference pattern of swirls. Any piece of this pattern, or hologram, will reconstruct the three-dimensional image of the object when placed in a coherent light beam like a laser.

Adopting the hologram as a model for many brain processes, Pribram proposed that connections in the brain are not limited to the linear computer type but are also formed by paths traversed by light. Light waves are encoded to form a mental hologram, which can then be projected in a way that decodes, or deblurs, the image. Holographic information processing is by no means limited to the process of seeing. Hearing, tasting, smelling, and remembering depend on the brain's performing complicated mathematical calculations on the frequencies it receives. Though these mathematical processes bear little resemblance to the perceived world, they enable us to construct sense-perceptible objects out of frequencies or blurs (Ferguson 1978, p. 10).

A distribution pattern similar to a hologram explains how a specific memory is not localized but scattered over large areas of the brain. This illustrates how Pribram's theory, which is supported by extensive research, explains aspects of mental functioning that have baffled investigators.

Since the brain mathematically constructs the world of objects by interpreting frequencies, the question arises: Might the universe itself resemble a hologram, a realm of frequencies and potentialities underlying an illusion of concreteness? Might the blur of the hologram be more basic to the universe than the material things that the "lens" of our decoding process brings into focus? Physicist David Bohm, a former colleague of Einstein's and a professor at London University, considers the universe to be structured on the same general principles as the hologram (Bohm 1971). He regards the ordinary "unfolded" order that we see as a manifestation of the basically "enfolded" "holomovement," the flowing movement of which involves folding and unfolding (R. Weber 1978, p. 28). In short, the brain appears to be a hologram interpreting a holographic universe.

Pribram has synthesized his theory with Bohm's and has speculated on the following unifying metaphysical implications. Transcendental experiences that have yielded extraordinary insights suggest access to the frequency domain, the ultimate reality. Phenomena of altered states of consciousness, which reflect altered brain states, may result from a literal attunement to this reality. If individual brains are bits of a more encompassing hologram, they might have access under certain circumstances to all the information in this hologram. Coincidental occurrences that seem to have meaningful connectedness may result from the patterned, purposeful character of the frequency domain. If precognition, psychokinesis, telepathy, healing, and other psychic events are in a dimension transcending our ordinary notions of space and time, their occurrence, Pribram observes, presupposes no need for measurable energy to travel from here to there (Ferguson 1978, p. 12). Furthermore, a holographic model helps explain to mathematicians why the operations of their brains often faithfully describe the fundamental order of the universe they perceive. Mental properties may be the pervasive organizing principle of the universe, which includes the brain (Pribram 1978, p. 15).

Pribram, once a staunch behaviorist, believes that we are in the middle of a paradigm shift that embraces all of science. Willis Harman, however, is not convinced that the shift is sufficiently basic. He objects to the holographic interpretation of consciousness in terms of something else that is ultimately quantifiable. Holographic theories, he maintains, are not yet the new science that treats consciousness more as a cuase than as an effect to be explained away (Harman 1978, p. 97). He claims that the correspondence between various states and contents of consciousness—the primary data of experience—and aspects of the physical brain is only partial (Harman 1979, p. 15). Extrasensory perception furnishes evidence that mind is spatially and temporally extended and is ultimately predominant over the physical. Moreover, minds are joined, as indicated by recent research on telepathic communication. Such conclusions lead Harman to regard holographic theory as an extension of the present paradigm, instead of an additional, complementary paradigm in which consciousness is the primary focus. To seek this complementary paradigm is to take what he views as the preferable path open to science as a social institution exerting profound effects upon human affairs (pp. 75, 76).

Since an adequate assessment of Pribram's holographic model and Harman's alternative would require extensive argumentation, I will confine myself to a few brief observations. Pribram, and to a somewhat lesser extent Bohm, has made a credible case for some of the basic features of a holographic model. The experimental evidence supporting holographic characteristics of brain functioning appears to warrant fundamental changes in psychology and related disciplines. Moreover, the consequences for both physical science and everyday life are significant and might prove to be profound. Most, but not all, physicists today are less inclined to accept a holographic or holonomic model than to search for fundamental building blocks of matter. The eventual outcome of disagreements among them remains rather conjectural. So does the extent to which extra-sensory phenomena can be corroborated. By apparently authenticating the in-sightfulness of experiences of oneness with the universe, holographic theory at least begins to bridge the gaps between scientist and mystic and between Wester-ner and Easterner. "In the holographic domain," Pribram (1978) writes, "each organism represents in some manner the universe, and each portion of the uni-verse represents in some manner the organisms within it" (p. 17). Yet even if holographic theory can integrate science, philosophy, and religion, this capacity does not guarantee that extensive integration will occur in most people's con-scious experience and that the currently dominant societal paradigm will be re-placed by a holographic one.

Still problematic is the inference from holographic characteristics of men-tal processes to the conclusion that the brain is a hologram interpreting a holo-graphic universe. Such comprehensive holographic theory calls for much further development and testing.

One wonders whether all versions of holographic theory will be as anti-thetical to the causal efficacy of conscious processes as Harman assumes. Of course, Harman's claims need to be scrutinized as rigorously as the claims made by Pribram and Bohm.

Our excursion into holographic theory has underlined the great potential for scientific and societal change,* as well as the highly uncertain question of whether—and if so, how—such change will occur. Now we turn our attention to normative assumptions in Harman's forecast of the coming transformation.

Normative Assumptions

The normative differences that separate Harman's analysis of value change from Herman Kahn's analysis are striking.† Whereas Harman pins his hopes on

---

*Other candidates for paradigm change include Nobel laureat Ilya Prigogine's mathe-matical theory of "dissipative structures": Nonequilibrium structures that evolve to progres-sively higher levels of self-organization by drawing on larger structures, thus locally running contrary to the second law of thermodynamics (Prigogine, Allen, and Herman, 1977).

†At the White House Conference on the Industrial World Ahead (February 7-9, 1972), the opposing views of two principal speakers, Willis Harman and Herman Kahn, were juxta-posed in an interesting way. Harman's paper was entitled "Key Choices of the Next Two Decades (An Exploration of the Future)"; Kahn's, "The World of 1990." Whereas Harman (1970b) had argued that the United States "will never again unify around 'business as usual'" (p. 293), Kahn presented a business-as-usual surprise-free projection. Kahn (1972) felt justi-fied in making this forecast of a relatively continuous future because "the events which we associate with various kinds of protest movements and with the counterculture seem now to have more or less topped off," as have "many pollution-type issues" (p. 1).

the most promising aspects of contemporary youths' rejection of the establishment orientation, Kahn feeds his fears on the most threatening. Kahn opposes Harman's "New Reformation" with his "counterreformation." Kahn and B. Bruce-Briggs (1972) write:

> Apparently we today are viewing pronounced tendencies toward a *late sensate* culture, particularly in the culture area of Northwestern Europe (formerly Protestant Europe . . . and in overseas settlements . . .), which has a very pronounced tendency toward what critics would call cynical, nihilistic, superficial, transient, disillusioned and alienated forms of cultural expression and social behavior. However, there are also strong movements in the world to counteract this movement. . . . In . . . the United States, there is a strong possibility of a powerful "counter-reformation," which might halt the further movement toward a late sensate society, at least for a time, and may affect its details for a longer period [Pp. 10–11]

Kahn, who advocates what he terms the "squaring of America" as an antidote to late sensate tendencies, is no less ideologically based than Harman, whose outlook has been significantly shaped by Aldous Huxley's "perennial philosophy" and Abraham Maslow's "self-actualization" psychology. This underscores the need for thorough analyses of the ways in which normative assumptions have molded incompatible forecasts, of the extent to which the assumptions can be justified, and of the means by which unwarranted ones can be improved.

Moreover, forecasters had best state their crucial assumptions and provide evidence that substantiates them or at least shows them to be reasonable. Harman (1976) has recently described some of the subjectively important events that have shaped his perception, including his experiences with what came to be called the "human-potential movement" (pp. xii, xiii). This makes it easier to ferret out normative and descriptive elements in his forecasts.

Assumptions about Likelihood

In his admittedly tentative earlier works, Harman appears to have overestimated the likelihood that a new trend and normative planning would lead to his preferred future. Should one really assume that there is "an inexorable quality to the driving force such that it probably could not be fundamentally diverted or stopped by anything less than an extremely repressive counterattack? (1970b, p. 285).

Although Kahn does not deny breaks with the past, he believes that Harman "overemphasizes many aspects of these changes" (p. 8). Kahn states: "I emphasize that there will be enormous continuity—in some ways more continuity than change" (p. 4).

Because of the self-fulfilling character of policy-oriented forecasts, forecasters may subconsciously adjust estimated probability in favor of their preferred futures. Even though this may shape people's expectations in ways that actually increase the probability that these futures will occur, these increases are typically less than the forecasters' estimates. Thus implicitly normative forecasts can deceptively masquerade as objective exploratory forecasts. Whether Harman made such a subconscious adjustment, the normative and descriptive elements in his earlier forecasts are excessively blurred.

Harman now regards his preferred future as less likely than he did before. In *Changing Images of Man* (Markley 1974), which records the results of the major research effort of the Social Policy Research Center of SRI, Harman is responsible for this concluding paragraph:

> One last word. The general tone of this work has been optimistic, which is fitting since there does indeed appear to be a path—through a profound transformation of society, the dynamics for which may already be in place—to a situation where the present major dilemmas of the late-industrial era appear at least resolvable. That optimism, however, relates to the potentialities only. It should not be mistaken for optimism that industrial civilization will develop the requisite understanding, early enough, to enable it to navigate these troubled waters without nearly wrecking itself in the process. In hoping this, some of us would be less sanguine. [P. 258]

A Major Contribution

The shortcomings of Harman's forecast do not prevent it from significantly enhancing our understanding of possible futures. His analysis of outmoded premises and interrelated dilemmas, which in certain respects parallels Bell's (1976) latest analysis of societal disjunctions, discloses the growing incapacity of the industrial-state paradigm to steer us through the troubled waters to which it has led. As he points out, the similarity of current world predicaments to earlier predicaments that precipitated large-scale sociocultural revolutions is indeed striking. Even some of the successful revolutions aroused so much turmoil that they almost ruined the societies in which they occurred. Thus Harman's acknowledgement of the difficulties inherent in making a rapid transition to transindustrial society is quite realistic.

Although somewhat less persuasive, Harman's presentation of the substitute paradigm does set forth a possible path to a better world order. Without this kind of creative effort to extricate the human species from the entanglements of the world macroproblem, a bleak, if not disastrous, global future seems unavoidable. Conversely, imaginative, realistic navigation may enable our species to escape between the Scylla of the fundamental dilemma and the Charybdis of excessive control into the open sea of ecologically feasible self-realization. An expanded image of human potentialities coupled with increased attention to neglected nonmaterial values would make the journey more enriching as well as safer.

If our extended analysis of the growth controversy in the next two chapters is correct, Harman's coming transformation will probably not occur during the next decade or two. Planetary limits are unlikely to push the dilemmas to a revolutionary threshold this soon. Turbulent change, which will continue, has not yet foreclosed as many options as Harman seems to believe. This provides the human species with limited time to implement the substantial changes needed to avoid global disasters and to diminish the traumatic character of the shift toward an appropriate paradigm.

7

MEADOWS'S "LIMITS TO GROWTH"

The future comes like an unwelcomed guest.
Ella Higginson

THE MEADOWS FORECAST

More widely publicized than the forecasts of Brzezinski, Kahn and Wiener, Bell, or Harman is that of Dennis Meadows's international team. *The Limits to Growth* (1972), a lucid paperback by Donella H. Meadows, Dennis L. Meadows, Jørgen Randers, and William W. Behrens III, has been translated into 29 languages and has sold well over 2.5 million copies. It warns that growth-induced ecological catastrophes could easily inflict a death blow on our golden age of material abundance, the likes of which the world would probably never again attain. Meadows's call for the stabilization of global economic growth challenges the esteemed civilizational principle of growth, thereby fueling the fires of the growth controversy. Technological optimists, growth-oriented economists, and leaders of poor nations view the Meadows forecast as undermining the world's hope for material development; limits-to-growth pessimists, as confirming their suspicion that unanticipated ecological consequences of technologies threaten global disaster.

The Club of Rome, an informal international organization alarmed by the ominous direction of global trends, commissioned the Meadow's team to carry out Phase I of the club's "Project on the Predicament of Mankind" at MIT. With the help of British scientist Alexander King, Italian economist and businessman Aurelio Peccei founded the Club of Rome in 1968. The club takes its name from the city to which Peccei invited 30 experts and leaders from ten countries.

Adopting a systematic approach to interconnected global problems, Peccei (1969) discerned a "world *problematique*." The Club of Rome needed to construct a model to elucidate this *problematique* and ways of coping with it.

Accordingly, the club consulted with systems analyst Jay Forrester of MIT. On the basis of his experience, but without conducting empirical research, Forrester (1971) devised a global computer model, "World2," which identifies specific components of the *problematique* and their interrelationships. After evaluating the assumptions of World2, the Meadows team constructed the "World3" model. The assumptions and coefficient values of World3 were, unlike those of World2, tied to the professional literature. Although the team members did eliminate Forrester's "quality of life" variable and treated the "crowding" variable some-what differently, World3 differs from World2 more because of their additions than deletions. They examined in some detail the basic subsystems that form sectors of the world system and constructed several subsystem models. Admitting that World3 is imperfect, oversimplified, and unfinished, they view it as the best available model for understanding long-range problems.

The "System Dynamics" Method

Forrester and the Meadows team employed the "system dynamics" method of computer simulation, which Forrester and other analysts at MIT had devel-oped to clarify the ways in which complex systems operate. Underpinning this method is "the recognition that the structure of any system—the many circular, interlocking, sometimes time-delayed relationships among its components—is just as important in determining its behavior as the individual components them-selves" (Meadows et al. 1972). Focusing on the structure of causal relationships distinguishes system dynamics from forecasting techniques that are preoccupied with statistical data. By programming a computer to trace the complicated im-pacts of interdependence upon a component whose trend lines were formerly extrapolated independently, the system dynamics method can call attention to counterintuitive system breaks as well as to cumulative functions.

Intuitively obvious "solutions" to social problems are prone to get snared in one of several traps set by the character of complex systems:

- Attempts to mitigate one set of symptoms may modify system-behavior in ways that result in unpleasant consequences.
- Efforts to produce short-term improvement frequently contribute to long-term degradation of desirable conditions and objectives.
- Local goals of parts of a system often clash with goals of the system as a whole.
- Dependence on intuition frequently leads decision-makers to inter-vene at points in a system where little leverage exists and where ex-penditures of effort and money have minimal effect. [Forrester 1971, p. 18]

Forrester argues that his process of computer modeling combines the main strength of human mentality—its ability to perceive the surrounding world—with the elimination of its main weakness—its inability to estimate the dynamic consequences of the complex interaction of the components of a system with each other over a period of time. Moreover, assumptions of computer models, unlike the often fuzzy assumptions of mental models, must be stated clearly. This promotes better selections from the vast array of fragments contained in mental models. For such reasons, computer models can surpass mental models and ought to replace them as guides to decision making (p. 51). This rejection of reliance on intuition strikes at the heart of genius forecasting and the Delphi technique.

A computer model, which should explicitly and accurately state theorectical assumptions concerning the operation of a real system, consists of a set of descriptions that tell the computer how each part of the system appears to act. This set of mathematical equations represents the modeler's best effort to quantify and express in function form the complex interrelated economic, political, organizational, technological, psychosocial, and other forces that govern systems behavior. In short, a forecaster constructs a computer model by, first, analyzing a complex system into components and causal interdependencies among them and, then, employing experience to assign appropriate equations to these relationships (pp. 15, 20).

A forecaster can program a computer to manipulate a model in ways that simulate various actual or possible behaviors of a system. By assigning to the components or variables those values likely to be obtained under different public or private policies, a forecaster can seek to project the likely outcome of each policy. Thus in principle the causal analyses afforded by the system dynamics method can provide policy planners with valuable information about the consequences of alternative policy choices.

Critics of Forrester's advocacy of computed models are quick to assert that such models are often invalidated by the so-called GIGO effect: garbage in, garbage out. They also point out that what is counterintuitive for some policy makers is not so for others or for model builders, who are typically quite aware of the ways in which the models they are constructing will behave. These general objections do not score against any particular model unless they are derived from detailed, cogent analysis of the model in question.

Recognizing that the task of modeling the world is difficult, the Meadows team does not treat the various World3 projections as detailed descriptions of the sequential results of different policies. Rather, the projections illustrate potential outcomes of the behavior of the world system. Yet the team does use World3 to suggest, for instance, the overall results of certain new technologies, the creation of which would be dependent on research and development programs initiated and sustained by policy choices.

Meadows's "World3" Model

The World3 model was designed to calculate likely consequences of the continued exponential growth of five interrelated global trends: industrialization, population, depletion of nonrenewable natural resources, pollution, and food production (in relation to malnutrition). Deceptively rapid exponential growth, which progressively reduces the doubling time of a trend, occurs when a quantity continues to increase by a constant percentage of the whole, as compound interest does. "Positive feedback loops" produce exponential growth. In such a loop, an increase in any element will start a series of changes that increase the originally changed element even more. Conversely, a "negative feedback loop," in which a directional change in one element is propagated until that element is changed toward the opposite direction, tends to regulate growth and promote the stability of a system (Meadows et al. 1972, pp. 31, 35).

Two dominant positive feedback loops have produced exponential growth in the world system: the loops governing capital accumulation and population growth (see Figure 7.1). Their impact depends not merely on their levels and rates of growth but also on the levels and rates of the corresponding negative feedback loops of depreciation and mortality, as well as on their interconnections with the rest of the model (see Figure 7.2). Capital investment has exceeded depreciation, and births have surpassed deaths in number. Investment has led to increased industrial output and then returned to increase itself, thus causing the world's industrial capital stock to grow exponentially. Since the global gain around the birth loop has declined only slightly since the year 1650 and the gain around the death loop has declined dramatically, population has grown at superexponential rates.

As growth pushes elements of a system near the carrying capacity of the environment, negative feedback loops become stronger and threaten to terminate growth. It is this increasing strength of negative feedback loops that Meadows considers so portentous. In short, a battle rages on this finite planet between the *forces of growth* and the *limits to growth*.

Having isolated natural resources, a healthy environment, and food as necessary conditions for industrial and demographic growth, the Meadows team sought to discover how much growth the global system could support. The causes of Meadows's five primary trends not only *stimulate* growth but, in their interrelationships, ultimately *limit* it. Exponential industrial and population growth generate in their wake exponential increases in depletion of nonrenewable natural resources, pollution, and, at least eventually, malnutrition. Continuing growth of the latter three trends would ultimately reach levels at which it would stop the growth of the former two (see Figure 7.3).

The time lags in the feedback pattern present considerable danger of counterintuitive "overshoots" of sustainable levels of industrialization and population, followed by disastrous collapses (pp. 156, 157). Forecasters who have simply extrapolated trends without taking into account their causally reinforcing and inhibiting interrelations have overlooked this danger. Thus the dominant behavioral mode of World3 is caused by three basic assumptions about the population-capital system: rapid growth, environmental limits, and feedback de-

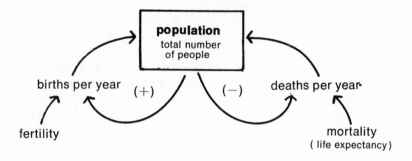

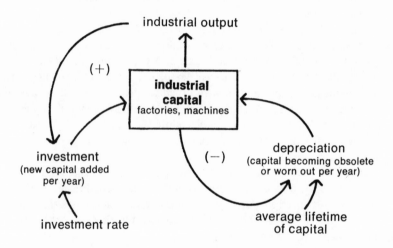

Figure 7.1. Population growth and capital growth feedback loops (Meadows et al. 1972, p. 95). (THE LIMITS TO GROWTH: *A Report for THE CLUB OF ROME'S Project on the Predicament of Mankind*, by Donella H. Meadows, Dennis L. Meadows, Jørgen Randers, William W. Behrens III. A Potomac Associates book published by Universe Books, New York, 1972, 1974. Graphics by Potomac Associates.)

lays (see Meadows et al. 1974, pp. 561–63, for a concise summary of the basic assumptions and conclusions of World3). Meadows and the coauthors of the team's technical report (1974) maintain:

A system that possesses these three characteristics—rapid growth, environmental limits, and feedback delays—is inherently unstable. Because the rapid growth persists while feedback signals that oppose it are delayed, the physical system can temporarily expand well beyond its ultimately sustainable limits. During this period of overshoot, the short-term efforts required to maintain the excess popula-

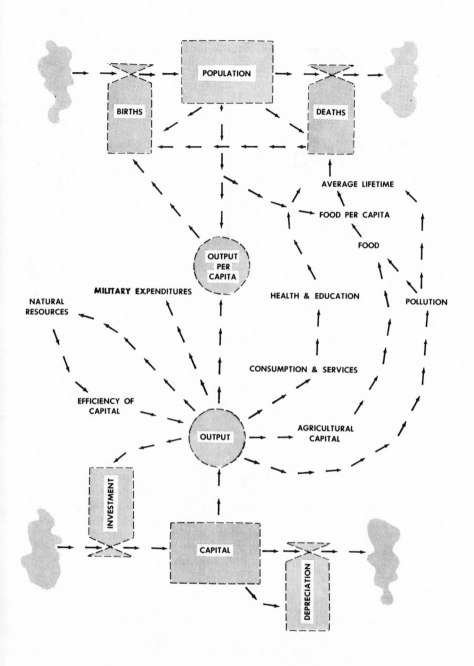

Figure 7.2. Basic interactions between population growth and capital accumulation (represented by horizontal rectangles) in Meadows's World3 model (Meadows 1971, p. 143). (Courtesy of THE FUTURIST, published by the World Future Society, 4916 St. Elmo Avenue, Washington, D.C. 20014.)

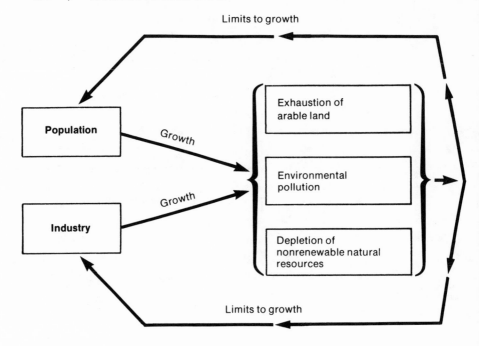

Figure 7.3. Simplified version of Meadows's World3 model, in which the global exponential growth of population and industrialization exhausts arable land, pollutes the environment, and depletes nonrenewable natural resources until these three derivative trends limit the growth of population and industrialization. (Constructed by the author.)

tion and capital are especially likely to erode or deplete the resource base. The environmental carrying capacity may be so diminished that it can support only a much smaller population and lower material standard of living than would have been possible before the overshoot. The result is an uncontrollable decline to lower levels of population and capital. [P. 562]

Results of Computer "Runs"

Since the Meadows team constructed the World3 model merely to clarify the directions toward which the world system is predisposed by the structure of its causal relationships, the computer runs do not constitute precise predictions that certain events will be triggered by a specific set of causes during a given year. Rather, the runs attempt to elucidate the basic tendencies of exponential growth and its limits during the next century. The exploratory runs of World3 turned out to be strikingly similar to those of Forrester's World2 model.

The Standard Run

The standard run assumes no major change in the physical, economic, and social relationships that have governed growth since 1900. Industrial output per capita, food per capita, and population grow exponentially until shortly after the year 2000, when a rapidly diminishing resource base causes the industrial output and food production to plummet downward. Soon afterward, pollution rises. Then population plunges (see Figure 7.4).

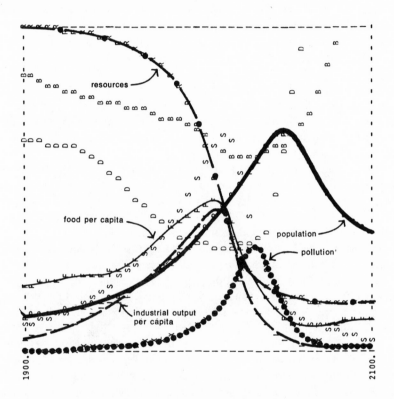

Figure 7.4. "Standard" run of Meadows's World3 model (Meadows et al. 1972, p. 124). (THE LIMITS TO GROWTH: *A Report for THE CLUB OF ROME'S Project on the Predicament of Mankind*, by Donella H. Meadows, Dennis L. Meadows, Jørgen Randers, William W. Behrens III. A Potomac Associates book published by Universe Books, New York, 1972, 1974. Graphics by Potomac Associates.)

Runs Assuming Technological Fixes

Repeatedly in the course of modern Western civilization, successful application of technological advances has pushed back limits to the growth of capital and population by weakening the restrictive negative feedback loops.

Could efforts to make significant technological changes in the present system promote continued global exponential growth without subsequent collapse? To answer this question, members of the Meadows team cumulatively introduced into World3 the four apparently feasible technological policies that seem best qualified to ensure such growth: "unlimited" resources, pollution controls, increased agricultural productivity, and "perfect" birth control (completely effective devices for optional use).

Team members investigated the consequences of technologically doubling the natural resource reserve assumed in the standard run. Indeed, industrialization reaches a higher level in this computer run. However, the enormous amount of pollution generated saturates the environmental pollution-absorption mechanisms, causing precipitous decline in the food supply, population, and industrial output. Even if "unlimited" nuclear energy would both double exploitable resources and make possible extensive recycling and resource substitution, a pollution crisis would still produce drastic reductions in food, industrial output, and population. Against technological optimists, the authors of *Limits* contend that unlimited resources fail to provide the key to sustainable growth in the world system (pp. 127, 132, 133).

What would happen if pollution controls were added? The Meadows team assumed that pollution generation per unit of industrial and agricultural output was reduced to one-fourth of its 1970 value. Industrial output per capita and population would rise to new heights, only to turn downward because of food shortages when all arable land had been cultivated (p. 137).

Suppose that technological progress, besides bestowing unlimited resources and pollution controls, would resolve food shortages by doubling the average land yield from 1975 on. Industrial output per capita would soar to prodigious heights. While each unit of production would generate less pollution, the total level would trigger an environmental crisis with accompanying reductions in food per capita and population (pp. 137, 138).

A model with unlimited resources, pollution controls, and fully effective birth control technology only averts collapse for an extra decade or two. This is because voluntary birth control unsupplemented by sufficient reductions in desired family size still yields an excessive amount of population growth. Decrease in food per capita occasions the crisis, in which pollution also plays a role (p. 139).

When unlimited resources, pollution controls, increased agricultural productivity, and perfect birth control devices are all simultaneously introduced into the model, the result is temporary achievement of a constant population with a global average income that nearly reaches the present U.S. level. Yet before the year 2100, industrial growth is halted, and the death rate rises as resources become depleted, pollution accumulates and food production decreases (p. 140). Hence, "even the most optimistic estimates of the benefits of technology in the model did not prevent the ultimate decline of population and industry and in fact did not in any case postpone the collapse beyond the year 2100" (p. 145). (See Figure 7.5.)

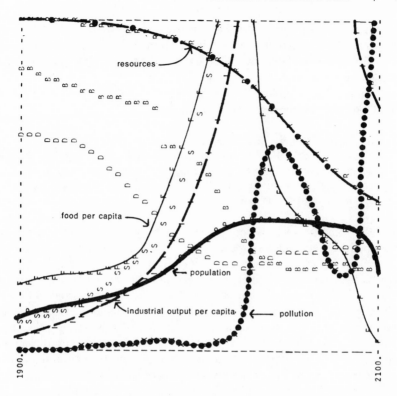

resources

food per capita

population

industrial output per capita

pollution

1900.

2100.

Figure 7.5. Run of the world model with "unlimited" resources, pollution controls, increased agricultural activity, and "perfect" birth control (Meadows et al. 1972, p. 127). (THE LIMITS TO GROWTH: *A Report for THE CLUB OF ROME'S Project on the Predicament of Mankind*, by Donella H. Meadows, Dennis L. Meadows, Jørgen Randers, William W. Behrens III. A Potomac Associates book published by Universe Books, New York, 1972, 1974. Graphics by Potomac Associates.)

Regardless of the many divergent forms that such a collapse might assume, "whatever fraction of the human population remained at the end of the process would have very little left with which to build a new society in any form we can now envision" (p. 170). This view of likely postcollapse situations is more persuasive than Jay Forrester's computer runs that show decided increases in the quality of life after collapses.

Basic Behavior of the World System

Though *purely technological strategies* can accelerate the rate of industrial and population growth and prolong their endurance, the Meadows team concluded, they *cannot prevent* subsequent *collapse* (pp. 140, 141). Moreover, such technologically induced extensions of the limits to growth in an overstressed system would construct an unstable superstructure that would be even more prone to sudden, precipitous decline. The closer the human race comes to growth limits, the less feasible technological solutions become. The Meadows team claims that these ultimate limits may be near.

Among the technological optimists quoted in *Limits* is R. Buckminster Fuller (1967), who triumphantly proclaims:

> Humanity's mystery of vast, inanimate, inexhaustible energy sources and the accelerated doing more with less of sea, air, and space technology has proven Malthus to be wrong. Comprehensive physical and economic success for humanity may now be accomplished in one-fourth of a century. [P. 48]

Yet if the Meadows team is correct, Thomas Malthus, the nineteenth century British political economist who issued dismal demographic predictions, has not been written out of the cosmic drama. Rather, he was temporarily upstaged in the West by a series of technological diversions that have vastly increased the amount of food that could be produced, distributed, and preserved to feed the swelling global population. The Meadows team contends that technological advance, until now so productive, may exhaust nonrenewable resources, generate a global pollution crisis, waste fertile soil, and increase population sufficiently to fulfill Malthus's ominous prophecy. Hence, Malthus may still reclaim the stage.

Whenever the World3 model was structured to assume either a continuation of present trends or any combination of feasible technological changes, computer runs suggested that the *basic behavioral mode* of the world system is *exponential growth of population and capital, followed by collapse*. The changing relation between planetary limits and human activities is rendering inappropriate the cultural principle that prescribes technological efforts to push back limits to growth. Such efforts have no impact on the essential problem, which is exponential growth in the finite and complex world system. Nonetheless, the Meadows team (1972) strongly believes that many technological developments—recycling, pollution control devices, contraceptives—will be absolutely vital to the future of human society, provided that they are combined with deliberate checks on growth (pp. 142, 145).

"Dynamic Global Equilibrium"

Members of the Meadows team regard a prolonged, unrestricted continuation of growth as impossible and a sudden, uncontrollable decline in capital and population as undesirable. Hence, they endorse the only other kind of alternative future that they deem possible: the difficult but worthwhile task of deliberately bringing a controlled end to growth. Accordingly, they formulated what is here regarded as a provisional catastrophist forecast that calls for extensive normative planning.

Equilibrium Runs

What evidence do the team members offer to support their contention that a no-growth world would avoid the disastrous consequences of uncontrolled growth? They revised the assumptions of World3 to reflect the rapid stabilization of population and industrial growth ("dynamic global equilibrium"), certain related technological innovations (such as recycling), and functionally beneficial value changes (for instance, keeping all input and output rates to a minimum) (pp. 156, 184). They found combinations of such assumptions for which computer runs show no collapse of industrialization and population. Rather, the runs indicate that the stabilized levels could be sustained long into the future in ways that would meet the basic material needs of all people. The sooner the world's people begin working to attain global equilibrium via a controlled, orderly transition, the better will be their chances of success (see Figure 7.6).

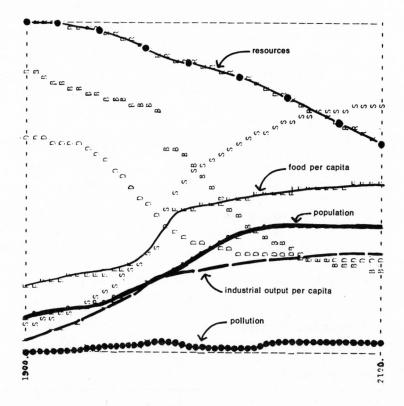

Figure 7.6. One stabilization run of World3 (Meadows et al. 1972, p. 168). (THE LIMITS TO GROWTH: *A Report for THE CLUB OF ROME'S Project on the Predicament of Mankind*, by Donella H. Meadows, Dennis L. Meadows, Jørgen Randers, William W. Behrens III. A Potomac Associates book published by Universe Books, New York, 1972, 1974. Graphics by Potomac Associates.)

One computer run was based on the following policies being enacted in 1975 unless otherwise specified:

Population stabilized and, in 1990, industrial capital stabilized;

Resource consumption per unit reduced to one-fourth its 1970 value;

Economic preferences shifted more toward the services (giving "desired" services per capita as a function of rising income);

Pollution generation per unit of industrial and agricultural output reduced to one-fourth of its 1970 value;

Capital diverted to produce sufficient food for all people, even if "uneconomic";

Highest priority assigned to soil enrichment and preservation; and

Average lifetime of industrial capital stock increased by better design and less obsolescence, thus enhancing the viability of a low final level of this stock (pp. 163, 164).

The run suggests that this set of policies could yield beneficial results for most people. The population, only slightly larger than that of 1970, has twice as much food per person and an average lifetime of 70 years. Services per capita have tripled. Even industrial output per capita substantially surpasses the present figure. The total average income per capita is approximately three times the present world average and half that of the United States today. Even though "resources are still being gradually depleted, as they must under any realistic assumption, . . the rate of depletion is so slow that there is time for technology and industry to adjust to changes in resource availability" (p. 166).

Since various societies might attain equilibrium by resolving the trade-offs differently, this run is intended to illustrate the levels of population and capital that are physically maintainable on the earth under the most optimistic assumptions. By modifying the unrealistic assumption that population and capital can be suddenly, absolutely stabilized, team members devised an equilibrium model in which capital and population are regulated within the natural delays of the system (pp. 166, 167). They assumed an average family size of two children, complete access to fully effective birth control, and an economic system that tries to keep average industrial output per capita around the 1975 level. The population level is much higher than in the previous run, while the industrial-output-per-capita level and the food-per-capita level are decidedly lower. Nevertheless, the last two levels are not only stable but higher than today.

Requirements for Equilibrium

To achieve and maintain the state of global equilibrium, the forces that tend to increase or decrease population population and capital need to be balanced carefully. Capital would be stabilized by reducing investment until it equals depreciation; population, by reducing births until they equal deaths (pp. 159, 162). This would weaken the two positive feedback loops that directly stimulate growth. Accordingly, two new links must be added to the global model: one to balance the positive and negative feedback loops in industry; the other, to balance the corresponding two loops in population.

A minimal set of three requirements characterizes the state of "dynamic global equilibrium": (1) constant size of the capital plant and the population; (2) minimum input and output rates of investment, depreciation, births, and deaths; and (3) adjustment of the levels of capital and population in a society and the ratio of the two (a trade-off relationship) to the values of that society (pp. 173, 174).

The minimization of input-output rates, and with it the rejection of gross national product as the chief criterion of economic success, would diminish both pollution and depletion of nonrenewable resources. Assigning paramount importance to the quality of stable capital stock and consumer goods rather than to the amount produced depends on a fundamental change in value-priorities.

Prospects for Increased Equality

Would dynamic global equilibrium destroy human freedom and perpetuate present inequalities? The authors of *Limits* argue that it need not. Within the requirements of global equilibrium, corporations could expand or fail, local populations could increase or decrease, and income could become more or less equally distributed. By revising the balance between its capital and population, a nation could alter its average standard of living. Inasmuch as only capital and population are held constant in the equilibrium state, any human activity could continue indefinitely, provided that it neither severely harmed the environment nor demanded a large flow of irreplaceable resources. Among the satisfying pursuits that could flourish are those of education, art, basic scientific research, music, religion, athletics, and social interactions. Emphasis would be placed on the services more than on industrial production. Because of technological progress, the services provided by a constant stock of capital could increase slowly (pp. 174, 175).

The authors claim that a society founded on equality is much more likely to evolve from global equilibrium than from the exponential growth that keeps widening the gap between rich and poor nations. Growth that led to a global collapse would produce scarcities, responses to which would probably exacerbate inequalities and restrict freedom. Conversely, the equilibrium state would remove two effective barriers to equality: lack of sufficient food and material production to maintain everyone at a subsistence level or higher and the promise promulgated by the myth that growth will lead to equality (pp. 178, 179).

The Meadows team recommends an egalitarian material standard of living for the world. To achieve this standard, massive international redistribution would be required. The United States would have to cut back to about half of its present standard.

Admittedly, there is no guarantee that the new society would be much better than, or even much different from, that which exists today. Yet "it seems possible . . . that a society released from struggling with the many problems caused by growth may have more energy and ingenuity available for other problems" (pp. 174, 175).

EVALUATION OF ASSUMPTIONS

The Forrester-Meadows forecasts generated a whole spectrum of responses: distressing perplexity, reactionary propheteering, reasoned defenses, caustic denunciations fathered by gut reactions, rational critiques, and revisions.* To explain the volume and intensity of the responses, we need to recognize that these forecasts challenge a fundamental principle of modern civilization: the principle encouraging indefinitely prolonged economic growth. Nothing short of drastic alteration of contemporary culture and institutions would prove efficacious for deliberately stabilizing growth.

Paradoxically, some of the critics of growth-oriented establishment values and lifeways are themselves certified pillars of the academic establishment. This is one reason why the growth controversy rapidly spread to include business and government opinion leaders.

Typical representatives of poor nations interpreted the proposal to limit growth as a subtle scheme by the world's wealthy nations to perpetually keep the Third World at subsistence standards of living. Despite the egalitarian recommendations made by the Meadows team, spokesmen for these nations at the United Nations Conference on the Human Environment (Stockholm, 1972) responded as if they were being bludgeoned by the Club of Rome. Indeed, Forrester's version of global equilibrium, based on his preferred computer run of World2, would decrease world food production and preserve gross inequalities between nations.

Whereas heated passion rather than cool reason served as a hallmark of the initial stage of the growth controversy, the more recent responses to the Forrester-Meadows forecasts tend to be less extreme, more objective, though no less vigorous. Let us see what cogent objections we can winnow from the chaff of emotion-laden misunderstandings. Most of the objections apply to Forrester's World2 as well as to the *Limits* version of World3 and also to the moderately

---

*For instance, the scathing reviews of *The Limits to Growth, Urban Dynamics*, and *World Dynamics* by economists Peter Passell, Marc Roberts, and Leonard Ross (*New York Times Book Review*, April 2, 1972) were answered by "a record outpouring of letters . . . pro and con" (July 30, 1972). Somewhat better reasoned is Burnham Beckwith's "The Predicament of Man? A Reply," written to answer three articles printed in the August 1971 issue of *Futurist* and accompanied by Dennis Meadows's "Response" (*Futurist*, April 1972). For an enlightening exchange between the University of Sussex group and Meadows, see Cole et al. 1973.

revised World3 of the teams' technical report (1974). Since many of these criticisms are so integral to the growth controversy; our extended analysis of them amounts to an evaluation of this controversy.

Goal and Procedure of Model Building

By ascertaining ways in which justifiable criticism of the World2 and World3 models may proceed, we will construct a framework within which to integrate and assess specific objections. We must take into account the primary explicit goal of Forrester and the Meadows team: to benefit decision makers by constructing models that adequately reflect the basic structural dynamics of the real world. The term *adequately* should be defined pragmatically in reference to those questions about the world's behavior for which answers are sought. Since Forrester and the Meadows team designed their models to provide an improved basis for framing policies that relate to economic and demographic growth, the degree to which these models are adequate must be judged in terms of this practical goal.

Obviously, the world is an extremely complex system in which a host of forces interact. Our understanding of the operation of many of these forces is still quite primitive. Not only are dominant causes hard to isolate but the qualitative character of some of them makes them hard to measure. Yet we would not be justified in a cavalier dismissal of the World2 and World3 models. A model of how the world works need not be perfect to fulfill its practical function.

The Forrester-Meadows computer runs do not pretend to predict accurately. Rather, the models purport to encapsulate the approximate behavior of several interrelated forces in the world system. Accordingly, runs attempt to calculate *upper limits* to the amount of industrial and demographic growth that the global system can support, either if present trends continue or if these trends are altered by various kinds of human intervention. Hence, the adequacy of the models depends on whether they come close enough to achieving this specific aim to warrant adoption of their conclusions as guides to policy formulation. To show that these models are inadequate, any objection must furnish convincing evidence that they seriously fall short of their practical goal.

To build a global model on the basis of data, one must first isolate the few key forces or "state variables" on which the behavior of the world system seems primarily dependent. Then one must measure the most important relationships among these dominant variables. Just as the behaivor of the resulting computer model stems basically from these dominant variables and their interrelations, so, we hope, the behavior of the world system is largely determined by a parallel structure. Especially crucial is the selection of all the dominant variables and only those. If Forrester and the Meadows team overlooked or misrepresented any such variables, they jeopardized their conclusions.

A model builder should accurately structure each of the dominant variables in regard to the causally relevant features both within it and between it and other variables. "Overaggregation" the insufficient differentiation of the variables—may render a model vague and unreliable. Accurate quantification of the levels of the dominant variables and of rates of flow between them (that is, the feedback loops) requires careful research in the real world.

Did Forrester and the Meadows team sample all relevant data, or was their selection somewhat hasty or unduly value laden? Did they interpret these data correctly, constructing models that:

Incorporate all and only the dominant variables that affect growth and its limits in the world system?

Accurately describe the growth structure and stabilization structure of each variable in terms of feedback loops?

Properly interrelate the variables in terms of the equations assigned to the causal links between variables in the feedback loops?

How warranted are the normative assumptions that underlie their general policy recommendations? Are these recommendations both feasible and preferable to alternatives? Can Forrester and the Meadows team justify their claim that, as guides to policy formulation, their computer models are superior to all competing verbal or mental models of long-term population and material growth? Although we cannot provide detailed answers to all these questions in the remainder of this chapter, we can marshal enough evidence to provide an overall evaluation of the Meadows model.

Importance of Assumptions

Boyd's Insertion of a Dominant Variable

Before Robert Boyd (University of California–Davis) and the Shell Oil group (the Netherlands) simultaneously published the results of computer runs of their models in 1972, critics of the Forrester-Meadows models had failed to substantiate their oft-voiced contention that substitution of technologically optimistic assumptions for the pessimistic assumptions of these models could generate computer runs showing extensive sustainable global economic growth.* Without commiting himself to the assumptions that ardent technological optimists make, Boyd sought to demonstrate that incorporation of their assumptions into World2 would yield runs indicative of the type of future that they envision. World3 ap-

---

*The Shell Oil model, more realistic than Boyd's model, indicated the possibility of safe, substantial industrial growth on the global level. Soon after the construction of these two models, Thomas Boyle (Lowell Conservatory, Flagstaff, Arizona) revised the Meadows model. According to the computer runs of Boyle's model, technological breakthroughs and appropriate policies could yield sizable industrial growth without a subsequent collapse.

pears to differ from World2 in no respect that would make his general conclusions inapplicable to it.

Boyd argues that technological optimists can reasonably object to the Forrester-Meadows decision to feed various technological assumptions into their models from outside, as it were, rather than treating science-based technology as an integral dominant variable in the world system. Forrester "invokes technology to, for example, reduce pollution output to some fixed fraction at some point in time . . . but this is hardly the constantly adjusting, powerful technology of the technological optimists" (Boyd 1972, p. 517). Hence, Boyd added a new state variable, technology (T), and multipliers to express the effects of technology on the other state variables. He also altered two questionable birthrate multipliers.

Boyd assumed that a sixfold increase in technology would produce an eightfold rise in the food ratio; a fourfold increase in technology, a decrease in both pollution output and natural resources input to zero (per unit material standard of living). The computer runs disclosed that "technology increases productivity, which . . . increases the material standard of living," which in turn "eventually drives birth rates low enough that a 'Utopian' equilibrium is reached" (pp. 517, 518).

Boyd's model makes simplistic, unrealistic assumptions about technological advance. Such factors as cost and lead time required for research, development, and implementation of technologies make these assumptions highly dubious. Yet certain later revisions of the Forrester-Meadows models, including that of the University of Sussex group in *Models of Doom*, show that plausible optimistic assumptions concerning technological growth can result in computer runs depicting much sustainable economic growth (Cole et al. 1973, pp. 516, 518).

Key Questions in the Growth Controversy

Since arguments that seem reasonable can be made by competent advocates of conflicting sets of assumptions, the Forrester-Meadows models cannot resolve the growth controversy. Boyd has centered attention on a crucial question in this controversy: *Which assumptions are more justifiable*: those of technological optimists, of limits-to-growth pessimists, or of forecasters who take intermediate positions?*

To serve as trustworthy aids to policy makers, computer models must have their assumptions justified. Otherwise, policy makers could be faced with equally plausible conflicting computer simulations corresponding to conflicting

---

*For an example of incompatible assumptions in the growth controversy, see "The Future of Man: Optimism vs. Pessimism" (*Futurist*, April 1972, pp. 62–66). The editor lists six points in terms of which he contrasts the technologically optimistic forecast of Burnham Beckwith with the technologically pessimistic forecast of Dennis Meadows (p. 55). Also, consult *The Next 200 Years* for an overview of four contrasting positions in the growth controversy (Kahn, Brown, and Martel 1976, pp. 9–20).

mental models. Yet the degree to which a model's assumptions can be justified should not be the sole criterion for evaluating its worth for policy formulation. When a forecast reveals a significant risk of unacceptable occurrences, it is *not* invalidated just because competing forecasts may be based on somewhat more justifiable assumptions and may have a better chance of being correct. To take an illustration from everyday life, a sensible family buys fire insurance and may install a smoke-detector, even though the probability of its house burning down is quite low. Thus a second crucial question arises in the growth controversy: Are projections of provisional ecological catastrophes *sufficiently plausible* to warrant major efforts to avoid them? Any adequate comparative evaluation of Meadows's pessimistic forecast and Herman Kahn's optimistic one (Kahn, Brown, and Martel 1976b) must be made in the light of both of these questions.

Since Boyd's technology variable assumes radical changes that reshape the trend of increasing industrialization, his model provides no evidence that a continuation of present trends (the standard run of the Forrester-Meadows models) would avoid global collapses of industry and population. Insofar as the standard run signals the danger of such collapses if decision makers fail to revise inappropriate policies, this run might promote policy revision. Nevertheless, the assumptions of the models still need to be justified if the dependability of the standard run is to be established. For these sets of assumptions to warrant action to avoid possible disaster, they must not be clearly mistaken in ways that would invalidate the projected collapses.

Forecasters who opt for much sustainable global growth are obliged to furnish convincing evidence that the World3 standard run greatly exaggerates the proximity of limits to growth or that major scientific-technological progress will probably stimulate extensive growth that will not be halted—as the other runs of World3 suggest—by the limits of resource depletion, environmental pollution, and inadequate food-producing capacity. Does the World3 model neglect or misrepresent important data and fail to encapsulate the basic dynamics of global growth? *Can full-fledged technological optimists justify their assumption that new technologies are likely to generate (1) abundant energy to obtain (2) plentiful raw materials and (3) produce sufficient amounts of food without (4) wrecking or dangerously altering the biosphere by pollution? Can they establish their other key assumption that these breakthroughs could be achieved in time to prevent disasters, would not cost too much for societies to afford, and could be implemented rapidly and effectively?* The last two questions focus attention on two crucial issues in the growth controversy: energy availability and the elasticity of sociocultural limits to growth. To sketch incomplete, but nonetheless warranted answers to these three questions in this chapter and the next, we begin by surveying the problems and prospects of the availability of natural resources (industrially important metals and energy sources), pollution control, and food production (see Jones 1977).*

---

*I provide a much more thorough, better-documented analysis of these ecological

Depletion of Industrially Important Metals

Prospects for Enhanced Availability

The Limits to Growth attaches much importance to the depletion of metals that provide raw materials for production. Easily accessible, high-grade reserves of many nonrenewable metallic ores are being, or already have been, quickly depleted. Understandably, analysts who consider only present usage rates and proved land reserves of relatively high-grade ores tend to conclude that the reserves of most of these metals—aluminum, chromium, copper, gold, tin, and so on—will be almost exhausted within a century. According to a Meadows table, derived from the U.S. Bureau of Mines, this would occur within 59 years (Meadows et al. 1972, pp. 56-60). A fivefold enlargement of these reserves would delay exhaustion for less than an additional 50 years. Another Meadows table estimates exhaustion of 18 important minerals within 150 years and of most of them within 100 years (Meadows et al. 1974, pp. 372, 373).

The problem of resource availability is, however, much more complicated. Although major increases in world resource use are likely, they might be substantially less than continually exponential during the next 50 or 100 years. Moreover, some of Meadows's estimates of known reserves are outdated and unduly conservative. In *The Next 200 Years* Kahn and his coauthors (1976b) note that Meadows's (1974) high figure for aluminum is based on a 1965 estimate of high-grade bauxite deposits (p. 90). The figure given in the 1973 U.S. Geological Survey publication (*U.S. Mineral Resources*) is more than twice as much. This later document argues that ten sources of aluminum other than bauxite provide the United States with virtually inexhaustible resources of aluminous material (see Table 7.1).

The seemingly generous Meadows figure of five times known reserves appears to be much too low for many of these metals. Further exploration has frequently expanded such reserves far beyond previous estimates (see Table 7.2). For instance, known reserves grew rapidly between 1950 and 1970, as illustrated by the 1,321 percent rise of estimated iron ore deposits. In large areas of the world, even the first few hundred feet of the earth's crust have not yet been well explored. Besides, exploration has shown that plentiful manganese nodules on the seabed contain nickel, copper, and many other metals.

Improved extraction and processing technologies that make feasible the economic use of lower-grade ores have also frequently enlarged the exploitable resource base. Recent developments suggest the likelihood of continued progress in this area.*

.

---

problems in "Current Prospects of Sustainable Economic Growth" (1977), sections of which I summarize here and revise to take into account developments since 1977.

*See pp. 37–38 of William Page's "The Non-Renewable Resource Sub-System" (Cole et al. 1973) for a summary of improvements in exploration, mining, and processing technology.

TABLE 7.1

Kahn's Adaptation of Meadows's Mineral Depletion Table

Resources	Average Annual Growth in Use (%)	Years Remaining Low	High
Aluminum	6.4	33	49
Chromium	2.6	115	137
Coal	4.1	118	132
Cobalt	1.5	90	132
Copper	4.6	27	46
Gold	4.1	6	17
Iron	1.8	154	n.a.
Lead	2.0	28	119
Manganese	2.9	106	123
Mercury	2.6	19	44
Molybdenum	4.5	65	92
Natural gas	4.7	19	58
Nickel	3.4	50	75
Petroleum	3.9	23	43
Platinum	3.8	41	49
Silver	2.7	15	23
Tin	1.1	62	92
Tungsten	2.5	27	n.a.
Zinc	2.9	76	115

Source: From Kahn, Brown and Martel 1976b, p. 89, adapted from Meadows et al. 1974, pp. 372–73. Adaptation from THE NEXT 200 YEARS by Herman Kahn, William Brown, and Leon Martel. Copyright © 1976 by Hudson Institute. By permission of William Morrow & Company; original reprinted from DYNAMICS OF GROWTH IN A FINITE WORLD by Dennis Meadows et al. by permission of The MIT Press, Cambridge, Massachusetts. © 1974 Wright-Allen Press.)

Eventually, huge additions to this resource base might be made by extracting minerals from higher-grade ordinary rock of the earth's crust, seawater, or heavenly bodies. As Gerald Feinberg (1972), a physicist, notes in his analysis of potentially available resources, all chemical elements exist in large quantities in the earth's crust. Although this crust is from 25 to 40 miles thick, typical mines today (excluding oil wells) descend not more than several hundred feet. Perhaps technological breakthroughs will make feasible extensive deep mining as well as the processing of both lower-grade ores and higher-grade common rocks to derive a spectrum of minerals. However, scientists and technologists can provide no guarantee that they will remove the present barriers of environmental impact and insufficient supply of affordable energy. The large-scale extraction of minerals from seawater is a further possibility. Another, which is plausible technologically but questionable economically, is the mining of the moon and asteroids for minerals. In Table 7.3, Kahn and his associates contrast Meadows's estimates of available land resources with estimates of ocean resources and resources in the earth's crust.*

Widespread recycling can enhance resource availability, as can the substitution of other metals or such synthetic materials as plastics for scarce metals. Industrialized countries could mine their large stocks of scrapped and relatively unused materials for new raw materials. Whereas the "recycle society" for which Glenn Seaborg (1975b) provides a working blueprint would recycle almost everything, World3 as presented in *Limits* allows for 75 percent recycling at most (Meadows et al. 1972, p. 140). Substitution, already practiced extensively, will assume increased importance. For instance, substitutes exist for each of the main uses of mercury, the extractable reserves of which may be practically exhausted in less than 50 years. The resource situation can be improved further by the manufacture of quality goods that last and by the development of technologies that do more with less resources.

TABLE 7.2

How Known Reserves Alter

Ore	Known Reserves in 1950 (1,000 Metric Tons)	Known Reserves in 1970 (1,000 Metric Tons)	Percentage Increase
Iron	19,000,000	251,000,000	1,321
Manganese	500,000	635,000	27
Chromite	100,000	775,000	675
Tungsten	1,903	1,328	− 30
Copper	100,000	279,000	179
Lead	40,000	86,000	115
Zinc	70,000	113,000	61
Tin	6,000	6,600	10
Bauxite	1,400,000	5,300,000	279
Potash	5,000,000	118,000,000	2,360
Phosphates	26,000,000	1,178,000,000	4,430
Oil	75,000,000	455,000,000	507

Source: From Kahn, Brown, and Martel 1976b, p. 92. (From THE NEXT 200 YEARS by Herman Kahn, William Brown, and Leon Martel. Copyright © 1976 by Hudson Institute. By permission of William Morrow & Company.)

---

*These estimates presuppose sufficient amounts of economically feasible energy for extraction and processing.

TABLE 7.3

Some Comparative Land and Sea Resources

	Land[a]	Ocean Nodules[b]	Sea Water[c]	Earth Crust[d]
Aluminum	3.6 billion	—	18 billion	80,000 trillion
Chromium	8.9 billion	—	80 million	110 trillion
Cobalt	11 million	3 billion	800 million	25 trillion
Copper	1.06 billion	3 billion	6 billion	63 trillion
Gold	50,000	—	8 million	3.5 billion
Iron	710 billion	130 billion	18 billion	58,000 trillion
Lead	1.8 billion	4 billion	60 million	12 trillion
Manganese	24 billion	160 billion	4 billion	1,300 trillion
Mercury	920,000	—	60 million	9 billion
Uranium	29 million[e]	—	6 billion	180 billion

[a]Dennis Meadows, *Dynamics of Growth in a Finite World.*

[b]Assumes 1 trillion tons recoverable ore. Uncertainties are large. But J. Mero estimates 1.6 trillion tons in the Pacific Ocean alone (John L. Mero, "Potential Economic Value of Ocean-Floor Manganese Nodule Deposits," in David R. Horn [ed.], *A Conference on Ferromanganese Deposits on the Ocean Floor* [Washington: The Office for the International Decade of Ocean Exploration, National Science Foundation, January 1972], p. 191).

[c]National Research Council, *Resources and Man* (San Francisco: W. H. Freeman, 1969).

[d]Upper layer only: 1 million trillion tons—about 4 percent of total (*U.S. Mineral Resources, 1973*).

[e]High estimate of U.S. resources at costs up to $100/lb.

Source: From Kahn, Brown, and Martel 1976b, p. 104. (From THE NEXT 200 YEARS by Herman Kahn, William Brown, and Leon Martel. Copyright © 1976 by Hudson Institute. By permission of William Morrow & Company.)

It seems quite probable that the potential availability of most metals is far greater than *Limits* suggests. On the basis of the conclusion drawn by Goeller and Wienberg (1975) from the U.S. Bureau of Mines data,* Kahn and his co-authors (1976b) maintain that more than 95 percent of the world metal demand is for five metals—iron, aluminum, silicon (a semimetal), magnesium, and titanium—that are inexhaustible (p. 101). The employment of advanced technologies and extensive recycling would probably make seven other metals inexhaustible. These are copper, zinc, manganese, chromium, lead, nickel, and tin. (This claim is questionable for lead, which is a relatively minor constituent of

---

*Goeller and Weinberg also emphasize the opportunities for resource substitution.

the earth's crust.) Granted the availability of sufficient amounts of relatively nonpolluting, reasonably priced energy, the long-term depletion problem focuses on metals that constitute less than 0.1 percent of the total demand by weight (p. 102).

Overaggregation of the Meadows Model

While *The Limits to Growth* and *Dynamics of Growth in a Finite World* do estimate the exhaustion of various minerals separately, the World3 model aggregates them into a 250-year global mineral supply at current consumption rates. As a given mineral becomes exhausted, World3 assumes, another can take its place until the overall mineral base becomes exhausted. World3 presupposes that the cost of exploiting remaining deposits and, hence, the cost of mineral substitution will undergo major increases. (For a summary of the World3 nonrenewable resources subsystem, see Page 1973, pp. 33–36.)

If distinctly limited resources constitute a unique, irreplaceable substance in a fixed, homogeneous reservoir, they cannot be extracted and consumed at exponential rates without soon undermining the industrial and demographic superstructure that has been erected upon them (Kahn 1972). However, the problems of the depletion of metallic ores, in particular, and of resource depletion, in general, are far too complex to treat accurately by lumping all resources together into World3's single resource variable. Hence, this variable needs to be differentiated extensively to account for updated estimates of proved reserves of each resource in various localities, increased efficiency in resource use, resource substitution, prices of raw materials, and the like. Indeed, long-range global models must omit irrelevant complexities; but disaggregation of the resource variable is by no means irrelevant, for it might suggest a significantly different type of answer to the questions about growth that World3 was designed to answer.

The Meadows team began this difficult task by developing and testing several disaggregated resource models. Yet the team's conclusion that disaggregation would not alter the behavior of the World3 model in fundamental ways can be traced to the dependence of their disaggregated models on data and assumptions that are subject to criticisms that we have already noted. Appropriate types of disaggregation would show that physical limits to extractable reserves of most metallic ores are much more remote than World3 suggests. Even in the most optimistic World3 computer run reported in *Limits*, resource reserves are only doubled by "unlimited nuclear power" (p. 140; also p. 132). Conversely, the Sussex team argues that a seemingly feasible sustained annual growth rate of 2.3 percent would increase in the static reserve index by a factor of ten over 100 years, thereby postponing the resource mode of collapse beyond the time horizons of World3 (Page, in Cole et al. 1973, p. 41). Furthermore, the operation of prices as allocators of diminishing resources renders the overshoot-collapse behavior of the model less likely. Rising prices generally stimulate efforts to expand supply, curtail consumption, or find an acceptable substitute.

The likely availability of much larger reserves than those estimated by the Meadows team makes World3's projected rise in the costs of supplying resources excessively steep. It can even be argued that such costs, as distinguished from artificially high prices set by cartels, might even remain roughly constant, as they have during the last 80 years. At any rate, an important feedback loop missing from the World3 resource subsystem is the effect of market conditions on the rate and direction of economically available reserves and on resource technology for increasing them.

Requirements for Availability

Thus World3's resource sybsystem, which especially influences the character of the computer runs, requires extensive revision. This casts serious doubt on the dependability of the runs, including the standard run, but does not force the conclusion that the problem of resource depletion can be safely ignored. The capacity of global reserves to meet foreseeable human needs for raw materials (see McHale and McHale 1975) provides no guarantee that sufficient supplies of metals will be made available. As easily accessible reserves of high-grade ores become depleted, unequally distributed locations of known reserves, higher prices, and limitations of current technologies will place added pressure on a number of metallic ores. Shortages and intensified international competition constitute a genuine threat.

Sustainable worldwide availability of the metals required for prolonged global industrial growth presupposes careful exploration aided by new technologies, development of improved extraction and processing technologies, enough reasonably priced energy to operate these technologies, adequate pollution control, and international access to reserves. One key question is whether a source of plentiful, environmentally acceptable, affordable energy will be harnessed. Another is whether institutional arrangements will be developed to manage resources in the interest of all peoples alive today as well as future generations.

Energy Resources and Technologies

Fossil Fuels

Within the time span of the World3 model, the depletion of nonrenewable energy resources—petroleum, natural gas, and uranium—poses an extremely serious problem that calls for immediate action. Yet *Limits*, written before the Arab oil crisis of 1973/74, places insufficient emphasis on the depletion of conventional fossil fuels and does not even list uranium in its resource table (pp. 56–59).

The energy-intensive global economy is heavily dependent upon petroleum. Hence, the imminent departure of the spectacular petroleum age will mark one of the major discontinuities in human history (see Figure 7.7). Assuming the relatively high estimate of 2,100 billion barrels of presently recoverable global

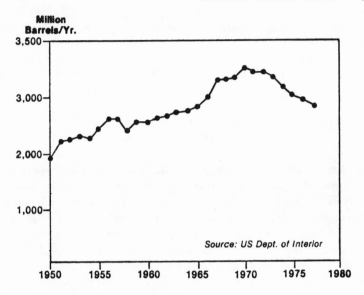

Figure 7.7. U.S. crude oil production, 1950–77 (L. Brown 1978, p. 103). (Courtesy of Worldwatch Institute.)

petroleum reserves, a continuation of petroleum production trends would cause world production to peak around the year 2000 and decline rapidly thereafter (Bethe 1976, p. 21). Already, U.S. production has dipped and the world price of petroleum has risen dramatically. The further problem of geopolitical accessibility arises from the location in the Middle East of 61 percent of the world's proved petroleum reserves that can be recovered by today's technologies.*

Even though coal could probably remain a major energy source until about the year 2300, it pollutes the air more than petroleum, costs more to extract and transport, and lacks as wide a range of uses. About 90 percent of currently exploitable deposits lie in the Soviet Union, North America, and China. While natural gas reserves are much harder to estimate, most experts think that competitively priced natural gas has distinctly less potential than coal as a future energy source.

The depletion of petroleum and natural gas makes mandatory:

The conservation of fossil fuels wherever feasible,
A transition to increased dependence on coal,

---

*Refer to Hubbert 1971; Surrey and Bromley, in Cole et al. 1973. For an analysis of the coal situation, consult Averitt (1973), pp. 133–42.

Increased use of "gasohol" (a mixture of oil and ethyl alcohol) in today's automobiles, and

Development of technologies to convert coal to synthetic gas and oil and to exploit such nonconventional hydrocarbons as heavy oil deposits, tar sands,
oil shales, and methane natural gas mixed with saltwater.

The extent to which technologies designed to accomplish these tasks will prove
to be both environmentally acceptable and economically feasible is still quite
conjectural.

At least for the next decade or two, the most promising fossil fuel technology is one overlooked by *Limits*: fuel emulsification. This simple, inexpensive
method of mixing typically immiscible substances such as coal, oil, and water
improves combustion thoroughness and reduces soot production. Additives that
remove sulfur dioxide make possible the emulsified use of high-sulfur coal that
cannot be burned safely in conventional systems. Moreover, an emulsion can be
tailored to existing boilers to avoid many problems of retrofitting. A low-cost
emulsifier for use in automobiles appears quite feasible. At current prices, savings
from using coal/oil/water emulsions as compared with oil may range from 13 to
37 percent. Since such emulsions burn less oil to produce an equivalent amount
of energy, they can both prolong the petroleum age and facilitate the switch to
extensive employment of coal (Dooher 1977; also see Essenhigh 1976).

New evidence, however, bids us take the presence of a fly in even the
emulsified ointment more seriously. Two reports by respected weather forecasters employing predictive atmospheric models conclude that average temperatures on the earth are likely to increase by up to 11 degrees Fahrenheit during
the coming century if fossil fuels, especially coal, are burned at growing rates
(Neustadtl 1977, p. 18). The National Academy of Sciences and Wallace C.
Broeckner of the Lamont Doherty Geological Observatory argue that such a
"greenhouse effect," induced by the carbon dioxide and water vapor released
when fossil fuels are burned, would begin to melt polar ice caps and raise sea
levels, decrease food production by moving agriculture to more acrid northern
soils, and change weather patterns in various ways. Although much further investigation should be conducted, these studies cast serious doubt on the advisability of recommending that fossil fuels constitute the predominant energy
source for large-scale industrial growth during the next few decades.

At any rate, fossil fuels can provide neither a geographically unrestricted
nor a long-term solution to the problem of energy supply. We urgently need new
energy technologies to fill the gap between reasonable demand for energy and
projected supply.

Uranium for Fission Reactors

Alarmed by diminishing reserves of conventional fossil fuels, higher prices,
and the threat of restricted geopolitical accessibility, many nations are turning to

nuclear fission reactors as an energy source. Consider, for instance, the energy projection for the United States that appears in Figure 7.8.

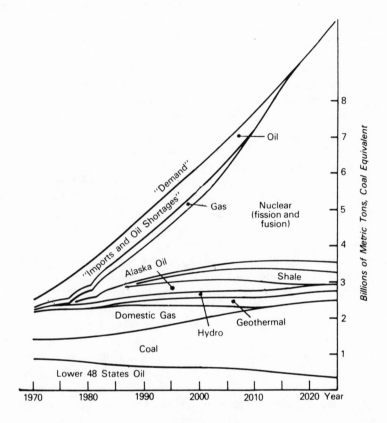

Figure 7.8. Energy supply distribution for nuclear option scenario. This graph gives projections made by the U.S. Atomic Energy Commission of energy demands in the United States from 1975 up to the year 2000 and how this demand could be met if the decision were made in favor of relying on nuclear energy production. By the year 2025 sole reliance on nuclear power would require more than 50 major nuclear installations, on the average, in every state of the union (Mesarovic and Pestel 1974, p. 133). (From MANKIND AT THE TURNING POINT by Mesarovic and Pestel. Copyright by Mihajlo Mesarovic and Edward Pestel. Reprinted by permission of the publisher, E. P. Dutton.)

However, unresolved safety problems beset the transportation of radioactive materials, the discard of highly toxic radioactive waste, and the supposed reliability of the Emergency Core Cooling System to prevent a disastrous reactor meltdown. Dangers stemming from inadequately trained personnel and, secondarily, from unsafe design were dramatized recently by the serious accident at Pennsylvania's Three Mile Island plant. The skyrocketing costs of nuclear plants are also putting a damper on plans for rapid implementation.

Projected shortages of uranium ore have stimulated efforts to develop and implement fuel reprocessing plants and fission "breeder reactors," so-called because they produce more plutonium fuel than they consume. Both technologies present extreme environmental dangers, for large amounts of plutonium would have to be kept from entering the biosphere for thousands of years and would also afford opportunity for the construction of inexpensive nuclear bombs.*

A somewhat more acceptable method of extending the life of the uranium supply (again, a technique neglected by *Limits*) is to shift from "light-water" reactors to "heavy-water" reactors. Then natural uranium, in which the concentration of fissionable U^{235} is only 0.7 percent, can be used as fuel instead of enriched uranium. Alternatively, a heavy-water reactor operated with enriched uranium and thorium added to convert into the separable isotope U^{233} would become a near-breeder, thus extending the uranium supply tenfold without encountering some of the major problems that plague the breeder. For instance, the enriched uranium-thorium reactor would produce even less plutonium than light-water reactors, and dilution of its fissionable U^{233} and thorium with enough nonfissionable U^{238} would prevent easy extraction for constructing nuclear weapons (Freiverson and Taylor 1976).

Like emulsification technology, heavy-water reactors, especially in the form of enriched uranium-thorium reactors, appear capable of making a major contribution to energy production during the next few decades. Such reactors might even serve as a keystone of a long-term solution to the energy problem. Yet this option could not be selected without making a Faustian bargain concerning safety problems. A global heavy-water reactor economy, contrary to the unfailing overshoot-collapse behavior of growth runs of the World3 model, not only would make possible much sustainable industrial growth but could also lead to a collapse precipitated by major accidents, the use of fissionable materials in war, or the undesirable consequences of eventually raising the temperature of the world's atmosphere. Thus the basic issue centers not on the *possibility* of such growth but rather on the *prospects* and *risks* of pursuing it. Because these risks are great, concerted efforts must be made to expand energy options. We need new energy technologies to generate large amounts of reasonably priced, relatively nonpolluting energy from sources other than conventional fossil fuels, uranium, and uranium isotopes.

Controlled Nuclear Fusion Reactors

The two leading candidates for generating plentiful, sufficiently clean energy are controlled nuclear fusion reactors and solar energy converters. Fusion

---

*For an overview of the problems of fission energy and ways of coping with them, consult *Nuclear Energy and National Policy* (1976). Of special interest is Alvin Weinberg's (1971) appraisal of the "Faustian bargain" made by opting for a fission economy.

differs from fission, which consists of splitting the nuclei of such heavy elements as uranium and plutonium to form lighter elements and free neutrons. Roughly speaking, fusion is the combination of two hydrogen nuclei to derive a single helium nucleus, a neutron, and a radiation loss of mass, which is converted into a large amount of energy. To achieve a fusion reaction, "heavy" hydrogen must be confined long enough at the proper density and at extremely high temperatures similar to those in the sun's interior.*

The fuel problems and environmental risks of fusion are far less than those of fission. One fusion fuel, deuterium, is abundant in seawater; the other, tritium, is derived from lithium. Although lithium deposits are somewhat limited, a fusion reactor can produce tritium at least to the extent that it is consumed. Tritium, which is not fissionable, is radioactive but not nearly as toxic or long-lived as plutonium. The walls of a fusion reactor would become radioactive, but this problem appears to be manageable. Furthermore, unexpected successes in generating extremely high temperatures have raised hopes of eventually achieving the deuterium-deuterium reaction, which, not even requiring tritium, might be harnessed to provide a virtually inexhaustible source of clean, abundant energy.

Researchers are improving various sorts of fusion devices, which fall into two broad categories: magnetic "bottles" and "inertial confinement" systems. The magnetic technology is closer to "break-even" power production, the point at which output of energy equals input. "Neutral beam injection," a new technology for firing a high energy beam into magnetically "bottled" (contained) "plasma" (hot ionized gas) to heat and enrich the plasma fuel, has made likely the production of break-even power by a magnetic reactor being constructed at Princeton University. The extent to which the break-even point may be surpassed remains unknown.

Demonstration of the technological feasibility of fusion power would provide no guarantee that the difficult tasks of engineering a reactor for commercial use and demonstrating its economic feasibility will be performed. Yet we may hope that the United States will begin commercial operation of a demonstration reactor by the mid-1990s. Extensive implementation on a worldwide scale would require several additional decades.

Inertia confinement refers to compressing or imploding a target by means, for instance, of lasers, electron beams, or heavy ion beams. In laser fusion, converging laser beams that form hot, dense plasmas implode hydrogen-containing fuel pellets. Commercial feasibility may be demonstrated during the coming century.

The beginning trend toward hybridization of fusion technologies promises to improve efficiency and decrease costs. A notable hybrid is Lawrence Livermore Laboratory's "Plasma Focus," which shoots an electron beam from a "gun"

---

*Rose and Feirtag (1976) present a balanced evaluation of the prospects for fusion power.

to create a magnetic containment field that induces fusion of the fuel pellet used in laser fusion.

Solar Energy Converters

Solar energy converters, another type of technology that *The Limits to Growth* neglects, draw on the renewable energy resource of sunlight. They pollute the environment less than any other energy source.* Unlike energy derived from fossil fuels, fission, and fusion, solar energy generated on the earth's surface would never raise the overall temperature of the earth's atmosphere (unless used extensively to heat things that release carbon dioxide). A temperature increase could touch off widespread climatic disturbances and eventually flood coastal cities by melting the Antarctic and Greenland icecaps. Such global thermal pollution may constitute the most intractable physical limit to the increasing use of fission, fusion, and, especially, fossil fuels, which emit carbon dioxide that gives the termperature an extra boost.

Expected decreases in the cost of the solar heating of buildings and increases in the cost of fossil fuels promise to make the former competitive for most of the United States within 40 or 50 years, if not sooner. An SRI project concluded that solar space heating is likely to dominate the market for new construction as soon as the year 2000 in those parts of the United States where alternative fuels are expensive (Reuyl et al. 1977, p. ix). Even now in sunny locations, government incentives can encourage investment in this renewable, clean form of energy. In *Energy Future: Report of the Energy Project at the Harvard Business School* (1979), coeditors Robert Stobaugh and Daniel Yergin conclude that the best hope for U.S. energy policy is to concentrate not only on using energy more efficiently but also on spreading low-technology solar energy faster.

In spite of the importance of the transition to solar heating and cooling, such energy consumption constitutes only about 10 percent of U.S. energy de-

---

*Amory Lovens (1977) explores solar and other "soft" energy technologies in some depth. Opposing the current U.S. "Hard Path" method of large-scale power systems dependent on exhaustible fuels, Lovens opts for the "Soft Path" that stresses diversity and smaller-scale investments in many relatively small components that operate on renewable resources. He argues that the soft path is less expensive in capital costs, has a better cash flow in delivered-energy price, and diminishes the chance of technical failure by spreading the risk among a wide range of relatively simple technologies that are known to work. Conversely, the failure of a huge, complex power station is like having an elephant die in the drawing room and needing to have another elephant handy to haul away the carcass. Among the available technologies that Lovens recommends are solar heating, wind pumps, and conversion of farm and forestry residues to liquid fuels. Although Lovens's soft path by itself appears incapable of meeting reasonable energy demand in a typical developed nation, it can meet a significant fraction of that demand and thus deserves adoption in conjunction with certain features of the hard path. The soft path is quite suitable for a typical developing nation.

mand. The large-scale conversion of solar energy into electric power is tech-nologically feasible but economically questionable. The various solar electricity technologies under investigation include:

Solar farms, on which hundreds of thousands of motor-driven mirrors would focus the sun's rays to produce high temperatures in a central solar furnace and boiler situated on top of a tower (Summers 1971);
Ocean thermal energy conversion plant ships that would first use sun-heated water on the ocean surface to boil ammonia at high pressure and drive turbines, and then would employ cold water pumped from the depths to re-liquify the exhaust gas and begin the cycle again (Schmidt 1976);
Photovoltaic cells, which convert the sun's rays directly into electric cur-rent (Murray and LaViolette 1977); and
Orbiting panels of cells that would convert solar energy into microwaves, which would be beamed to earth and converted to electricity (O'Neill 1975).

Ocean thermal energy conversion is particularly suited to the production of clean-burning hydrogen and, hence, to promoting the transition to an economy in which hydrogen would be the basic fuel for almost all purposes. The eco-nomic feasibility of photovoltaic cells, which can operate on any scale, would facilitate the decentralization of large-scale power production. This would in-crease energy independence, decrease vulnerability, and save the energy other-wise wasted by widespread transmission.

What about projected costs of solar electrical energy generation? Some experts seriously doubt that it can be made economically feasible, even in sunny areas near the equator (Pollard 1976). Sunlight is so diffuse that the solar thermal mirror technology, for instance, requires extremely large areas of costly collec-tion devices. Hans Bethe (1976) has estimated that solar electricity would be at least five times as expensive as nuclear energy. Yet other experts, such as John Holdren, argue that likely cost reduction in solar electric energy coupled with rising costs of coal and nuclear energy may make the former comparable in price by the 1990s. A study conducted by the International Institute for Applied Sys-tems Analysis indicates that substantial engineering advances, which seem feasible, would make possible a worldwide solar energy system serving over 10 billion people at the present per capita energy level of Western Europe. The transition to such a system would take at least a century (Weingart 1977). A 1977 Office of Technology Assessment report maintains that small solar equip-ment can probably supply electricity for between 5 and 15 cents per kilowatt hour, as compared with current residential rates of 3 to 4 cents. Hence, an in-crease in today's rates by a factor of 1.5 to 2.0 would make the solar alternative economically attractive.

Some of the solar technologies stand a better chance of becoming eco-nomically feasible than do others. Not only does the cost of orbital solar energy conversion appear to be downright prohibitive; such conversion, unlike its terrestrial counterpart, would add heat to the earth's atmosphere and is, therefore, limited by the heat-pollution ceiling. The cost of the mirror technology remains rather problematic, though such innovations as the construction of many modules of mirrors, each with its own tower, will probably reduce costs significantly. Perhaps the economic prospects of ocean thermal energy conversion and photovoltaic cells are better, though highly uncertain. Despite recent breakthroughs that promise sizable decreases in the costs of these technologies, solar electric energy may still be quite expensive. A question well worth asking is: At what price levels and during which periods of time could various regions switch to solar electric energy without excessively disrupting their economies. A recent SRI study suggests that by the year 2025 the United States could produce between a quarter and a third of its total energy by various types of solar energy generation, as shown in Figure 7.9.

Other Energy-Generating Technologies

Of special importance among other new energy technologies are geothermal wells, modern windmills, and bioconversion. Geothermal energy could be harnessed by drilling holes where there are hot rocks near the surface, piping down water that would return as steam, and using the steam to turn turbines for electric power generation. Since this technique might tap a renewable energy resource for large amounts of electric power, it deserves much further research. Still, a number of energy experts seriously question whether it could produce energy that is plentiful, safe, or inexpensive.

Wind energy possesses the advantages of being nonpolluting, inexhaustible, and capable of decentralized power generation. Its intermittance, like that of solar energy, creates problems of energy storage that raise costs. Modern types of windmills, which are radically different from those of the past, should be further developed and implemented to diminish the rate of use of exhaustible and polluting energy sources. Especially promising are new multivane wind generators, which tend to be stronger, more efficient, and cheaper than the three-or-four-vane models that have been in the spotlight. Even though estimates cover a fairly wide range, the total amount of energy that windmills can supply seems to be rather limited. Marshal Merriam (1977), who takes a rather optimistic view, maintains that wind power generators could eventually supply about 15 percent of the energy used in the United States today (pp. 28–39). This assumes that the energy grid could absorb all the power at the time it was produced.

Bioconversion, a supplementary energy source, converts organic matter into fuels or power by a number of processes. The use of dry organic wastes to generate power can also control pollution.

Other energy technologies, some of which are being researched today, may make significant contributions to energy generation. For instance, the possibility of emulsifying sewage sludge or plentiful wood oil to produce fuels deserves serious investigation.

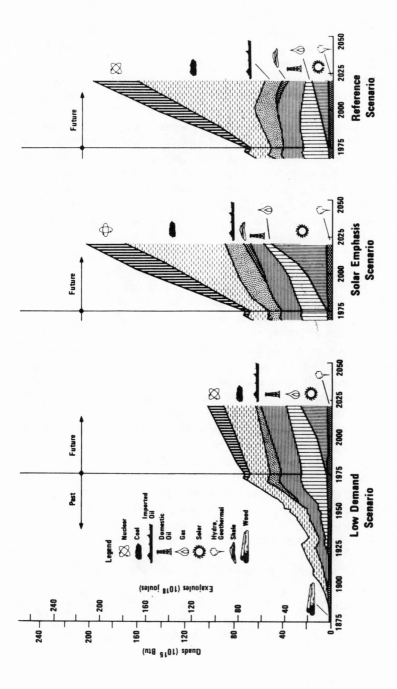

Figure 7.9. Three alternative energy futures projected by Stanford Research Institute's project, Solar Energy in America's Future (Reuyl et al. 1977, p. viii).

World Energy Outlook

Neither as bleak as the Meadows model suggests nor as bright as unbridled technological optimists maintain, the world energy outlook is fraught with highly uncertain promises and perils.* At least for the next two or three decades, during which reserves of conventional fossil fuels will dwindle and many of the new technologies will not yet be ready for full-scale implementation, energy demand will outstrip supply and the price of energy is quite likely to increase substantially. Energy conservation is mandatory, as is a mixed-energy economy consisting of a range of energy-generating technologies. In particular, we should implement coal/water/oil emulsification and low-technology solar energy conversion devices rapidly and extensively. To help bridge the gap between reasonable energy demand and supply, as well as to safeguard against the greenhouse effect from excessive dependence on coal, substantial implementation of the safer fission technologies will probably be needed (unless people generally become willing to make major reductions in demand and become much more conservation oriented). Among these technologies are heavy-water reactors operated with enriched uranium, thorium, and U^{238} but not breeder reactors or fuel reprocessing plants. Safety standards for fission technologies ought to be raised, in spite of the added expense. Such considerations may make advisable a temporary moratorium on the construction of U.S. nuclear plants as well as the closing down of a few existing ones.

Intensified efforts should be channeled toward improving solar electric energy conversion technologies and cutting their costs. In view of their ecological and social benefits, such technologies need to be implemented as soon as they become economically feasible, even if still somewhat more expensive than other energy sources. An unlikely but possible reduction in the cost of photovoltaic cells to commercially competitive levels during the next couple of decades would warrant crash programs geared to extensive implementation. Then fossil fuel and nuclear energy production could be gradually phased out.

Harnessing a source or combination of sources of abundant, clean, reasonably priced energy would resolve the long-range problem of energy shortages. Economically feasible solar electric energy would be much less polluting than the World3 model allows, could diminish shortages of raw materials instead of precipitating them, and would make possible a new stage of sustainable global industrial growth. Fusion could also promote such growth, assuming the likely manageability of radioactive pollution problems and the remoteness of an excessive warming of the earth's atmosphere.

If, conversely, plentiful, relatively nonpolluting, affordable energy turns out to be unattainable and a global heavy-water fission economy is deemed too risky, the human species will need to slow its industrial growth and then virtu-

---

*Overviews of the energy situation are provided by: Bethe 1976; Cook 1976; Hubbert 1971; Schmalz 1974; Seaborg 1975a.

ally stabilize it. This does not preclude substantial selective industrial growth oriented toward meeting basic human needs in poor countries, for such growth appears to be ecologically sustainable. In developed countries, some selective industrial growth employing energy-efficient, clean technologies that would not excessively diminish resources could probably continue. So could nonindustrial economic growth in the service sectors of the economy. Energy-efficient electronic information technology could facilitate such growth into a type of post-industrial society.

Thus the Meadows team need not have advocated the stabilization of economic growth. By aggregating the various forms of economic growth instead of adequately differentiating them, World3 ignores crucial distinctions among kinds of industrial growth and between industrial growth and nonindustrial economic growth. The types of growth that we must curtail for ecological reasons are only those that excessively deplete nonrenewable natural resources, dangerously pollute the environment, place undue strain on food-producing capacity, or have other consequences that are clearly undesirable ecologically. This leaves room for considerable sustainable selective economic growth regardless of whether the vision of abundant, relatively nonpolluting, affordable energy proves to be illusory.

Nonetheless, current energy policy should seek to minimize the economic dislocations that would result if such energy is not forthcoming. Planned reductions in industrial expansion can proceed much less traumatically than the involuntary reductions that have already begun. Even if abundant energy becomes available for extensive implementation in the next century, some energy shortages still appear unavoidable during the rest of this century. Hence, both long-term uncertainties and short-term supply problems make it advisable for developed countries to curtail some kinds of industrial growth and to reduce their overall growth rates somewhat.

Pollution Control

Types of Pollution

Environmental pollution is so integral to the problems of resource extraction and energy generation that a number of examples have already been mentioned. Among the many other kinds of pollution are:

Local "heat islands" arising from large-scale energy use, even if solar converters would constitute the major energy source;

Threatened impairment of the ability of the atmosphere's ozone layer to screen out much of the incoming carcinogenic ultraviolet radiation—thereby inducing major increases in skin cancers and genetic mutations in fetuses—caused by the discharge of fluorocarbons contained in aerosol sprays, large fleets of supersonic transport planes, or global nuclear war;

Automobile exhaust and emissions from industrial combustion as well as from the refinement and preparation of volatile chemicals; release of such toxic metals as lead, mercury, and cadmium into the atmosphere and waterways;

Industrial pollutants that now endanger phytoplankton, the microscopic plants that float on the ocean surface and interact with sunlight to produce one-fourth of the oxygen that human beings breathe;

Huge amounts of solid waste deposited on the ground or dumped into rivers, lakes, and oceans;

Accumulation of organic wastes in bodies of water in which circulation is minimal, thus decreasing oxygen concentration (to zero in parts of the Baltic Sea) and making it difficult or impossible for most forms of acquatic life to survive; and

Extensive disturbance of the preexisting environment by strip mining.

Meadows's Treatment of Pollution

The section on pollution in *Limits* (pp. 69-86), one of the better parts of the book, calls attention to the wide range of pollutants and to the general paucity of knowledge concerning them. The authors acknowledge that "we have almost no knowledge about where the upper limits to ... pollution growth curves may be" (p. 69). They perceive that natural delays in ecological processes (the extended time required for some pollutants to exert their full environmental impact) increase the likelihood that necessary control measures will be underestimated. For instance, a Randers-Meadows computer study (1971) indicated that, despite the assumption of a rapid decline in the world dichloro-diphenyl-trichloro-ethane (DDT) application rate beginning in 1970, the amount of DDT in fish would continue to rise for 11 years as DDT made its way to the oceans and passed through the food chain (p. 82).

In short, decision makers might fail to appreciate the seriousness of pollution problems until it was too late to prevent disasters by introducing remedial measures. Hence, World3's overshoot-collapse behavior, which is caused by delays in feedback, is more plausible for pollution than for nonrenewable metal resource depletion.

Limits's admission of lack of information about pollution presents a striking contrast to World3's pollution subsystem. The pronounced weakness of the data base that is relevant to the long-term, global consequences of pollution makes it extremely difficult, if not impossible, to construct a reliable computer subsystem. Yet the Meadows team felt obliged to insert this subsystem to make the model ecologically comprehensive.

The need to quantify and the emphasis on delays led to a decision to restrict the pollutants considered to physiologically measurable, persistent ones with an appearance delay of over a year. Thus the team excluded such important pollutants as sulfur dioxide.

As Marstrand and Sinclair maintain in *Models of Doom* (Cole et al. 1973), several of the assumptions of the pollution subsystem are vulnerable to objections (see pp. 80-89 for a list and an analysis of the key assumptions of the pollution subsystem of World3). For instance, the assumption that the generation of persistent pollution results from industrial and agricultural activities neglects pollution derived from consumer activities, including driving automobiles. Moreover, data fail to supply convincing evidence for the assumption that pollution will grow at the same rate as industrial and agricultural output. The recent English antipollution legislation, for instance, allowed production to increase while pollution decreased markedly (Cole et al. 1973, p. 86). The assumption that the upper bound of pollution is 25 times the 1970 level, though not asserted dogmatically and mitigated by computer runs made at higher levels, cannot be substantiated. Thus the exceptionally weak data base results in rather arbitrary assumptions.

Furthermore, serious problems arise from the decision to aggregate under the single concept of "pollution" a changing mix of divergent pollutants that exhibit a wide range of effects at different places and times. The notion of a composite trend triggering global disasters fails to do justice to this consideration. Disasters are more likely to strike locally or regionally as a result of a given pollutant or class of pollutants. Moreover, the numbers assigned to the trend of aggregate pollution are quite arbitrary in World3, as are the numbers adduced for its consequences of increased death rates and land infertility.

Other questionable assumptions of World3 concern the cost and efficacy of pollution abatement measures.

Cost and Potential Effectiveness of Pollution Control Measures

A number of analysts, including Lincoln Gordon (1976) of Resources for the Future, assert that World3 overestimates the cost of pollution control. Gordon argues that rich countries can attain reasonable protection against major health hazards and impairment of productivity at costs not exceeding 2 or 3 percent of the GNP (p. 5). Indeed, during the 1970s many industrialized countries have made significant progress toward controlling air and water pollution at affordable costs.

However, recent evidence suggests that the chemical contamination of biological systems is far more serious than previously recognized. *Consumer Health Product Hazards*, a scholarly volume published by The MIT Press, expresses concern that the proliferation of chemicals manufactured and used in mass consumption societies has proceeded without previous careful analysis of ways in which these chemicals interact to form compounds that induce harmful mutations and such degenerative diseases as cancer (Epstein and Grundy 1974). Medical authorities generally agree that between 60 and 90 percent of all human cancers stem from environmental causes. In particular, data disclose significant correlations between the output of the chemical industry and the incidence of cancer. Animal experiments furnish evidence that many chemical-laden consumer products, including nearly all commercial hair dyes, dispose human beings toward contracting cancers.

Toxic polychlorobiphenyls (PCB) have invaded a number of bodies of water in the United States. Recent studies suggest that the carcinogen asbestos now contaminates much of the nation's fresh water. Even the disease-controlling chlorine present in much drinking water apparently forms cancer-causing substances, as a report to the Environmental Protection Agency (EPA) by the National Research Council observes. Until an effective substitute is devised, refusal to use chlorine would raise the annual global total of some 10 million deaths directly attributable to waterborne intestinal diseases. (Actually, developing countries need much more chlorination, since about 70 percent of the world's population is still without safe, dependable fresh water.)

These few examples illustrate how biological contamination could decrease life expectancy and undermine the quality of life in mass consumption societies. This danger makes mandatory extensive research concerning, and control of, the production and release of polluting chemicals into the environment. Regulatory agencies should place restrictions on the marketing of products containing chemicals that have not been sufficiently tested for their environmental impacts. Although this transition will be difficult and expensive, it must be made.

Other appropriate measures would at least initially increase the cost of pollution abatement. One example is a shift toward the manufacture of long-lived quality products, thereby curtailing the pollution that stems from excessive numbers of quickly obsolescent items that are soon discarded. Another is the necessary increase in recycling. Recycling could be facilitated, Glenn Seaborg (1975b) observes, by building products with standardized, replaceable parts that can be easily repaired with basic tools. The coding and tagging of everything in regard to its material content would greatly decrease the cost of materials separation. Consumers could return old items for standard trade-in prices.

If enough affordable energy became available, plasmas (hot ionized gases) made at much lower temperatures than fusion plasmas might be used to recycle virtually all discarded material goods. A plasma torch would vaporize, dissociate, and ionize solid wastes in such a way as to permit the recovery of valuable elements and compounds for reuse (Gough and Eastland 1971). The economic feasibility of such a torch is questionable, and the heat disposal problem has not been resolved.

Also requisite is the willingness to replace dirty technologies with cleaner ones or at least to make the dirty ones safer and to forgo such dangerous technologies as the breeder reactor and nuclear fuel reprocessing plants. The safety of fission energy generation would be enhanced, for instance, by building new reactors underground and by improving the Emergency Core Cooling System and methods of radioactive waste disposal.

To promote the rapid, effective development of pollution control technologies and implementation of various strategies, the government needs to fund suitable programs and to enforce antipollution laws and taxes without exception. Government incentives can enable businesses to make expensive changes without fearing bankruptcy. Underpinning this overall effort should be comprehensive programs to monitor the levels of various pollutants and to investigate both long- and short-term dangers of projected increases.

The cost of the pollution abatement required to meet reasonable standards may run considerably more than 2 or 3 percent of the GNP of industrialized countries. Yet this does not justify the World3 assumption that societies aided by technological advance will be unable to afford a reduction of pollution below one-quarter of the present (1970) amount per unit produced (Meadows et al. 1972, pp. 136, 140). If, for instance, ultraclean solar electrical energy becomes reasonably priced, greater pollution reduction appears quite likely. The amount of selective industrial growth that such energy (and probably economic fusion energy as well) could promote without being halted by global pollution far exceeds the upper limit that World3 computes for industrial growth (pp. 136, 140).

Even if societies find that they cannot afford to decrease undifferentiated pollution below the Meadows estimate, control of the most dangerous kinds of pollutants by substantial expenditures on intelligently designed programs seems quite feasible. Thus World3, besides overestimating the likely cost, underestimates the potential effectiveness of pollution control measures. Overaggregation and questionable assumptions of the pollution subsystem of World3 conceal a wide range of alternative futures that could result from different pollutants, technologies, and policies.

In summary, pollution could precipitate disasters and limit industrial growth by rendering its environmental, social, and personal costs so exorbitant that societies would discontinue it. The level of growth at which this limit would prevail depends significantly on changeable sociocultural practices. Implementation of appropriate corrective measures would apparently permit substantial selective industrial growth accompanied by diminishing environmental deterioration.

Potential Food Production

Since food is essential for human survival and well-being, the need for an adequate supply of nutritious, equitably distributed food assumes paramount importance. Food production almost doubled from 1950 to 1975 while population increased by 59 percent. Nonetheless, food shortages continue to plague the contemporary world.* The authors of *Limits* observe:

> No one knows exactly how many of the world's people are inadequately nourished today, but there is general agreement that the

---

*For overviews of the world food situation, see Borgstrom 1973; L. Brown 1974, 1972; Eckholm 1976; Ehrlich, Ehrlich, and Holdren 1973; Kahn, Brown, and Martel 1976b; McHale and McHale 1975; Ward and DuBois 1972; T. Wilson 1974; Wittwer 1974.

number is large—perhaps 50 to 60 percent of the population of the less industrialized countries [estimated by the President's Scientific Advisory Panel on the World Food Supply, 1967], which means one-third of the population of the world. [P. 46]

Recent estimates include the following (Hughes and Mesarovich 1978, pp. 31, 32):

Between 600 and 759 million people were malnourished in 1976 (World Bank study).

355 million in Asia are malnourished (recent Asian Development Bank Survey).

One billion suffer from malnutrition, 400 million of which live on the edge of starvation; in India, 1 million children die of starvation each year (Jean Mayer 1976).

The global food situation worsened after *Limits* was written. World food stocks shrank from 105 days' consumption in 1961 to about a month's supply in 1975 (see Figure 7.10). Erratic weather conditions resulted in regional crop shortfalls, while shortages of higher-priced energy and petroleum-based nitrogen fertilizers intensified food production problems. Agricultural yields have begun to rise again, but the world fish catch, which increased from 21 to 70 million tons annually between 1950 and 1970, has shown no signs of returning to its exponential growth (see Figure 7.11).

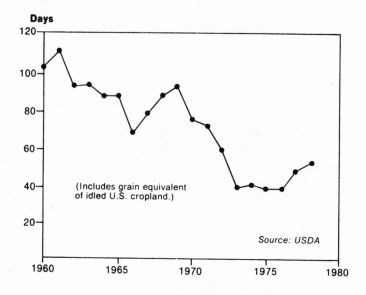

Figure 7.10. World grain reserves as days of World Consumption, 1960–78 (L. Brown 1978, p. 132). (Courtesy of Worldwatch Institute.)

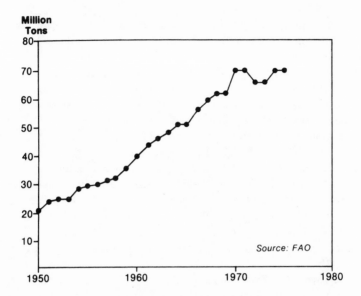

Figure 7.11. World fish catch, 1950–75 (L. Brown 1978, p. 19). (Courtesy of World-watch Institute.)

Some experts forecast increases in world food production of about 3 percent annually during the next several decades, compared with the current yearly population growth rate of about 1.8 or 1.9 percent. However, a continuation of gross inequalities of distribution and high levels of wastage would seriously restrict widespread availability of food. Accordingly, the Food and Agricultural Administration of the United Nations estimates that the world food deficit by 1985 appears likely to increase to approximately 76 million tons a year, which is close to the subsistence minimum of 400 million people. Hence we need to investigate possibilities of sustainably expanding food production, preservation, and distribution. We begin by considering criticisms that *Models of Doom* (Cole et al. 1973) levels against the agricultural subsystem of World3.

Diminishing Returns from Investment?

World3's agricultural subsystem, which assumes the possibility of major increases in world food production, displays more optimism about the potential food supply than the main section on food in *Limits* (pp. 46-54) might lead one to expect. Although computer runs assuming continued exponential growth show that the shortage of food could precipitate collapse, this does not occur in the most optimistic run until the world's population soars to about 20 billion people. Even then, the crucial cause of collapse is not the physical inability to raise more food but the diminishing returns of capital investment in agriculture.

In *Models of Doom*, Marstrand and Pavitt (Cole et al. 1973) question the claim that, in principle, diminishing returns would allow no higher level of food production than that set by World3 (pp. 56-65) (see pp. 56-58 for a summary of the key assumptions, structure, and behavior of World3's agricultural sub-system). The model's assumption that each major increase in food production will require a substantially greater increment of investment depends largely on other assumptions that it makes about the projected costs of developing arable land and of boosting land yields. World3 employs worldwide averages of arable land, development costs for new arable land, crop yields per unit of land, and costs of increasing yields. Marstrand and Pavitt contend that this process of world averaging produces excessively low estimates of affordable increases in land development and crop yields. This is because averaging assumes that invest-able resources will continue to be divided in the present suboptimal way among nations, instead of being concentrated in regions where the potential is highest and costs are lowest. As politically realistic as world averaging may be, it under-estimates the physically possible increase in agricultural output per unit input (pp. 59, 60).

Marstrand and Pavitt conclude that two plausible new assumptions—the technological progress in land development techniques and plant varieties and the rational worldwide use of agricultural resources—lead to sufficiently optimistic estimates of development costs and land yields to make any physical limits to agricultural production recede beyond the time horizon of the World3 model (p. 64). The factors relevant to large increases in the world food supply are, how-ever, more complex than either World3 or the Marstrand-Pavitt critique of it suggests.

Short-Term Prospects

Prospects of enlarging the food supply during the rest of this century depend principally upon *increasing crop yields on already cultivated land in developing regions* and on advances in the storage and distribution of food (Thomas Wilson 1974). Higher yields per unit of land can be achieved by such strategies as:

Use of the Green Revolution's new seeds of high-yield varieties of grain;
Employment of chemical fertilizers and pesticides, but with due concern for long-term pollution problems;
Annual multiple cropping in the tropics and subtropics;
Selection and widespread use of technologies appropriate to the basic needs of specific peoples in poor countries; emphasis on labor-intensive "intermediate" technologies to provide employment and make the problems of energy cost and pollution generation manageable (Schumacher 1973);
Development of new technologies and affordable types of currently expensive technologies;
Farming systems research, coupled with its application (Wittwer 1975);
Agricultural education of rural citizens in poor nations; and

Land redistribution in countries that have inequitable land ownership systems, thus increasing the motivation of farm workers.

By focusing on the first two strategies, neither the authors of *Limits* nor their Sussex critics present a comprehensive, balanced assessment.

Application of existing technologies to improve the storage and transportation of food could bring about major reductions in food wastage in developing countries. The loss of stored foodstuffs to rodents, insects, and birds in Asia is estimated at 40 percent. World3 bypasses the problem of wastage, as does the Marstrand-Pavitt critique.

Even more crucial is the problem of gross inequalities in distribution of the global food supply. Although the calorie and protein levels of global food production total more than twice the per capita requirements of the world's population (McHale and McHale 1975), undernutrition still prevails in many poor countries. Apart from the rise in food requirements springing from rapid population growth, the world food problem is basically one of distribution. Consider, for instance, the present dependence of the world on North American grain (see Table 7.4). The centrality of the distribution problem is not at all clear from the over-aggregated World3 model or from the Sussex critique.

Preference for beef in many developed countries illustrates how food production and distribution are skewed in favor of the rich. Animals consume as much as 90 percent of North American grain, but the meat that beef cattle supply amounts to only about one-seventh of the food they eat. Hence, a decision by North Americans to eat less meat while maintaining grain production levels could free much grain for export.

TABLE 7.4

The Changing Pattern of World Grain Trade[1]

Region	1934–38	1948–52	1960	1976[2]	
		(Million tons)			
North America	+ 5	+23	+39	+56	+94
Latin America	+ 9	+ 1	0	+ 4	− 3
Western Europe	−24	−22	−25	−30	−17
E. Europe and USSR	+ 5	—	0	0	−27
Africa	+ 1	0	− 2	− 5	−10
Asia	+ 2	− 6	−17	−37	−47
Australia and N.Z. +	+ 3	+ 3	+ 6	+12	+ 8

[1] Plus sign indicates net exports; minus sign, net imports.
[2] Preliminary estimates of fiscal year data.
Note: From L. Bown 1978, p. 135. (Courtesy of Worldwatch Institute.)
Source: Derived from FAO and USDA data and author's estimates.

Neglect of Limits and Agricultural Technologies

The Meadows presentation and the Sussex reply neglect additional forces that could limit agricultural food production as well as important technologies for increasing it. Such forces include a possible continuation of recent climatic aberrations, the threatened scarcity of reasonably priced fresh water for irrigation, and shortages of affordable energy for growing, transporting, processing, and storing food. If, for instance, the progressive cooling of the Northern Hemisphere continues (a trend that began around the middle of the century and has not yet been counteracted by a carbon dioxide greenhouse effect), climatic changes will make it more difficult to increase the world's soil-based food production. Moreover, irrigation water is already running low in many areas, especially where deforestation and overgrazing have led to the advance of deserts. (The seriousness of the freshwater problem is recognized in *Limits* but is not incorporated into World3 from which the forecast is primarily derived [pp. 52–54]). The rise in energy costs interferes with efforts to make extensive desalination of seawater economically feasible, to expand capital-intensive agriculture, and to transport huge amounts of grain over vast distances.

The extent to which such forces will restrict the food supply depends in part on the technologies employed. Yet neither the Meadows nor the Sussex team supplies a detailed analysis of the potential of present and prospective technologies for increasing food production. Despite their importance, the first three of the following technologies (Wittwer 1975) are not even mentioned in *Limits* or *Models of Doom*:

Minimal or zero-tilling expands the supply of arable land by making possible the cultivation of slopes of up to 15 percent gradient without significant erosion and with less use of energy and fresh water.

Drip or trickle irrigation, a veritable "Blue Revolution," supplies water to crops through plastic pipes with openings, thus using less than half as much water as traditional irrigation and being less expensive in its total costs.

Enhanced photosynthetic efficiency in carbon dioxide fixation by conventional crops could probably be accomplished by major research and development programs, thereby increasing yields.

Plant strains with a capacity for nitrogen fixation, a distinct possibility that warrants R&D programs, would relieve the pressure on supplies of nitrogen-based fertilizers, decrease the use of fossil fuels and pollution, and reduce costs.

Relatively inexpensive desalinization, which would probably become feasible if abundant affordable energy were harnessed, would make it possible to greatly expand the supply of arable land by farming deserts.

Neglected Soilless Technologies

Both the Meadows team and their Sussex critics devote insufficient attention to the long-range potential of feasible food-producing technologies that do not require arable land. Suppose that the extensive, widespread use of such technologies becomes economically feasible and socioculturally acceptable. This would circumvent the exhaustion of arable land, which constitutes the chief limit on which the agricultural subsection of World3 is based. Among the strategies for benefiting from existing and plausible soilless technologies are the following:

The large-scale processing of various species of fish, land animals, and plants that are not currently eaten into protein-rich, inexpensive powder;

Extensive production of modified natural foods, including relatively cheap high-protein meat substitutes made from soybeans, and the promising "single-cell protein" (grown either in a petroleum-based medium or by the conversion of cellulose [derived by recycling municipal and agricultural waste or from paper or wood] into glucose that microbes then transform into high-protein food) (Kahn, Brown, and Martel 1976b, pp. 132, 133);

Eventual mass production of various synthetic foods, provided that enough energy is available and that long-term research proves them to be nutritious and noncarcinogenic;

Further development of capital-intensive hydroponic farming, the technique of growing plants in tanks of water with chemicals added, with the hope that technological progress and cost reduction will someday make possible the production of large amounts of grain in desert areas (pp. 127–32);

Production of much reasonably priced, nutritious food by raising prolific algae in shallow artificial ponds and then converting them into a variety of foods acceptable to people of different cultures;

Development of fish farming in areas where nutrient-rich, deep ocean water is near the shore (accomplished by pumping this water into concrete pools to grow unialgal diatom cultures that are then introduced into fish tanks); and

Fishing for plentiful krill, a hitherto bypassed edible fish species in Antarctic waters—but only to the extent that this can be done without undermining the diet of whales.

The long lead times required for research and development, capital accumulation, production, and widespread implementation of new technologies make it unlikely that several of these strategies will have significant impact during the rest of this century. Within the constraints of what societies can afford, crash programs for processing various species into powder, modified natural foods (especially single-cell protein), and algae farming seem warranted. Krill could be fished in the near future.

Redesigning the World Food System

The level at which physical limits to feeding the world's population would assert themselves depends significantly on human ingenuity and practices. Societies could make such progress toward alleviating undernutrition by redesigning the global system of food production, storage and transportation, processing, and distribution (McHale and McHale 1975). The basic goal would be to supply, in a sustainable manner, *adequate amounts of nutritious food to undernourished people at prices they can afford.* To attain this goal, appropriate technologies need to be researched, developed, and implemented rapidly. Increased regional self-sufficiency in food production would cut the energy costs of transportation and reduce dependence on the energy-intensive agriculture of North America. For emergency use, a reliable world grain reserve should be established. Improved processing efficiency, some experts estimate, could diminish energy use by as much as 35 percent and waste and effluents by 80 percent; and it could increase processing yields by 5 to 20 percent (Wittwer 1975).

To bring about such changes quickly and effectively, powerful but elastic sociocultural limits to the global food supply must be stretched. Failure to make appropriate changes in institutions and policies would speed the human species toward premature encounters with physical limits to growth. Hence, any treatment of physical limits is incomplete unless it analyzes their interconnections with sociocultural limits. Neither the Meadows nor the Sussex team performed this task in detail, though the former calls attention to the need to do so.

A fog of uncertainty obscures detection of the precise stringency of physical limits, the feasibility of various technologies, and the extent to which sociocultural limits will be stretched. For all we know, world food production and distribution might unfold as any of a number of quite different alternative future histories.

Could optimum use of the world's food-producing capacities temporarily support nearly 20 billion people, as World3 suggests? Perhaps so, though such a high level could probably not be sustained unless plentiful, relatively clean, reasonably priced energy were harnessed. Even if such energy were to make possible the extensive implementation of desalination, hydroponic farming, synthetic food production, long-range transportation of the foodstuffs, and similar techniques for expanding the world's food supply, at some level physical limits would prevail against a growing population. Moreover, the sociocultural problems inherent in any attempt to feed 20 billion people well, or even to maintain them at the subsistence level, boggles the mind. To facilitate efforts to provide nourishing food for everyone, tandem efforts must be made to *stabilize the world's population at as low a level as is compatible with acceptable means.* Hence, Meadows's advocacy of global population stabilization is well-founded.

Overaggregation Again

Regional Disasters More Likely

From a perspective quite different from that of Marstrand and Pavill, Draper Kauffman has mentioned to me another facet of overaggregation that weakens World3. The model's overaggregation of food and of population creates the misleading impression that population would grow enormously before insufficient food applied a brake. More likely than this gigantic overshoot-massive-collapse mode of behavior is a series of increasingly common local and regional famines that hopscotch around the globe. Consequently, death rates would increase substantially in most of the areas that now have the highest population growth rates. This could induce lower birthrates and stimulate population control programs. Despite the need for capital investment to increase agricultural productivity, Kauffman maintains, responses to the various problems resulting from rising death rates would soak up much of the available capital. Paradoxically, this danger of becoming enshared in a number of regional Malthusian traps reduces the likelihood of large-scale global overshoot and collapse.

We can interpret the seemingly incompatible objections raised by Marstrand and Pavitt and by Kauffman, who disagree as to whether overaggregation renders World3's runs excessively pessimistic or optimistic, in a way that makes them consistent. Worldwide averaging does ignore the potential of optimally differentiated agricultural investment, which might increase the world's soil-based food production beyond the limits suggested by World3. Whereas Marstrand and Pavitt focus on this possibility allowed by physical limits, Kauffman centers attention on the regional dangers inherent in a continuation of socioculturally conditioned trends. Thus the overaggregation of the agricultural subsystem of World3 produces results that are too pessimistic in one respect and too optimistic in another.

The Disaggregated Mesarovic-Pestel Model

Treatment of the world as a single unit ignores the bipolarity between rich and poor countries, which display striking contrast in regard to population growth, food production, nonrenewable natural resource deposits, resource consumption, pollution generation, wealth, and income and capacity for technological innovation. Various regions of the world are so diverse in both population and food production that they need to be differentiated in any forecast of world futures. Mihajlo Mesarovic and Eduard Pestel (1974) sought to perform this kind of differentiation in their global model and forecast, which they describe in *Mankind at the Turning Point*, the second report to the Club of Rome.* To avoid treating the world as a homogeneous system misleadingly characterized in terms of averages, they constructed a computer model of the world as a multilevel system of ten diverse, relatively homogeneous interacting regions: (1) North America, (2) Western Europe, (3) Japan, (4) Australia and South Africa, and the rest of the market economy of the world, (5) Eastern Europe including the Soviet

---

Multilevel Computer Model of World Development System, the six-volume technical report by Mesarovic and Pestel, poses an obstacle to the interested reader, for it is an anthologized collection of papers rather than a systematic report.

Union, (6) Latin America, (7) North Africa and the Middle East, (8) Tropical Africa, (9) South and Southeast Asia, and (10) China. Each region is represented on six levels: the individual, group, demoeconomic, technology, ecology, and geophysics strata. Interconnections and exchange mechanisms express the interdependence of the regional models (pp. 12, 40, 46).

Unlike the Forrester-Meadows models that treat the entire world system as overshooting its limits at one time and then collapsing, the Mesarovich-Pestel model depicts diverse regions as encountering different limits for different reasons at different times. The resulting catastrophic collapses, many of which could occur long before the middle of the next century, would be experienced throughout the world system in a variety of ways, depending on the interrelationships of the constituent parts (pp. 36, 34, 45, 54). Computer-tested scenarios suggest that a continuation of current undifferentiated growth, like cancerous growth, would lead to such disasters. For instance, if a population equilibrium were implemented in South and Southeast Asia in 1995 instead of 1990, the estimated penalty would be more than 150 million additional child deaths (p. 128).

Yet Mesarovic and Pestel regard a rapid stoppage of growth as unnecessary and undesirable. What is required is controlled, differentiated growth that would achieve a better balance between population growth and food, resources, energy, and wealth. Such "organic sustainable growth" should proceed according to a global "master plan" that would encourage each functionally interdependent region or group of nations to make its own contribution to the organic development of mankind (pp. 7, 9, 144–48). A five-point program emphasizes a global approach, investment aid to developing countries, balanced economic development for all regions, an effective population policy, and worldwide diversification of industry (p. 127). The recommended scenario, aimed at significantly reducing the gap between rich and poor nations by the year 2025, requires at least $250 billion annual aid from developed to developing regions during the period from 1975 to 2000 (pp. 60–64). Conflict must be replaced by global cooperation that would benefit all by promoting the harmonious operation of the differentiated world system.

The balanced, differentiated economic growth advocated by Mesarovic and Pestel is definitely more realistic and desirable than the Forrester-Meadows proposal to rapidly stabilize global economic growth. Yet Lincoln Gordon (1976) observes that the supposedly "undifferentiated growth" that they attack is a caricature of the past and present, and the "organic growth" they advocate is an imprecisely defined prescription for the future (p. 4). Thus they need to specify precisely the ways in which growth ought to become increasingly differentiated.

The Mesarovic-Pestel model improves upon the World2 and World3 models in several respects, including regional disaggregation with the accompanying diversification of problems, potential disasters, and specific interrelated remedial measures. The modeling structure is more complex, sophisticated, and closer to the structure of the real world. The model is being used by a number of decision makers in various parts of the world.

Although the Mesarovic-Pestel model constitutes a salutary first step in the construction of regional, multilevel, hierarchical computer models of the world system, it is not without serious flaws. Its assumptions, some of which are dubious, strongly predispose it toward the generation of provisional catastrophist scenarios. Mesarovic and Pestel appear to underestimate the amount of sustainable global industrial growth that could be brought about by the wise use of present and prospective technologies. Their analysis of the energy situation, though crucial to the model, is exceptionally weak (pp. 130–42). Their recommended intermediate strategy of supplementing oil with coal and liquified coal would fall far short of meeting reasonable energy requirements, particularly since many countries lack adequate coal deposits. Yet they assert that "nuclear energy [fission and fusion] —the technology optimists' magical and dangerous solution—may never be needed" (p. 139). Their long-term energy strategy of building solar energy farms in oil-producing regions makes long-term energy prospects dependent on a technology that (1) might not become economically feasible; (2) is probably not the most promising type of solar electric energy converter; and (3) is highly centralized, prone to disruption, and subject to major transportation costs. Such weaknesses underline the need for model builders to engage in extensive research and to draw careful inferences after examining all relevant data.

The weaknesses of the Mesarovic-Pestel forecast cannot be reduced to shortcomings of the model. Many of the authors' conclusions and recommendations are not directly derived from their models' behavior.

As Frank Snowden Hopkins (1975) observes, the Mesarovic-Pestel proposal of relatively unconditional, massive development aid ignores the psychological and cultural complexities involved in political decision making. This unrealistic recommendation might easily promote "inaction in the less developed world which is not encouraged to help itself by affecting needed reforms, and inaction in developed countries which are told that the price of global reform is so impossibly high (in one scenario, $500 billion annually toward the end of a 50-year development period) that they will feel that no effective help can or should be provided" (p. 262). To facilitate major increases in development aid, proposals must keep costs within bounds that developed countries can manage. Such proposals also need to provide assurance that developing countries will assume responsibility to use the funds wisely and to reduce the gross domestic inequalities that so hinder development. Thus the Mesarovic-Pestel normative plan for differentiated growth is implausible in some respects, though insightful in others.

Conclusion

Upshot of the Objections

Our evaluation has disclosed significant shortcomings in the data base of World 3 and in some of the assumptions that are integral to the structure of the model. Key objections center on World3's:

Overestimation of the proximity of physical limits to the availability of nonrenewable metal resources,
Underestimation of the benefits available from science-based technology,
Treatment of the highly differentiated world as a single unit, and
Overaggregation of complex notions such as economic growth and pollution.

Such objections marshal weighty evidence against the claim that economic growth must be stopped within three decades to avert a subsequent gigantic collapse of the global economic system.

This is not to say that ardent advocates of huge amounts of global industrial growth have shown that such growth would be sustainable. They can argue cogently that World3 greatly exaggerates the depletion of metals and the accompanying imminent danger of an overshoot and collapse of global economic growth. However, assuming a continuation of present trends, it is not obvious that World3 overrates the threat of encountering the limits to environmental pollution and economically feasible food production. Admittedly, pollution disaster is more likely to be triggered by specific pollutants, most of them regional in their primary effects, than by the total amount of global pollution. Similarly, inability to produce sufficient amounts of reasonably priced food would probably not precipitate a single world population collapse but, instead, the starvation of sizable portions of expanding populations in poor areas with limited food-producing capacity. Yet the very real danger of such disasters makes it clear that Meadows's warnings must not be dismissed as those of an alarmist crying "Wolf!" when there is no wolf. Disasters stemming primarily from sociocultural constraints could occur long before the times suggested by the runs of the Meadows model.

Technological optimists present a convincing case against World3's suggestion that the optimal application of the best prospective technologies could not prevent a collapse of a growing global economic system during the next century. They cannot, however, conclusively establish their own assumption that abundant, affordable energy will be harnessed to provide plentiful raw materials and sufficient amounts of food without dangerously affecting the biosphere. We may hope that this will occur, but to base all policies concerning industrial and population growth on such an uncertain assumption would be foolhardy. Furthermore, the projected cornucopia of technological optimists presupposes the success of major efforts to stretch current sociocultural limits to the research, development, and widespread, effective implementation of the necessary technologies. Without such efforts, which require departures from what have been known as the business-as-usual and politics-as-usual approaches, current patterns of industrial and population growth would take their toll.

Meadows's technical report does present computer runs that, like Robert Boyd's, depict an enormous amount of continuing, sustainable industrial growth.

However, Meadows and his coauthors emphasize that they attained these runs only by making the untenable assumptions that technologies can be developed to erode limits with no delays and no physical costs anywhere in the system and that technology will advance at 4 percent each year without cost. Countering these assumptions, they argue that successful advances in technology are subject to decreasing returns, increasing costs, and physical laws (Meadows et al. 1974, pp. 510-37). Short-term technological solutions unaccompanied by social policies merely postpone an ultimate decline by shifting the limiting force from one sector to another.* Thus runs that take these constraints into account show the overshoot-decline mode of behavior.

This analysis elucidates the systemic operation of sociocultural limits to growth, the need for social as well as technological policies, and the danger of overshoots and collapses. Yet is still underestimates the potential benefits of feasible technologies. In addition, delays and acceptable costs are much more relative to what societies are willing to do and to their competence than the Meadows analysis might lead one to believe. Many of World3's estimates of the delays required to obtain promising technologies appear to exceed the time that would probably be consumed by large-scale, effectively coordinated research, development, and implementation programs. Highly motivated affluent societies could finance a number of programs of this sort, especially by curtailing expenditures elsewhere. Since much uncertainty remains as to whether the required technologies can and will be developed and effectively implemented, the Meadows team could have enhanced the credibility of its forecast by placing more emphasis on the sociocultural limits to growth and on the prospects of stretching these elastic limits.

Relevance to Policy Formulation

The assumptions of both ardent technological optimists and limits-to-growth pessimists are less justifiable than the assumptions of those who take an intermediate position that combines moderate technological optimism with an emphasis on sociocultural limits to growth. Thus World3 falls short of the goal of benefiting decision makers by adequately reflecting the structural dynamics of growth in the real world. The lack of clearly dependable long-range global computer models does not justify use of World3 for formulating policies in response to such issues as resource depletion. Although typically less precise or less comprehensive, mental or computer models that make assumptions that are more warranted are preferable.

---

*Forrester has publicly acknowledged (for instance, at the opening session of the Second General Assembly of the World Future Society [June 1975]) that optimistic Herman Kahn appears to be roughly correct about which technologies are technically feasible. Granted that much global economic growth is in principle possible, Forrester deems it undesirable because he believes that accompanying system stresses would outweigh its benefits.

This does not mean, however, that the Meadows model has no worth for assessing overall policy objectives. It does provide insight into certain dangers inherent in a continuation of present trends and intertwined problems. In a general way, the projections of provisional ecological disasters arising from pollution and from population growth outdistancing food production are sufficiently plausible to warrant major efforts to avert such disasters. Moreover, the Meadows team suggests some of the changes that societies need to make to avoid undesirable futures. These warnings and suggestions should not go unheeded by those policy makers who still adhere to a business-as-usual or a politics-as-usual orientation.

The normative plans of Forrester and of the Meadows team for the rapid stabilization of economic and population growth differ significantly from each other but are both open to convincing objections. From similar models, Forrester and the Meadows team derive radically different policy suggestions concerning food production and inequalities. Forrester's preferred computer run cuts world food production 20 percent, whereas the Meadows team favors increases in food production. Forrester's world would largely perpetuate current inequalities; Meadows's world would redistribute available wealth in egalitarian fashion. Contrasting value-priorities led Forrester and the Meadows team to devise such different kinds of no-growth computer runs.

Neither Forrester nor Meadows sets forth a future that is both desirable and feasible. Their recommendations that growth be rapidly stabilized are unattractive (especially Forrester's recommendation) and politically unrealistic (especially Meadows's). Any policy that intentionally decreases world food production by 20 percent, as in Forrester's favored run, would be denounced by many outraged citizens of both industrialized and less-industrialized countries. The Meadows team formulated no plausible scenario for implementing its recommendation of voluntary redistribution of available wealth. Moreover, it is hard to imagine how the drastic measures required to stabilize global economic growth could be promptly implemented without severe restrictions on freedom.

The Forrester-Meadows forecasts present a sobering warning but *not a sufficiently convincing case to halt economic growth.* To a considerable extent, beneficial economic growth in the service sectors of the economy could continue even if industrial growth needed to be stopped. Moreover, proposals that advocate global industrial equilibrium face this dilemma: Either they overstate their pessimistic case or they prove to be impractical in the real world at the present time. In view of the powerful motivation toward continued industrial growth, what short of the near-demonstration that such growth must soon precipitate catastrophes might summon sufficient countermotivation to stabilize it rapidly? Even then, curtailment of the threatening types of industrial growth would take precedence over its stabilization as an aggregated whole.

Nevertheless, if efforts to harness plentiful, relatively clean, affordable energy fail, a virtual stabilization of global industrial growth might well become an advisable policy objective. Hence, we had best begin to explore the concept of global industrial equilibrium, as Forrester and the Meadows team have done. At the present time, uncertainties concerning the future energy supply make it appropriate that industrial growth become increasingly selective and that it proceed at somewhat slower rates in developed countries.

When we recognize that appropriate normative and institutional changes would permit sustainable global economic growth—including substantial selective industrial growth—the recommendation of sudden stabilization loses whatever attractiveness it had. In particular, less-industrialized nations will refuse to relinquish such growth. The next chapter provides evidence that the extensive changes required to achieve this kind of growth are much less drastic than those accompanying rapid stabilization.

Contributions Made by Forrester and Meadows

It is much easier to criticize a global computer model than to construct one that is decidedly superior. The world system is so complex, diverse, and susceptible to a wide range of future developments that any modeler of its growth dynamics is confronted by a task comparable in difficulty with that of Hercules.

The pioneering attempts that Forrester and the Meadows team made to model the structural dynamics of global growth have encountered convincing objections. Yet these objections need to be tempered by recognition of the immature state of computer modeling of complex systems around 1970, the general deficiencies and inconsistencies in available data and inferences from them, and the deadlines as well as the limited funds of the project. The major deficiencies evident from today's perspective should not lead us to underestimate the importance of the contributions made by Forrester and the Meadows team. The outpouring of controversy touched off by their forecasts has issued in a greatly increased knowledge of global ecological problems and prospects, though many uncertainties remain. This knowledge has enhanced our perception of the need for a comprehensive systems approach to cope with these serious interrelated problems. Accordingly, few forecasters any longer extrapolate global trends as little affected by intervening factors and delays in feedback. Emphasis has shifted toward modeling that involves normative forecasting and planning. In short, the World2 and World3 models have served as stepping stones for the construction of improved global models.

Owing to its interesting subject matter, fluent style, and startling conclusions—as well as to the masterful promotional campaign staged by the Club of Rome—*Limits* has exerted considerable influence on public opinion. The dangers of encountering limits to continual exponential growth on our small planet—depicted so graphically by the repeated doubling of a lily that quickly expands to the borders of its pond (p. 29)—have been dramatized in ways that have begun to reshape people's outlooks. In conjunction with the energy crisis of 1973/74 and the many other forces that stimulated this change in consciousness, *Limits* played a significant role.

8

KAHN'S REPLY:
"GENTLE SATURATION"

> The world's great age begins anew,
> The golden years return,
> The earth doth like a snake renew
> Her winter weeds outworn
> Lydia Huntley Sigourney

GENERAL RECOGNITION OF DISCONTINUITIES

Despite the acknowledged danger of nuclear war, the climate of opinion during the early and middle 1960s was conducive to the optimistic projection of developmental futures from established trends. This wave of optimism was broken on the rocks of adversity. Since the late 1960s, pollution problems have aroused much concern about possible environmental catastrophes. International news during the 1970s has been dominated by such upsetting occurrences as:

The Arab oil embargo and the fourfold increase in oil prices,
Resulting energy shortages and the instability of the international monetary system,
Increased costs and shortages of a number of natural resources,
Combined recession, inflation, and unemployment,
Severe food shortages in several developing countries,
The plight of populous resource-poor developing countries, and
Nuclear proliferation.

Occurrences of this sort focused attention upon the interplay of pressures generated by phenomenal technological, industrial, and population growth in the heterogeneous, limited global system. By 1974, the United Nations had convened world conferences on the environment (Stockholm, 1972), population

(Bucharest, 1974), and food (Rome, 1974). Increasing awareness of interrelated global problems that might trigger disasters was nourished by the widely publicized growth controversy. Although cogent objections to the Forrester-Meadows models emerged, the projection of turning-point futures had nonetheless become much more plausible.

Lester Brown (1975), who left the Overseas Development Corporation to become founder and president of the Worldwatch Institute, persuasively articulated the widespread perception that "we may be on the verge of one of the great discontinuities in human history—economic, demographic, political." Among the many discontinuities that Brown views as contributing to this prospective overall discontinuity are shifts:

In rapid global economic and population growth to decelerating rates,
In political power from industrial countries to raw material suppliers, and
In emphasis from economic growth to distribution, from supply expansion to
    demand conservation, and from access to international markets to access
    to suppliers (p. 123).

Brown argues that a continuation of the 4 percent global economic growth rate attained during the third quarter of the twentieth century is rendered untenable by pollution, rising costs of resources, and lack of an abundant supply of low-cost energy. He maintains that population growth is now slowing because of declining birthrates in some countries and rising death rates in others. The soaring world price of food is forcing millions of people below the survival level of food intake. Such departures from past trends suggest "that the fourth quarter of this Century will not be merely an extrapolation of the third; 'business as usual' assumptions about the future will no longer suffice" (p. 123). What is called for is a global approach to population policy and to the management of such vital resources as the oceans, climate, energy, and food (p. 124).

KAHN'S RESPONSE

The Current Historical Turning Point

Well into the 1970s, Herman Kahn continued to formulate forecasts diametrically opposed to those made by Brown, Forrester and Meadows, and many other ecological provisional catastrophists. Kahn confined himself to setting forth minor revisions of the 1967 Kahn-Wiener forecast and to criticizing claims made by proponents of limits to growth. Subsequently, however, he made a startling announcement. In "A World Turning Point—and a Better Prospect for the Future" (1975), Kahn and William Brown claimed that "the 1975-1985 decade now appears destined—in certain ways—to mark one of the most important turning points in world history" (p. 23). The trends of global population, gross world product (GWP), and GWP per capita have been growing at unprecedented rates: about 2, 5,* and 3 percent annually, respectively. These trends have already started or are soon likely to begin a rather slow, long-term decline in their growth rates.

Kahn and Brown remark: "If this decline actually occurs, then the scholars and publicists who have extrapolated trends on the basis of recent all-time high rates . . . will have suggested incorrect expectations about the world's future and the underlying mechanisms at work" (p. 23). This observation is intended as a critique of forecasts that project exponential growth as continuing until stopped by physical limits. Yet it implicitly acknowledges that Kahn's prior analysis of the multifold trend (1967 [with Weiner], 1972 [with Bruce-Briggs]) needs to be revised. He had maintained that the constituents of this trend are likely to continue at least until the year 2000, after which some may saturate or begin to recede. His present affirmation of an imminent, persistent slowdown in the rates of global economic and population growth runs contrary to his previous forecasts.

Slower Growth to Postindustrial Affluence

The dramatic opening of the Kahn-Brown essay conveys the impression that Kahn has revised his image of the most likely future much more than the remainder of the essay discloses. The projected reduction in growth rates is so gradual that it permits extensive economic and population growth. Envisioned economic growth proceeds through a superindustrial period into a global postindustrial era of abundance.

This forecast, which takes the form of a scenario, is developed in detail by Kahn, William Brown, and Leon Martel of Hudson Institute in *The Next 200 Years* (1976b). They maintain that growth rates will soon begin to decrease until they level off about 100 to 200 years from now. Acknowledging uncertainty, they estimate that the inflection point of the population growth curve (the point at which slower growth begins) will occur from 1976 to 1980. The growth of GWP may reach its inflection point about a decade or two later. Thus upcoming growth is more likely to follow flattened S-shaped curves than to be either exponential or sharply curtailed (pp. 5, 26, 27).

Kahn, Brown, and Martel locate the inflection points near the midpoint of their postulated "great transition" from 1776 to 2176 (see Figure 8.1). "Future ages," they contend, "will undoubtedly look back at what happened in these four centuries of economic development and technological advancement as mankind's most effective and pervasive transformation—from a world basically inhospitable to its few dwellers to one fully commanded by its expanded multitudes" (p. 24). This transition to a postindustrial society will constitute a watershed of history comparable with the agricultural revolution that began about

---

*L. Brown's estimate is 4, not 5, percent.

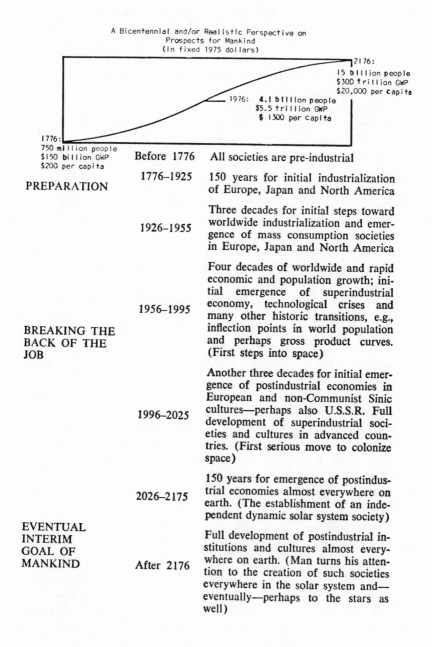

A Bicentennial and/or Realistic Perspective on
Prospects for Mankind
(In fixed 1975 dollars)

2176:
15 billion people
$300 trillion GWP
$20,000 per capita

1976: 4.1 billion people
$5.5 trillion GWP
$ 1300 per capita

1776:
750 million people
$150 billion GWP
$200 per capita

	Before 1776	All societies are pre-industrial
PREPARATION	**1776–1925**	150 years for initial industrialization of Europe, Japan and North America
	1926–1955	Three decades for initial steps toward worldwide industrialization and emergence of mass consumption societies in Europe, Japan and North America
BREAKING THE BACK OF THE JOB	**1956–1995**	Four decades of worldwide and rapid economic and population growth; initial emergence of superindustrial economy, technological crises and many other historic transitions, e.g., inflection points in world population and perhaps gross product curves. (First steps into space)
	1996–2025	Another three decades for initial emergence of postindustrial economies in European and non-Communist Sinic cultures—perhaps also U.S.S.R. Full development of superindustrial societies and cultures in advanced countries. (First serious move to colonize space)
	2026–2175	150 years for emergence of postindustrial economies almost everywhere on earth. (The establishment of an independent dynamic solar system society)
EVENTUAL INTERIM GOAL OF MANKIND	**After 2176**	Full development of postindustrial institutions and cultures almost everywhere on earth. (Man turns his attention to the creation of such societies everywhere in the solar system and—eventually—perhaps to the stars as well)

Figure 8.1. The great transition (Kahn, Brown, and Martel 1976b, p. 6). (From THE NEXT 200 YEARS by Herman Kahn, William Brown, and Leon Martel. Copyright © 1976 by Hudson Institute. By permission of William Morrow & Company.)

10,000 years ago and with the industrial revolution. In a service economy that emphasizes quaternary activities, many of which are akin to leisure activities, increasing numbers of people will do things for their own sakes. Accordingly, the authors call attention to great similarities between their view of a likely post-industrial society and many preindustrial societies. They believe that at least for a time most people will enjoy postindustrial society, though it will not be a utopia (pp. 8, 20-24).

More specifically, the "earth-centered" perspective of the Kahn-Brown-Martel scenario (as contrasted with the "space-bound" perspective that is mentioned but not developed [for example, p. 4]) assumes that during the next 200 years: (1) the world population curve flattens out at least for awhile at 15 billion people, give or take a factor of two (that is, a range from 7.5 to 30 billion); (2) the per capita product at $20,000 (in fixed 1975 dollars), give or take a factor of three; and (3) the GWP at about $300 trillion, give or take a factor of five (p. 7). Although the possible ranges of variability are admittedly larger, the authors regard these figures as quite plausible. They maintain that global resources will be more than sufficient to sustain, for an indefinite period of time and at high standards, the levels of population and economic growth projected (p. 27).

Kahn, Brown, and Martel expect postindustrial society and culture to be present almost everywhere on earth. They hope that the great abundance will result in prosperity for almost everyone, reduced competition, and relative peace (p. 8). In view of the "enormous power to direct and manipulate both man and nature, . . . [the] great issues will still be the very questions that confront us now: Who will direct and manipulate, and to what ends?" (p. 226).

Kahn and his coauthors sketch this scenario to show that the means are available to negotiate the transition from present problems to a prosperous "growth" world that they favor. They consider their scenario to be "much more likely to occur [than doomsday scenarios] or to be relatively representative of what does occur" (p. viii). Merely "the application of a modicum of intelligence and good management in dealing with current problems can enable economic growth to continue for a considerable period of time, to the benefit . . . of mankind" (p. 4).

Causes of Declining Growth Rates

The postulated reduction of global economic and population growth rates is basically separate from the recession of the mid-1970s. Even though the possibilities of resource scarcity, pollution, famine, poverty, and overcrowding could hinder growth, they should be seen as temporary or regional phenomena that society must deal with (p. 8). Projections from present trends indicate that declining rates of growth will probably stem more from a slowing of demand than from intensified difficulties in obtaining physical supplies (p. 7). Accordingly, Kahn and Brown (1975) contend, "Changing priorities and values appear to be the most relevant, in a causal sense, to the more or less gradual decrease in growth rates which we should expect" (p. 24). Kahn, Brown, and Martel (1976b) maintain that this leveling tendency

> will be a social consequence of such factors as modernization, literacy, urbanization, affluence, safety, good health and birth control, and government and private policies reflecting changing values and priorities (accompanied by the increasing desire of vested interests to protect their status quo from external pressures for expansion). [P. 8]

Exponential growth of the world's population appears to be stopping now, but not for reasons associated with desperate physical limits to growth (p. 30). The economic and social development of developing countries is bringing about lowered birthrates by decreasing desired family size. This tendency of parents with rising incomes to want fewer children can be traced to the reduced value of children as economic assets, coupled with the increased cost of rearing them and the erosion of traditional religious and social pressures for having large families. Thus in developing countries economic growth is ushering in the "demographic transition": the decrease in population growth rates that has occurred and seems likely to continue during the successive stages from preindustrial to postindustrial society. Since "the problem of exponential population growth appears almost to be solving itself," the authors argue, "the population worries and alarmist exhortations of the 1960's and 1970's may well be recorded as an amusing episode in human history" (p. 30). (See Figure 8.2.)

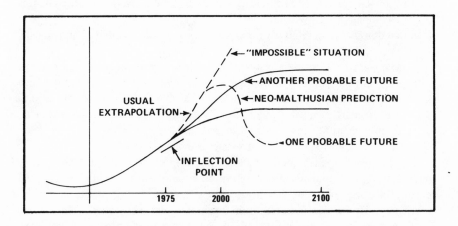

Figure 8.2. Contrast between a neo-Malthusian projection of coninued exponential growth of population, followed by collapse, and Kahn's projected slowdown of the growth rate resulting in a gradual leveling off of growth (*Futurist*, December 1975, p. 3). (Courtesy of THE FUTURIST, published by the World Future Society, 4916 St. Elmo Avenue, Washington, D.C. 20014.)

Because of the beneficial consequences of the rapid, sustained economic growth that the authors expect in most developing nations, they claim that even a projected world population of 30 billion would be compatible with an optimistic earth-centered scenario (p. 34). Moreover, they believe that the apparently feasible migration of people to space colonies could easily encourage a new cycle of safe population growth (p. 31).

Nonetheless, rapid population growth can reduce the rate of economic growth, and local famines are possible. To speed the demographic transition, policies should be oriented primarily toward economic development in those areas where birthrates are still very high (p. 213). Antinatalist programs can also be useful in reducing the rate of population growth, though they do not always have significant impact (p. 212). *The Next 200 Years* is less critical of such programs than is "A World Turning Point," in which Kahn and Brown (1975) remark: "At least in the short and medium run, direct government programs intended to reduce population growth rates (except for programs that disseminate family planning information) are remarkably ineffective" (pp. 24–25).

The projected decline of the global economic growth rate depends on declining rates in developed countries. After worldwide development has essentially been completed, many economies will achieve a more or less steady state (Kahn, Brown, and Martel 1976b, p. 50). Kahn and his coauthors list five cumulative, accelerating reasons why they consider this likely:

A remote upper limit to economic growth,
Diminishing returns from increasingly costly factors of production,
Decrease in the marginal utility of wealth and production,
Opposition by many vested interests either to growth itself or to the changes
    accompanying growth, and
Eventual dominance of relatively nonproductive quaternary activities (pp. 50–54).

The authors place relatively little emphasis upon the first two reasons. They maintain that, in view of the flexibility of modern economies and the huge surplus of land, energy, and resources available, the limitations set by scarcity should not usually prove dominant. Moreover, past experience suggests that increased investment, technological progress, and other innovations may often reduce costs proportionate to the investments made in them.

Although the fifth reason will become important eventually, the closely related third and fourth reasons appear to be most decisive in the projected decline of the economic growth rate. As affluence becomes more normal or customary, its further increase often seems less desirable when other desires must be sacrificed to achieve it. Indeed, the flower children of the 1960s have faded. Yet the culture of the Atlantic-Protestant culture area (Scandanavia, Holland, England, the United States, Canada, and Australia) has taken some steps away from the work and achievement ethic and probably will not return to anything like its former state. This shift in priorities and values should continue as increased Social Security, welfare, and insurance provide more protection against most of the vagaries of life.

Furthermore, the authors expect an increasing desire to leave things as they are. As people get richer, they tend to be satisfied with their quality of life. Hence, change-oriented technical and economic efficiency will be given much less weight.

Kahn and his coauthors note that in many countries, at something like $1,000 to $2,000 per capita, the upper middle class tends to fare worse as the country as a whole does better. They agree with Joseph Schumpeter's observation that one good maid is worth a household full of appliances. Such considerations lead them to "believe that one of the major reasons for the objections to growth by elites arises directly out of this class interest" (p. 53). In "A World Turning Point," Kahn and Brown appear to be saying that the disillusionment with economic growth manifested by many members of the upper middle class in developed countries is the primary contributor to the anticipated decline in the global economic growth rate (for example, p. 28).

Rapid Economic Growth in Most Developing Countries

Resource-intensive economic growth of developed countries requires such resources as raw materials, inexpensive workers, and tourist attractions from abroad. Developing countries that have these resources can obtain the capital, markets, and technology needed for their economic growth. Hence, Kahn and his coauthors (1976) regard the arithmetically widening economic gap between developed and developing countries as the central reason for projecting rapid growth in the latter (p. 34). Accordingly, "the clearest moral and political argument for further growth in the developed world (and against artificial and forced limitation) is that it aids the poor both within and outside the developed countries" (p. 19). The disproportionate character of such growth for the next 100 years or more "should not be disastrous either morally or politically since there are very few peasants, workers or even businessmen in developing nations who care much about gaps" (p. 49). The authors claim that, despite the slowly decelerating global economic growth rate, most developing countries are likely to undergo rapid, sustained growth (p. 34) (See Figure 8.3.) The growth of "non-coping" developing countries (those with per capita incomes below $400 and with large balance-of-payments deficits) seems likely to proceed at slower rates until late in the next century and then increase speed dramatically (p. 55). The present 100-to-1 ratio of per capita product between the wealthiest 10 percent and poorest 20 percent of the world population could shrink to about 5 to 1 by the year 2100, give or take a factor of two or three (pp. 55, 57). Even if a ratio similar to 100 to 1 persists, the absolute standard of living of people in poor countries would probably exceed that of Greece or Spain today (p. 57).

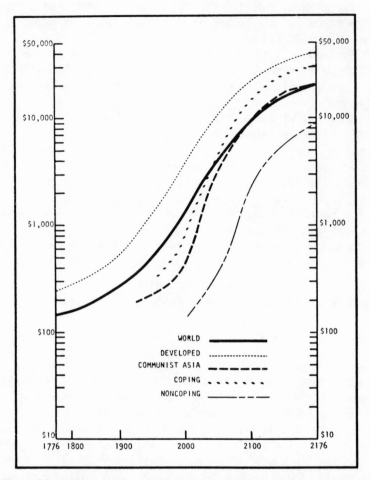

Figure 8.3. Kahn's estimate of gross world product per capital, 1776–2176 (Kahn, Brown, and Martel 1976b, p. 56). (From THE NEXT 200 YEARS by Herman Kahn, William Brown, and Leon Martel. Copyright © 1976 by Hudson Institute. By permission of William Morrow & Company.)

Supposed Physical Limits

Energy Supply

Kahn and his collaborators argue that the primary factor limiting growth is the amount of growth that people want rather than insufficient energy availability, depletion of nonrenewable raw materials, pollution, or inadequate food production. They admit that the future well-being of the human race is intimately linked to prospects for an abundant supply of energy at reasonable prices (p. 59).

Many uncertainties concerning cost, development, time, environmental impact, and, in some cases, technical feasibility enter into their survey of various technologies for generating solar, geothermal, fusion, and fission energy. "Until the development of eternal power sources has been accomplished on a large commercial scale—which will probably occur by the middle of the next century if not sooner—the world's best hope lies in the use of fossil fuels, especially coal" (p. 65). The world will probably lean heavily on shale oil, with nuclear power as a possibly important adjunct (p. 67). Even the "serious possibility of a moratorium one day being placed upon the construction or use of nuclear energy plants, at least in the United States, . . . need not affect future growth possibilities" (p. 66).

The authors contend that "energy costs as a whole are very likely to continue the historical downward trend indefinitely" (p. 58). Oil prices, which they seriously doubt will stay very high for more than 5 or 10 years, "might easily return to something like $3-7 [per barrel] in the Persian Gulf" long before the 15 or 20 years required to amortize major new coal investments has elapsed (p. 60). Still, the world can successfully adjust to the $12-per-barrel price if necessary (pp. 60, 65). The path to abundant energy may not be smooth. However, "except for temporary fluctuations caused by bad luck or poor management, the world need not worry about energy shortages or costs in the future" (p. 83).

Available Raw Materials and Pollution Control

The authors' long-term analysis of the feasible supply of raw materials, pollution control, and food production depends crucially on the availability of an abundance of affordable energy. Their assessment of nonrenewable metal resources, presented in the preceding chapter as a critique of Meadows's treatment, concludes that:

> 99.9 percent of the probable future demand for metals . . . [perhaps
> 15 to 60 times that of today] is clearly satisfiable at least for a
> world of 15 billion people and $300 trillion GWP—and this con-
> clusion does not depend upon the considerable resources of outer
> space. [P. 102; also see p. 87).

In view of the uneven distribution of raw minerals, cartels might occasionally be able to extract higher prices than usual from customers (p. 87).

Since the late 1960s, remarkable progress in controlling pollution has been made in North America, northwestern Europe, and Japan. Attainment of reasonable environmental standards, not the growth-hampering and sometimes impossible standards of certain environmentalists, is probable within 10 or 15 years and almost certain by the year 2000 (pp. 147, 162). Even though the authors admit the possibility of major environmental catastrophes, they "estimate the odds at five to one or better that all the serious long-terms problems will be successfully dealt with in due course—and at a cost that is acceptable in most people's judgments" (p. 166). Furthermore, "it seems quite probable that, within a century or so, man will be able to prevent" genetic damage caused by radiation or chemical pollution—or by pollution generally" (p. 173). Hence, "calculations from accumulated damage 10 to 100 generations from now will probably turn out to be irrelevant" (p. 173).

Food Production

The authors maintain that "the world is likely to be much better fed 100 years from now than it is today; after 200 years, current American standards, or even better, could very well be the norm" (p. 111) (See Figure 8.4.) They claim that their argument is based on reasonable management coupled with conservative expectations of technological advance—not on exceptionally fortunate technological breakthroughs, even though some now seem inevitable (p. 107).

According to the authors' calculations, expansion of tillable acreage, multicropping, and increased yield per crop could multiply current world food production by a factor of 20 to 110 (p. 126) (See Table 8.1.) Moreover, technologies like the "nutrient-film technique," a variety of hydroponic farming, may eventually make possible the large-scale production of grains in desert regions at

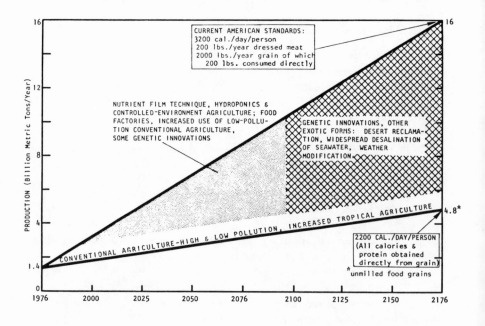

Figure 8.4. Kahn's "reasonably optimistic" scenario for equivalent grain production, 1976–2176, for feeding the world's population (Kahn, Brown, and Martel 1976b, p. 134). (From THE NEXT 200 YEARS by Herman Kahn, William Brown, and Leon Martel. Copyright © 1976 by Hudson Institute. By permission of William Morrow & Company.)

TABLE 8.1

Kahn's Estimate of Potential Increases in Food Production

	Conservative	Optimistic
1. Increased agricultural land harvested	factor of 2.5	4
2. Multicropping	factor of 1.5	2
3. Average yield per crop: Improved use of		
fertilizer	factor of 1.5	2
irrigation	factor of 1.5	2
HYVs	factor of 2	2.5
Other inputs	factor of 1.2	1.4
Multiplicative totals	factor of 20	110

Note: The estimate also includes the possibility of opening new tropical lands that lend themselves to both multicropping and the entire input package of high-yielding varieties.

Source: From Kahn, Brown, and Martel 1976b, p. 126. (From THE NEXT 200 YEARS by Herman Kahn, William Brown, and Leon Martel. Copyright © 1976 by Hudson Institute. By Permission of William Morrow & Company.)

costs not more than five times today's (p. 131). Furthermore, it appears likely that palatable, nutritious foods can be mass-produced in more or less automated factories (p. 111). Advanced technology would be used to extract low-cost food from almost any organic matter, including wood, leaves, cellulose, petroleum, and even agricultural and urban wastes. Especially encouraging is the progress being made in the production of single-cell protein (pp. 132, 133). Elsewhere, Kahn and Brown (1975) argue that techniques being developed could produce almost limitless amounts of edible, perhaps very palatable, foods (p. 38). Kahn, Brown, and Martel (1976b) conclude that "the prospect of an abundant supply of food for future generations is not in any reasonable sense limited by existing resources" (p. 111).

To reduce the likelihood of regional famines, developing countries must make institutional reforms to improve their own agricultural sectors while surplus-food-producing nations build stockpiles that can be drawn upon in periods of emergency (p. 121). Indeed, a tremendous effort is needed to produce and distribute sufficient food for an expanding population (p. 138). Yet "from the vantage point of the year 2176, 20th Century concerns about food may appear merely as a temporary detour of imagined or real troubles on the road to success" (pp. 111, 112).

Dangers of Pessimism

The authors' long-term optimism does not keep them from recognizing the possibility of serious short-term anomalies, dislocations, and crises, any one of which could greatly complicate the process of making the transition. Among these potential difficulties are retarded economic growth, energy shortfalls, raw material shortages, temporary but intense pollution, environmental surprises, regional overpopulation, local famines, and—most fearful of all—large-scale thermonuclear war (p. 211).

The authors maintain that acceptance of their position provides the best hope of both reducing the possibility of such occurrences and of mitigating the consequences if any occur (p. 211). Since the more intractable, basic problems usually lie less in the nature of things than in recent or current policies, unnecessarily poor administration, or sometimes just plain bad luck, rather straightforward, practical solutions can be found in most cases (p. 20). In particular, economic growth is needed to reduce the population growth rate voluntarily, resolve pollution problems, tap new energy sources and increase the supply of resources, stimulate food production, and raise the living standards of poor people.

The chief danger, Kahn and his coauthors believe, is that the reaction against economic growth could be carried much too far. They claim that "any concerted attempt to stop or even slow 'progress' appreciably . . . is catastrophe-prone" (p. 165). Not only would it impede the resolution of current problems; it might encourage hopelessness, thus becoming a self-fulfilling prophecy that would lead to the kind of disasters it was intended to prevent (p. 8). Moreover, it would probably require extraordinarily repressive governments or movements, as well as a repressive international system (pp. 165, 174). Finally, "mankind is involved in a process that probably cannot voluntarily and safely be stopped or prematurely slowed down significantly, even if there are good arguments for doing so" (p. 164). Kahn and his coauthors hope that the potential for a future of unprecedented material abundance will not be stifled by foolish political behavior or misplaced concern about nonexistent or badly formulated growth issues (pp. 20, 24, 25).

A "Space-Bound" Perspective: A New Stage of Growth

"Within the last two years," the authors point out, "a growing number of serious scholarly studies have not only asserted a technical feasibility for colonization in space, but have also indicated an economic viability" (p. 31). As an alternative to the "earth-centered" perspective of their book, Kahn, Brown, and Martel suggest a "space-bound" perspective to which they are somewhat more inclined (pp. 4, 5). An especially vigorous effort in extraterrestrial activities early in the twenty-first century would be oriented toward the eventual establishment of large autonomous colonies in space. These colonies would process

raw materials, produce energy, and manufacture durable goods both for indigenous consumption and export to earth or other colonies. The authors maintain that such developments, which would involve substantial migration from
earth, could result in radically new patterns of population and product growth:

> A new S-shaped curve may start sometime in the 21st Century,
> representing the colonization of the solar system and eventually
> generating growth rates that we would not even try to estimate; per-
> haps later, when the transition was near completion, yet another
> curve would begin, representing the colonization of interstellar
> space, a task that may be as open-ended as . . . the universe. [Pp. 5, 7]

The exploitation of space could serve as a major positive economic and
technological influence on the earth-centered perspective (p. 24). Besides, it
could provide an exciting, challenging frontier for those achievement-oriented
young people who otherwise might find postindustrial society boring. Extraterrestrial self-sustaining communities could even function as a lifeboat for spaceship earth if a highly improbable, massive ecological calamity occurred on the
latter (pp. 222, 224).

EVALUATION OF THE KAHN-BROWN-MARTEL FORECAST

Methodological Ambiguities

Kahn, Brown, and Martel (1976b) perceive that an inaccurate, morale-
eroding image of the future can function as a self-fulfilling prophecy. They also
observe that projecting a persuasive image of a desirable, practical future is extremely important to high morale, dynamism, consensus, and, in general, for
helping the wheels of society turn smoothly (pp. 209–11). Nonetheless, they
emphatically state that their being convinced of the truth of their future-oriented
message constitutes a prerequisite for circulating it to improve morale. In other
words, the virtue of their projected image of the future is that it "may prove
accurate, or at least [be] about the most plausible image one can develop now"
(p. 209).

Their earth-centered scenario, which sets forth a cornucopian future as
more likely than a disastrous one (p. viii) and as a highly desirable goal, appears
to function as both an exploratory and a normative forecast. It seems to be intended primarily as an exploratory forecast. Yet in response to a review, Kahn,
Brown, and Martel present the scenario as possible, desirable, and realistically
attainable (1976a). The reader could easily get the impression that they first
selected a goal and then sought to show that its attainment is feasible enough to
warrant its pursuit. Still, unlike many normative forecasts that prescribe drastic
institutional changes or revolutionary technologies, the scenario is quite in line
with ongoing tendencies (1976b, p. 4).

At any rate, the scenario is beclouded by a methodological ambiguity that makes it difficult for the analyst to discern the ways in which it serves as an exploratory and as a normative forecast. We here evaluate the scenario as primarily an exploratory forecast from which the authors derive deeply felt, policy-oriented recommendations. The normative assumptions of this scenario, which does not profess to be value free, are considerably less implicit and, hence, less deceptive than those of the Kahn-Bruce-Briggs forecast (1972).

Another ambiguity concerns the extent to which the scenario rests upon an analysis of trends. In answer to a criticism of their scenario as being based on the mechanical extrapolation of past trends, Kahn, Brown, and Martel assert that the exact opposite is the case (1976a). They state that their scenario, instead of extrapolating growth trends, suggests that these trends are soon likely to pass through their inflection points and thus change significantly.

However, reliance on trends permeates *The Next 200 Years* (1976b). How can a reader even suspect that Kahn has abandoned his emphasis on long-term trends as the most basic devices for forecasting? Consider, for instance, the following remark: "Hudson projections based on current trends point to the conclusion that growth is likely to continue for many generations, though at gradually decreasing rates, which we expect to result more from a slowing of demand than from increased difficulties in obtaining physical supplies" (p. 7). Hence, one is forced to conclude that Kahn now refuses to apply the term *qualified trend extrapolation* to his method merely because the basic trends projected are soon likely to begin an extremely slow decline. This rather arbitrary linguistic decision, probably made to distinguish the forecast from one of continued exponential growth, does not conceal the striking similarities between Kahn's past and present methodology.

"New Wine in Old Wineskins"

Just as Kahn's methodology has changed much less than his rhetoric suggests, so his basic image of the type of earth-centered future that seems more likely than any other* has undergone decidedly less revision than the reader might suspect initially. Four salient novelties in *The Next 200 Years* are the space-bound perspective, the proximity of the inflection points of the exponential growth curves, the comparatively turbulent character of the projected transition to global postindustrial society, and the adaptive theory of value change. The

---

*For brevity, this expression is sometimes condensed to "image of the most likely future." In spite of their occasionally guarded statements, Kahn, Brown, and Martel appear to believe that their overall image of the earth-centered or space-bound future is not only more likely than any one of the other available images but also (at least in many of its basic features) likely.

first, however, is not examined in detail, and the third amounts to relatively minor setbacks coupled with the quite unlikely possibility of major global catastrophes. The second, which articulates changes that most affect the basic forecast, brings such a gradual slowdown of growth that the attainment of a world of unprecedented material abundance still appears likely. Whereas the term *historical turning point* leads one to expect rapid, profound change, the scenario of the earth-centered perspective is relatively continuous with the historically grounded present. Continuity is especially evident in Kahn's latest treatment of the multifold trend (1976b, pp. 182-84).* Not until this last item in the list of constituent elements is there even a tentative major revision: "perhaps a slowing down in next two or three decades—at least in some areas" (p. 184).

As early as 1967, Kahn stated that some of the trends might begin to level off after the year 2000 (Kahn and Wiener 1967). What he has done now is to place the probable turning point of the exponential economic and population growth trends before the year 2000 and perhaps as early as the present. This revision enables him to answer critics of *exponential* growth in a way that permits retention of nearly all the basic motifs of his previous global forecasts (Kahn and Wiener 1967; Kahn and Bruce-Briggs 1972). Without imputing motives to Kahn, it is interesting to observe that the historical turning points conveniently coincide with the U.S. bicentennial (despite the footnoted qualification on page 5 of *The Next 200 Years* and the guarded language of the last item in the multifold trend [quoted above]).

Thus Kahn's image of the most likely future still boils down to relatively continuous development to affluent global postindustrial society. This image is antithetical to images of dramatic planned intervention to rectify interrelated global problems and to shape a desirable world future that would be quite discontinuous with long-term trends.

Kahn acknowledges that certain changes in priorities and, later, in values are needed to circumvent Malthusian traps and to make a successful transition to postindustrial society. Yet he claims that these changes have already begun to occur as by-products of economic development. Generally speaking, he thinks that this ongoing developmental process can be counted on to lead people to adapt their normative orientations satisfactorily to the changing world. This adaptive theory of value change, the fourth of the novelties in *The Next 200 Years*, lies at the heart of Kahn's projection of relatively continuous development.

---

*For simplicity's sake, Kahn's name will often be used without mention of Brown and Martel, and reference to their book—*The Next 200 Years*—will appear as "Kahn 1976b" in the remainder of the book.

Adaptive Value Change

Increasing economic growth that yields rising per capita income, Kahn contends, will quite naturally produce two types of normative change. People in developed countries will tend to attach less importance to acquiring increased quantities of material goods, and typical parents in developing countries will want to have fewer children. Thus the global trend of GWP per capita will reduce the growth rates of both the GWP trend and the population trend by inducing appropriate changes in priorities and values. To put it differently, the projected decline in growth rates is attributable primarily to spontaneous corrective measures arising from the trends themselves rather than to shortages, real or imagined disasters, and planned human intervention. Paradoxically, people are becoming most alarmed about the adverse consequences of growth just when it is losing its explosive character through natural processes (Kahn and Brown 1965, p. 31).

Kahn's adaptive theory of value change is based on an implicit model that is diametrically opposed to the Forrester-Meadows overshoot-collapse models. Unlike futurists who foresee obsolete values promoting growth until it disastrously surpasses the global carrying capacity during the next century, Kahn views growth trends as if they were equipped with built-in safety valves that keep them from exploding. The result is a self-corrective, adaptive model of value change. This model suggests that the best overall policy is to let nature take its course rather than to attempt to persuade people to change their values.

Does Kahn's safety valve model reflect the systemic behavior of the modeled phenomena well enough to improve the quality of policy making? To answer this question cogently, one must investigate whether each of the two projected normative changes is:

Rooted in historical processes,
Authenticated by the most plausible interpretations of contemporary developments,
Distorted by an overaggregated analysis,
Likely to follow the trajectory projected by Kahn or to be diverted from this course by intervening factors, and
Likely to occur in time to prevent disasters and promote the quality of life or needs to be fostered by planned intervention.

It is also relevant to inquire whether the structural dynamics of Kahn's model replicate ways in which dangerously outmoded values have been updated in time to avert threatened disasters.

Decreasing Worth of Further Economic Growth

Kahn's forecast that the rate of economic growth is soon likely to begin a gradual decline depends largely on postulated normative changes induced by the increasing affluence of the upper middle classes in developed countries. He contends that this affluence will put a damper on the growth rate by decreasing the marginal utility of wealth and production and by encouraging a tendency to protect what has been acquired (1976b, pp. 50-53).

Affluent individuals and upper classes have frequently lost their taste for rapid economic growth. Moreover, typical societies and civilizations that have become relatively rich tend sooner or later to rest on their laurels, instead of maintaining their rates of growth. These historical considerations support the inference that eventually, in the absence of unusual circumstances, increasingly affluent industrialized countries will probably reduce their growth rates voluntarily. However, Kahn's inference that the appropriate type of normative change is soon likely to gather enough momentum to bring about this persistent, widespread decline rests on a shaky historical foundation.

The Recent Recession: How Relevant?

The long-term tendency toward decreasing birthrates in industrialized countries has not been paralleled by a corresponding reduction in economic growth rates. Conversely, economic growth reached unprecedented heights for over two decades after World War II. Yet the rate increase of the planetary product plummeted from about 6.8 percent in 1973 to 2.6 percent in 1974, when the combined GNPs of Western developed nations were close to zero growth. Clearly, the oil price hike exerted a much greater impact on this world recession than did an upper middle class rejection of growth values. Hence, the recession, which has led many forecasters to expect reduced rates of growth, provides little or no evidence for Kahn's projected decline of economic growth rates.

If anything, the recession counts against Kahn's expectations. It seems to have upgraded the value of economic growth in the perception of many disenchanted youths who had taken affluence for granted. Furthermore, rising oil prices render quite problematic a crucial assumption of his forecast: the availability of enough reasonably priced energy within the next two decades to fuel the large amount of economic growth needed to reach levels of affluence at which the projected normative change seems most plausible.

As we noted in Chapters 5 and 6, Daniel Bell suggests that the United States may be experiencing a climacteric, Willis Harman stresses the danger of imminent societal breakdown, and Jay Forrester forecasts the likelihood of another depression in the near future. As the Fall 1978 Conference Board meeting on the international business outlook, the most encouraging forecast was mildly pessimistic. The main reason for the expectation of significantly slower economic growth rates is that world trade, the chief stimulus to prosperity in rich and poor nations since World War II, may continue to expand at only half of the 10 percent rate that it attained during the 1960s. Other forces that restrain the growth rate include trade imbalance, the weakening of the dollar, foreign exchange turmoil, high-priced energy, public sector deficits, changes in the work force, sluggish investment, and poor productivity. The small amount of economic growth projected for the industrial world would raise unemployment and do little to lower inflation rates (*Business Tomorrow*, Spring 1978, p. 11). Regardless of whether such forces make a major depression probable during the 1980s, they count against Kahn's projection.

Recent Antigrowth Ideology: A Wave of the Future?

How convincing is Kahn's "sociology of knowledge" analysis that recent upper-middle-class objections to economic growth are forerunners of the imminent, slowly increasing normative change that he projects? Shortcomings of this analysis are evident in the following passage:

> Most of the current no-growth advocates [characteristically, members of the upper middle class, p. 166] argue for a redistribution of resources as opposed to continued growth as a means of improving the current quality of life. But we have argued that many of these "reformers" do not mean what they say. They already have a high standard of living and do not see any real future gain for themselves if others improve their economic standards—although they may not recognize these as their true feelings. [P. 165]

Thus the authors lead the reader to believe that the supposed concern of many no-growth proponents for a more equitable distribution of resources conceals their self-serving subconscious motivation to preserve their own wealth at the expense of poor people. Virtually no evidence is presented to support this serious allegation. One suspects that a careful analysis would reveal it to be not merely a gross oversimplification but a caricature of nearly all of the accused. Indeed, a conservative motif is present in the no-growth orientation. Yet some conservatives, such as Jay Forrester, do not propose redistribution. Many no-growth or slow-growth advocates indicate by their overall behavior deep concern not only about preserving a viable environment for themselves but also about sustainably meeting the pressing needs of the world's poor people.

The nonmethodological assumptions implicit in this passage and others (for example, pp. 142-46) appear to have exerted a strong influence on the forecast of value change. Even the tone of the presentation, as evidenced by the statement that "some of the more militant environmentalists" "might even be labeled 'bigoted'" (p. 143), conveys the impression that the analysis may amount to little more than an ad hominem argument.

Attacks on growth by members of upper middle classes, though sometimes directed against exponential growth as a whole, have sprung up in response to specific adverse consequences of certain kinds of growth. For instance, Barry Commoner (1971), an ecologist, has centered the blame for pollution problems in the United States on the use of technologies introduced after World War II. The critique of growth voiced by U.S. neo-Marxist youths during the 1960s can be traced to their perception of the "one-dimensional," insufficiently satisfying, inadequately distributed, excessively technocratic and militaristic nature of contemporary growth (see Marcuse 1964).

Neither ecologists nor neo-Marxists would be satisfied with Kahn's reduced rates of growth, which would fail to correct the perceived ills. However, technological and sociocultural changes that would ameliorate these ills might lead many ecologists, neo-Marxists, and other upper-middle-class members to favor accelerated growth. Whereas they view current patterns of growth as antithetical to the quality of life and self-actualization, quantitative growth of appropriate kinds could enhance the quality of life and provide new opportunities for their self-actualization.

Suppose, for instance, that Kahn is correct in assuming that pollution will be controlled at acceptable prices and abundant, inexpensive, clean energy will be harnessed. Would this not restrain increasing "localism" (the propensity of people in a community to prevent the incursion of new industry), which is due largely to the perception that such technologies as nuclear fission installations endanger areas where they are constructed? Would not many vested interests regard the new energy supply as an opportunity for their safe, rewarding growth?

Overaggregation of Kahn's Critique

This evaluation of the conflict between Kahn and the growth antagonists has already pointed to an Archilles' heel in his arguments against them. Although he is fond of castigating the Forrester-Meadows models for overaggregation, he makes a similar mistake in formulating his answer to the critics of exponential growth. Just as some of them assumed that exponential growth is the primary culprit, so his basic response implicitly makes the same assumption. Ecological problems stem more from specific kinds of economic growth than from its undifferentiated exponential character.

The question of how values concerning economic growth may, should, and will change is intimately intertwined with the ways in which prospects for selective growth will be perceived and acted upon. This important, probably crucial dimension of prospective normative change is quite foreign to Kahn's overaggregated model.

Not only does Kahn's oversight render his model untrustworthy for forecasting normative change; it also creates the misleading impression that the supposed safety valves (the projected normative changes that reduce the rates of growth) can be relied upon to prevent disasters. Reduction in the rate of economic growth unaccompanied by appropriate changes in its character could easily trigger disasters. Kahn fails to provide an adequate account of the types, amounts, and rates of normative change needed to cope with interrelated global ecological problems.

How can Kahn think that his favored kind of normative change would proceed without provoking reactions that could easily alter its supposedly gradual, relatively continuous trajectory? For instance, the occurrence of the disasters threatened by a continuation of relatively undifferentiated growth would induce normative changes unanticipated by Kahn's model. Any adequate model of value change must be much more sensitive to the feedback provided by human responses to possible occurrences. Among the results of such sensitivity are a wide range of possible normative changes and much uncertainty.

Desire for Smaller Families

Kahn contends that the demographic transition is the major factor accounting for both the recent decline in the world population growth rate and the likelihood that the trend's inflection point will have been reached by 1980 (p. 30). In short, economic growth and concomitant social developments are leading parents to want fewer children. Kahn relies primarily on this nearly automatic growth-induced normative change to ameliorate population problems.

Modern history discloses that the demographic transition accompanied by rising food production generally prevented major famines and dying off in currently developed countries. A notable exception is the 1845 Irish potato famine in which as many as 500,000 people may have died. Nonetheless, the demographic transition is a well-authenticated historical pattern that provides the major piece of historical evidence for Kahn's safety valve model.

How applicable to the future of populous developing countries is this historical precedent? To supply background information relevant to answering this question, a brief overview of population problems is in order.

Overview of Population Problems

The upsurge in the world's population since World War II has resulted from a major imbalance between birth- and death-rates. Because of malaria control and better health care, more children survive and have a higher life expectancy. In many parts of the developing world, birthrates have not diminished nearly enough to balance the dramatic decline in death rates. As the large numbers of children have become adults and reproduced at traditional levels, exponential population growth has unfolded.

At the current world population growth rate of about 1.8 or 1.9 percent annually, approximately 1 million people are added every four and a half days. If this rate continues, the 1976 population of 4 billion people will swell to 5 billion before 1990. Suppose this rate were maintained for a little over 1,000 years. There would be a billion-billion people—some 1,700 for each square yard of the earth's surface! Obviously, this astronomical figure will never be reached. Such physical limits as insufficient supplies of food, fresh water, space, and, more generally, a livable environment would intervene if population growth were not deliberately restricted. Thus the important question is *when, at what levels,* and *by what means* global population growth will be limited and *with what differential effects on various regions* (see Figure 8.5).

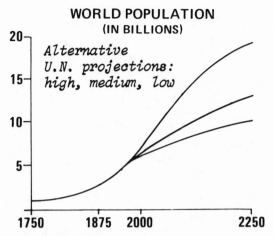

WORLD POPULATION
(IN BILLIONS)

Alternative U.N. projections: high, medium, low

20
15
10
5

1750   1875   2000   2250

Figure 8.5. UN projections of world population growth (in billions) (*Futurist* December 1975, p. 285). (Courtesy of THE FUTURIST, published by the World Future Society, 4916 St. Elmo Avenue, Washington, D.C. 20014.)

The high population growth rates of many developing countries could easily lead to large-scale regional mortalities from famines (see Figure 8.6). Moreover, these rates exacerbate a wide range of vexing problems, including undernourishment, illiteracy, unemployment, environmental deterioration, accelerated urbanization, and the widening gap between developed and resource-poor developing countries. Kahn's analysis neglects these problems.

Consider, for instance, excessive rates of urbanization. In 1920 about 19 percent of the world's population lived in urban environments, including small towns. By 1960 this figure had risen to 34 percent. The United Nations forecasts that as many as 2 billion people in developing countries may reside in urban areas by the turn of the century, compared with an estimated 775 million in 1975. Only 23 cities in developing regions had populations over 1 million in 1959, but the number may swell to 264 million by the year 2000. Already, mushrooming cities are characteristically surrounded by sprawling shanty towns that are without food and water supplies, sewers, medical and health services, shops, schools, and garbage collection. Many of the people who have flocked there from depressed hinterlands have been unable to secure regular jobs. The unbridled growth of cities to gigantic proportions could make it virtually impossible for agriculture and industry to keep pace with the demand for basic food, goods, and services. Curtailing high population growth rates constitutes a key requirement for reducing the urban influx to manageable rates (L. Brown 1972, p. 228). Instead of mentioning this, Kahn (1976b) and his coauthors confine themselves to this general, insufficiently differentiated answer to the issue of

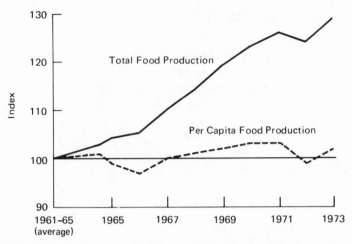

Figure 8.6. Developing countries: population growth absorbs food production increases (L. Brown 1974, p. 104). (Reprinted, by permission, from Lester R. Brown, IN THE HUMAN INTEREST. W. W. Norton & Company, Inc. Copyright © 1974 by W. W. Norton & Company, Inc.)

crowding: "There is plenty of room in almost all countries for everyone to have a suburban lifestyle" (p. 32).

Stabilization at 15 Billion: Plausible?

Since many pressing problems are worsened by runaway population growth, the need for lower rates eventuating in population stabilization has become obvious. Less evident are the levels at which world population could be sustained, either at high material standards of living or at subsistence standards. If the unfolding of the demographic transition is incompatible with the attainment of a stabilization level that provides acceptable living standards, emphasis on other voluntary strategies for decreasing birth rates is mandatory. Can Kahn, who places his bet on the demographic transition, substantiate his estimate of stabilization at about 15 billion people with a per capita annual income of approximately $20,000?

The higher the level at which stabilization occurs, the greater the pressure on the vital resources of food, energy, raw materials, and information. Excessive pressure of these resources deprives those coming into the world as well as those already inhabiting it. Hence, the global population needs to be stabilized at a level that clearly permits the basic resource needs of all people to be met sustainably. The quality of life, including the global material standard of living, would be enhanced by voluntary population stabilization at a relatively low level.

It would be extremely difficult to supply 15 billion people with sufficient food, energy, raw materials, and information. This could be done eventually—though a $20,000 per capita income remains speculative—if a source of clean, abundant, inexpensive energy were harnessed and if unprecedented progress were made in lessening political and economic constraints on an equitable distribution of resources. However, this scenario is too permeated with time delays and risks to make reliance on it tenable for current goal setting, especially since the well-being of billions of people is at stake.

Even more unjustifiable is Kahn's assertion that a population of 30 billion would be compatible with an optimistic earth-centered scenario (p. 34). By comparison, stabilization near the 7.5 billion bottom level that Kahn allows would greatly enhance projects for human dignity and world peace. Yet he fails to draw attention to the world of difference between the top and bottom levels. Moreover, he furnishes no convincing evidence that the demographic transition can proceed fast enough to achieve the bottom level.

Kahn's affluent world of 15 or 30 billion people is rendered still less plausible by his grossly overaggregated estimate of the number of people that can be maintained at high living standards. Global figures concerning expected reductions in the population growth rate fail to convey important information about how much growth would occur at what rates in which localities. According to UN estimates, a fourfold growth of the present world population would probably involve nearly tenfold growth in Africa, over sevenfold in Latin America, and almost sixfold in South Asia. The likelihood that regional food production and food import capability would keep pace with such skyrocketing population growth is extremely doubtful. Yet as Lincoln Gordon (1976) observes, Kahn does not even discuss the grim regional implications of his 15 billion figure (p. 4).

Suppose that Kahn is correct in his expectation that increasing affluence will soon result in the population growth rate taking a permanent downward course. Even then, his stress on this inflection point creates the dubious, probably mistaken, impression that the projected slowdown will both steer clear of almost all Malthusian traps and proceed at a rate sufficient to permit the amount of economic growth needed to keep itself going. The demographic transition is likely to occur too slowly in many populous developing countries to warrant Kahn's complacency.

Obstacles to the Demographic Transition

A balanced treatment of the demographic transition weighs its promising potential against the obstacles that prevent if from becoming a remedy. Objections to its alleged adequacy to arrive at an acceptable stabilization level must not be allowed to obscure its crucial role as a contributor to the achievement of such a level. One reason why economic growth should be encouraged in poor regions is that rising material standards of living generate a range of changes that promote voluntary reductions in fertility rates. While increased per capita income tends to be closely correlated with the desire for smaller families, the former takes time and the latter often takes even more time to catch up to the former. Increasing prosperity in developing countries is not always correlated with falling birthrates, as illustrated by data from Mexico, Brazil, oil-rich Arab nations, and several African nations during the last 10 to 20 years (Prehoda 1977b, p. 14). Moreover, the point at which fertility rates tend to be lowest is in the neighborhood of $1,000 annual per capita income. Income in many populous developing countries is presently far less.

Rapid economic growth is itself hindered by the population explosion that it is supposed to defuse. The gains that many countries register in GNP are often drastically reduced on the per capita level by large numbers of offspring. Thus high birthrates constitute a major impediment to the process by which the demographic transition occurs. A further obstacle in many developing countries is the momentum of population growth. A large segment of the population has yet to reach prime reproductive age—about 36 percent of all people living today are under 15 years of age. Even if each pair would only have two children, today's population could double in less than 40 years. Not only will there be more prospective parents and more children to feed, clothe, and educate; the available manpower source will triple if population doubles, precipitating grave unemployment problems. Given the momentum of population increase and the economic problems that it leaves in its wake, many poor areas might suffer major increases in mortality rates before they came close to an annual per capita income of $1,000.

Thus high birthrates and the momentum of population growth will probably put a damper on the high rates of economic growth that Kahn projects for developing countries. Consequently, he appears to overestimate the rate at which the demographic transition is likely to occur and underestimate its stabilization level. In view of the obstacles that hinder this transition, it is highly unlikely to follow the smooth trajectory that he plots. Moreover, in many heavily populated countries, worsening problems, die-offs, and planned intervention to reduce birthrates by various means may conjointly play a more important role than the demographic transition in limiting population growth.

The Demographic Transition: Predominent Cause of Reduced Growth?

Questions arise as to whether the chief cause of the recent decrease in the global population growth rate is the demographic transition and whether this decline indicates the imminence of the inflection point of the population growth curve.

Most demographers agree that the mid-1970s mark a dip in the world population growth rate from about 2 percent annually to around 1.8 or 1.9 percent. This reduction has come in the wake of:

Major shortfalls in food production, accompanied by widespread hunger and
    undernourishment in populous developing countries;

The energy crisis and the quadrupling of oil prices;

A slowdown of global economic growth;

Increasing sensitivity to limits to growth; and

Concerted efforts to implement family planning and to establish services re-
    quired to satisfy basic human needs.

Accordingly, this decrease in the growth rate is probably due much less to increasing affluence than to

Rising death rates stemming from regional shortages of reasonably priced food
    (L. Brown 1975, pp. 123, 124);

Successes of family planning programs in a number of developing countries (L.
    Brown 1973, p. 152; Ravenholt 1976, pp. 64-68); and

Efforts to meet basic human needs, as in the Peoples Republic of China, without
    necessarily raising per capita income substantially (L. Brown 1973; Cleve-
    land 1977).

This analysis scores decisively against Kahn's contention that the predominant cause of the decline is the demographic transition. Thus this decline,
the centerpiece of his supposed evidence that the demographic transition is
about to bring the population growth curve to its inflection point, paradoxically
proves to be damaging to the very inference he drew from it. The curve may be
near its inflection point but not for the main reason that he proposes. Hence,
his causally flawed model is undependable for charting future tendencies.

Finally, there is no guarantee that the global birthrate will not rise again.
Even if it does not, breakthroughs that control the aging process might so lower
death rates that population growth would be accelerated.

Strategies for Stabilization: Guaranteed Living Standards and Family Planning

Unless population growth is voluntarily limited, its consequences will limit
it by misery and death. Desirable results of declining birthrates in developing
countries include much better prospects for economic growth, for sufficient
food to meet the nutritional needs of their citizens, and for the ability to cope
with many other problems that are worsened by excessive rates of population
growth. People need to search for acceptable ways of rapidly curtailing and then
stabilizing global population growth at a relatively low level.*

----

*Some futurists, such as Garrett Hardin and Robert Prehoda, argue that the world's
population already exceeds its optimum level. Much more optimistic than Hardin regarding

The challenge is to *isolate factors* that are *correlated with reductions in the desired family size* and the birthrate and then to *create conditions in which parents will want to limit the size of their families.* On the one hand, safe economic growth and its accompaniments—including women's liberation, increased non-family-oriented occupational choices, rising levels of literacy, and better education—constitute a rewarding goal for developing countries. On the other, guaranteed minimum living standards supplemented by effective family planning programs need to be implemented to achieve major reductions in the desired family size and to make available technologies by which people can limit reproduction, regardless of whether extensive industrialization occurs.

At the United Nations World Population Conference in Bucharest (August 1974), representatives of poor countries insisted that population control can only be brought about in the context of economic and social development. Moreover, future-oriented studies conducted by John McHale, Lester Brown, Mihajlo Mesarovic and Eduard Pestel, Harlan Cleveland, and others provide persuasive evidence that major increases in the food supply and economic development are mandatory for voluntary, humane population stabilization. This, however, does not mean that developing nations are obliged to follow the Western example of extensive industrialization.

Recent research points to a common denominator in developing countries that have experienced significant sustained reductions in fertility levels without previously undergoing major increases in per capita income. This shared characteristic is access for the lowest income groups to resources required to meet basic needs. Statistics, however scanty, suggest that *societies that have taken steps to ensure minimum living standards* in the form of guaranteed incomes, food supply, health and social services, unemployment and welfare services, education, and old-age insurance generally *show declining fertility rates at lower socioeconomic levels.* Conversely, those developing societies that place the entire

---

technological potential, Prehoda (1977b) assumes what he terms a "technophilic-Malthusian perspective." He concurs with Konrad Lorentz's judgment that "overpopulation is really the root of all evil" but also maintains that a population of optimum size would eventually allow our descendants to create an exotic supertechnological utopia (p. 12). He advocates enforcement of negative population growth (NPG), deliberately reducing population in size by reducing the birthrate, during a century of transition. Even though he stresses the importance of behavioral research to show how NPG might win general acceptance in diverse societies, he agrees with Hardin that:

> If NPG will require fertility coercion during the century of transition, then it should be based on . . . "mutual coercion, mutually agreed upon by a majority of the people affected." [P. 13]

The strategies for population stabilization that I recommend avoid coercion, which could easily open a Pandora's box comparable with the one that has been opened by exponential population growth.

responsibility for gaining a subsistence on the shoulders of individual citizens tend to have persistently high rates at these levels.

Guaranteed access to basic goods and services tends to reduce the desired family size of couples who still fall far short of an annual income of $1,000. No longer do they need to have many children to make sure that a few survive to adulthood. Nor do they require a large number of male offspring to eke out a subsistence and to support them in their waning years.

Admittedly, guaranteed minimum standards of living could be abused and eventually exploded by delays in the drop of desired family size. People might still want to have many children, even when they have no pressing need for large families. They could continue to be motivated by the dictates of their religion, social custom, and status, or they might simply act out of ignorance of changing conditions. If too many services were provided free, the costs of having extra children might not become clear enough to many parents and the desired family size might not decline sufficiently. Efforts to implement minimum standards of living, therefore, need to be designated and administered wisely as well as combined with vigorous programs in family planning.

Some developing nations would be able to finance the implementation of a guaranteed living standard, as the Peoples Republic of China has done. However, many resource-poor nations would need outside assistance. International cooperation would be required to shift funds from rich countries and multinational corporations as well as to use these funds effectively.

Developed countries would find it impossible to isolate themselves from the serious global problems that would result from continuous population growth. Lester Brown (1973) maintains that we may witness the emergence of a situation in which it will be in the best interest of rich countries to launch a concerted attack on global poverty. His normative plan would establish a global minimum standard of living to meet the basic needs of all people (pp. 322–25). Since the benefits of effective implementation may be very great, the feasibility of such plans needs to be investigated thoroughly.

Guaranteed minimum standards of living must not be viewed as a substitute for, but as a supplement to, family planning and population stabilization programs. Family planning is oriented toward meeting the needs of individuals and families by preventing unwanted pregnancies. The United Nations's World Population Plan of Action affirms the basic right of individuals as well as couples to decide freely and responsibly on the number and spacing of their children.

The traditional value attached to large families and to competitive population growth among social groups has become counterproductive, not merely to the well-being of the human race collectively but also to that of the individuals that comprise it. Information and educational services can be provided by family planning programs to clarify the real material interests of people in changing socioeconomic circumstances. Yet the immediate challenge is not so much to change poor people's attitudes toward family planning as to supply them with the necessary information and contraceptives. Family planning programs, espepecially when accompanied by programs designed to satisfy basic human needs, have proved to be much more successful recently than the Kahn-Brown-Martel analysis might lead one to suspect (Ravenholt 1976, pp. 64–68). Adults in developing countries generally want to have fewer children than the average couple. Contrary to the oft-expressed assertion that people in developing countries typically oppose or ignore efforts to institute family planning programs, a 1971 UN report states:

> Studies carried out recently in many of those countries have revealed widespread interest in family planning. Although it is difficult to generalize in view of the different social, economic, and cultural conditions prevailing in the various countries, the over-all picture shows that about three quarters of the population approves of family planning; three fifths are interested in learning about family planning, about half of those with three or more children do not want more childbirths, but that only one tenth practice some form of family planning.

In view of the widespread desire for smaller families and the high acceptance rate of contraceptive use, several family planning experts have estimated that the use of present types of contraceptives by all who would like to restrict their family size might cut the global birthrate by as much as 50 percent. According to the United Nations Fund for Population Activities, only about $2 billion per year would be required to make family planning services universally available in developing countries.

Thus the chief problem is the insufficient supply of effectively mobilized family planning programs. To resolve this problem, national leaders of developing countries would have to become sufficiently convinced of the worth of these programs to implement them. In addition, developed countries would need to offer active assistance. To avoid political entanglements, aid from developed countries could be channeled through UN agencies and such informational nongovernmental organizations as Planned Parenthood.

Since formidable obstacles obstruct the path to rapid stabilization of the world's population by voluntary means, many uncertainties permeate efforts to attain this desirable, but evasive, goal. Nevertheless, cooperative, effective pursuit of the strategies mentioned above might even achieve stabilization at a level of 8 billion people or less during the next century.

Historical Inadequacy of Kahn's Safety Valve Model

Kahn's inferences to gradual voluntary reduction of economic growth in developed countries and to a successful demographic transition in developing countries clearly rest on a shakey historical foundation. This makes one wonder whether the very structure of his safety valve model is, from a historical perspective, conducive to anticipating the types of normative change that seem most plausible. He does admit that continual exponential growth would precipitate disasters eventually and that appropriate changes in the values that promote such growth are therefore needed. In numerous historical instances, failure to revise outdated societal values has contributed significantly to disaster. Does the dynamic structure of Kahn's model replicate ways in which dangerously outmoded values have been changed to prevent disasters?

A prolonged time lag in normative adaptation to new situations seems to be much more common than the spontaneous, sufficiently rapid, yet gradual and quite continuous, relatively uniform, widespread adaptation that Kahn envisages. Often the need to adjust values rendered obsolete by changed situations has not attracted sufficient attention until crises have made relatively smooth adaptation unfeasible. Even when the need for change has been perceived in time, various dissenting groups have frequently adopted conflicting sets of values. Not all, and sometimes none, of these sets have been optimal. Relatively nonadaptive normative changes have often prevailed over competing changes that would have been more appropriate. In short, normative change in such situations is typically delayed, turbulent, and particularly difficult to forecast.

Indeed, one can find many historical examples of gradual normative change that proved to be adaptive. These examples, however, are hardly comparable with the contemporary global ecological situation. More plausible than the kind of change depicted by Kahn's model are two frequent patterns of rapid, extensive normative change: (1) disaster dramatizes the obsolescence of old values and points to appropriate new ones, and (2) confronted by the threat of disaster, people of divergent orientations realize that only by cooperation can they avert common disaster and attain mutually beneficial goals.

The former can be illustrated by the potato famine in Ireland, in response to which this Catholic country reduced its population by massive immigration to the United States, disapproval of excessive reproduction within marriage, delay of the customary age of marriage, and retention of strict taboos against extramarital sex. The latter pattern of change is exemplified by the heroic collective effort of England's people to repel Hitler's onslaughts during World War II. Another example is provided by the collaborative, intense efforts of the basically nonmilitaristic scientists who worked on the Manhattan Project to devise the atomic bomb as a countermeasure to Hitler's "U Project."

Kahn's Model: Misleading for Policy Making

Kahn's safety valve model of adaptive value change, in summary, is based on one primary overpowering cause—global economic growth. Such growth induces two virtually universal normative changes: the decreasing worth of additional economic growth for affluent people and the desire for fewer children by poor people whose incomes are rising. These changes safely guide economic and population growth along smooth trajectories of very gradual decline in their growth rates. Kahn uses his model to project this departure from exponential growth, coupled with modest technological progress and a modicum of intelligent management, as likely to lead to an affluent, ecologically thriving, global postindustrial society.

Thus the methodology that Kahn used to devise his earth-centered scenario for the world during the next 200 years comes uncomfortably close to simple trend extrapolation from the two trends of GWP and global population (and a third, GWP per capita, which is derived from the other two). Extrapolation of this sort is unreliable for formulating a long-range, comprehensive forecast. Even though the trends of economic and population growth are instances of the long-term trends that Kahn has regarded as the basic devices for forecasting, his scenarios depend on the turning points and subsequent deceleration of these two trends. Such changes in trends are more difficult to forecast than the continuation of trends in the absence of contravening factors. One turning point is hypothesized as about a decade away; the other as having just begun or as likely to occur by the end of this decade. Hence, the turning points themselves are quite conjectural. Since the rationale for extrapolating declining trajectories of the trends is especially weak, Kahn's high level of confidence in his scenario is surprising.

Moreover, Kahn's model oversimplifies and incorrectly analyzes the causes that produce the two trends. Whereas it attributes the recent decrease in the population growth rate to the economic growth that brings about the demographic transition, careful analysis discloses that other causes are probably more responsible for what may be the beginning of a turning point. The projected downturn in the economic growth rate, which is treated as distinct from the recent recession, also flows from the model's overaggregated, highly questionable causal analysis.

The assumption of the relatively constant rates and directions of the two trends becomes even more dubious when juxtaposed with the usual variability of normative change. Such change often follows an action-reaction pattern and is sometimes revolutionary. The smooth rates and directions of the two trends could be altered by other trends or the interrelated problems of the complex global system. In short, Kahn's model neglects many factors that could intervene in different situations and at various times to affect the trends significantly.

Upon analysis, Kahn's model boils down to little more than his attempt to refute neo-Malthusians by turning their objections to exponential growth into an argument against them. On one hand, he contends that they wrongly project growth at exponential rates; on the other, that naturally occurring normative changes are likely to produce very slow reductions of growth rates, thus functioning as safety valves that permit enormous amounts of sustainable economic and population growth. However, Kahn's methodological and nonmethodological assumptions make his model and the earth-centered scenario derived from it distinctly misleading. Similarly, his space-bound scenario, which subsequently takes off from the earth-centered scenario upon which it is constructed, is undermined by its dependence on these assumptions. Regardless of whether he can justify the scenarios' further assumptions of pronounced ecological optimism and a planned business-as-usual approach, the adaptive value change expressed by his safety valve model renders these scenarios counterproductive guides for policy formulation. Reliance on what almost amounts to a "pre-established harmony" between the global ecological situation and appropriate normative changes encourages dangerous inaction at a time when intelligent planned intervention is urgently needed.

Ecological Assumptions

Despite Kahn's disclaimers, his earth-centered scenario depends on extreme optimism concerning prospects of rectifying global ecological problems by relatively conventional means. His underestimation of these problems and his excessive technological optimism concerning energy prospects become clear when his claims are evaluated in the light of the preceding analysis of the growth controversy (Chapter 7). Yet Kahn's assumptions about energy are so crucial to his scenarios that they warrant special attention. Moreover, our analysis of his treatment of one ecological problem—that of rapid population growth—needs to be supplemented by a brief examination of his expectations of increased food production.

Energy Availability

Kahn assumes that reasonably priced, abundant, inexhaustible energy will probably be available by around the middle of the next century or sooner. He also presupposes that the energy supply in the meantime will be adequate to fuel safely the extensive economic growth that he projects. Hence, he forecasts the availability of plenty of energy for resource extraction, pollution control, and food production.

However, nearly every leading energy expert, such as Glenn Seaborg or Hans Bethe, would reject Kahn's claims that resolution of the problem of world energy sufficiency will require no more than a decade or two (Kahn and Brown 1975, p. 39) and that failure to obtain an abundance of commercially used energy from new sources during the next century is almost inconceivable (p. 40). Kahn admits many near-term uncertainties concerning particular energy technologies but asserts that the overall energy prospects are very encouraging. Yet many experts maintain that much of the uncertainty extends to these prospects.

Kahn (1976b) regards solid fossil fuels, especially coal, as the world's best hope prior to the advent of inexhaustible energy (p. 65). But, he never comes to grips with the extremely uneven geopolitical distribution of coal deposits and the desire of many nations to avoid increased dependence on imported fuel. Furthermore, two recent projections of the extent to which the large-scale burning of fossil fuels would raise the temperature of the earth's atmosphere have cast serious doubt on the advisability of relying on coal as the predominant interim energy source for the huge amount of economic growth that Kahn forecasts (Neustadt 1977, p. 18).

Kahn (1976b) overlooks coal/oil/water emulsification, the most promising of the fossil fuel technologies that can be widely implemented in the near future. Instead, he declares that the world will probably be heavily dependent on shale oil (p. 67), the first commercial feasibility of which his estimate locates in the year 1985 (p. 82). In a footnote, however, he concedes that the commercial extraction of oil from shale "may well not be competitive with other alternatives for decades" (p. 64). He acknowledges that the conversion of coal to liquid and gaseous fuels and the extraction of oil from shale and tar sands encounter difficulties that lie in their near-term economic viability, optimum rates of development, and associated environmental, land-use, and allocation problems (p. 65).

These admissions weaken his argument that indigenous fuel supplies and competitive sources will probably result in major reductions in the Organization of Petroleum Exporting Countries's (OPEC) oil prices. Especially dubious is his claim that these prices appear unlikely to remain high for more than five or ten years and could easily drop to from $3 to $7 a barrel in Persian Gulf nations long before 15 or 20 years have elapsed (p. 60). Using the World Integrated Model, a highly differentiated second-generation version of the Mesarovic-Pestel computer model, Barry Hughes and Mihajlo Mesarovic (1978) tested this scenario (p. 8). Computer runs show that oil prices in a free market scenario rise throughout the end of this century to a level 50 percent higher than current prices in real terms. They climb even more rapidly after the turn of the century because of more severe supply constraints. When political actions are assumed to reduce the price of oil to $8 a barrel in ten years and to $3 a barrel in the year 2000, an oil shortage develops quickly as demand outstrips supply. After testing a large number of energy scenarios with alternative assumptions, Hughes and Mesarovic concluded: "The expectation that oil prices 'might easily return' to the pre-1973 level is not based on any apparent evidence or logical analysis" (p. 8). (See Figure 8.7.)

The balance-of-payments problems of many oil-importing countries render problematic Kahn's claim that within a decade an adequate adjustment will be made if oil prices happen to remain high. Robert Stobaugh and Daniel Yergin (1979), coeditors of the report of Harvard Business School's extensive Energy Project, show that the costs and dangers of heavy dependence on imported oil are far greater than most U.S. citizens have realized. The more oil that importing nations buy from the OPEC cartel, the more readily the cartel can raise the world price of oil. Despite the disadvantages of making its economy increasingly dependent on decisions made in oil producing and exporting nations, the United States in 1979 imported an estimated 47 percent of the oil it consumed as compared with 24 percent in 1970. The recent stoppage of oil exports from Iran and the rise in oil prices by OPEC countries to a range from $24 to $30 a barrel have

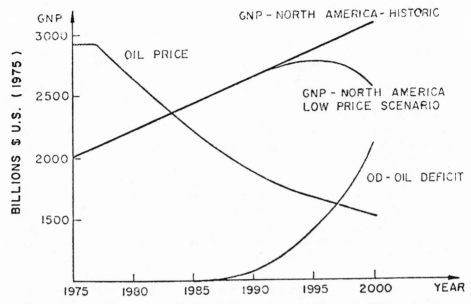

Figure 8.7. Computer run indicating that low oil prices would rapidly deplete reserves and bring about a decline in U.S. GNP (Hughes and Mesarovic 1978, p. 9). (Courtesy of the BULLETIN, published by the World Future Society, 4916 St. Elmo Avenue, Washington, D.C. 20014.)

rekindled the public awareness, originally sparked by the 1973–74 Arab oil crisis, of the drawbacks of excessive dependence on foreign oil.

Additional doubts are rasied by another of Kahn's assertions: "If oil in the Persian Gulf were to disappear over the next 10 years, the immediate and obvious need for coal would dictate that adjustments be made quickly and effectively" (1976b, p. 21). To replace oil imports with an equal amount of nuclear energy production, Western Europe would have to construct 3,000 nuclear plants of 1,000-megawatt size between 1977 and 1978, or nearly one per day. The Hughes-Mesarovic model indicates that "the effect of eliminating in 10 years what amounts to nearly 80% of world oil trade—or 50% of the energy supply in Western Europe—is that the world economic system simply collapses" (1978, p. 9). Similarly, Stobaugh and Yergin (1979) conclude that it is only romanticism to think that the United States could halt the rise of oil imports through the four conventional domestic energy sources: oil, natural gas, coal, and nuclear plants. (Stobaugh and Yergin do recommend reduction in U.S. oil imports— much slower than that envisioned by Kahn—attained much more by conservation and by accelerating the transition to solar energy than by relying on programs to develop synthetic fuels.)

Kahn's treatment of fission power is quite balanced, yet he does not even mention the promising thorium-converter reactor that would use the isotope U^{233} diluted with nonfissionable U^{238}, thus decreasing weapons-making capability and burning uranium with such efficiency that breeder reactors would not be needed. Moreover, he is overly confident that adequate alternatives to fission energy will be available during the rest of this century for industrialized countries that lack coal deposits. To make matters worse, the harnessing of an alternative source of affordable, plentiful energy for extensive use during the next century is far from certain.

Not only does Kahn sometimes fail to estimate the costs of possible energy technologies; some of his estimates are already obsolete on the low side (L. Gordon 1976, p. 5). For instance, one of his charts shows the cost of photovoltaic, ocean thermal, and even the bottom range of solar thermal energy conversion technologies to be roughly equal to the cost of conventional energy technologies by the year 2020 (Kahn 1976b, p. 70). The figures given for wind or bioconversion technologies are even lower. One way of making a case for some of these estimates is to assume the cost of conventional energy generation will rise substantially. This, however, conflicts with Kahn's position that energy costs will probably decrease.

This chart illustrates Kahn's tendency to underestimate not just the costs of new technologies but also the time needed to research, develop, and implement them. Indeed, this process can often be accelerated by crash programs. Yet Kahn bypasses the pressing problem of whether enough capital will be available for the huge amounts of investment that they require. Finally, even a high level of funding does not guarantee rapid development and implementation of a new technology, as demonstrated by problems encountered in the development of the breeder reactor.

Furthermore, Kahn tends to exaggerate potential power production. For instance, many energy experts do not expect that geothermal energy will be harnessed on the scale that he envisions and that it may well be the first of the eternal energy sources to achieve large-scale power production (p. 75).

Otherwise, Kahn's treatment of the various solar, geothermal, and fusion technologies is generally lucid, balanced, and accurate. Major difficulties arise not so much from the analysis of individual technologies as from the summary of global resources (pp. 82, 83). Despite the many uncertainties that pervaded their examination of the individual technologies, Kahn and his coauthors conclude that they expect all but one of 16 major energy sources to be "commercially feasible before 2050, and most of them by the year 2000" (p. 83). (See Table 8.2.) The only exception is geothermal energy derived directly from deep molten rock.

The summary of prospective energy sources presented in Table 8.2 does not follow from the prior analysis on which it is supposedly based. In a number of respects, the list and its accompanying explanation appear to be incompatible

TABLE 8.2

Kahn's Summary of Global Energy Resources

Source	Long-Term Potential (Est.)	1st Commercial Feasibility (Est.)	Problem Areas[a]
Hydroelectric	.1 Qe/yr.	Current	C
Oil & Natural Gas	30 Q	Current	E
Tar Sands & Oil Shale	30–2,000 Q	1985	C,E
Coal & Lignite	200 Q	Current	E
U–235 (Free World)	15 Qe	Current	E
U–235 (Ocean)	3,000 Qe	Current	C,E
Uranium for Breeders	> 100,000 Qe	1995	C,E
Li–6 (D–T Fusion Reactor)[b]	320 Q	1995–2005	C,E,T
Deuterium (D–D Fusion Reactor)	> 1 billion Q	2020–50	C,E,T
Solar Radiation (1% of Surface Energy)	30 Q/yr.	1980–2000	C,T
Ocean Gradients	20 Qe/yr.	2000	C,T
Organic Conversion	1.2 Q/yr.	1975–90	C
Geothermal—Magma	> 1 billion Q	?	C,E,T
Hot Dry Rock	> 100,000 Qe	1990–95	C,E,T
Liquid-dominated	> 1,000 Qe	1980–85	C,E
Dry Steam	1 Qe	Current	—

[a]C = cost, E = environment, T = technology.

[b]Li–6: The lithium isotope used to breed tritium in first-generation fusion reactors. World resources might be 10 times greater than shown.

Source: Kahn, Brown, and Martel 1976b, p. 82. (From THE NEXT 200 YEARS by Herman Kahn, William Brown, and Leon Martel. Copyright © 1976 by Hudson Institute. By permission of William Morrow & Company.)

with the analysis. In short, the extreme technological optimism expressed by this list constitutes an unsupported, basically unsupportable declaration of faith.

Planning should guard against the possibility of not acquiring the plentiful, relatively nonpolluting, economical energy that Kahn's scenarios presuppose and should also take into account the likelihood of some energy shortages during the next two decades. Therefore, contrary to Kahn's position, policies of selective industrial growth and slower rates of industrial growth appear to be advisable for industrialized countries while they research and develop alternative energy sources. Kahn seriously underestimates the urgent need for energy conservation (p. 61).

Raw Materials and Pollution

Kahn argues cogently that physical limits to nonrenewable metals have been grossly exaggerated by such forecasters as Dennis Meadows (see Chapter 7). His analysis of prospects for enhancing the supply of raw materials is quite enlightening. Still, the amount required by his scenarios presuppose the harnessing of abundant, sufficiently clean, affordable energy. He also tends to underestimate costs and minimizes sociocultural constraints on technological possibilities. Kahn's claim that pollution will be manageable in his envisioned growth world and that the cost of curtailing it will even decline during the next century (p. 139) is rooted in his questionable assumptions that (1) "technology can solve or alleviate almost all pollution problems" (p. 151), (2) people will take advantage of this technological potential, and (3) clean, plentiful energy will become available (p. 155).

Recent evidence suggests that the chemical pollution of biological systems is more serious than most experts had thought (Epstein and Grundy 1974; also, see Chapter 7). Hence, Kahn probably underestimates the difficulty of controlling pollution adequately and the necessary cost. The amount of worldwide economic development that he projects needs to be accompanied by much additional progress in protecting organisms and their environments from chemical contamination. Scientifically based concern about "such things as genetic damage caused by radiation or chemical pollution" must not be dismissed on Kahn's (1976b) supposition that "within a century or so, man [probably] will be able to prevent such damage" (p. 173).

Food Production

Kahn presents a valuable survey of techniques for greatly expanding the food supply. His analysis, however, is marred by a number of deficiencies. For instance, he probably underrates the extent of malnourishment when he approvingly mentions a recent Food and Agriculture Organization (FAO) estimate that only 10 percent of the world population has an insufficient protein-energy supply (p. 109, source unspecified). The World Bank estimated that between 600 and 759 million people were malnourished in 1976, whereas Jean Mayer argues that about 1 billion suffer from malnutrition (see Chapter 7). The rising prices of food, as illustrated by soybean prices, have exacerbated the malnutrition of poor people (see Figure 8.8).

The highly optimistic land assessment study of project MOIRA (Model for International Relations in Agriculture) calculates that, adjusting for soil conditions and water constraints, Africa has a total potential of 317.5 million hectares, not 500 to 700 million yet to be developed as Kahn indicates (Hughes and Mesarovic 1978, p. 13). Kahn contemplates the development of tens of millions of hectares of arid land by means of low-cost irrigation. His plan for double-cropping requires the irrigation of three-fourths of the 3.19 billion hectares to be brought under cultivation. Conversely, the MOIRA project calculates that

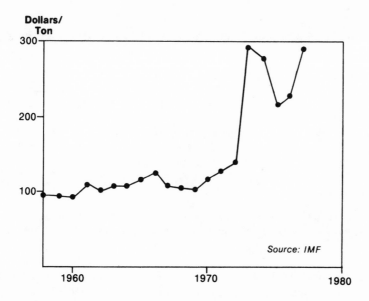

Figure 8.8. World price of soybeans, 1958–77 (L. Brown 1978, p. 175). (Courtesy of Worldwatch Institute.)

only 470 million hectares can potentially be irrigated, and the U.S. Department of Agriculture estimates that irrigation facilities in developing countries are unlikely to expand at a rate greater than 1 percent a year from 1975 levels (p. 14). Fresh water is becoming more scarce than Kahn intimates, and energy-intensive desalinization is still costly. Hence, the tapping of abundant, inexpensive energy is one prerequisite for the feasibility of Kahn's plan. At least for the next two or three decades, developing countries need to implement such energy-efficient "intermediate" or appropriate technologies (Schumacher 1973) as trickle irrigation (see Table 8.3).

In their reply to the Hughes-Mesarovic critique, William M. Brown and Leon Martel (1978) state that the MOIRA study estimates Africa's potential agricultural land at 761.2 million hectares *before* correction is made for soil deficiencies and the need for irrigation (p. 20). Brown and Martel believe that within the next 200 years these deficiencies and this need for irrigation could be taken care of by sufficient investment and technological advance. One wonders how the requisite level of investment would be generated.

Kahn's focus on technologies for producing conventional and unconventional foods unconventionally calls attention to opportunities that are too often overlooked. However, "Kahn is far too glib in his easy assertions of unconventional food factory production as a solution already in sight for the early twenty-first century" (L. Gordon 1976, p. 5). Kahn's (1976b) "reasonably optimistic

TABLE 8.3

Estimated World Irrigated Land Area, 1900–75, with Projections to 2000

Year	Irrigated Area	Average Annual Increase
	(MILLION HECTARES)	(PERCENT)
1900	40	
1950	110	1.9
1975	200	2.6
2000 (projected)	260	1.1

Note: From L. Brown 1978, p. 141. (Courtesy of Worldwatch Institute.)
Source: *FAO Production Yearbook*, and author's estimates.

scenario" assumes that by the year 2025 advanced agricultural technology alone will more than double the total world grain production in 1975 (p. 134). However, this energy-intensive technology will probably produce far less unless much larger amounts of affordable energy become available. Even if powered by such energy, the hydroponic farming that Kahn expects to become competitive on a large scale during the next century might be up to five times more expensive than today's soil-based techniques in regard to yield per acre (pp. 130, 131).

The future of synthetic food is more problematic than Kahn suggests. In view of the carcinogenic character of a number of food additives, synthetic food requires extensive testing before being placed on the market.

The major weakness in Kahn's presentation is that theoretically possible food production is not linked closely enough to necessary economic inputs. When all of the problems of food production and distribution are taken into account, it is not at all clear that 15 billion people would be adequately and sustainably nourished. Hughes and Mesarovic (1978) tested Kahn's scenario (Kahn 1976b, p. 134) to find what inputs into the agricultural sector would be needed to reach that level and whether one can realistically expect those inputs to be available at the appropriate times and in the quantities required. According to their computer runs, "The immense investment required . . . could not be generated internally within developing countries, nor could it be expected to derive from transfers of resources from the developed world" (p. 12). (See Figure 8.9.)

Even if Kahn's scenario were economically feasible, it would still require substantial revision to cope with other sociocultural constraints. Such countervailing forces as narrowly perceived competitive self-interest, unwise decision making, and inefficiency can be weakened but will, nevertheless, continue to thwart the aim of employing available funds optimally. Moreover, many current sociocultural constraints would have to be loosened to achieve equitable distri-

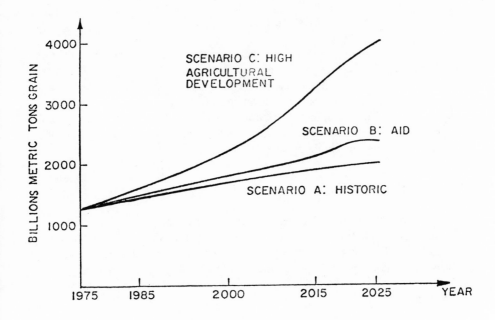

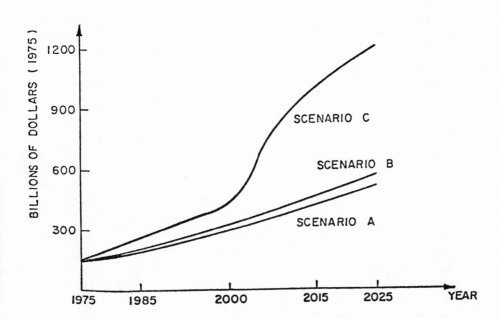

Figure 8.9. Computer runs of three agricultural development scenarios, showing the projected production and costs of each (Hughes and Mesarovic 1978, pp. 11, 12). (Courtesy of the BULLETIN, published by the World Future Society, 4916 St. Elmo Avenue, Washington, D.C. 20014.)

bution of food to 15 billion people, including those at low levels of income in developing countries. Thus major reforms, not just Kahn's "reasonable management" and moderate technological progress, are needed to take increased advantage of what is technologically and economically feasible. In view of the restrictions on food production and distribution capacity, efforts to expand the food supply and distribute it equitably must go hand in hand with family planning programs oriented toward decreasing the birthrate.

The Development Gap

Kahn relies on the widening income gap between developed and developing nations to promote rapid, sustained economic growth in most of the latter (p. 34) (see Table 8.4). He argues that by the year 2000 perhaps more than two-thirds of mankind will have passed the level of $1,000 per capita income (p. 48).

TABLE 8.4

GNP per Capita in 20 Most Populous Countries

Country	Dollars
United States	6,640
Fed. Rep. of Germany	5,890
France	5,190
Japan	3,880
United Kingdom	3,360
Italy	2,770
USSR	2,300
Spain	1,960
Mexico	1,000
Brazil	900
Turkey	690
Philippines	310
People's Rep. of China	300
Thailand	300
Egypt	280
Nigeria	240
Indonesia	150
India	130
Pakistan	130
Bangladesh	100

Note: L. Brown 1976, p. 196. (Courtesy of THE FUTURIST, published by the World Future Society, 4916 St. Elmo Avenue, Washington, D.C. 20014.)
Source: World Bank.

What an accomplishment this would be is dramatized by the International Labor Organization's estimate that two-thirds of the population in the developing market economies—about half of the world population—had per capita incomes of less than $200 in 1972 (Hughes and Mesarovic 1978, p.5). Hence two questions arise: Can enough investment be generated between now and the year 2000 to fulfill Kahn's expectation? If so, what changes, if any, would that volume of investment require in national and international policies?

The Hughes-Mesarovic Critique of Kahn's Scenario

To answer the questions posed above, Hughes and Mesarovic programmed their World Integrated Model with a historic trend scenario for Africa and South Asia. This scenario, which is based on a continuation of past policies and world economic relationships, makes rather optimistic assumptions concerning regional efforts at self-development. The computer run suggests that by the year 2000 the average annual per capita income will have reached only $400 in Africa and $200 in South Asia (in 1975 dollars). The combined population of these two regions will comprise about 30 percent of the world's population by the year 2000. Since other regions may also fall short of Kahn's target and such regions as Latin America are characterized by huge income disparities, Hughes and Mesarovic conclude: "It is quite evident that the Hudson Report argument regarding the level of global development by the year 2000 is not based on current facts and trends" (p. 5).

Next, Hughes and Mesarovic sought to ascertain the magnitude of change in the world economic order needed to reach Kahn's goal. They assumed that the necessary investment in Africa and South Asia would come from the developed market economies in proportion to their GNPs. "Assuming rather efficient use of the transferred funds and an optimal schedule of such transfers, the annual increment needed . . . would be on the order of 140 billion dollars by the year 2000, with the total transfer of resources reaching a level of nearly 2.5 trillion dollars" (p. 5). By then, cumulative transfer from North America alone would reach nearly $1 trillion, the equivalent of about 60 percent of the total current U.S. GNP. Even by 1990, the transfer from North America would surpass the cost of its imported oil (pp. 5, 6).

To what extent could funds be transferred effectively from developed to developing countries by means of the "forces" or economic measures—for instance, foreign aid, export of labor, and tourism (Kahn 1976b, pp. 35-49)—that take advantage of the development gap to promote the growth of developing countries? After conducting scenario runs to answer this question, Hughes and Mesarovic (1978) concluded:

> *Our analysis of the assumptions underlying the Hudson Institute scenario for rapid economic transition indicates that there are impediments—economic, not to mention political (e.g., the imposition of what would amount to a $1,000 tax per family per year in the United States to support foreign aid) and physical (e.g., the interna-*

> *tional transport of 70 to 100 million people each year as "guest laborers" or tourists)—of such magnitude that none of the measures cited (in isolation or in combination) could realistically be expected to provide conditions for achieving the Hudson target. The argument that such a scenario should be expected to occur over the next 25 years is without foundation. [P. 6]*

Much further analysis would be required to establish just how reliable the Hughes-Mesarovic scenarios are. Brown and Martel (1978) maintain that their own current lack of knowledge of the techniques and data or which the Hughes-Mesarovic critique rests "is by no means resolved by their [Hughes and Mesarovic's] footnote which informs the reader that their printouts, data, and assumptions can be obtained upon payment of a presumably nominal fee" (p. 17). Indeed, Brown and Martel score a limited number of points against the critique, to a considerable extent because Hughes and Mesarovic had to translate the assertions of *The Next 200 Years* into specific numerical terms to apply computer analysis. However, the Hughes-Mesarovic scenarios generally appear to be much more dependable than the overall development scenario set forth by Kahn, Brown, and Martel. The implausibility of this scenario up to the year 2000 undermines the further projection of steady progress to a superaffluent world by 2176.

The Gap: Promise or Peril?

Despite the unfeasible character of his scenario, Kahn makes certain supportable claims that score against those neo-Malthusians who have taken opposing positions. He correctly asserts that the development gap typically contributes to the economic growth of developing nations. Moreover, he detects several forces that aid this growth. As Lincoln Gordon (1976) also argues, cooperative attempts by developing nations to decouple from the markets and technology of the industrialized world in order to "correct the world's economic imbalances" would risk forfeiting a major potential force for accelerated development (p. 4). More important than reducing this gap are absolute increases in living standards aimed at meeting the basic needs of poor people in developing countries.

Nevertheless, Kahn creates the impression that the best way for the poor countries to get rich is for rich countries to get rich faster. Gordon detects "a ring of Victorian upper-class smugness" in this claim that "the best the North can do to promote development in the South is to focus exclusively on . . . [its] own prosperity" (p. 6). Historical evidence suggests that the developmental effects of income gaps work best with middle-class countries that are not far behind the leaders (p. 5). The poorest populous countries, which need growth the most, may continue to stagnate in poverty. The World Bank estimated in 1967 that 750 million people with a present average per capita income of less than $100 have little more than a faint promise of a $2 annual increase over the next decade (Hughes and Mesarovic 1978, p. 5). They are locked into a set of circumstances that they cannot break out of by themselves. Unless birthrates in South

Asia are brought down, such stagnation in a Malthusian trap seems more likely than Kahn's scenario (L. Gordon 1976, p. 5). In tropical Africa today, government complacency about high birthrates threatens to exacerbate development problems when the high mortality rates are greatly reduced through public health measures within the next decade or two. Even Kahn admits that the non-coping developing countries seem likely to grow at slower rates until late in the next century (Kahn 1976b, p. 55). Since such a large percentage of the human race resides in these countries, the need to devise feasible, acceptable programs of planned intervention to meet basic human needs is especially urgent.

Furthermore, Kahn underrates the dangers to world solidarity inherent in the expanding development gap. His projections of the extent to which the development gap may expand should be viewed against the background of the intensifying interpenetration of the world's divergent regions, growing awareness of absolute and relative deprivation, rising demands for equality, and spreading capacity to build nuclear weapons. The gap then begins to take on the ominous appearance of an unstable, potentially earth-shattering fissure between an affluent North and an impoverished South. This impression is greatly intensified by the untenability of Kahn's projection that by the year 2000 two-thirds of the world's people may have annual per capita incomes of over $1,000. Grandiose expectations that are subsequently dashed by brute facts often trigger devastating consequences. If bitter experience drives representatives of poor nations to the conclusion that their promised growth is not promoted sufficiently by the maximum growth of rich nations, they will denounce the evasive promises as another version of specious Western ideology designed to further the interest of the rich at the expense of the poor. Thus the growth ideology would join the ranks of the antigrowth ideology. Clearly, this would undermine prospects for a cooperative, peaceful world.

Normative Forecasts for Coping with the Gap

Among the growing number of normative forecasts devised to cope with the development gap are those made by Lester Brown and teams headed by two Nobel Prize winners, Wassily Leontief and Jan Tinbergen. These forecasts, though markedly different in their aims and in some of their assumptions and conclusions, advocate the reduction of the development gap as an especially important goal. They agree that drastic institutional reforms promoting intelligent international and national cooperation are required to reach this goal. These reforms would stretch unduly restrictive sociocultural limits to growth. A brief overview of the Leontief and Tinbergen forecasts will not only disclose alternatives to Kahn's orientation, but also to Brown's.

The Future of the World Economy (1977) records the outcome of research by economist Wassily Leontief's UN team concerning the prospects of sustained accelerated development of poor countries during the remainder of this century. The Leontief model of the world economy divides the world into

15 economic regions, each of which is characterized in terms of 45 sectors of economic activity.

The Leontief team concluded that physical limits need not prevent rapid development that would begin to close the gap between developed and developing countries between now and the year 2000. Substantial investment could increase land productivity from 60 percent to 100 percent to provide sufficient food for an expanding population. Pollution is a grave problem that is nonetheless technologically manageable at a relatively high, but not unbearable, cost. World mineral consumption is projected to grow so rapidly that from three to four times the quantity of minerals consumed throughout the history of civilization will be consumed during the last 30 years of the twentieth century. Yet known reserves of metallic minerals and fossil fuels are generally sufficient to supply rapidly increasing world needs until the year 2000 and probably into the early portion of the twenty-first century, though prices will rise significantly and regional shortages could occur. Moreover, smooth transitions to dependence on new energy sources are by no means guaranteed.

Thus the chief limits to the economic growth advocated by this normative forecast are political, social, and institutional. The accelerated development of poor countries accompanied by a substantial narrowing of the average income gap that separates them from rich countries could be obtained only by the combined satisfaction of two general conditions. One is far-reaching political, social, and institutional changes within developing countries; the other, significant changes in the world economic order.

A crucial requirement is that developing countries devote 30 to 40 percent of their gross product to capital investment. This necessitates drastic measures of economic policy in the fields of taxation and credit. Only by reducing the share of their income that is now channeled into personal consumption could they increase their rate of total saving enough to have sufficient funds for investment. Furthermore, to attain a 50 percent reduction of the income gap between developed and developing countries by the year 2000, higher growth rates in developing countries would have to be combined with slightly lower ones in developed countries.

At the request of the Club of Rome in 1974, the Dutch economist Jan Tinbergen assembled a team of 21 scholars to formulate a normative forecast for the next few decades (*RIO: Reshaping the International Order*, 1976). As distinguished from the Leontief report's emphasis on what developing nations can do to promote their accelerated economic growth, the Tinbergen report's focus is primarily on what the developed West can do to meet the basic needs of impoverished people. The fundamental aim of the world community should be to achieve a life of dignity and well-being for all world citizens (Tinbergen et al. 1976, p. 61). This requires the creation of an equitable social order, both internationally and nationally. "Society as a whole must accept the responsibility for guaranteeing a minimum level of welfare for all its citizens" and "aim at equalizing opportunities within and among nations" (p. 63).

The Tinbergen team is distinctly less optimistic than the Leontief team about prospects for resource availability, pollution control, and food production and, hence, about prospects for rapid, sustainable industrial growth in developing countries. Mass consumerism in industrialized countries, stimulated by artificially generated demand, has brought enormous waste in a needy, finite world. Both to avoid turning the oceans into "the ultimate cesspool" and to promote the equitable distribution of their mineral wealth, they need to be treated as "a common heritage." Moreover, rich nations should help poor nations become increasingly independent in food production and could also free more grain for export by putting a ceiling on their own meat consumption. "Without international and, where necessary, national reforms, the humble wheatsheaf seems destined to become a powerful weapon of economic warfare and the hungry millions of Africa and Asia, pawns in the game of international politics" (pp. 30, 31). Furthermore, "support should be given to all efforts to establish a negotiated timetable for constructive reductions in military budgets with the simultaneous and effective transfer of resources thus released to constructive civilian uses, including developmental purposes" (p. 167). World military expenditures are now approaching $300 billion a year.

The Tinbergen team traces the current world economic crisis to the inability of the present international system to promote the best interests of an increasingly interdependent world. What is required are fundamental institutional reforms oriented toward creating a new international order from which all would benefit. These reforms include:

An International Industrial Development Bank,
A system for international taxation that would be handled by a World Treasury,
The creation of an international reserve currency by an International Central
    Bank,
A World Energy Research Authority, and
A Disarmament Agency.

A major objective of many reforms of this sort would be to promote the equitable development of the world's poor people, not a "catching up" with wasteful aspects of Western life. "Nor can mass poverty necessarily be attacked through high growth rates, the advantages of which will eventually 'trickle down' to the masses" (p. 71). What is produced and how it is distributed is more important than high growth rates of production.

To investigate how income disparities might be reduced significantly, Tinbergen and his colleagues constructed scenarios based on alternative assumptions about population growth, food production, and income growth (pp. 88, 93). The team concluded that the 13-to-1 real income differential between the richest 10 percent and the poorest 10 percent of the world's population could be reduced to 13-to-4 over a 42-year period by:

A 5 percent growth rate in per capita incomes in Third World countries,
A growth rate of only 1.7 percent in industrialized countries (about half the existing rate, so as to attain zero growth in approximately 40 years),
A maximum growth in world food production of 3.1 percent a year (compared with about 2.7 today), and
A population growth of 0.1 percent less than the "low" UN forecasts (p. 93).

Among the objections raised against the Leontief forecast is the following: problems engendered by such large-scale gorwth might eventuate in unmanageable ecological crises beyond the forecast's relatively short-term time horizon. Typical critics of the Tinbergen forecast argue that it fails to supply feasible scenarios for implementing its recommendations in the arena of international politics. Regardless of whether these objections are justified, such normative forecasts supply insights into alternative ways of coping with the development gap.

Kahn's Neglect of Crucial Sociocultural Limits

Restrictive Sociocultural Forces

Kahn's forecast exhibits considerable insight into technological possibilities. Suppose that unqualified acceptance of his promissory note concerning these possibilities could be justified. This would not imply that human beings would necessarily make the major economic and political changes needed to develop and fully implement these technologies rapidly. A crucial reason why Kahn's forecast is misleading for policy making is that it tends to underestimate current sociocultural (particularly, economic and political) forces that interfere with efforts to develop the best feasible technologies and to adopt ecologically appropriate practices. These sociocultural constraints (Hirsch 1976; Miles 1976) constitute the primary barriers to sustainable economic growth today.*

In his own way, Kahn focuses on sociocultural constraints. He attributes many basic difficulties to shortcomings of recent policies and poor management. However, his growth scenario explicitly assumes only a modicum of intelligence and good management to provide prudent guidance along the present course (Kahn 1976b, pp. 7, 156). His projection of the almost-automatic gradual oc-

---

*Rufus Miles's *Awakening from the American Dream—The Social and Political Limits to Growth* (1976) analyzes determinants that have made U.S. society highly vulnerable to further sabotage and social deterioration. Although his outlook appears to be overly pessimistic, Miles's insightful delineation of social and political limits supplies an antidotal additive to Kahn's undiluted technological optimism.

Another pessimistic work that balances Kahn's lopsided approach is Fred Hirsch's *Social Limits to Growth* (1966). Hirsch argues that growing material affluence exacerbates frustration, since an increasing proportion of the additional goods, services, and facilities that consumers seek cannot be acquired or used by all without spoiling them for each other.

currence of normative changes needed to enhance the safety of growth glosses over many of the dangerously outmoded cultural beliefs, values, goals, institutions, and policies that need to be revised rapidly. Appropriate changes would promote intelligent, cooperative planned intervention aimed at decreasing the probability of premature encounters with limits to growth. Inherent in this aim would be the effort to remedy interrelated global problems sufficiently to guide the human race into a rewarding future of sustainable selective economic growth coupled with voluntary population stabilization at a relatively low level.

Kahn's *World Economic Development* (1979) is more tentative, somewhat less optimistic, and more concerned with sociocultural limits to growth than is *The Next 200 Years*. His treatment of specific aspects of economic development is enhanced by attention to cultural differences and frequent acknowledgment that bad management or bad luck could interfere with the realization of his projections. One subsection of chapter 3 focuses on "Social Limits to Growth." Kahn has become distinctly less optimistic about the short-term future, which is characterized by the growing pains of an emerging superindustrial economy, malaise, institutional problems, and inflation. He still projects a world of $20,000 per capita annual income "as perhaps 'the most probable situation'" (p. 73). However, he now regards world population as leveling off at 10 billion people instead of 15 billion and GWP as being correspondingly reduced from his previous estimate to $200 trillion (p. 73). The postulated reduction of likely global population by a third certainly improves the scenario. Its credibility, however, is diminished by Kahn's belief that

> very little ingenuity soon demonstrates that as far as we know today this kind of a world does not present us with extraordinarily difficult technological or economic problems, given reasonably good management. We tentatively conclude that even if the management is not good but not really bad, we could probably get from here to there, not necessarily smoothly and perhaps with a lot of tragedy on the way. [P. 73]

Moreover, Kahn still presumes "that far away the safest, most normal and reasonable path is to go along with what might be thought of as the 'natural' path, where natural forces do the slowing down, not government programs" (p. 73). Thus Kahn has not changed his basic position, though he has improved it by qualifying it. It remains open to the objection that he shortchanges the force of sociocultural limits to growth and the need for fundamental planned changes.

Deficiencies in the Kahn-Brown-Martel (1976b) forecast stemming from neglect of sociocultural limits to growth have been unveiled, for instance, by the critique of his safety valve model and by the Hughes-Mesarovic arguments against the feasibility of his scenarios. Other examples include the analysis of costs and delays that seem likely to retard the development and implementation of many technologies that he anticipates. Among the sociocultural factors that limit technological advance are:

Inadequately funded, poorly coordinated research and development programs;

Shortages of investment capital;

Inferior design and unanticipated consequences of a new technology;

Excessive cost of initial outlay or maintenance;

Inadequate government incentives, such as laws and taxes, to develop and rapidly implement nonpolluting and pollution-control technologies;

Skillful opposition to a commercially competitive new technology by vested interests, to whom its adoption brings the depreciation of present capital; and

Loss of control over a technology when it becomes an economic necessity by being absorbed into a social system.

Additional sociocultural hindrances to the amount of sustainable growth that the purely technological viewpoint leads one to expect include:

Difficulty in managing today's large, complex systems, which tend toward relatively low performance as they become more incomprehensible, and toward vulnerability to disruption as a result of increasing levels of interdependence (see Schwartz, Teige, and Harman 1977, p. 277);

Counterintuitive behavior of complex social systems: obscurity of some of the critical pressure points at which such systems are highly sensitive to policy changes;

Excessive compartmentalization of aspects of problems as a consequence of institutional boundaries devised for less tightly coupled societies, instead of sufficiently comprehensive approaches to problem solving (p. 278);

Loss of shared societal purpose that balances individual desires and the general well-being and that, thereby, supports the efficacy and legitimacy of basic societal institutions (p. 278);

Corporate, regional, and international pursuit of short-range, self-centered goals to the detriment of other parts of the system and of the system as a whole in the long run; and

The tragedy of the commons, which occurs when a shared environment—air, rivers and lakes, the oceans and their resources, space, and the like—is overexploited for short-term self-interest.

Outmoded Beliefs and Values

Many sociocultural limits to growth can be traced beyond current policies and institutions to cultural beliefs and values that, though outmoded or otherwise inappropriate, continue to shape the goals of economic and political systems (Jones 1975b, 1977, 1978, 1980b). The most basic value and corresponding goal is the maximization of both economic growth and political power. This presently challenged goal has been achieved primarily by maximizing the growth of technology. Optimism concerning economic growth is rooted in the belief that science and technology can continually enhance the material standard of living. To expand their own political power in the competitive arena of international policies, nations rely on economic growth and on increasingly destructive weapons derived from technological sophistication.

Historically, Eastern civilizations have tended to value harmony with nature. By contrast, Westerners have been culturally oriented toward controlling nature by technology. Rational bourgeois capitalism and the nation-state that arose in Europe during early modern times depend on competitive self-interest to supply the motivational power for economic and political growth. Adam Smith's "invisible hand" seemed to guide private self-interest to unwittingly serve the common good. Despite warnings by Thomas Malthus and John Stuart Mill, the principles that governed business and politics treated the global system (technically the earth-sun system) as if it were an unconditionally "open system." Such a system would have an unlimited supply of usable energy, unlimited reservoirs for resource extraction, unlimited potential for food production, and unlimited sinks for pollution absorption. Technological breakthroughs were counted on to surmount any limits to growth. Regardless of whether this belief in an unconditionally open system was explicitly articulated, in practice the earth was treated as if it were unlimited in its capability to support continual industrial growth. Thus little responsibility was assumed for the adverse consequences of economic and political behavior on people at that time, on future generations, and on the exploited environment.

These increasingly obsolete beliefs, values, and goals direct current economic and political systems toward crisis-prone growth and away from sufficient emphasis on safe growth. Although new technologies might make possible much sustainable industrial growth by harnessing a source of abundant, non-polluting energy at reasonable prices, this by no means implies that the earth-sun system is unconditionally open. Since it is not, wasteful behavior needs to be curtailed and efficient design encouraged in order to do more with less energy and resources.

Many cultural traditions have inculcated desires for large families, or at least for many male offspring, which were considered to confer palpable benefits. Even though these traditions in many developing societies have continued to guide people's thoughts and behavior long after changing environmental circumstances had rendered them inappropriate, significant reductions in desired family size have started to occur.

Several inappropriate beliefs and values that have long characterized industrial societies have also begun to change rather dramatically. One is the "open-system" belief; another, the value expressed by the "technological imperative," the assumption that what can be done technologically should be done. This imperative, which ignores limits to growth, is being replaced by technology assessment, which evaluates feasible technologies in order to choose between them. Although definitely improved by such action-guiding changes, contemporary economic and political systems still need to be revised extensively.

Inappropriate "Linear" Economies

Increased material production and consumption constitute overriding goals in both capitalist and socialist economic systems. Economic progress in market-economy countries is primarily measured by annual increases in GNP; in centrally planned socialist countries, by production quotas over the last year or within a given multiyear plan. Judging the success of an economy in terms of increases in production and consumption creates a demand for the increased turnover of material goods. The production of quality goods that last would lead to less consumption, less production, and less profit. Hence, the values of product durability and quality have been downgraded, and the useful practice of built-in obsolescence has become an important instrumental value. This practice also stems from the value-laden belief that what is new is better than what is old.

Built-in obsolescence and the creation of artificial demand result in the waste of natural resources and the acceleration of pollution, not only by producers but also by consumers who discard obsolete products into the environment. Yet at least initially, concern about resource use and environmental quality raises the costs of production and consumption and diminishes output.

In view of the illimitable, reckless character of existing economic systems, Kenneth Boulding (1970) colorfully depicts them as "cowboy economics." Such economic systems, whether capitalist or socialist, rely on a relatively "linear economy" or an "open materials economy." Raw materials are extracted to maximize production and subsequent consumption, both of which increase pollution. The economy, which presupposes that the global system is unconditionally open, is linear or open for two reasons. First, nonrenewable natural resources are not conserved by limited, efficient use and recycling. Second, pollution is not minimized by recycling and emission controls. Hence, inputs from the environment result in excessive resource depletion; the return of wastes to the environment, in pollution. By contrast, outputs in a "circular" economic system would not be eventually discarded as rubbish but would be recycled for further production (see Figure 8.10).

As long as resources are only mildly depleted and the environment is relatively unpolluted, raw materials and waste disposal may be inexpensive or free. Thus limits to growth seem quite irrelevant. However, the situation has changed. Pollution has accumulated and resource shortages accompanied by price hikes have begun. The beliefs and values that shape linear economics are being rendered increasingly obsolete by unanticipated consequences of maximizing the flow of materials through the economy. Self-interested decisions of producers and consumers have promoted profitable linear economies, only to have Adam Smith's invisible hand replaced by the invisible foot that is leading private self-interest to kick the common good to pieces. In an overly exploited environment, the continued pursuit of what is good in the short run for producers and consumers may be disastrous for the whole system—and thus for all who participate in it—in the long run.

Because of their excessively linear character, present economic systems

LINEAR ECONOMIES

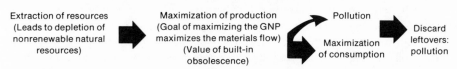

Extraction of resources
(Leads to depletion of
nonrenewable natural
resources)

Maximization of production
(Goal of maximizing the GNP
maximizes the materials flow)
(Value of built-in
obsolescence)

Pollution

Maximization
of consumption

Discard
leftovers:
pollution

CIRCULAR ECONOMIES

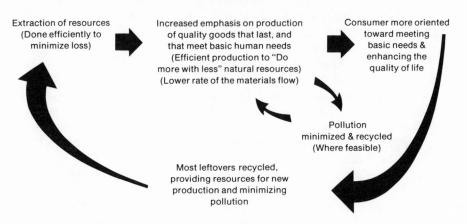

Extraction of resources
(Done efficiently to
minimize loss)

Increased emphasis on production
of quality goods that last, and
that meet basic human needs
(Efficient production to "Do
more with less" natural resources)
(Lower rate of the materials flow)

Consumer more oriented
toward meeting
basic needs &
enhancing the
quality of life

Pollution
minimized & recycled
(Where feasible)

Most leftovers recycled,
providing resources for new
production and minimizing
pollution

Figure 8.10. Linear and circular economies.

have prematurely started to encounter limits to growth. Clearly, such systems artificially restrict the amount of sustainable global industrial growth by imposing unnecessary sociocultural constraints.

Inappropriate Nationalistic Goals

The primary goals of national leaders can be grouped under four headings: (1) maximization of national wealth and income, (2) maximization of national power, (3) increase in population (in some instances), and (4) sovereign independence. As manifested in policies, these goals are characterized by a short-term perspective.

One, if not the, primary domestic goal of virtually all national governments is growth of GNP (or of a similar measure). Like businesses, national governments have typically treated the global system as if it were an unconditionally open system capable of supporting unlimited national growth. Growth of a nation's income and wealth has, at least until very recently, almost always taken precedence over environmental concerns. Moreover, the ecological consequences of a nation's economic or military activity can extend far beyond its borders, as exemplified by air and water pollution and overfishing of the oceans. On the basis of such evidence, Richard Falk (1972, 1975) argues convincingly that the calculus of national self-interest discourages ecological self-restraint.

In the competitive arena of international politics, governments aspire to increase their own economic and military strengths. Gains in relative power are frequently made at the expense of other nation-states. This can be illustrated in the economic realm by the undesirable consequences of the fourfold increase in oil prices; in the military realm, by wars. Paradoxically, competitive increases in national defense budgets are often disadvantageous to all nation-states involved. Many nation-states have promoted population growth to increase their productive capacity and political power. Even in a number of developed nations—among them Romania, the Soviet Union, Israel, Canada, and Japan—policies have recently encouraged a high rate of population growth.

Sovereign independence, which constitutes the most fundamental goal, means that the government of a country is not accountable to any secular or spiritual authority outside its borders and is free to manage its territory, the lives of its people, and its institutions solely with regard to its national interest. This autonomous pursuit of national self-interest induces international friction, since the constraints of the international system prevent the simultaneous satisfaction of all national designs for power and wealth. Despite increasing ecological, economic, and political interdependence, national governments still behave as if they were sovereign and independent of the rest of the world.

Typically, the time horizon of national decision makers is no longer than their political life expectancy. Thus terms of office exercise a strong influence on choice of policies, which are generally selected to maximize short-term payoffs.

A continuation of today's nationalistic goals would prove counterproductive. For instance, if increasingly scarce natural resources were withheld from a nation because of its policies, such misuse of resources as a political weapon could provoke military warfare. The pursuit of short-term national self-interest could eventuate in collective calamity. Despite this danger, there is as yet no effective system of laws for the resolution of national disputes over natural resources, food, or pollution.

Toward a Planetary Ecological Ethic

Current economic and political systems consist of relatively independent, autonomous parts, each using a relatively linear economy to pursue competitively its own growth interests. Although the beliefs, values, and goals that shape and guide these systems have previously produced much beneficial growth, they are generating undesirable consequences that are rendering some of them increasingly obsolete. Not only are they speeding the human race toward confrontations with present-day limits to growth; they are also interfering with movement toward a harmoniously interacting world order. Hence, reliance on a business-as-usual and a politics-as-usual orientation would probably worsen interrelated global problems rather than produce a cooperative world future of sustainable selective growth.

What is needed is an appropriate revision of the increasingly obsolete beliefs, values, and goals that guide sociocultural systems, institutions, policies, and behavior. To an appreciable extent, this revision has begun. It may gain momentum, thereby promoting the mandatory transition from wasteful linear economies toward recycled circular ones and from narrowly defined national self-interest toward ecologically responsible international cooperation.

Many of the appropriately revised beliefs, values, and goals are evident from the analysis of inappropriate ones (for example, Ferkiss 1969, 1974; Harman 1976). Elsewhere, I have attempted to identify these revisions and integrate them into a provisionally formulated planetary ecological ethic (Jones 1975b, 1978).* Compared with the unrestricted quantitative growth orientation, this sustainable selective growth ethic would relate human beings to the environment and to each other in a more satisfactory manner. The ethic, established on the primary moral principles of beneficence and justice, would promote the equitably distributed satisfaction of basic human needs by selective growth in ecologically and socially sustainable societies. *Selective growth* is defined to encompass the kinds of qualitative and quantitative growth that promote human well-being within the boundaries imposed by the finite planetary support system. Such growth also manifests concern for nonhuman sentient life.

The ethic would articulate world interest on global ecological issues, thus facilitating efforts to match basic human needs with feasible technologies that are safe, with acceptable means of implementation, and with plausible strategies for coping with nontechnological problems associated with growth. Accordingly, it would prescribe desirable goals for the human race and rules for attaining them but would allow choice between various permissible trade-offs and would encourage cultural diversity on nonglobal issues. Hence, it would help its proponents adapt the goals and strategies of their different regions to diverse environmental and sociocultural conditions in ways that are compatible with the long-term well-being of the human race.

Although many of the values, goals, and rules that characterize the ethic are quite abstract and general, they can be interpreted by customs, laws, and policy objectives to furnish beneficial guidance in specific situations. However, formidable sociocultural barriers now block voluntary implementation of a planetary ecological ethic. Authoritarian attempts to impose it would undermine its moral character, abrogate freedom, and provoke rebellion. Voluntary support can be buttressed by sanctions but not effectively replaced by them.

Sustained discussions involving representatives of many cultures and

---

*I selected the "good reasons approach" of contemporary philosophical ethics (Brandt 1959, pp. 241–70; Frankena 1973, pp. 107–16; Rawls 1971; summary in Washburn and Jones 1978) as a credible method for formulating a planetary ecological ethic (Jones 1978). This approach provides a set of overlapping methods for making rationally justifiable normative claims.

nations would be required to make a planetary ecological ethic sufficiently agreeable to divergent groups to be implementable on a broad scale. The ethic would not have to be institutionalized formally in the international and national arenas to become useful in rechanneling behavior toward ecologically desirable goals. At first, it could be regarded primarily as a guide for personal action. Efforts could be made to implement some of its objectives on the local and regional levels. Especially important to the growth of commitment to the ethic and its accompanying objectives is widespread awareness of the sustainable, humane, satisfying type of future that could be reached by feasible steps. Also crucial to cooperative implementation of the ethic is enlargement of self-interest to include a rewarding future for the human species.

Global Goals

The social sciences and history furnish convincing evidence that what happens in societies depends significantly on the character of their goals (Polak 1973). In this technologically shaped, finite, diverse but progressively interconnected world, complex global problems have made mandatory the cooperative pursuit of global goals for the collective well-being of humanity (Laszlo et al. 1977). Such shared targets could either be derived from a formally institutionalized planetary ecological ethic or, alternatively, from appropriate piecemeal normative changes in various cultures. Adoption of ecologically appropriate global goals would stretch the sociocultural constraints that now unnecessarily, but effectively, restrict the level of sustainable economic growth as if they constituted a straightjacket. Among the crucial interrelated global goals that can be derived from a planetary ecological ethic are the following:*

1. Selective economic growth concentrated in the service sectors of developed countries (thereby using less energy, consuming less nonrenewable resources, and causing less pollution than undifferentiated growth) and aided by the use of electronic information technology (especially computers linked with communications media)
   a) Growth in the quantity and quality of services
   b) Movement into forms of postindustrial society that involve considerable public participation in preference-rating and decision-making processes
   c) Slower rates of industrial growth (at least temporarily), which must become more selective

------

*This list of global goals closely resembles that formulated by the Club of Rome's Goals for Global Society Project, in connection with which I served as a Research Fellow at UNITAR of the United Nations. These goals are not, of course, exhaustive of all needed goals, nor is this the only plausible categorization. Each goal involves more specific recommendations. The ways in which some of the goals overlap others reflects their interrelationships.

2. Economic growth in developing countries to meet the basic needs of all their citizens (includes, but does not necessarily emphasize, industrial growth, which should be selective)
   a) Choice among alternative patterns of development that are ecologically acceptable
   b) Appropriate types of aid from developed countries; investigation of the feasibility of a global minimum standard of living
3. A transition from wasteful linear economies toward conservation-oriented circular economies, which are based on recycling and on producing long-lived quality goods rather than on maximizing GNP (thus increasing the safety of industrial growth and raising its level of sustainability)
   a) Resource conservation, coupled with increased resource availability (achieved through conservation, technological progress, and political agreements)
   b) Protection of the environment from excessive pollution (attained by monitoring, legislating and taxing, recycling, and switching to clean technologies)
   c) Safe growth of the world's energy supply, including:
      (1) Wise use of fossil fuels, with emphasis on emulsification and on the restraint required to avoid triggering an atmospheric greenhouse effect
      (2) Rapid development of ecologically and economically acceptable alternative energy technologies, among which, we may hope, will be a source of clean, abundant, reasonably priced energy
      (3) Special attention to lowering the cost of solar photovoltaic energy conversion, the ideal source of electrical energy generation for decentralized energy control and environmental protection
      (4) Intensified efforts to facilitate cost-efficient conversion to an economy dependent on clean-burning hydrogen
      (5) Careful, limited use of selected fission technologies (as needed, while vigorous efforts are made to implement emulsification rapidly and to develop clean energy technologies) but refusal to implement breeder reactors and fuel-reprocessing plants
4. Stabilization of the world monetary system (through domestic reforms to cope with inflation, recession, and unemployment and international reforms to create a hard crisis-proof currency available to both rich and poor countries as a medium of foreign exchange)
5. Containment of nuclear proliferation, major progress in defusing potential nuclear holocaust, curtailment of the transfer of conventional arms, and movement toward efficient peace keeping and eventual disarmament
6. Production and distribution of nourishing food for everyone (attained by such means as increased crop yields per unit of already cultivated land in developing countries, employment of agricultural technologies most appropriate to the needs of specific peoples, advances in the storage of food and its distribution at affordable prices, establishment of adequate world food reserves, and accelerated development and implementation of new technologies)

7. Stabilization of the world's population at as low a level as is compatible with voluntary means, including concerted efforts to make family planning services universally available and to establish other services to meet basic human needs
8. Reduction of runaway urbanization in developing countries to manageable rates (by upgrading rural areas, creating agro-industrial complexes away from major urban areas, providing public information, relocating squatters in designed settlements, and decreasing the population growth rate)
9. Widespread recognition, especially by national and corporate leaders, of the urgent need for cooperative efforts to cope with interrelated global problems; revitalization of existing international institutions and creation of new ones; and adoption of policies oriented toward global goals

Strategies for Implementation

These global goals cannot properly be dismissed as the product of wishful thinking. At least to a significant extent, they apparently could be attained by intelligent, cooperative efforts. Yet the paths leading to them are cluttered with obstacles. Despite the pressing need for representatives of various cultures and people generally to engage in much further analysis of appropriate global goals and subsidiary objectives, the most crucial problems concern implementation.

To give rise to workable policies, global goals must be operationalized by practical definitions and workable strategies. Just as a skeleton needs to be fleshed out to convey an accurate guide to the identity of a person, so these abstract goals must be characterized precisely and joined to feasible, acceptable implementation scenarios that specify realistic steps by which they may be reached. Such scenarios would take into account the potential for constructive change as well as expected opposition by vested interests and by any conflicting political-ideological orientations.

These scenarios would delineate both technological and nontechnological changes. Attainment of many global goals depends significantly on the adoption of appropriate technologies. Sociocultural hindrances to the rapid research, development, and implementation of such technologies can be reduced substantially by adequately funded, skillfully coordinated R&D programs. In today's mass-consumption societies, the lack of sufficient investment capital for many worthwhile R&D projects dramatizes the need for cooperative saving and investment of the money saved. This in turn depends on shared commitment to desirable long-range goals. Obviously, motivation is crucial in the establishment and success of R&D projects.

Efforts to loosen sociocultural constraints must be oriented toward improving inappropriate policies, institutions, incentives, economic and political systems, cultural beliefs and values, and, ultimately, perceptions and conceptions of the world and of one's place in it. Institutional reforms to combat entrenched sociocultural constraints should not seek to achieve perfectionist, unrealistic objectives but rather to make enough progress in lessening these constraints to bring about a satisfying future of sustainable growth. Current government institutions would have to be revamped and supplemented by new ones. The role of governments in coordinating the transition to sustainable growth would extend far beyond the establishment of R&D projects. During disruptions stemming from the termination of ecologically unsound practices and the transition to preferable technologies, governments would be called upon to protect affected business from bankruptcy, to help manufacturers convert to different kinds of production, and to retrain displaced workers as well as locate jobs for them.

While such undertakings require increases in some types of centralized governmental decision making, electronic information technology could be employed to decentralize decision making wherever feasible. Effective government leadership, which might be possible without a massive swelling of government budgets, could foster popular willingness to endure necessary disruptions. To prevent repressive rule invoked to marshal united responses to worsening problems (Heilbronner 1974), every effort must be made to secure the voluntary public cooperation that a successful transition presupposes in democratic societies.

New international agreements and institutions are needed to:

Manage international dislocations resulting from huge transfers of assets to oil-producing countries,
Guarantee equal access to scarce resources,
Check any mad scramble for such resources and for export markets,
Establish a world food reserve for aiding famine-stricken areas,
Rectify the diversified manifestations of the problem of the commons, and
Perform many other tasks.

Strong international institutions would be mandatory. However, a full-fledged world government would probably be unnecessary. Even though decisions that concern world interest should doubtless be influenced by a broad-based assessment of popular sentiments, international institutions would make and enforce such decisions. These institutions should be designed to be representative as well as efficient.

This transition to sustainable selective growth, equitable distribution, and global security seems bound to be turbulent. It could be traumatic. Knotty problems arise not only from powerful antagonists pursuing narrowly defined self-interest but also from the haze of uncertainty that envelops the issue of just how to proceed. Judged from the interrelated perspectives of conceptual orientation (Ackoff 1970, 1974; Michael 1968, 1973; Ozbekhan, 1968) and practical experience, the capacity for planned change appears to have increased. Yet as Donald Michael (1968, 1973) points out, the human race is still poorly equipped to engage in the type of long-range planning required to cope with enormous upcoming changes. The scale and pace of the planning needed to ameliorate intertwined global problems is unprecedented. In view of the many pitfalls that beset such planned change, concerted efforts to make major improvements in the planning and implementation processes are mandatory.

Among futurists who opt for large-scale intervention, strategies for planned change range from basically incremental approaches to relatively radical ones. For instance, Harlan Cleveland (1977, 1978, with T. Wilson) of Aspen Institute proposes numerous changes, the accumulation of which would reform the present international system. Conversely, Richard Falk (1975, 1976), who served as research director of the U.S. team of the Institute for World Order's World Order Models Project (WOMP), advocates changes that tend to be more revolutionary. Like Cleveland, Falk sets forth a fairly detailed normative plan that includes a preliminary set of strategies for implementation.

Although no author is cited in "The Planetary Bargain" position paper (1975), much of the credit should go to Cleveland, director of the Aspen Institute Program in International Affairs. This essay focuses on the need to develop multilateral planetary bargaining among decision makers in the world system. Aimed at the humanistic management of interdependence, such bargaining would promote a "revolution in fairness" that would meet minimum human needs and keep industrialized societies from advancing beyond prudent limits in using scarce resources. International institutions in a new international order would make those decisions about trade, investment, and money that can no longer be left prudently to single nation-states.

Compared with reforms recommended by Falk and other members of the Institute for World Order, these reforms still operate within the framework of the nation–state system. Elsewhere, Cleveland and Thomas W. Wilson (1978) declare: "National governments will still be the basic building blocks of world order, but they will increasingly find themselves exercising their sovereign right to collaborate in getting things done that simply cannot be done by translating 'independence' as 'isolation'" (p. 37). The effective governance of prudent, purposeful growth to meet basic human needs and maximize options is less dependent on how things are organized, they maintain, than on how well the participants in the process of planning and implementation understand the process of which they are a part. Thus lifelong education, whether gained by reschooling or on the hoof, is mandatory for overcoming the limits to governance inherent in the outmoded character of today's ineffective political institutions (pp. 31, 41). Only in this way can the ascending value of "humangrowth"— selective, purposeful, ecologically responsible, equitably distributed growth "as if people mattered"—be sufficiently converted into institutions and policies by a pluralistic world society (pp. 9, 31, 37, 41).

Falk's "relevant utopia" is a reformed world designed to promote the actualization of four central values agreed upon by WOMP participants: peace, social and economic well-being, basic human rights and political justice, and environmental quality that includes conservation. Falk argues that contemporary elites and institutions are inadequate for making the requisite reforms. He recommends "central guidance" to create a unified capacity for the formation, coordination, and implementation of appropriate policies, with the accompanying dilution of national sovereignty in the policy-making process. Global, regional, and transnational actors would come to exert much more influence in the world order system than nation-state actors. Inappropriate nationalist imperatives would be modified. Still, central guidance would depend on minimum coercion and bureaucracy to coordinate activities of smaller collective entities in the world system.

In spite of fundamental differences between the approaches of Cleveland and Falk, large areas of agreement offer the opportunity for programs designed to make significant reforms. Yet these differences pose a dilemma that must be addressed. On the one hand, relatively piecemeal, incremental reforms may prove insufficient to ameliorate interconnected global problems. On the other, attempts to bring about basic systemic reforms could easily backfire or might succeed at the price of resorting to authoritarian control. While much additional analysis is necessary, this dilemma seems to call for a judicious combination of incremental reforms, which are safer, whenever they appear to be sufficient to attain global goals. When efforts to bring about change that is more revolutionary become mandatory, they ought to be tempered by realism, a concern to gain widespread support, and an aversion for using brute force. Integral to the success of both types of reforms are changes in consciousness that motivate cooperative efforts.

Wise Use of Motivational Resources

The problem of motivation lies at the heart of implementation difficulties. The successful ongoing pursuit of global goals requires extensive local, national and international cooperation. How, if at all, can people be motivated to cooperate intelligently in ways likely to produce the needed changes? How limited are motivational resources?

The open, nondictatorial use of motivational resources to facilitate implementation of goals and subsidiary objectives is itself a goal. To achieve it, a threefold motivational task needs to be performed: (1) objective payoffs must be altered (for instance, by laws and taxes) so as to encourage ecologically sound behavior and discourage the opposite, (2) self-interest must be reconceptualized to overlap more with cooperatively sought collective well-being, and (3) commitment to collective well-being must be viewed as subjectively rewarding.

A motivational orientation aligned to accomplishing this task supplies a master key for overcoming such excessively restrictive sociocultural constraints as the problem of the commons. Appropriate changes in policies and institutions can spring from underlying changes in perception and motivation.

The adjustment of rewards and punishments required to combat pollution in a market economy furnishes an illustration of how the first part of this task can be performed. Strong international institutions would be needed to enforce necessary regulations on the international level.

To accomplish the crucial second part of the task, one must show how self-interest is becoming increasingly intertwined with the well-being of the human race. The common interests that unite people should be interpreted as more important than current divisive interests. History has repeatedly demonstrated that rapid, effective *shifts from action governed by conflicting self-interest to collective action directed toward common goals can be sparked by this shared perception of a changed situation: Only by cooperation can mutual disaster be avoided and mutually beneficial goals achieved.* Persuasive evidence supports the claim that *only by intelligently working together* can human beings avert unprecedented collective suffering and successfully make the transition to a satisfying future of sustainable global economic growth.

This type of cooperative orientation typically arises only after a crisis has occurred. A subtle danger of interrelated global problems is that they may not be perceived as constituting a crisis demanding unprecedented cooperation until after disaster has become unavoidable. Will human beings envisage likely consequences of these problems vividly enough to mobilize constructive collective action while the problems are still manageable? This is the primary challenge of the next few decades.

The third part of the task requires recognition that a morally good person—one who is willing to do his (her) duty even if refusing to do it would bring more objective gain—can enjoy a satisfying life. Since self-actualization is frequently enhanced by constructive commitment to the well-being of a collectivity, subjective gain can be viewed as outweighing an objective loss. Empathetic acceptance of the obligation to contribute to human well-being can give rise to a feeling of unity with a meaningful whole. Thus people can find purpose in life by choosing to be responsible members of the world system. Having become valuable moral resources, such people possess the virtue of integrity.

Performance of this threefold task by leaders and by people generally would make duty and perceived self-interest coincide more extensively than they do today. Societal rewards and punishments, likely objective gains and losses, and subjective gains and losses would encourage cooperative behavior that promotes sustainable economic growth and discourage behavior that conflicts with it. Rather than continuing to be dominated by the "zero-sum game mentality" according to which some nations must be losers when others are winners, national leaders and citizens might explore the possibility of synergistic exchange agreements between developed and developing countries (L. Brown 1972, 1976). For instance, the former might supply scientific and technical assistance, economic advice, educational aid, clean technologies, and family planning personnel as well as contraceptives. In exchange for these benefits, developing countries might agree to supply natural resources at mutually acceptable prices, sign trade agreements, renounce possession of nuclear weapons, and make major efforts to increase their food-producing capacities while reducing their birthrates. Actual agreements would, of course, have to be far more specific, detailed, and complex. Yet mutually beneficial exchange agreements, whether formal or relatively informal, could help to resolve interconnected global problems sufficiently to usher in a satisfying global era of sustainable selective growth.

APPENDIX TO CHAPTER 8:
KAHN'S "SPACE-BOUND PERSPECTIVE"

Although Kahn, Brown, and Martel concentrate on their "earth-centered" scenario in *The Next 200 Years* (1976b), they seem to prefer their "space-bound" scenario "that assumes a much more vigorous effort in extraterrestrial activities early in the 21st century, including the eventual establishment of large autonomous colonies in space" (p. 4). Does this proposed migration into space provide Kahn and his coauthors with a workable escape hatch from the objections leveled against their earth-centered scenario? No. Kahn's space-bound perspective is seriously weakened by the untenable assumptions that it shares with his earth-centered perspective and appears to be even more vulnerable to objections based on sociocultural limits to growth.

The leading advocate of rapid, large-scale space colonization is Princeton physicist Gerard O'Neill. According to his multistage program, a "Model 1" space colony resembling a giant wheel could be operational by 1988. It would house approximately 10,000 people inside a mile-long cylinder with a radius of several hundred feet. By 1996 its residents could construct a much larger "Model 2," from which "Model 3," several miles long and housing perhaps a million people, could be completed by around 2002. Beginning about 2014, the work force of a parent colony could build a daughter colony within six years solely by use of its own resources coupled with materials from outer space. O'Neill (1976) calculates that by about 2050, space colonies could absorb the population increase of both the earth and the colonies and that population density thereafter could be decreased (pp. 25–33).

Whereas part of the necessary technology is presently available, the rest would be developed subsequently. O'Neill estimates that his program would cost approximately $5 billion a year (in 1972 dollars). The colonies could begin to pay for themselves as they beamed solar energy to collectors on earth and exported to earth products that can be manufactured more effectively and less expensively in space (pp. 25–33).

Much of O'Neill's proposed program seems to be technologically feasible, but it minimizes sociocultural constraints. John Holt (1976) estimates that O'Neill's program would take perhaps 2 to 4 times as much time and 10 to 20 times as much money (p. 44). Even if Holt's price tag is too high, O'Neill's is probably far too low. Moreover, solar energy converters in space would probably be excessively expensive (Chapter 7). Yet they might become affordable eventually, as might the mining of the moon and the asteroids for raw materials. Besides, some kinds of manufacturing and scientific experiments can best be conducted in space. This, however, is by no means equivalent to large-scale space colonization.

Holt counters the claim that relatively small space colonies would be self-sufficient and self-sustaining by contending that too many different kinds of materials have to be manufactured, distributed, and fixed (p. 46). If correct, Holt's argument counts against O'Neill's position; if incorrect, the likely consequences of self-sufficiency could be even more damaging. A large number of economically and politically self-sufficient space colonies could become involved in space wars and place the earth in constant danger. Paul Csonka (1977) argues persuasively that, contrary to O'Neill's expectation of cultural diversity and peace, economic incentives as well as cultural and racial hostilities would probably trigger aggression (pp, 287–88). One reason is that occupation of a colony would be both faster and cheaper than construction of a new one; another, that competition for the most desirable raw materials could result in raids on each other's installations.

Furthermore, Garrett Hardin, Csonka, and Holt stress the threat of political and social instability in space colonies that, like ships at sea, would be extremely vulnerable to sabotage. The most likely kinds of government would involve rigid, harsh discipline by authoritarian hierarchies.

O'Neill's program presupposes that human behavior is mostly rational and generous in that it furthers the best interests of the human race (Csonka 1977, p. 286). However, "premature large-scale space colonization would amount to exploitation on a cosmic scale of oppression, suffering, and disorder—the very qualities which characterize most human behavior today" (p. 290). Csonka concludes:

> Before large-scale space exploration is undertaken in the far distant future, we need to solve three problems: (1) how to settle conflicts (e.g., concerning the distribution of resources) nonviolently *and* justly, (2) how to safeguard the right of self-determination of various groups (on Earth and in space colonies) without opening the door to perpetual turmoil, and (3) how to limit population growth and waste production to avoid finding ourselves in desperate situations leading to desperate actions. [P. 290]

In a somewhat similar vein, Holt (1976) objects that O'Neill's program constitutes a diversion of resources, energy, money, scientific talent, and attention from coping with pressing problems on earth (p. 44). The expectation that the problem of limits to growth will be solved in space may lead people to act as if they need not learn to live within these limits on earth. Certainly space colonization provides no workable strategy for coping with the pressing problem of world population expansion, which requires remedial action now. Even if shooting large groups of poor people from developing countries into space became economically feasible, one wonders whether they would want to go and whether their lifeways are suitable to success in such colonies.

9

CONCLUSION: PROSPECTS FOR IMPROVING FORECASTING

> We can only pay our debt to the past by putting the future in debt to ourselves.
>
> Tweedsmuir

Our exploration of the alternative futures projected by representative forecasters has confirmed our initial claims that:

Consequences of the revolution in science-based technology make long-range, comprehensive forecasting and planning mandatory.

The task of making such forecasting reliable is an extremely difficult one.

Futurists have significantly improved forecasting, though serious weaknesses remain.

These weaknesses could be partially overcome, thus rendering forecasting more reliable.

The aim of our critique of the methodological and nonmethodological assumptions that bias forecasts has been to improve forecasting. Instead of cavalierly debunking forecasts as specious expertise or worthless ideology, we have examined them for ways of controlling turbulent change. Past and present developments influence ongoing processes, increasing the plausibility of some alternative futures and decreasing that of others. Accordingly, improvements in data collection, theories, and inferences to alternative futures make forecasting a more dependable instrument for planning and decision making.

Overall progress in forecasting has followed more of a zigzag path than a linear trajectory. Proposed correctives for perceived weaknesses have often been too extreme or have generated other problems. Moreover, different forecasts formulated at any given time display various degrees of sophistication. Yet a state-of-the-art comparison of forecasting today with forecasting several years ago shows that futurists have substantially enhanced their methodology and, to a somewhat lesser extent, their forecasts. For instance, interrelated world problems have dramatized the appropriateness of holistic methods. Some of the most recent attempts to model complex systems display definite advances. Furthermore, the gathering of data and the evaluation of assumptions have raised the growth controversy to a higher level. Most of today's forecasts about the consequences of growth are superior to forecasts made during the late 1960s and early 1970s.

Nevertheless, our survey of forecasts has revealed that competent futurists continue to formulate incompatible and even diametrically opposed forecasts. Policy makers often lack sufficient rational grounds for choosing among these forecasts. Thus *futurists face this dilemma*: specialized, short-range forecasts—though more reliable because of less likelihood of error—fail to meet the pressing need for long-range, comprehensive planning; macroforecasts, designed to satisfy this need, tend to resemble pseudoscientific speculation and, therefore, alienate policy makers. By uncovering, analyzing, and improving both methodological and nonmethodological assumptions that shape forecasts, futurists could take lengthy strides toward resolving this dilemma.

METHODOLOGICAL IMPROVEMENTS

Of crucial importance is the construction of better models for anticipating possible discontinuous changes, including normative changes, in complex systems. Such systems are especially hard to model, because their behavior is affected by the complicated interaction of numerous forces of various weights. Perhaps the best available method is Stanford Research Institute's FAR, which deserves further development. So do computer modeling, "retrospective forecasting," the "method of movement," and "catastrophe theory," among others.

The restrospective forecasting pioneered by Nazli Choucri (1976) and Robert North constructs models that, when "run backwards" on a computer, accurately depict past dynamic systems out of which present systems have been generated. These historically oriented models may then be used for forecasting. Insufficiently known is Michel Massenet's (1963) method of movement, which facilitates detection of changes that, though just beginning today, may exert enormous impact in the future. Rene Thom's (1975) catastrophe theory can help forecasters to visualize the various forms that system breaks can take.

In spite of Hasan Ozbekhan's (1968) major methodological contributions, normative forecasting and planning calls for much further development. Relevant to attaining this goal are the improvements in planning methodology set forth by Russell Ackoff (1970), Donald Michael (1973), Donald Schoen (1971), and others. I have argued elsewhere (Washburn and Jones 1977) that employment of the "good reasons approach" of philosophical ethics could enhance the goal selection process. Various improvements in the normative forecasting-planning process could increase both the feasibility and likelihood of avoiding disasters and attaining preferable options.

However, we should not expect forecasting to become the science that a few of its most ardent advocates have envisioned. The credibility of forecasting depends crucially on the forthright acknowledgement of its weaknesses and limitations. The requisite shift toward relatively objective methods that can be checked and improved will not even eliminate the need for intuitive genius forecasting. Generally speaking, policy decisions had best be founded on a comparative use of various methods. Methods can be weighted on the basis of which is most useful for the specific forecasting task.

EXPLICATION OF NONMETHODOLOGICAL ASSUMPTIONS

Major improvements in methodology—even if universally adopted—would certainly not eliminate incompatibilities among forecasts. Forecasters who employ the same method can derive conflicting forecasts. Even when exploratory forecasts resemble each other, accompanying policy recommendations may diverge radically. Such incompatibilities result from clashing nonmethodological assumptions that typically can be traced to different perceptions of the world and the human situation. Especially important are various beliefs about causality, which differentially affect judgments about the directions in which trends are likely to proceed and about the human ability to shape the future.

Although the movement from genius forecasting toward computer modeling and other formalized methods is turning some implicit nonmethodological assumptions into explicit ones, implicit assumptions still play leading roles in distorting forecasts. To make forecasting more trustworthy, assumptions about technology, human nature, societies and cultures, polities, economies, causality, time, history, values, and the like must be detected, assessed, and improved.

Since the goal of value-free exploratory forecasting has proved more elusive than a ball of mercury, forecasters should explicate their own normative orientations and estimate the influence on their forecasts. This practice promotes the separation of exploratory and descriptive elements in forecasts. Since judgments of desirability often subtly influence judgments of probability and vice versa, such a separation enhances the trustworthiness of forecasts.

Beginning efforts to provide systematic procedures for evaluating nonmethodological assumptions include those of Wendell Bell, James A. Mau, Bettina J. Huber, and Menno Boldt (1971), David C. Miller and Ronald L. Hunt (1973), and Ian Miles (1978). Their lists of assumptions can help decision makers and people generally to become aware of the kinds of implicit assumptions that often distort forecasts. Aided by appropriate check lists, forecasters could try to uncover and evaluate their own assumptions as part of the forecasting process. What is needed to improve this technique is the specification of categories of assumptions, application of this list of categories to explicate implicit assumptions, detection of omissions or other weaknesses in the present list, reformulation of this list, reapplication, and so on.

Recent work in decision analysis points to the dependence of forecasts on "inquiring models" and explanatory models of reality, which are often left implicit. Integral to inquiring models are different styles of information collecting and evaluating (Mendell 1978). Forecasters had best become more explicit about the steps of, first, deciding how much they know, second, selecting a model, and, finally, deriving a forecast (*Science and Cybernetics* September 1968, pp. 333ff).

IMPROVEMENT OF NONMETHODOLOGICAL ASSUMPTIONS

Having explicated their own assumptions, separated normative from descriptive elements, and interrelated the assumptions, forecasters can formulate an assumption-explicit forecast. Better yet, they can begin by critically assessing their own assumptions and rejecting the ones that they cannot justify. Forecasters need to evaluate their descriptive assumptions (or descriptive elements of assumptions) in terms of the best available data and theories of the natural and social sciences. Moreover, they may fruitfully explore the extent to which their normative assumptions depend on their beliefs about the world. (When conflicting normative assumptions of different forecasters arise from incompatible factual beliefs—exemplified by divergent beliefs about the likely consequences of continued economic growth—one way to resolve the disagreement is to present evidence that induces agreement in belief.) Then forecasters can test their normative assumptions by applying the good-reasons approach, which provides a nonarbitrary method for guiding choices and for resolving many, though not all, moral disputes (Brandt 1959, Frankena 1973; Rawls 1971). A related technique for reaching rational decisions on the basis of estimates of desirability and probability is Bayesian decision analysis (Ashley 1978).

Obviously, the data and theories of many disciplines are useful for evaluating descriptive assumptions. Yet the subject matter of a given forecast renders some disciplines more relevant than others. A necessary condition for the reliability of comprehensive forecasts of sociocultural change is that they be founded upon an understanding of contemporary developments as rooted in the past. The most important research in historical sociology provides comparative historical analyses of changing societies, cultures, and civilizations, thereby elucidating current processes and the alternative directions in which they might move. This extremely broad discipline is particularly suitable for assessing and improving assumptions about sociocultural structures and processes, including assumptions about value change.

Unfortunately, historical sociology is generally neglected by contemporary futurists, few of whom have a thorough background in either history or sociology. Most of them furnish little evidence of being well-acquainted with the works of such perceptive diagnosticians of sociocultural change as Max Weber, Sir Henry

Sumner Maine, Marcel Mauss, Emile Durkheim, Ernest Barker, Jacob Burkhardt, Johan Huizinga. Charles Moraze, Joseph Levenson, Benjamin Nelson, and Joseph Needham. Several futurists do draw on contributions made by Pitirim Sorokin, Edward Tiryakian, and Alexis de Tocqueville.

Analysis of the forecasts made by the RAND Delphi panelists, Brzezinski, Kahn and Wiener, Kahn and Bruce-Briggs, Forrester and the Meadows's team, and Kahn, Brown, and Martel (and to a lesser extent, forecasts by Bell and Harman) discloses that each forecast is handicapped by at least one of the following shortcomings in its analysis of sociocultural change:

Neglect of the action-reaction pattern of change,
Failure to note the importance of conflicts between trends,
Faulty treatment of certain crucial historical developments and omission of
    reference to others,
Faith that change will almost inevitably proceed rationally,
Excessive optimism concerning the potential of technological breakthroughs,
Unrealistic belief that human beings can create a near-utopia,
Reduction of value change to a function of technological change, and
Lack of a holistic systems approach that estimates the results of the interaction
    of all relevant causal factors.

Each of these shortcomings reflects unjustifiable assumptions concerning sociocultural change. An important source of unreliable forecasting is the attempt to map past, present, and possible sociocultural processes by imposing excessively intuitive, alien theoretical frameworks on data that are selected rather arbitrarily. Hence, reference to the best work in historical sociology could help to explicate and adjudicate conflicts among incompatible assumptions. Futurists could improve their methodological as well as their nonmethodological assumptions in this way.

Upsetting developments during the last few years have underlined the need for better methods of anticipating discontinuous changes, including possible and probable changes in priorities and their influence on such factors as pollution and technological progress. A key question in the growth controversy has become: To what extent can unnecessarily restrictive *sociocultural* limits to economic growth (especially, inappropriate values and priorities) be loosened to permit additional sustainable growth? Most futurists seem insufficiently equipped to answer this difficult question optimally. Knowledge supplied by historical sociology could help them to represent the relationships between historical developments with more accuracy, to correct erroneous assumptions, and, hence, to forecast feasible and likely normative changes with more dependability. What is needed is extensive comparative research to ascertain causal relationships between macrophenomena (psychological, social, economic, political, technological, and environmental phenomena), particularly as these relationships have affected normative changes in historical processes.

Furthermore, investigation of the actual experiences of people in specific spatio-temporal locations could serve as an antidote to totalistic propensities that squeeze data into simplified schematic molds, thereby distorting the past, homogenizing the present, and truncating the diverse range of alternative futures. Variabilities in the mixes of economic, political, social, and cultural elements in different civilizational settings call for recognition. In short, futurists could improve their long-range, comprehensive forecasts by relying more on the comparative-historical-differential sociology of civilizational patterns, complexes, and encounters (Nelson 1974, pp. 137–41).

I regard the writings of Benjamin Nelson—especially in the area of historical sociology—as constituting an important opening toward the kind of theoretical and substantive macrohistorical approach needed to enhance the trustworthiness of forecasting. To explicate the most crucial changes of our time, he maps the sociocultural world in terms of several interrelated revolutions that differ in point of historical origin, rate of increase, stage of development, extent, causal efficacy, and interrelations of reinforcement or interference. His approach helps to elucidate, for instance, current anomie, changing priorities, and responses to increased contacts on the intersocietal and intercivilization levels (see the Bibliography).

A CRUCIAL CHALLENGE

All of the forecasts we have examined make valuable contributions to our understanding of alternative future histories. Yet our analysis has furnished evidence that some of these forecasts provide better guidance for planning and decision making than others. To be sure, unresolved conflicts among forecasts and corresponding uncertainties remain. Nevertheless, in the preceding chapter we concluded that efforts to cope with the world macroproblem require the adoption and pursuit of a set of interrelated global goals. The general direction of appropriate change is sufficiently clear to warrant major policy changes by governments, corporations, and other institutions.

The amelioration of the world macroproblem and the possibility of achieving a satisfying global postindustrial age, however, require major improvements in forecasting, planning, and implementation of plans. Such improvements appear feasible but depend on concerted societal efforts. In short, attractive options for the world's future are still open though not easy to achieve.

Thus consequences of the revolution in science-based technology—the nuclear age, the space age, the electronic age, and the ecological age—have made forecasting and planning mandatory for coping with complex, interrelated problems and for attaining desirable but elusive goals. Our analysis has shown that:

The need is enormous,
The task is difficult,

The potential for improvement is substantial, and
The challenge is great.

Therefore, the only tenable response to the current shortcomings of the fore-casting–planning process is a wholehearted effort to improve it.

BIBLIOGRAPHY

Ackoff, Russell L. 1974. *Redesigning the Future. A System's Approach to Societal Problems.* New York: John Wiley & Sons.

——. 1970. *A Concept of Corporate Planning.* New York: Wiley-Interscience.

Amalrik, Andrei. 1970. *Will the Soviet Union Survive until 1984?* New York: Harper & Row.

Amara, Roy C., and Gerald Selancik. 1972; "Forecasting: From Conjectural Art toward a Science." *Futurist*, June, pp. 112-17.

Ament, R. H. 1970. "Comparison of Delphi Forecasting Studies in 1965 and 1969." *Futures*, March, pp. 35-44.

Ascher, William. 1978. *Forecasting: an Appraisal for Policy-Makers and Planners.* Baltimore, Md.: Johns Hopkins University Press.

Ashley, Richard K. 1978. "Beyesian Decision Analysis in International Relations: The Analysis of Subjective Processes." In *Forecasting in International Relations*, edited by Nazlo Choucri and Thomas W. Robinson, pp. 149-71. San Francisco: W. H. Freeman.

Averitt, Paul. 1973. "Coal." In *United States Mineral Resources*, edited by Donald A. Brobst and Walden P. Pratt. Washington, D.C.: U.S. Government Printing Office.

Ayres, Robert U. 1979. *Uncertain Futures: Challenges to Decision-Makers.* New York: John Wiley & Sons.

——. 1969. *Technological Forecasting and Long-Range Planning.* New York: McGraw-Hill.

Baier, Kurt, and Nicholas Rescher, eds. 1969. *Values and the Future: The Impact of Technological Change on American Values.* New York: Free Press.

Barnea, J. 1976a. "Reclaiming and Recycling of Used Materials." *Important for the Future.* New York: United Nations Institute for Training and Research.

——. 1976b. "Towards Mass-Produced Low Cost Solar Cells." *Important for the Future.* New York: United Nations Institute for Training and Research.

Bauer, Raymond A., ed. 1966. *Social Indicators: A First Approximation.* Cambridge: Massachusetts Institute of Technology Press.

Beckwith, Burnham P. 1972. "The Future of Man: Optimism v. Pessimism." *The Futurist.* April, pp. 62–64.

———. 1968. *The Next Five Hundred Years: Scientific Prediction of Major Social Trends.* New York: Exposition Press.

Bell, Daniel. 1976. *The Cultural Contradictions of Capitalism.* New York: Basic Books.

———. 1973a. *The Coming of Post-Industrial Society: A Venture in Social Forecasting.* New York: Basic Books.

———. 1973b. "A Rejoinder." *Social Research*, Winter, pp. 745–60.

———. 1971. "Foreword." In *The Future of U.S. Government*, edited by Harvey Perloff. New York: Braziller.

———. 1968a. *Toward the Year 2000.* Boston: Houghton Mifflin.

———. 1968b. "The Trajectory of an Idea." In *Toward the Year 2000: Work in Progress*, edited by Daniel Bell. Boston: Houghton Mifflin.

———. 1967a. "Introduction." In *The Year 2000: A Framework for Speculation on the Next Thirty-Three Years.* New York: Macmillan.

———. 1967b. "Notes on Post-Industrial Society." *Public Interest*, no. 6, pp. 24–35, no. 7, pp. 102–18.

———. 1965. " The Study of the Future." *Public Interest.* no. 1, pp. 119–30.

Bell, Wendell, and James A. Mau, eds. 1971. *The Sociology of the Future: Theory, Cases and Annotated Bibliography.* New York: Russell Sage Foundation.

Bell, Wendell, James A. Mau, Bettina J. Huber, and Menno Boldt. 1971. "A Paradigm for the Analysis of Time Perspectives and Images of the Future." In *The Sociology of the Future: Theory, Cases and Annotated Bibliography*, edited by Wendell Bell and James A. Mau. New York: Russell Sage Foundation.

Bendix, Reinhard. 1974. "Review of Daniel Bell's *The Coming of Post-Industrial Society.*" *Contemporary Sociology*, March, pp. 99–101.

Berger, Stephen D.1974. "Review of Daniel Bell's *The Coming of Post-Industrial Society,*" *Contemporary Sociology*, March, pp. 101–5.

Bestuzhev-Lada, Igor V. 1970. "Utopias of Bourgeois Futurology." *New Times: A Soviet Weekly of World Affairs*, August 12.

Bethe, Hans. 1976. "The Necessity of Fission Power." *Scientific American*, January, pp. 21–31.

"Blueprint for Survival." 1972. *The Ecologist*, January, entire issue.

Bohm, David. 1971. *Causality and Chance in Modern Physics*. Philadelphia: University of Pennsylvania Press.

Boguslaw, Robert. 1965. *The New Utopians*. Englewood Cliffs, N.J.: Prentice-Hall.

Borgstrom, George. 1973. *Focal Points: A Global Food Strategy*. New York: Macmillan.

Boulding, Elise. 1970. "Futurology and the Imagining Capacity of the West." In *Cultural Futurology Symposium, Pre-Conference Volume of the American Anthropological Association*.

Boulding, Kenneth. 1978. *Stable Peace*. Austin: University of Texas Press.

——. 1970. "The Economics of the Coming Spaceship Earth." In *The Futurists*, edited by Alvin Toffler. New York: Random House.

——. 1965. *The Meaning of the Twentieth Century*. New York: Harper & Row.

Boyd, Robert. 1972. "World Dynamics: A Note." *Science* 177 (August 11): 1516–19.

Brandt, Richard. 1959. *Ethical Theory*. Englewood Cliffs, N.J.: Prentice-Hall.

Bright, James R., ed. 1968. *Technological Forecasting in Government and Industry*. Englewood Cliffs, N.J.: Prentice-Hall.

Brown, Harrison. 1978. *The Human Future Revisited: The World Predicament and Possible Solutions*. New York: W. W. Norton.

——. 1954. *The Challenge of Man's Future*. New York: Viking Press.

Brown, Harrison, ed. 1967. *The Next Ninety Years*. Pasadena: California Institute of Technology.

Brown, Harrison, James Bonner, and John Weir. 1957. *The Next Hundred Years*. New York: Viking Press.

Brown, Lester. 1978. *The Twenty Ninth Day*. New York: W. W. Norton.

——. 1976. "The Limits to Growth of Third World Cities." *Futurist*, December, pp. 307–15.

——. 1975. "The Discontinuities before Us." *Futurist*, June, pp. 122–31.

——. 1974. *In the Human Interest.* New York: W. W. Norton.

——. 1973. "Rich Countries and Poor in a Finite, Interdependent World." *Daedalus*, Fall, pp. 153–64.

——. 1972. *World without Borders.* New York: Random House.

Brown, William M., and Leon Martel. 1978. "A Response to Critics of *The Next 200 Years*", *World Future Society BULLETIN*, November–December, pp. 16–20.

Brzezinski, Zbigniew. 1968a. "America in the Technetronic Age." *Encounter*, January, pp. 16–26.

——. 1968b. *Between Two Ages: America's Role in the Technetronic Age.* New York: Viking Press.

Chou, Marylin, David P. Harmon, Jr., Herman Kahn, and Sylvan H. Wittwer. 1977. *World Food Prospects and Agricultural Potential.* New York: Praeger.

Choucri, Nazli, and Thomas W. Robinson, eds. 1978. *Forecasting in International Relations.* San Francisco: W. H. Freeman.

Clarke, Arthur. 1973. *Profiles of the Future: An Inquiry into the Limits of the Possible.* Rev. ed. New York: Harper & Row.

Cleveland, Harlan. 1977. *The Third Try at World Order: U.S. Policy for an Interdependent World.* n.p.: Aspen Institute for Humanistic Studies.

Cleveland, Harlan, and Thomas W. Wilson, Jr. 1978. *Humangrowth.* n.p.: Aspen Institute for Humanistic Studies.

Coates, Joseph. 1972. "The Future of the U. S. Government." *Futurist*, June, pp. 104–8.

——. 1971. "Technology Assessment: The Benefits . . . the Costs . . . the Consequences." *Futurist*, December, pp. 225–31.

Cole, H. S., Christopher Freeman, Marie Jahoda, and K. L. R. Pavitt, eds. 1973. *Models of Doom: A Critique of the Limits to Growth.* New York: Universe Books.

Cole, Sam. 1977. *Global Models and the International Economic Order.* New York: Pergamon Press.

Commoner, Barry. 1971. *The Closing Circle.* New York: Bantam Books.

Conger, D. Stuart. 1974. *Social Inventions.* Canada: Saskatchewan New Start.

Cook, Earl. *Man, Energy, and Society.* San Francisco: W. H. Freeman.

Cornish, Edward. 1979. "The Great Depression of the 1980's: Could It Really Happen?" *Futurist.* October, pp. 253–380.

———. 1977. "What Shall We Call the Study of the Future?" *Futurist*, February, pp. 44–50.

Cornish, Edward, ed. 1978. *The World of Tomorrow.* Washington, D.C.: World Future Society.

Cornish, Edward, and members of the staff of the World Future Society. 1977a. *An Introduction to the Study of the Future.* Washington, S.C.: World Future Society.

———. 1977b. *The Study of the Future.* Washington, D.C.: World Future Society.

Csonka, Paul L. 1977. "Space Colonization: An Invitation to Disaster?" *Futurist*, October, pp. 285–90.

Cummings, Ronald G., et al. 1979. "Mining Earth's Heat: Hot Dry Rock Geothermal Energy." *Technology Review*, February, pp. 58–78.

Daly, Herman, ed. 1973. *Toward a Steady-State Economy.* San Francisco: W. H. Freeman.

de Jouvenel, Bertrand. 1967. *The Art of Conjecture.* New York: Basic Books.

de Jouvenel, Bertrand, ed. 1965. *Futuribles: Studies in Conjecture.* Vol. 2. Genoa, Italy: Droz.

———. 1963. *Futuribles: Studies in Conjecture.* Vol. 1. Genoa, Italy: Droz.

de Tocqueville, Alexis. 1966. In *Democracy in America*, edited by J. P. Mayer and Max Lerner. New York: Harper & Row.

Deutsch, Karl W., Bruno Fritsch, Helio Jaguaribe, Andrei S. Markovits. 1977. *Problems of World Modeling: Political and Social Implications.* Cambridge, Mass.: Bollinger.

Dickson, Paul. 1977. *The Future File: A Guide for People with One Foot in the 21st Century.* New York: Rawson.

Didsbury, Howard J. 1979. *Student Handbook for the Study of the Future.* Washington, D.C.: World Future Society.

Dooher, John. 1977. "Feasibility Study of Using a Coal/Water/Oil Emulsion as a Clean Liquid Fuel." Paper prepared for the U.S. ERDA, Adelphi University, Garden City, N.Y.

Dror, Yehezkel. 1971. *Ventures in Policy Sciences.* New York: American Elsevier.

Drucker, Peter F. 1968. *The Age of Discontinuity: Guidelines to Our Changing Society.* New York: Harper & Row.

Duhl, L. J. 1967. "Planning and Predicting: Or, What to do When You Don't Know the Names of the Variables." *Daedalus* 96 (Summer): 779–88.

Duncan, Otis Dudley. 1969. "Social Forecasting: The State of the Art." *Public Interest*, no. 17, (Fall), pp. 88–118.

Durkheim, Emil, and Marcel Mauss. 1971. "Note on the Notion of Civilization." Translation, with introduction by Benjamin Nelson. *Social Research* 38 (Winter): 1808–13.

Eastlund, Bernard J., and William Gough. 1971. "The Prospects of Fusion Power." *Scientific American*, February, pp. 50–64.

Eckholm, Erik. 1976. *Loosing Ground: Environmental Stress and World Food Prospects.* New York: W. W. Norton.

Edison Electric Institute. 1976. *Economic Growth in the Future: The Growth Debate in National and Global Perspective.* New York: McGraw-Hill.

Ehrlich, Paul, Anne Ehrlich, and John Holdren. 1973. *Human Ecology: Problems and Solutions.* San Francisco: W. H. Freeman.

Elgin, Duane S., and Arnold Mitchell. 1977. "Voluntary Simplicity: Life-Style of the Future?" *Futurist*, August, pp. 200–9.

Ellul, Jacques. 1964. *The Technological Society.* New York: Knopf.

Encel, Solomon, Pauline K. Marstrand, and William Page. 1976. *The Art of Anticipation: Values and Methods in Forecasting.* New York: Pica Press.

Epstein, S. S., and R. Grundy. 1974. *Consumer Health Product Hazards.* Cambridge, Mass.: MIT Press.

Essenhigh, R. H. 1976. "Combustion of Oil/Water and Emulsions." Paper presented at the Central States Section Meeting of the Combustion Institute, Battelle Memorial Laboratories, Columbus, Ohio, April 5–6.

Etzioni, Amitai, 1974. "Review Symposium." *Contemporary Society*, March, pp. 105–7.

——. 1968. *The Active Society*. New York: Free Press.

Ewald, W. R., Jr., ed. 1968. *Environment and Change: The Next Fifty Years.* Bloomington: Indiana University Press. (Papers commissioned by the American Institute of Planners' two-year consultation, 1966.)

Falk, Richard. 1976. "A World Order Analysis of Nuclear Proliferation." *Forum* 8 (October): v–111–v–116.

——. 1975. *A Study of Future Worlds.* New York: Free Press.

——. 1972. *This Endangered Planet: Prospects and Proposals for Human Survival.* New York: Random House.

Fan, John C. C. 1978. "Plugging into the Sun." *Technology Review*, August–September, pp. 14–37.

Feinberg, Gerald. 1974. "Some Hopes and Doubts about Technological Answers to Future Material Problems." Unpublished paper.

——. 1972. "Some Considerations on a Long-Term Future Materials Policy." Paper presented at the Conference on Society and Growth, Minneapolis, Minn., June 23.

——. 1968. *The Prometheus Project: Mankind's Search for Long-Range Goals.* New York: Doubleday.

Ferguson, Marilyn. 1980. *The Acquarian Conspiracy: Personal and Social Transformation in the 1980's.* New York: J. P. Tarcher/St. Martin's.

Ferguson, Marilyn. 1978a. "Karl Pribram's Changing Reality." *Re-vision*, Summer/Fall, pp. 8–13.

Ferguson, Marilyn. 1978b. "A New Perspective on Reality." The Special Updated Issue of the *Brain/Mind Bulletin. Re-vision*, Summer/Fall, pp. 3–7.

Ferkiss, Victor C. 1977. *Futurology: Promises, Performance, Prospects.* Beverly Hills, Calif.: Sage.

——. 1974. *The Future of Technological Civilization.* New York: George Braziller.

——. 1969. *Technological Man: The Myth and the Reality.* New York: New American Library (Mentor).

Forrester, Jay W. 1978. "Changing Economic Patterns." *Technology Review.* August–September, pp. 46–53.

———. 1971. *World Dynamics.* Cambridge, Mass.: Wright-Allen Press.

———. 1970. "The Counterintuitive Behavior of Social Systems." *Technology Review*, January.

Forrester, J., D. Gabor, et al. 1972. (Letters). *Science*, April 14, pp. 109–10.

Fowles, Jib, ed. 1978. *Handbook of Futures Research.* Westport, Conn.: Greenwood Press.

Frankena, William K. 1973. *Ethics.* Englewood Cliffs, N.J.: Prentice-Hall.

Freeman, Christopher, and Maria Jahoda, eds. 1978. *World Futures: The Great Debate.* New York: Universe Books.

Freiverson, H. A., and Theodore B. Taylor. 1976. "Security Implications of Alternative Fission Futures." *Bulletin of the Atomic Scientists*, December, pp. 14–18.

Fuller, R. Buckminster. 1969. *Utopia or Oblivion: The Prospects for Humanity.* New York: Bantam Books.

———. 1967. *Comprehensive Design Strategy, World Resources Inventory, Phase II.* Carbondale, Ill.: University of Illinois.

"Fusion Power Comes Closer to Reality," Unsigned. 1976. *Futurist*, February, pp. 45–46.

Futurist. 1972 and 1971. Articles on technology assessment, February, pp. 16–32, and December, pp.225–52, respectively.

Gabor, Dennis. 1972. *The Mature Society.* New York: Praeger.

———. 1970. *Innovations: Scientific, Technological and Social.* New York: Oxford University Press.

Gappert, Gary. 1974. "Post-Affluence: The Turbulent Transition to a Post-Industrial Society," *Futurist*, October, pp. 212–16.

Goeller, H. E., and A. Weinberg. 1975. "The Age of Substituability." Eleventh Annual Foundation Lecture presented before the United Kingdom Science Policy Foundation Fifth International Symposium, A Strategy for Resources. Eindhoven, The Netherlands, September 18.

Gompert, David C., et al. 1977. *Nuclear Weapons and World Politics.* New York: McGraw-Hill.

Gordon, Lincoln. 1976. "Limits to the Growth Debate." *Resources for the Future*, Summer, pp. 1ff.

Gordon, Theodore J. 1972. "The Current Methods of Futures Research." In *The Futurists*, edited by Alvin Toffler, pp. 164–89. New York: Random House.

———. 1967. "Forecasters Turn to 'Delphi.'" *Futurist*, February, pp. 164–89.

———. 1965. *The Future*. New York: St. Martin's Press.

Gordon, Theodore J., and Olaf Helmer. 1966. "Report on a Long-Range Forecasting Study". In *Social Technology,* New York: Basic Books.

Gough, William. 1973. "The Promise of Fusion Power." *Futurist*, October, pp. 211–15.

Green, Philip. 1968. *Deadly Logic.* New York: Schoken Books.

Greenwood, Ted., Harold A. Feiverson, and Theodore B. Taylor. 1977. *Nuclear Proliferation.* New York: McGraw-Hill.

Groethuysen, Bernard. 1968. *The Burgeoise: Catholicism versus Capitalism in Eighteenth Century France.* Translated by Mary Ilford. New York: Holt, Rinehart and Winston.

Hamil, Ralph. 1970. "The Cloudy Future of Communism." *Futurist*, December, pp. 213–15.

Hardin, Garrett. 1973. "The Tragedy of the Commons." In *Toward a Steady-State Economy*, edited by Herman Daly, pp. 133–48. San Francisco: W. H. Freeman.

Hardin, Garrett, and John Baden. 1977. *Managing the Commons.* San Francisco: W. H. Freeman.

Harman, Willis. 1979. "Broader Implications of Recent Findings in Psychological and Psychic Research." *Institute of Noetic Sciences Newsletter*, pp. 14–16.

Harman, Willis. 1978. "Willis Harman Comments." *Re-vision*, Summer/Fall, p. 97.

———. 1977a. "The Coming Transformation." *Futurist*, April, pp. 106–12.

———. 1977b. "The Coming Transformation." *Futurist*, February, pp. 4–12.

———. 1976. *An Incomplete Guide to the Future.* San Francisco Book.

——. 1972a. "Agenda for Business: Choices for the Near-Term Future." Paper prepared by the EPRC of Stanford Research Institute, Menlo Park, Calif. June.

——. 1972b. "Key Choices for the Next Two Decades (An Extrapolation of the Future)." Paper prepared for the White House Conference on the Industrial World Ahead, February 7–9; partially reprinted in *Fields within Fields . . . Within Fields*, edited by Julius Stulman. Vol. 5. New York: World Institute Council.

——. 1970a. *Alternative Futures and Educational Policy.* Menlo Park, Calif.: Stanford Research Institute, Educational Policy Research Center, February, 6747–RN–6,

——. 1970b. "Policies for National Unification." *Journal of Creative Behavior*, 4 (Fall): 283–93.

——. 1969. "The New Copernican Revolution." *Stanford Today*, Winter.

Hartke, Vance. 1972. "Toward a National Growth Policy." *Futurist*, December, pp. 240–42.

Hauser, Philip M. 1968. "Chaotic Society." Address given August 28, 1968. *Vital Speeches* 35 (October 15): 22–32.

Hayashi, Yujiro, ed. 1970. *Perspectives on Postindustrial Society*. Tokyo:University of Tokyo Press.

Hayes, Denis. 1977. *Rays of Hope: The Transition to a Post-Petroleum World*. New York: W. W. Norton.

Heilbronner, Robert L. 1974. *An Inquiry into the Human Prospect*. New York: W. W. Norton.

Helmer, Olaf. 1976. "Forward." In *The Delphi Method: Techniques and Applications*, edited by Harold A. Linstone and Murray Turoff. New York: American Elsevier.

——. 1974. *The Future State of the Union and Its Relevance to the Planning Process*. Los Angeles: University of Southern California, Center for Futures Research Publication.

Helmer, Olaf, with contributions by Bernice Brown and Theodore Gordon. 1966. *Social Technology*. New York: Basic Books.

Helmer, Olaf, and Nicholas Rescher. 1960. "On the Epistemology of the Inexact Sciences." Report R–353. Santa Monica, Calif.: Rand Corporation, February.

Heppenheimer, T. A. 1977. *Colonies in Space.* Harrisburg, Pa.: Stackpole.

Hess, H. 1976. "Geothermal Energy: Prospects and Limitations." *Sierra Club Bulletin*, November/December.

Hirsch, Fred. 1976. *Social Limits to Growth.* Cambridge, Mass.: Harvard University Press.

Holt, John. 1976. "Space Colonies Are Absurd." *New Age*, December, pp. 44–47.

Hopkins, Frank Snowden. 1975. "The Limitations of World System Models." *Futurist*, October, pp. 258–62.

Hubbert, M. K. 1971. "The Energy Resources of the Earth." *Energy and Power.* A *Scientific American* Book. San Francisco: W. H. Freeman.

Huber, Bettina J. 1971. "Studies of the Future: A Selected and Annotated Bibliography." In *The Sociology of the Future*, edited by W. Bell and J. A. Mau. New York: Russell Sage Foundation.

Huber, Bettina J., and Wendell Bell. 1971. "Sociology and the Emergent Study of the Future." *American Sociologist*, November, pp. 287–95.

Hughes, Barry B., and Mihajlo Mesarovic. 1978. "Testing the Hudson Institute Scenarios: Is Their Optimism Justified?" *World Future Society BULLETIN*, November–December, pp. 1–15.

Humphrey, Hubert H. 1972. "Whither We Are Tending: An Effort to Make the U.S. Government Look to the Future." *Futurist*, December, pp. 236–38.

Huxley, Aldous. 1945. *The Perennial Philosophy.* New York: Harper.

———. 1932. *Brave New World.* New York: Harper & Row.

Ikle, F. Charles. 1967. "Can Social Predictions Be Evaluated?" *Toward the Year 2000: Work in Progress, Daedalus*, Summer, pp. 733–58.

International Institute for Environmental Affairs. 1973. *World Energy, the Environment, and Political Action.* New York: IIEA.

James, Mark. 1978. "Moving Toward Fusion: 200 Megawatts and Beam Heat." *Technology Review*, February, p. 58.

Jantsch, Erich. 1968. "Integrating Forecasting and Planning through a Function-Oriented Approach." In *Technological Forecasting for Industry and Government*, edited by James R. Bright. Englewood Cliffs, N.J.: Prentice-Hall.

——. 1967. *Technological Forecasting in Perspective*. Paris: Organization for Economic Cooperation and Development.

Jones, Thomas E. 1979a. "The Futurist Movement: A Brief History." *World Future Society BULLETIN*, July–August, pp. 13–26.

— —. 1979b. "Today's Obsolescent Aspirations." *World Future Society BULLETIN*, November–December, pp. 19–26.

——. 1978. "Toward a Planetary Ecological Ethic." Finalist paper in the Alternatives to Growth 1977 essay contest. Condensed version printed in *World Future Society BULLETIN*, September–October, pp. 9–19.

——. 1977. "Current Prospects of Sustainable Economic Growth." *Goals in a Global Community*, edited by Ervin Laszlo and Judah Bierman. Vol. 1. The Original Background Papers for *Goals for Mankind*: A Report to the Club of Rome. New York: Pergamon Press.

——. 1975a. "Outmoded Aspirations." *The Centrality of Science and Absolute Values*. Vol. 2. Proceedings of the Fourth International Conference on the Unity of the Sciences. New York: International Cultural Foundation.

——. 1975b. "Toward a Future of Selective Growth." *The Next 25 Years: Crisis and Opportunity*, edited by Andrew Spekke. Washington, D.C.: World Future Society.

Jungk, Robert. 1968. "About 'Mankind 2000.'" *Planning for Diversity and Choice*, edited by Stanford Anderson. Cambridge: M.I.T. Press.

Jungk, Robert, and Johan Galtung, eds. 1968. *Mankind 2000*. Oslo Norway: Universitetsforlaget.

Kahn, Herman. 1979. *World Economic Development*. New York: Morrow.

——. 1972. "The World of 1990." In *White House Conference on the Industrial World Ahead*. Rochelle Park, N.J.: Emanuel.

——. 1970. *The Emerging Japanese Superstate: Challenge and Response*. Englewood Cliffs, N.J.: Prentice-Hall.

——. 1961. *On Thermonuclear War*. Princeton N.J.: Princeton University Press.

Kahn, Herman, and William Brown. 1975. "A World Turning Point—and a Better Prospect for the Future." *Futurist*, December, pp. 289–92.

Kahn, Herman, William Brown, and Leon Martel. 1976a. "Future Hope," *Time Magazine*, May 24.

——. 1976b. *The Next 200 Years*. New York: Morrow.

Kahn, Herman, and B. Bruce-Briggs. 1972. *Things to Come*. New York: Macmillan.

Kahn, Herman, with the collaboration of Basil Candela and Marcello de Leva. 1972. "Some Notes for a Paper on Resources, Power, and Other Depletion and Scarcity Type Issues." Paper Prepared by the Hudson Institute, Croton-on-Hudson, New York.

Kahn, Herman, and John B. Phelps. 1979. "The Economic Present and Future: A Chartbook for the Decades Ahead." *Futurist*, June, pp. 202–22.

Kahn, Herman, and Anthony J. Wiener. 1967. *The Year 2000: A Framework for Speculation on the Next Thirty-Three Years*. New York: Macmillan.

Keller, Suzanne. 1972. "The Utility of Sociology for Futurism." *1972 American Sociological Association Seminar on the Sociology of the Future*. Minneapolis University of Minnesota Press.

Kneese, A., and Charles L. Schultze. 1975. *Pollution, Prices, and Policy*. Washington, D.C.: Brookings Institution.

Krutch, Joseph Wood. 1968. "What the Year 2000 Won't Be Like." *Saturday Review*, January 20.

Kuhn, Thomas S. 1967. *The Structure of Scientific Revolutions*. Chicago: University of Chicago Press.

Landsberg, Hans H., L. L. Fischman, and J. L. Fischer. 1963. *Resources in America's Future. Patterns of Requirements and Availabilities 1960–2000*. Baltimore: Johns Hopkins University Press.

Lasswell, H. O. 1966. "The Garrison State." *American Journal of Sociology*, 46: 157–66.

——. 1962. "The Garrison-State Hypothesis Today." *Changing Patterns of Military Politics*, edited by Samuel P. Huntington, pp. 51–71. New York: Free Press.

Laszlo, Ervin, et al. 1977. *Goals for Mankind: A Report to the Club of Rome*. NewYork: E. P. Dutton.

Lawrence Livermore Laboratory. 1977a. "Glasses for High-Powered Fusion Lasers." *Energy and Technology Review*, September.

——. 1977b. "Neutral Beams for Magnetic Fusion." *Energy and Technology Review*, September.

Leontief, Wassily, et, al. 1977. *Future of the World Economy: A United Nations Study*. India: Oxford University Press.

Levenson, Joseph. 1968. *Confucian China and Its Modern Fate: A Trilogy*. Berkeley: University of California Press.

Levy-Pascal, A. Ehud. 1979. "Will the Rising Price of Energy Push Us Over the Cliff?" *Futurist*, December, pp. 477–80.

——. 1976. *An Analysis of the Cyclical Dynamics of Industrialized Countries*. Washington, D.C.: U.S. Central Intelligence Agency.

Linstone, Harold A., and Murray Turoff. 1975. *The Delphi Method: Techniques and Applications*. Reading, Maine: Addison-Wesley.

Lovens, Amory B. 1977. *Soft Energy Paths*. Cambridge, Mass.: Ballinger.

Lovens, Amory B., and John H. Price. 1975. *Non-Nuclear Futures: The Case for an Ethical Energy Strategy*. Cambridge, Mass.: Bollinger.

Lund, R. 1977. "Making Products Live Longer." *Technology Review*, January, pp. 48–55.

McEachron, Norman B., and Connell F. Persico. 1971. *Forces for Societal Transformation: Historical Background and Theoretical Framework*. Menlo Park, Calif.: Stanford Research Institute, Educational Policy Research Center, June, 6747-RN–12.

McHale, John. 1977. *Futures Directory*. Boulder, Colo.: Westview Press.

——. 1976. *Changing Information Environment*. Boulder, Colo.: Westview Press.

McHale, John, and Magda McHale. 1975. *Human Requirements, Supply Levels, and Outer Bounds*. New York: Aspen Institute.

——. 1972a. *A Continuation of the Typological Survey of Futures Research, U.S.* Project report to the Division of Mental Health Programs. Washington, D.C.: National Institute of Mental Health.

——. 1972b. *World Facts and Trends*. New York: Macmillan.

——. 1972c. "The Changing Information Environment." *Information Technology*, p. 193.

——. 1970. *The Ecological Context*. New York: Braziller.

——. 1969. *The Future of the Future.* New York: Braziller.

Madden, Carl. 1972. *Clash of Culture.* Washington, D.C.: National Planning Association.

Maine, Henry Sumner. 1970. *Ancient Law.* Gloucester, Mass.: Peter Smith.

Marcuse, Herbert. 1964. *One-Dimensional Man.* Boston: Beacon Press.

Marien, Michael. 1976. *Societal Directions and Alternatives: A Critical Guide to the Literature.* Lafayette, N.Y.: Information for Policy Design.

——. 1973a. "Daniel Bell and the End of Normal Science." *Futurist,* December, pp. 262–68.

——. 1973b. "Herman Kahn's *Things to Come.*" *Futurist,* February, pp. 7-15.

——. 1972. *The Hot List Delphi.* Syracuse, N.Y.: Educational Policy Research Center.

Markley, O. W. 1976. "Human Consciousness in Transformation." In *Evolution and Consciousness: Human Systems in Transition,* edited by Erich Jantsch and C. H. Waddington, Reading, Mass.: Wesley.

——. 1974. *Changing Images of Man.* Policy Research Report 4. Menlo Park. Calif.: Stanford Research Institute, Education Policy Research Center.

——. 1971. *Alternative Futures: Contexts in Which Social Indicators Must Work.* Menlo Park, Calif.: Stanford Research Institute, Educational Policy Research Center, February, 6747–RN–11.

Marks, Robert. 1960. *The Dymaxion World of Buckminster Fuller.* Carbondale: Southern Illinois University Press.

Marstrand, Pauline K., and K. L. R. Pavitt. 1973. "The Agricultural Sub-system." In *Models of Doom,* edited by H. S. Cole, Christopher Freeman, Marie Jahoda, and K. L. R. Pavitt. New York: Universe Books.

Marstrand, Pauline K., and T. C. Sinclair. 1973. "The Pollution Sub-system." In *Models of Doom,* edited by H. S. Cole, Christopher Freeman, Marie Jahoda, and K. L. R. Pavitt. New York: Universe Books.

Martin, James. 1978. *The Wired Society.* Englewood Cliffs, N. J.: Prentice-Hall.

——. 1977. *Future Developments in Telecommunications.* 2d ed. Englewood Cliffs, N.J.: Prentice-Hall.

Martino, Major Joseph. 1969. "Evaluating Forecasts," *Futurist* June, p. 75.

——. 1967a. "An Experiment With the Delphi Procedure for Long-Range Forecasting." Unpublished paper prepared for the Air Office of Scientific Research, n. p.

——. 1967b. "Forecasting Hastens Technological Progress." *Futurist*, December, p. 96.

Maslow, Abraham H. 1962. *Toward a Psychology of Being*. New York: D. Van Nostrand Company.

Massenet, Michael. 1963. "Introduction à une sociologie de la prévision." Futuribles/no. 70. *Supplement to Bulletin SEDEIS*, 2, 857, June 20.

Meadows, Dennis. 1972. "The Future of Man: Optimism vs. Pessimism." *Futurist*, April, pp. 64–66.

——. 1971. "The Predicament of Mankind." *Futurist*, August, pp. 137–44.

Meadows, Dennis, ed. 1977. *Alternatives to Growth–I: A Search for Sustainable Futures*. Cambridge, Mass.: Ballanger Books.

Meadows, Dennis, et al. 1974. *Dynamics of Growth in a Finite World*. Cambridge, Mass.: Wright-Allen Press.

Meadows, Dennis, et al. 1973. *Toward Global Equilibrium: Collected Papers*. Cambridge, Mass: Wright-Allen Press.

Meadows, Donella H., Dennis L. Meadows, Jørgen Randers, and William W. Behrens III. 1972. *The Limits to Growth: A Report for the Club of Rome's Project on the Predicament of Mankind*. New York: Universe Books.

Mendel, Arthur P. 1969. "Robots and Rebels." *New Republic*, January 11, pp. 16–19.

Mendell, Jay S. 1978. "The Practice of Intuition." In *Handbook of Futures Research*, edited by Gib Fowles, Westport, Conn.: Greenwood Press.

Mendlovitz, Saul H., ed. 1975. *On the Creation of a Just World Order: Preferred Worlds for the 1990's*. New York: Free Press.

Merriam, Marshal. 1977. "Wind Energy for Human Needs." *Technology Review*, January, pp. 28–39.

Mesarovic, Mihajlo, and Eduard Pestel. 1974a. *Mankind at the Turning Point*. New York: E. P. Dutton.

——. 1974b. *Multilevel Computer Model of World Development System*, 6 vols. Laxenburg, Austria: IIASA.

Michael, Donald N. 1973. *On Learning to Plan—and Planning to Learn*. San Francisco: Jossey-Bass.

———. 1968. *The Unprepared Society: Planning for a Precarious Future*. New York: Basic Books.

———. 1965. *The Next Generation. The Prospects Ahead for the Youth of Today and Tomorrow*. New York: Random House.

Miles, Ian. 1978. "The Ideologies of Futurists." In *Handbook of Futures Research*, edited by Gib Fowles. Westport, Conn.: Greenwood Press.

———. 1975. *The Poverty of Prediction*. Lexington, Mass.: Lexington Books.

Miles, Rufus E., Jr. 1976. *Awakening from the American Dream—The Social and Political Limits to Growth*. New York: Universe Books.

Miller, David C., and Ronald J. Hunt. 1973. *Futures Studies and Research Curriculum Guide*. San Francisco: DCM Associates.

Miller, Marvin. 1979. "The Nuclear Dilemma: Power, Proliferation, and Development." *Technology Review*, May, pp 18–29.

Moore, Wilbert E. 1966. "The Utility of Utopias." *American Sociologist Review* 31 (December 31): 765–72.

———. 1964. "Predicting Discontinuities in Social Change." *American Sociological Review* 29 (June): 331–38.

Moore, Wilbert E., and Eleanor B. Sheldon, eds. 1968. *Indicators of Social Change: Concepts and Measurements*. New York: Russell Sage Foundation.

Mumford, Lewis. 1962. *The Transformation of Man*. New York: Collier, 1962.

Murray, Bruce C. 1975. *Navigating the Future*. New York: Harper & Row.

Murray, Robert H., and Paul A. LaViolette. 1977. "Assessing the Solar Transition," *Goals in a Global Community*, edited by Ervin Laszlo and Judah Bierman, Vol. 1. New York: Pergamon Press.

Needham, Joseph. 1954–74. *Science and Civilization in China*, 5 vols. in 9 pts. New York: Cambridge University Press.

Nelson, Benjamin. 1974. "Sciences and Civilizations, 'East' and 'West': Joseph Needham and Max Weber." In *Philosophical Foundations of Science, Boston Studies in the Philosophy of Science*, edited by Raymond J. Seeger and Robert S. Cohen, pp. 445–93. Vol. 11. Dordrecht, Holland: D. Reidel.

——. 1973. "Civilizational Complexes and Intercivilizational Encounters." *Sociological Analysis*, 34 (Summer): 79–105.

——. 1969. *The Idea of Usury: From Tribal Brotherhood to Universal Otherhood*, 2d ed., enl. Chicago: University of Chicago Press.

——. 1968. "Scholastic Rationales of 'Conscience', Early Modern Crises of Credibility, and the Scientific, Technocultural Revolutions of the 17th and 20th Centuries." *Journal for the Scientific Study of Religion* 7: 157–77.

——. 1965. "Self-Images and Spiritual Direction in the History of European Civilization." In *The Quest for Self-Control: Classical Philosophies and Scientific Research*, edited by S. Z. Klausner. New York: Free Press.

——. 1964. "Actors, Directors, Roles, Cues, Meanings, Identities: Further Thoughts on Anomie." *Psychoanalytic Review,* 51 (Spring): 135–59.

Neustadtl, Sara Jane. 1977. "New Heat in Climate Prediction," *Technology Review*, October/November, p. 73.

"The Next Five Centuries: A Prospective History Based on Current Events." 1968. Unsigned review of *The Next 500 Years*, by Burnham Bechwith, *Futurist*, October, pp. 85–89.

Nisbet, Robert. 1972. "The Attractive and Utterly Fallacious Time Machine: Futurology," *Intellectual Digest*, May, pp. 40–42.

——. 1971. "Has Futurology a Future?" *Encounter*, November.

——. 1969. *Social Change in History*. New York: Oxford University Press.

——. 1968. "The Year 2000 and All That." *Commentary*, June, pp. 60–66. (Replies in September issue.)

Norman, C. 1976. "Federal Safeguards on Industrial Chemicals: A Vote for Foresight." *Technology Review*, December, pp. 6–7.

North, Robert C. 1978. *The World That Could Be*. New York: W. W. Norton.

——. 1968. "Some Observations on Forecasting Based on Lessons from Retrospective Analysis." In *Forecasting in International Relations*, edited by Nazli Choucri and Thomas W. Robinson, pp. 269–77. San Francisco: W. H. Freeman.

Nuclear Energy and National Policy, 1978. A statement by the National Policy Committee of the Committee for Economic Development. n.p.: Georgian Press.

330 / OPTIONS FOR THE FUTURE

Ogburn, William F. 1964. *On Culture and Social Change*. Chicago: University of Chicago Press.

O'Neill, Gerard K. 1977. *The High Frontier: Human Colonies in Space*. New York: Morrow.

——. 1976. "Space Colonies, The High Frontier." *Futurist*, February pp. 25–33.

——. 1975. "Space Colonies and Energy Supply to the Earth." *Science*, December 5, pp. 943–47.

Ophuls, William. 1977. *Ecology and the Politics of Scarcity*. San Francisco: W. H. Freeman.

Orwell, George. 1956. *1984*. New York: Harcourt, Brace, and World.

O'Toole, James. 1975. *Energy and Social Change: Summary of First Twenty Year Forecast Project*. Los Angeles: University of Southern California, Center for Futures Research Publication.

Ozbekhan, Hasan. 1968. *The Triumph of Technology: 'Can' Implies 'Ought,' "* In *Planning for Diversity and Choice*. Cambridge: Massachusetts Institute of Technology Press.

Page, William. 1973. "The Non-Renewable Resource Sub-system." In *Models of Doom*. edited by H. S. Colle, Christopher Freeman, Marie Jahoda, and K. L. R. Pavitt. New York: Universe Books.

Passell, Peter, Marc Roberts, and Leonard Ross. 1972. *"The Limits to Growth, Urban Dynamics, World Dynamics."* New York, *Times Book Review*, April 2 pp. 1ff.

Peccei, Aurelio. 1969. *The Chasm Ahead*. London: Macmillan.

Perloff, Harvey S., ed. 1971. *The Future of U.S. Government: Toward the Year 2000*. New York: Braziller.

Pirages, Dennis, ed. 1977. *Sustainable Society: Implications for Limited Growth*. New York: Praeger.

Pirages, Dennis, and Paul Ehrlich. 1973. *Ark II: Social Response to Environmental Imperatives*. San Francisco: W. H. Freeman.

The Planetary Bargain: Proposals for a New International Economic Order to Meet Human Needs. 1975. n.p.: Aspen Institute for Humanistic Studies Program in International Affairs.

Platt, John. 1975. "The Future of Social Crises." *Futurist*, October, pp. 266–68.

——. 1974. "World Transformation: Changes in Belief Systems." *Futurist*, June, pp. 124–25.

——. 1972. "Councils on Urgent Studies." *Science*. August 25. pp. 670–76.

——. 1969. "What We Must Do." *Science*, 166 (November 28): 1115–21.

——. 1966. *The Step to Man*. New York: John Wiley and Sons.

Polak, Fred. 1973. *The Image of the Future*. San Francisco: Jossey-Bass.

Pollard, William C. 1976. "The Long-Range Prospects for Solar Energy." *American Scientist*, 64 (July-August): 424–29.

Prehoda, Robert W. 1977a. "Principle of Optimigation." *World Future Society BULLETIN*, July-August, pp. 6–12.

——. 1977b. "The Technophilic-Malthusian Perspective," *World Future Society BULLETIN*, September-October, pp. 10–160.

——. 1967. *Designing the Future: The Role of Technological Forecasting*. Philadelphia: Chilton.

Pribram, Karl H. 1978. "What the Fuss Is All About." *Re-vision*, Summer/Fall, pp. 14–18.

——. 1977. *Languages of the Brain*. Monterey, Calif.: Brooks Cole.

Prigogine, Ilya. Peter M. Allen, and Robert Herman. 1977. "Long Term Trends and the Evolution of Complexity." *Goals in a Global Community*, edited by Ervin Laszlo and Judah Bierman. Vol. 1: The Original Background Papers for *Goals for Mankind*: A Report to the Club of Rome. New York: Pergamon Press.

Randers, Jørgen, and Dennis L. Meadows. 1971. "System Simulation to Test Environmental Policy. I: A Sample Study of DDT Movement in the Environment." Cambridge, Mass.: Massachusetts Institute of Technology, Mimeographed.

Ravenholt, R. T. 1976. "Winning the Battle against Overpopulation," *Futurist*. April, pp. 64–68.

Rawls, John. 1971. *A Theory of Justice*. Cambridge, Mass.: Harvard University Press.

Renfro, William L. 1978. "The Future and Congressional Reform," *American Bar Association Journal*, April, pp. 561–63.

Rescher, Nicholas. 1969. "What is Value Change? A Framework for Research." *Values and the Future*, edited by Kurt Baier and Nicholas Rescher, New York: Free Press.

Reuyl, John S., et al. 1977. "Solar Energy in America's Future: A Preliminary Assessment." 2d ed. ERDA Contract E (04-3)-115, SRI Project URU-4996. Menlo Park, Calif.: Stanford Research Institute, March.

Rhyne, Russell. 1971. *Projecting Whole-Body Patterns—The Field Anomaly Relaxation (FAR) Methods.* Menlo Park, Calif.: Stanford Research Institute, Educational Policy Research Center, February, 1971, 6747-RM-10.

Richta, Radovan, and a research team. 1968. *Civilization at the Crossroads: The Social and Human Implications of the Scientific and Technological Revolutions.* Czechoslovakia: n.p.

Riegel, M. 1976. "Space Debate," Interviews with John Holt and Gerard O'Neill. *New Age*, December, pp. 44-47.

Rose, D. J., and M. Feirtag. 1976. "The Prospect for Fusion." *Technology Review*, December, pp. 21-43.

Rosen, Stephen. 1971. "Inside the Future." *Innovation*, February.

Roszak, Theodore. 1972. *Where the Wasteland Ends: Politics and Transcendence in Post-Industrial Society.* New York: Doubleday.

Sakharov, Andrei D. 1970. *Progress, Coexistence and Intellectual Freedom.* New York: W. W. Norton.

Salk, Jonas. 1973. *Survival of the Wisest.* New York: Harper & Row.

Schmalz, Anton B., ed. 1974. *Energy: Today's Choices, Tomorrow's Opportunities.* Washington, D.C.: World Future Society.

Schmidt, J. C. 1976. "Ocean Energy." *Johns Hopkins Magazine*, March, pp. 32-35.

Schramm, L. W. 1970. "Shale Oil." *Mineral Facts and Problems*, Washington, D. C.: U.S. Government Printing Office.

Schoen, Donald A. 1971. *Beyond the Stable State.* New York: Random House.

Schumacher, E. F. 1973. *Small is Beautiful: Economics as if People Mattered.* New York: Harper & Row.

Schwartz, Peter, Peter J. Teige, and Willis Harman. 1977. "In Search of Tomorrow's Crises," *Futurist*, October, pp. 269–73 (also, edited summary of future problems, pp. 274–78).

Science and Cybernetics, December 1968, pp. 333ff.

Seaborg, Glenn. 1975a. Opportunities in Today's Energy Milieu". *Futurist*, February, pp. 22–37.

——. 1975b. "Toward a Recycle Society." Paper presented to the Conference on Facing a World of Scarce Resources, Los Angeles, Calif., March 21.

——. 1974. "The Recycle Society of Tomorrow." *Futurist*, June, pp. 108–15.

Shane, Harold G. 1973. *The Educational Significance of the Future*. Bloomington: Indiana University Press.

Shubik, Martin. 1971. "Modeling on a Grand Scale." *Science*, December 3, pp. 1014–15.

Skinner, B. F. 1971. *Beyond Freedom and Dignity*. New York: Knopf.

——. 1948. *Walden Two*. New York: Macmillan.

"Slow Economic Growth: Future Normal." 1978. (unsigned) *Business Tomorrow*, (Spring): 11.

Somit, A. 1976. *Political Science and the Study of the Future*. New York: McGraw-Hill.

Sorokin, Pitirim A. 1962. *Social and Cultural Dynamics*. Vol. 1. New York: Bedminster Press.

Spekke, Andrew. ed. 1975. *The Next 25 Years: Crisis and Opportunity*. Washington, D.C.: World Future Society.

Starr, Paul. 1978. "Medicine and the Waning of Professional Sovereignty," *Daedalus* 107 (Winter): 175–93.

Stearns, Peter N. 1974. "Controversy." *Society*, May/June, pp. 10–22. Review of Daniel Bell's *The Coming of Post-Industrial Society*.

Stiefel, Michael. 1979. "Soft and Hard Energy Paths." *Technology Review*, October, pp. 56–66.

Stine, G. Harry. 1975. *The Third Industrial Revolution*. New York: Putnam.

Stobaugh, Robert, and Daniel Yergin, eds. 1979. *Energy Future: Report of the Energy Project at the Harvard Business School.* New York: Random House.

Summers, C. M. 1971. "The Conservation of Energy." In *Energy and Power, A Scientific American Book.* San Francisco: W. H. Freeman.

Surrey, A., and A. Bromley. 1973. "Energy Resources." In *Models of Doom*, edited by H. S. Cole, Christopher Freeman, Marie Jahoda, and K. L. R. Pavitt. New York: Universe Books.

Taviss, Irene. 1969. "Futurology and the Problem of Values." *International Journal of Social Sciences* 21. No. 4: pp. 574-84.

Taylor, Theodore B., and Charles C. Humpstone. 1973. *The Restoration of the Earth.* New York: Harper & Row.

Technology Review. 1972. *Energy Technology to the Year 2000.* Cambridge, Mass.: Technology Review.

Theobald, Robert. 1976a. *An Alternative Future for America's Third Century.* New York: Swallow.

——. 1976b. *Beyond Despair.* Washington, D.C.: New Republic.

——. 1967. "Planning with People." In *Environmental Change: The Next Fifty Years*, edited by William W. Ewald. Bloomington: Indiana University Press.

Theobald, Robert, and J. M. Scott. 1972. *Teg's 1994: An Anticipation of the Near Future.* New York: Swallow Press.

Thom, Rene. 1975. *Structural Stability and Morphogenesis: An Outline of a General Theory of Models.* Translated by D. H. Fowler. Reading, Mass.: W. A. Benjamin.

Thompson, Sir George. 1973. *The Foreseeable Future.* Rev. ed. Cambridge, England: Routledge & Kegan Paul.

Tilton, Timothy A. 1973. "The Next Stage of History?" *Social Research.* (Winter): 728-45.

Tinbergen, Jan, coordinator; Anthony J. Dolman, editor; Jan van Ettinger, director. 1976. *RIO: Reshaping the International Order. A Report to the Club of Rome.* New York: Dutton.

Toffler, Alvin. 1976. "The American Future Is Being Bumbled Away." *Futurist*, April, pp. 97-102.

——. 1975. "What is Anticipatory Democracy?" *Futurist*, October, pp. 224–29.

——. 1972. *The Futurists*. New York: Random House.

——. 1970. *Future Shock*. New York: Random House.

Touraine, Allain. 1971. *The Post-Industrial Society*. Translated by F. X. May-hew. New York: Random House.

U.S. Geological Society. 1973. *U.S. Mineral Resources*. n.p.: U.S. Geological Society.

U. S. National Goals Research Staff. *Toward Balanced Growth: Quantity with Quality*. Washington D.C.: U.S. Government Printing Office.

Vickers, Geoffrey. 1970. *Freedom in a Rocking Boat: Changing Values in an Unstable Society*. Hammondsworth, England: Penguin Press.

——. 1968. *Value Systems and Social Processes*. New York: Basic Books.

von Neumann, John. 1955. "Can We Survive Technology?" *Fortune*, June, pp. 106–8.

Ward, Barbara, and Rene Dubos. 1972. *Only One Earth*. New York: W. W. Norton.

Ward, Jonathan. 1972. "The Squaring of America." *Intellectual Digest*, September, pp. 16–19 (Interview with Herman Kahn).

Washburn. Michael, and Thomas E. Jones. 1978. "Anchoring Futures in Preferences." In *Forecasting in International Relations*, edited by Nazli Choucri and Thomas W. Robinson. San Francisco: W. H. Freeman.

Watt, Kenneth E. F. 1974. *The Titanic Effect*. Stamford, Conn.: Sinauer Association.

Weber, Max. 1958a. "Author's Introduction." *The Protestant Ethic and the Spirit of Capitalism*. Translated by Talcott Parsons. New York: Charles Scribner's Sons.

——. 1958b. *Essays in Sociology*, Trans. by H. W. Gerth and edited by C. W. Mills, New York: Oxford University Press.

Weber, Renee, 1978. 'The Enfolding-Unfolding Universe: A Conversation with David Bohm." *Re-vision*, (Summer/Fall): 24–51.

Weinberg, Alvin. 1971. "Can We Live with Fission?" Paper presented to the American Association for the Advancement of Science, Philadelphia, December 27.

——. 1967. "Can Technology Replace Social Engineering?" *BULLETIN of American Scientists*, 22: pp. 4–8.

Weingart, Jerome. 1977. "The Helios Strategy—A Heretical View of the Role of Solar Energy in the Future of a Small Planet." Prize-winning essay, Alternatives to Growth '77 contest.

Whitmore, William F. 1978. "OTEC: Electricity from the Ocean," *Technology Review*, August-September, pp. 14–37.

Wiener, Anthony. 1973. "The Future of Economic Activity." *Annuls of the American Academy of Political and Social Science*, July, pp. 47–61.

——. 1969. "The Rocky Road to Utopia," *Futurist*, February, pp. 7–9.

Wiener, Norbert. 1948. *Cybernetics*. New York: John Wiley and Sons.

Williams, Robert H., ed. 1978. *Toward a Solar Civilization*. Cambridge: Massachusetts Institute of Technology Press.

Wilson, Carroll L., project director. 1977. *Energy: Global Prospects 1985–2000*. Report of the Workshops on Alternative Energy Strategies. New York: McGraw-Hill.

Wilson, Ian. 1971. "The New Reformation: Changing Values and Institutional Goals." *Futurist*, June. pp. 105–8.

Wilson, Kenneth D., ed., 1977. *Prospects for Growth*. New York: Praeger.

Wilson, Thomas W., Jr. 1974. *World Food: The Political Dimension*. n.p.: Aspen Institute for Humanistic Studies.

Wilson, Thomas W., Jr., ed. 1972. *World Energy, The Environment and Political Action* International Institute for Environmental Affairs, New York: WEEPA.

Winthrop, Henry. 1968. "The Sociologist and the Study of the Future." *American Sociologist*, 2, May: 136–45.

Wittwer, Sylvan H. 1974. "Maximum Production Capacity of Food Crops." *Bioscience* 24: pp. 216–24.

World Energy, the Environment and Political Action. 1973. New York: International Institute for Environmental Affairs.

World Future Society. 1977. *The Future: A Guide to Information Sources*. Washington, D.C.: World Future Society.

Young, Michael. 1963. *The Rise of Meritocracy 1870–2033. An Essay in Education and Equality*. Baltimore: Penguin Books.

Young, Michael, ed. 1968. *Forecasting and the Social Sciences*. London: Heineman.

Zaltman, Gerald, and Robert Duncan. 1977. *Strategies for Planned Change*. New York: Wiley-Interscience.

INDEX

Ackoff, Russell, 306
affluence and leisure, 51, 52, 69, 87, 92–93, 123–24, 137, 139–40, 164–65, 191–201, 244–246
agriculture: *see* food production
alienation: Bell's pessimism, 122; Brzenzinski's expectation, 71, 77; Harman's optimism, 182; Kahn and Wiener's forecast, 87–88, 89, 92, 93; Kahn's counter-trend, 181–85; Mendel's revolutionary optimism, 82–83; Kahn, Brown, and Martel's analysis, 248–49
alternative futures: comparative overviews of forecasts, 41–43, 147–49; continuous and discontinuous futures, 25; developmental and turning-point futures, 23; tree of future histories, 18
Amara, Roy, 30
Ament, Robert, 53
American Academy of Arts and Sciences, 'Commission on the Year 2000': 6, 27–43
assumptions: importance of in the growth controversy, 204–6; methodological and non-methodological, 31, 307–10; the need to analyse, 31–33; of particular forecasters, *see* CONTENTS
authoritarianism: authoritarian future projected, 156–57; technocracy, 111–12, 120, 134
automation: 41, 42, 50–51, 52, 89, 92

Behrens, William H., III, 188
Bell, Daniel, 1, 7; evaluation of others forecasts, 61–62, 82, 124
Bell, Daniel, 1973 forecasts of: axial analysis central to forecasting,

126–27; axial principles and structures, 112, 114–16; axial principles and social disjunctions, 125–27, 135–37; establishment orientation of, 136–37; methodology employed, 112, 114; methodological advances, 125–26; neglect of alternative futures and other methodological shortcomings, 130–31, 136–37; post-industrial society, *see* post-industrial society and culture; compared with Brzezinski's forecast, 111–12
Bell, Daniel, 1976 forecast analyzing cultural contradictions of capitalism, 137–42
Bell, Wendell, 307
Bendix, Reinhard, 140
Bestuzhev-Lada, Igor, 81
Bethe, Hans, 219
bias, normative, *see* normative bias
bioconversion, 220
birth control, *see* population
Bohm, David, 182, 183, 184
Boldt, Menno, 307
Boulding, Kenneth, 292
Boyd, Robert, 238; revision of Forrester's World 3 model, 204–6
breeder reactors: dangers of, 12; energy producing capacity, 214–16; potential weapons use, 57; risks associated with deployment, 297; *see also* nuclear technology
Brown, Harrison, 5
Brown, Lester, 57, 227, 268, 269
Brown, William, forecast of, *see* Kahn's forecast with Brown and Martel
Bruce-Biggs, B., *see* Kahn's forecast with Bruce–Biggs
Brzezinski, Zbigniew: forecast of,

68-84; inadequate methodology of, 74-76; predicted technetronic age, 69-74; criticisms of,
Bell's, 114-118; Ellul's, 79-81;
Ferkiss', 80; Bestvzev-Lada's, 81;
Touraine's, 81-82; Mendell's, 82-
84

California Institute of Technology,
5-6
Center for the Study of Social Policy, 6, 148
change: consequences of shortsighted
planning 8-9; continuous contrasted with discontinuous, 125-
27, 242-44, 258, 309; dice-game
model of, suggested by Nisbet,
108-9; forecasting and planning,
role of in controlling, 13-14; increasing pace of, 87; institutionalization of, 86-87; Kahn on
priorities, 258; motivation to,
301-2; need to control, 1, 3, 8-
14; possibility of chaos resulting
from, 168; pre-crisis management
of, 13-14, 69; process of, 77;
socio-cultural, fundamental, 174-
87; a strategy for, 169-71; see
technology
Choucri, Nazli, 306
class conflict, Marxist and neo-
Marxist perspectives on, 81-82
Cleveland, Harlan, 268; forecast of,
300-1
Club of Rome, 6, 34, 148, 188
coal, 213-14, 222, 273-74
Coates, Joseph, 7-8
collective goals, conflict with individual ends, 141; see goals
collective goods and rights, 120
Commoner, Barry, 261
communications media, see computers, information
communism: comparison with democracy, 93-94; decision making
processes within Communist
societies, 16
computers: conferencing, 133-34;
used for modeling, 189-90; and
telecommunications, 133; fore-

casts related to, 69, 74, 89
conservation, 214, 297
controversies among futurists, 26-27,
42-43, 147-48; see growth controversy, participation, meritocracy
cooperation: need for increased
international, 295; strategy for
obtaining, 236-241
Cornish, Edward, 4, 176-78
counterculture: countercultural attempts to reverse trends, 101-
2; in post-industrial society, 121;
normative changes generated by,
106
cross-impact matrix method, 20, 45,
62-64
culture: 11, 129, 137; antinomian,
120-21, 134; conflict with
social structure, 126; cultural
contradictions of capitalism, 137-
142; cultural traits and their impact upon forecasting, 109; high,
101; outdate cultural premises,
158, 290-96; sensate, 87-88, 96-
97, 185; supposed uniformity and
uni-directionality of U.S., 101-2,
135
Cybernation, 41, 132; see automation

Dalkey, Norman, 45
DDT, see dichloro-diphenyl-trichloro-
ethane
decentralization, 164-65; 132-34;
299; see decision making and
planning, urbanization
de Jouvenal, Bertrand, 6
desalinization, 232
decision making and planning: centralized or decentralized, 16, 78,
87, 132-34, 299; elite or participatory, 16, 23, 71, 296; impact of
electronic information technology
upon, 43; narrow perspective, 8-
9; pre-crisis management, 13-14;
processes in democratic and communist nations, 15-16; processes
in the international system,
299-301

Delphi forecasting: cross-impact method as supplementing, 45, 62-63; description and evaluation of 1963/64 RAND forecast, 45-67; need for holistic systems approach, 61-64; technique summarized, 20, 44-45

democracy, compared to: authoritarian technocracy, 111; communism, 16, 93-95; meritocracy, 132; technocratic totalitarianism, 134; see decision making and planning

demographic transition, 247, 261-67

depression, possibility of during the 1980s, see inflation and recession

desalinization, 232

detente, 95

developed and developing nations, gap between: 71, 88-92, 249, 269-70; analysis of Kahn's projection concerning, 282-84; dangers inherent in this gap, 284-85; means of coping with the gap, 201, 285-88

developmental futures: def. and overview, 23-25, 41-43

dichloro-diphenyl-trichloro-ethene, 224

dilemmas: basic, see Harman-SRI forecasts

disasters, forecasts of ecological, 168; regional compared to global, 234-37; and value change, 271; see ecology, provisional catastrophism

disjunctions, social, see Bell, Daniel, 1973 forecast of

ecology: ecological ethics, 136-37, 164, 292-96; energy, 212-223, 273-77, food production, 227-34, 278-81, population, 262-70; raw materials and pollution, 206-12, 223-27, 278; equilibrium, 198-201; problems re, 130-31, 159; importance of assumptions in the controversy concerning, 204-6; processes, and delays in feedback within, 224; projected

catastrophes, 27-28, 147-48, 168, 188, 191-98

economic growth: among the affluent, 139, 196-201, 258-59; among developing nations, 248-49, 280-88; commitment to, 138-39, 196-98; danger of reacting against, 254; distribution and redistribution of, 51-52, 88-92, 159, 198-202, 260-61; exponential, 123-24, 130; forecasters' comments upon, 89, 165-67, 223, 248-62; interaction with population growth, 265-66; in linear and circular economies, 292, 296-97; selective and sustainable, 238, 296-97; see economic systems

economic systems, types of: automated, 52; circular, 292, 296-97; inappropriately linear, 292; one-dimensional, 83

education, importance of: 169, 300

Educational Policy Research Center (EPRC), 6

electronic information technology, see computers, information, participation

Ellul, Jacques, forecast of, 79-81

emulsification, fuel, 214, 274

energy: alternative technologies, 172, 212-22; increasing cost of, 176, 250-51; need for conservation of, 222; prospects for abundant, 176, 222-23, 273-77; "soft path", 218; and growth of, 250-51, 273-78, 297; world energy outlook, 50-51, 222-23

environmental pollution: chemical contamination of biological systems, 225-26, 278; control of, and cost of control, 223-27, 297; greenhouse effect, 214; protection from, 297; threat to ozone layer, 223

equality: the need for, 287-88, 299-301; prospects for, 200-1; as projected in various forecasts, 69-71, 77, 130, 132, 134; of results and of opportunity, 130, 134

equilibrium, dynamic global, 200-1,

239–40

ethics: communal, in post-industrial society, 121; ecological, 164, 292–96; good reasons approach, 306–7, 308; Protestant, 134–35; self-realization, 164; transcendentalist, 121, 135; work and achievement, shift from, 249

exploratory forecasting, 17–18

eugenics, 52, 89

Falk, Richard, 194; forecast of, 300–1

family planning, 267, 269–70; and desire for smaller families, 262, 269–70

Feinberg, Gerald, 208

Ferguson, Marilyn, 182, 183

Ferkiss, Victor, C., 80–81

fertilizers and chemical pesticides, 230

Field Anomaly Relaxation Method (FAR), 152

fish farming, 233

fission, see nuclear technology

food: Blue Revolution, 232; distribution patterns, 231, 297; emerging technologies and techniques of production, 232–34, 252–53; factors bearing upon potential for increasing production, 223, 227, 230–32; Green Revolution, 230; redesigning the world food system, 233–34; sociocultural restraints upon production, 280; soil-less food production, 233; synthetic foods, feasibility of, 280; projected consequences of increasing agricultural productivity, 190, 200; wastage in developing countries, 231

forecasting: analysis of forecaster assumptions, 31–33; as an art, 109, 305, 306; a central goal of, 14–15; continuous and discontinuous futures, 25–26; problems posed by counterintuitive behavior of social systems, 62, 189–90; criteria for evaluating,

28–31; developmental and turning point futures, 23; difficulty of, 305; goals of modeling, 202–4; historical sociology and forecasting, 308–10; methods of, 16–18; improvements in, 14–15, 125–26, 305–6, 310; need to explicate and improve non-methodological assumptions, 307–10; need to aid planning in controlling change, 13–14; prediction, compared to projection, 66–67, 109; self-fulfilling character of assumptions, 16, 29, 161, 185–86; surprise-free projection, 88–93, 94–95, 103–4; utility and accuracy of, 28–29

forecasting methods: cross-impact matrices, 20, 62; Delphi poll, 20, 44–67; exploratory, 17–18; Field Anomaly Relaxation (FAR) modeling, 152; intuitive genius forecasting, 16–17; 26–28; modeling, 19–20, 201–4, 306–7; normative, 21–22; scenario writing, 21, 112, 246, 255–56; systems dynamic modeling, 189–90; trend extrapolation, simple and qualified, 19, 102–4, 106–9, 255–7

forecasts, described and evaluated in detail: of Daniel Bell, 1973 and 1976 forecasts, 111–142; Zbigniew Brzezinski, 68–84; Willis Harman-SRI, 150–87; Herman Kahn, William Brown, and Leon Martel, 86, 243–303; Kahn and B. Bruce-Briggs, 85–86, 105–6; Kahn and Anthony Wiener, 85–110; Dennis Meadows team, 188–208; 210–41; Mihajlo Mesarovic and Eduard Pestel, 235–39; 1963/64 RAND-Delphi conducted by Ted Gordon and Olaf Helmer, 44–66

Forrester, Jay, 148, 188–205, 261; on complex systems behavior, 62; compared to Meadows, 239–41; on the possibility of another depression, 176–78

Forrester-Meadows forecasts: based on World2 and World3 models, 188-201; compared to the Mesarovic-Pestel computer model, 236; evaluations of, 123-24, 202-39; revisions of World2 suggested by Boyd, 204-5

fossil fuels, 212-14, 273-74

Fuller, R. Buckminster, 6, 28, 42, 124, 198

fusion reactors, 12, 50, 217; *see* nuclear technology

futures: *see* alternative futures

Futures Group, the, 6

future shock, 9, 153; reduced rate of, 13

futurism: characteristics, 4; comparison with science, 4-5; critics of, 7; disagreements within, 6, 22-28; a central goal of, 14; origin and development of, 5-7; rapid growth of explained, 7-8; strands of U.S., 27-28, 33-34; study of, 3, 4; unifying traits of, 4-5

genetic control, possibilities of, 89

genius forecasting, 16-17, 44-45, 67, 75

geothermal wells, 226

goals: global-international, 287, 296-98; implementation of global goals, 298-302; individual and social, 162-63; nationalistic, 293-94

Goeller, H. E., 210

Gordon, Lincoln, 236, 284

Gordon, Theodore, 6; Delphi forecast conducted by 44-67

Gordon–Helmer RAND Delphi forecast: assumptions analysed, 53-67; comparison to forecast conducted by Martino, 61; conceded methodological deficiencies, 64-65; forecasts for years 1984, 2000, and 2100, 47-52; methodology employed, 45-47; problems anticipated, 51-52; process of selecting panel members, 60-61

green revolution, 230, *see* food

gross world product (GWP), 93, 244

growth: desirable and adverse consequences of, 11, 12, 242-43; competing values and costs involved, 159; economic, *see* economic growth; industrial, 222-23, 238, 257; industrial colapse projected, 191-96; limits to *see* limits to growth; population, *see* population growth; selective, 295, 296-97, 219; sociocultural restraints upon, 227; stabilization of, 176, 198-201, 222-23, 237-41; stoppage of, upper-middle class affiliation with, 259-61; stopping or reversing ecological damage, 147-48; sustainable, 222-23, 236, 238, 299

growth controversy, 6-7, 26-27, 147-49, 204-6, 309; *see* limits to growth

Harman, Willis, 6, 23, 25, 148; forecast of, 150-85

Harman-SRI forecasts: assumptions evaluated, 171-87; coming societal transformation projected, 165-66; and evaluated, 174-87; comparison with Kahn's and Meadows' forecasts, 148, 150-51; SRI's five alternative U.S. futures projected, 152-57; methodology employed, 151-52; New Reformation and New Age premises, 161-62; new society, 153; the 'industrial state' paradigm and its basic dilemmas, 159-61; spiritual and moral crisis of civilization, 157; a world 'macroproblem,' 150-51, 153, 157-59

Hartke, Senator Vance, 15

Harvard Business School, Energy Project, 274, 275

Heilbronner, Robert, 299

Helmer, Olaf, 5, 6; Delphi forecast of, 44-67

Holdren, John, 219

holistic systems approach, need for, 61-64, 80

holographic paradigm, possible emergence of, 181-84

Hopkins, Frank Snowden, 237
Huber, Bettina J., 307
Hudson Institute, 5, 27
Hughes, Barry, evaluation of Kahn's
    forecasts re: agriculture, 280, 282;
    oil price increases, 274; develop-
    ment gap, 283-84
Human Environment, United Nations
    Conference on the, 202
Humphrey, Senator Hubert, 15
Hunt, Ronald L., 307
Huxley, Aldous, 163, 185
hydroponic farming, 234, 252-53

images: of economic man, 175; of
    the future and their importance,
    169, 253; of man in the future,
    163-64
industrialization: internal contra-
    dictions of, 150, 158-61; relation
    to nationalism, 100; as a trend,
    86
inflation, and recession, 139-40,
    156-57, 274-75
information: accumulation of, 87; in-
    formation and knowledge socie-
    ties, 12, 114-16, 123, 134; elec-
    tronic information technology,
    15-16, 22, 41; importance of in
    post-industrial society, 114, 130,
    172; relation to control and
    power, 69; value of, 41-42, 78-79
Institute for the Future, 6, 30, 53
Institute for World Order, 300
intellectual technology, 22, 42, 115-
    16
International Futuribles Committee,
    6
international system: need for inter-
    national agreements and institu-
    tions, 299; need for reform of,
    287-88; problems of, 138; value
    change and the, 136

Japan, rise of, 89, 92-93, 94-95
Jouvenal, Bertrand de, 6

Kahn, Herman, 5-6, 23-25; alone or
    in conjunction with Anthony J.

Wiener, B. Bruce-Briggs, William
    Brown, and Leon Martel on: anti-
    growth ideology, 260-61; adap-
    tive value change, 258-72; causes
    of declining economic and popu-
    lation growth rates, 246-49;
    detente, 95; developing nations,
    249-51; the development gap,
    282-85; economic growth, 148,
    257, 259; energy, 250-51, 273-
    77; forecast in World Economic
    Development, 289; limits to
    growth, 243-55, 289; nuclear war
    and arms control, 56, 92-93; nu-
    clear power and technology, 250-
    51, 274-76; other forecasts, 150-
    52, 207-9; population growth rate
    decline, 261-70; post-industrial
    affluence, 244-46; post-industrial
    society being ushered in by the
    multi-fold trend, 86-93, 256;
    raw materials supply, and pollu-
    tion, 210, 217; rectifying ecolo-
    gical problems, 273-82; socio-
    cultural limits to growth, 288
Kahn, Herman, forecast with William
    Brown (1975), 243-44
Kahn, Herman, forecast with William
    Brown and Leon Martel (1976),
    243-55; assumptions analysed,
    255-302; current historical turn-
    ing point seen, 243-44; methodo-
    logy, 255-57; novel characteristics
    discussed, 256-57; pessimism
    feared as self-fulfilling, 254; pro-
    jected post-industrial affluence,
    244-46; space-bound perspective,
    254-55; supposed physical limits
    to growth, 250-53
Kahn, Herman, forecast with B.
    Bruce-Briggs (1972), 85-86, 105-
    6; conservativism of, 105-6;
    'counter-reformation' opposing
    late sensate culture endorsed by,
    105; normative bias in, 105-6;
    technological crisis, 105
Kahn, Herman, alternative futures
    (canonical variations), 93-94;
    assumptions evaluated, 95-107;

comparison with Kahn-Bruce-Briggs forecast (1972), 85–86, 105; evaluated by other forecasters, 123–24, 165–67; forecast with Anthony Wiener (1967), 85–110; importance of, 85–86; likelihood of surprise-free projection, 94; multifold trend, extrapolated to post-industrial culture, 86–93; positive features of, 109; surprise-free projection to the year 2000, 88–92, and to the early 21st century, 92–93, with canonical variations, 93–94; U.S. prospects in early 21st century, 94–95

Kahn, Herman, forecast in *World Economic Development* (1979), 289

Kauffman, Draper, 235
Keynes, John Maynard, 124
King, Alexander, 188
knowledge, *see* information
Kuhn, Thomas, 158

land redistribution, 230
lasers, 89
Leontief, Wassily, 285–86
limits to growth, factors relevant to: energy supply and growth, 212–23, 250–51, 273–77, 297; food production, 227–35, 278–82, *see* food; forecasters' assumptions concerning growth, role of in influencing outcomes of forecasts, 204–6; pollution, 223–27, 278; proximity of, 175–76; raw minerals availability, 207–12, 278; sociocultural forces, 239, 286–88; technological change, prospects for alternative energy technologies, 172, 212–23; *see* growth controversy

limits to growth, forecasters: perspectives: author's, 176, 207, 214–23, 237–41, 288–302, 309; Bell's, 130; Harman's, 175–76; Kahn's, 250–54; Leontief's, 285–86; Meadows', 188–202; Tinbergen's, 287

Lovens, Amory, 218

malnutrition, 278, *see* food
Malthus, Thomas, 227–28, 291
Marien, Michael, 105–6
Markley, O. W., 23, 148, 150, 186, *see* Harman-SRI forecasts for details
Marstrand, 224, 230, 235
Martel, Leon, forecast of, *see* Kahn's forecast with Brown and Martel
Martino, Major Joseph, Delphi forecast conducted by, 61
Maslow, Abraham, 185
Marxists, and neo-Marxists, 7; objections to Brzezinski's forecast, 81–84; ideological class struggle in post-industrial society, 81–82
Massachusetts Institute of Technology (MIT), 6, 28, 34, 148
Massenet, Michael, 306
Mau, James A., 307
McHale, John, 28, 74, 79–80
Meadows, Dennis, 23, 26, 34, 148, 188–205
Meadows, Dennis, forecast based on computer model assembled by Club of Rome team, 190–201; assumptions evaluated, 201–41; comparisons with other forecasts, 148, 239–41, 278; 'dynamic global equilibrium' or growth stabilization, endorsed as desirable goal, 198–201; ecological catastrophe feared, 194–98; exponential growth, effects of, 190; methodology, 189–94; policy suggestions, 239–41; results of computer runs, 194–201; shortcomings in data base, 237–38
Meadows, Donella, 188
megalopoli, 87–88, *see* urbanization
Mendel, Arthur, 7; forecast of, 82–84
Mendell, Jay, 308
meritocracy: concept of meritocratic elite, 26–27, 69–71, 76–79, 111–12, 117–18, 120, 131; decreased public participation expected, 69–71, 122–23; democracy seen com-

patible with, 69, 71; elitism vs. populism, 120; evaluations of, 69, 78, 80-84, 299-301; perceived stimulus to alienation, 82; as a trend, 86

Mesarovic, Mihajlo: support of sustainable organic growth, 236; computer model with Eduard Pestal, 235-37; use of Mesarovic-Hughes model to criticize the Kahn-Brown-Martel forecast, 274-75, 280-82; methodological strengths and weaknesses of Mesarovic-Pestel model, 237; Mesarovic-Pestel model compared with Forrester-Meadows' models, 236-37

methods, forecasting, 14-22, see forecasting methods

Michael, Donald, 299, 306
Miller, David C., 307
Mitchell, Arnold, 148
modeling, 19-20, 148, 306; goals and procedures of, 202-04; use of computers in, 189-92; non-mathematical FAR, 152

multifold trend: described, 86-93, 257; evaluated, 95-104, 103, 165-67, 257

National Environmental Policy Act, 15
nationalism: goals of, 293-94; interaction with modernization and industrialization, 100; Cleveland and Falk concerning, 299-301; plans for coping with, 300

Nelson, Benjamin, 32, 126, 310
Nisbet, Robert, 7, critique of Kahn and other forecasters, 106-9
normative biases, in forecasts: Bell's, 136-37; Brzezinski's, 79; Kahn's and Bruce-Briggs', 105-6; Harman's, 182-86; Meadows' and Forrester's, 239-40; Kahn's, Brown's, and Martel's, 258

normative forecasting and planning, 21-22, 198, 299-301
North, Robert, 306
nuclear technology: arms control, 92-93; balance of terror, 10-11,

13; emerging fission and fusion energy technologies, 1, 214-18; evaluated, 275-76; power, 89, 250-51; proliferation, 57, 297; safety problems of, 214-16; war, 56-57, 99

ocean thermal energy conversion (OTEC), 219-20, see solar energy
Office of Education, U.S., 152
oil, 212-14, 242-43, 250-51, 273-76, 275
OPEC, see oil
optimism vs. pessimism, 22-26, 42-43, 53, 59-60, 79-81, 82-83, 137-42, 147-48, 153, 175, 185-87, 204-5, 206, 238-39, 254-55, 276, 289
Ozbekhan, Hasan, 306

paradigm change (see Harman-SRI forecasts; holographic paradigm)
participation, in private and public decision making: as an axial principle of Bell's analysis, 112-14, 114-16; controversy over, 26-27, 111; impact of electronic information technology upon, 42; possibility of increasing amounts of, 77-79; see decision-making
participation controversy, 26-27, see participation, meritocracy
PCB, see polychlorobiphenyls
Peccei, Aurelio, 188
Pestel, Eduard, 268; see Mesarovic-Pestel forecast
Pfaff, William, 99
photovoltaic cells, 219, see solar energy
planning: need for, 299-301; participatory, 78; see decision making, participation in public and private decision making, normative forecasting and planning
pollution, environmental, see environmental pollution
polychlorobiphenyls, 226
population: 262-73; birth control, 248; family planning and control, 50, 87, 262, 269-70; food pro-

duction and, 234; growth of, and consequences of, 50–51, 92–93, 98, 190–91; growth rates, 52–58, 87, 246–48, 262, 266–68, 269–76; strategies for stabilization of, 267–70; 298; relation to guaranteed living standards, 267–70; threat posed by excessive growth, 192–98, 262–64

postindustrial society and culture: 22–23, 41–43; affluence, level of, 87, 244–46; culture of, 88–92, 102, 120–21; Bell's forecast of, 111–42; centrality of knowledge to, 22–23, 114-16, 128–30, 172; consequences of, 142; decision making and public participation in, 132–34; economic growth of, 69, 71, 89–92, 123–24, 139, 244–46; elitism vs. populism in, 120; emergence and development of, 114–15; growth of, 244; as an 'ideal' type, 112, 125, 127; ideology, role of and effect upon class conflict, 81–84, 117–18; as information society, 114–16; intellectual institutions in, and intellectual technology, 42, 69, 71, 92, 114–18, 130; polity of, and need for revising the U.S. political system, 120, 140–41; problems in, 121–23; service and knowledge orientation of, 80, 92, 112–24, 246

Pribram, Karl, 181–83

Protestant ethic: compared to hedonism, 184, 138; forecasters' comments upon, 96–97, 121, 134–35

provisional catastrophism, 26, 29, 34, 147–48, 198

psychic phenomena, 180, 182–83

RAND Corporation, 5, 6, 42, 45, *see* Gordon-Helmer RAND Delphi forecast

Randers, Jorgen, 188

recycling, 208–9, 226, 292–93, 297

raw materials: projected consequences of depletion, 190–91; conservation, 297; criticism of Meadows' forecast of resource scarcity, 206–12; distribution of, 51–52, 159, 260–61; pollution as restraint upon extraction and production, 278; projected availability, 206–12

resources, *see* energy, raw materials

Rhyne, Russell, 148

revolutionary change: potential for evaluated, 174; sociocultural revolutions, 69, 82–84, 96, 103, 165–66, 200–1; youth as a source of support for, 71, 82–84

Sakharov, Andrei, 6

satellites, solar energy, 219

scenario writing, 21, 112, 241, 256

Schumacher, E. F., 230

Seaborg, Glenn, 209, 226

Selancik, Gerald, 30–31

selective growth, 222–23, 238, 288, 294–95, 296

self-interest: economic, 292–93; microdecisions based upon, 159–61; national decisions based upon, 293–94; reconceptualization of, 301–2

sensate cultures, 86–88, 95, 96, 101, 102, 185

single cell protein, 233, 253

Smith, Adam, 291

social engineering, 87, 96

social structure: changes leading to postindustrial society, 114–23, 127–28; centrality of knowledge in postindustrial society, resulting in the rise of a professional-technical class, 69, 116; widening gap between meritocratic elite and the non-elite, 71, 76–79, 117–20, 131–34; the need for control mechanisms, 77, 123–24, 131–32, 139; three aspects of, 112, 114; social structure contrasted to culture, 11, 121, 123; *see* meritocracy, participation

society: basic changes in U.S., 89–93,

202; technological, 27–28, 124

value change: adaptive, 258; in basic
values, 135, 161–62; 166–67, 207–
71, 301–3; and declining growth
rates, 246–49; and ecological-in-
ternational problems, 125–37;
patterns of rapid, 270–71, 302;
and technological development,
75; evaluation of unity and de-
cisiveness of contemporary, 181–
82
values: differences among forecasters, 79–80, 82–84, 136–37,
182–85, 239–40, 300; New Age,
161; appropriate, 295–6; outmoded, 157–58, 290–91; sensate
and late sensate, 86–88, 104–6,
120–21, 137–39

war: danger and likelihood of, 50,
56, 99; nuclear, 56, 99; prevention, 51, 297
Weber, Max, 96, 308
Wiener, Anthony J., 25–26, 33, 43,

85; *see also* Kahn-Wiener forecast
for details
Wilson, Thomas W., 300
windmills, modern, 220
work: in automated economy, 52;
in a service economy, 116; changes
in nature of, 134–35; social forces
undermining, 138; work-roles
dilemma, 160–61; *see* postindustrial society and culture, meritocracy, social structure
World Future Society, 6
world macroproblem: causes, 157–61;
global goals designed to ameliorate,
310; Harman's and SRI's treatment of, 150–61
World Order Models Project (WOMP),
300
World2, Forrester's computer model,
188–205; Boyd's revision of, 204–
5
World3m Meadows computer model,
188–205

Yergin, Daniel, 274

ABOUT THE AUTHOR

THOMAS E. JONES teaches courses on the future at Polytechnic Institute of New York, where he is Adjunct Associate Professor in the Graduate School of Management, and at the New School for Social Research. He is a consultant to the Hudson Institute and to UNITAR (United Nations Institute of Training and Research. He belongs to the International Platform Association and lectures frequently on future-oriented topics.

Dr. Jones served as a consultant for revision of the United Nation's *World Plan of Action* in 1977. As a member of the Club of Rome's Goals for Global Society Project, he was appointed Research Fellow at UNITAR of the United Nations in 1975 and also worked at the International Institute for Applied Systems Analysis (Luxenburg, Austria) and Aspen Institute (Colorado). In 1974–75 he engaged in research for the National Science Foundation to formulate methods for detecting, evaluating, and reducing implicit assumptions that deceptively bias forecasts. He regularly conducted a "Futures" seminar for IBM from 1973 to 1976. Since 1974 he has served on the Board of Advisors of the World Future Society's New York City Chapter, of which he has been vice-president.

Dr. Jones has presented papers on the future at numerous conferences. Many of his essays are published as articles in such scholarly journals as *Philosophy Forum, Sociological Inquiry, Journal of Value Inquiry*, and the *World Future Society BULLETIN.* He has also contributed chapters to such books as *Forecasting in International Relations* (1973, chapter coauthored by A. Michael Washburn), *Goals in a Global Community* (1977), and *The Next 25 Years: Crisis and Opportunity* (1975).

Dr. Jones received an M.A. from Harvard University and a Ph.D. from Johns Hopkins University in philosophy and a D.S.Sc. (Doctor of Social Science) in sociology from the New School for Social Research, Graduate Faculty.